Back Channel: The Vietnam Betrayal

Back Channel:

The Vietnam Betrayal

William Bertram MacFarland

DEDICATION

Respectfully dedicated to the more than 2,000,000 citizens killed in the Vietnam War and to the more than 3,000,000 wounded as well as to the countless millions more who were their friends and families.

Over 58,000 of those killed and over 300,000 of those wounded were Americans. All of this death, pain and sorrow can be laid squarely at the feet of one man — who betrayed us all.

CONTENTS

ACKNOWLEDGMENTS

Cover design by Mel B. Jones.

My sincerest thanks to my editor, friend and fellow author, Trish Jackson, who transformed my bumbling initial manuscript into the polished jewel that it has become.

xiii

Prologue

Johnson and the early Vietnam years

My name is William Bertram MacFarland. I am a patriot, a soldier, a spy and an assassin. I served as a Special Assistant to President John F. Kennedy who became a cherished and trusted friend and who included me as a member of his extended family.

When I met with President Johnson shortly after President Kennedy's funeral, he shocked me by refusing to accept my resignation as Special Assistant to the President. Johnson was well aware of my habit of collecting biographical and work-related information on most of the members of the Kennedy Administration with whom I regularly worked. I have always found doing that sort of 'homework' to be of immense usefulness. I had been a back channel to the leaders of several countries, a 'fly on the wall' and an occasional negotiator for Kennedy. A thorough knowledge of the other person's background and mind-set is essential for a smooth and productive negotiating process.

An unsought by-product of doing that kind of research is that sometimes, I came across information that I wish I hadn't. Everybody makes bad decisions now and again, and I don't know anybody who hasn't done something, sometime in their life, that they sincerely regret, and wish that somehow they could take back or undo. When you find someone who consistently and *consciously* does things that cover the gamut, from clearly unethical to downright criminal, that's scary, and Johnson scared the hell out of me. I had strong reasons to believe that he had been complicit in at least nine murders over the course of his political career.

He is unfortunately not alone in his lack of compunction about permanently silencing inconvenient but credible voices that could expose misdeeds, lies, deeply immoral and/or unethical conduct and/or outright criminal behavior. It is shocking when heads of state are so silenced, but countless more have perished at the hands of their 'leaders'. Though more common in countries led by dictators and despots, such quiet assassinations have been carried out many times by every single government in Europe—as well as here in the United States. This book and the ones to follow are going to step on some very powerful toes. It is well that I have accumulated my 'insurance documents.'

I have never, ever shared my background research papers and notes with <u>anyone</u>. Nor have I *ever* used them as a personal threat by hinting, "Hey, I know a few things about you that I bet you wish I didn't." Collectively however, the now vast assemblage of those research documents, which I have gathered over the past 50 years, constitutes my 'insurance policy.' They all reside in a very large safe deposit container in the vault of a well-known Western European bank—the key to which is held by an equally well-known law firm in that country. Should I, or anyone else on a list that I have provided to that law firm, die unexpectedly or suspiciously, they will launch a detailed and scrupulous investigation of the death in question. If they decide, in their sole discretion, that the death was not either accidental or natural—they will release the *entirety* of my research papers to the public. Many, many reputations will be ruined forever. Even the reputation of the United States itself will be badly tarnished. I hope and pray that such release will never be necessary. Absent anything unnatural however, the papers will be totally destroyed fifty years after my demise.

The death of President Kennedy changed everything for me. I no longer wanted anything at all to do with government service. I just wanted to live the rest of my life as a normal, private citizen. The frenetic activity of a Special Assistant to the President had been exhilarating, and the feeling of being intimately involved at the center of the ever-changing drama of world events was intellectually and emotionally intoxicating. I don't think I have ever been so totally absorbed on so many different levels. I don't usually sleep for more than four hours per day but I sincerely begrudged Morpheus his brief quasi-diurnal reign.

For those of us lucky enough to have worked in the Kennedy administration, it really was Camelot. I think it was the happiest time of my life, but it was all over after the assassination. Literally overnight, the environment in the White House had not only become totally reversed, but the hostile and antagonistic attitude of Johnson towards me was threatening and toxic. It wasn't quite the same sense of betrayal and aloneness that I had felt when I was being transported by the KGB to Lubyanka—but it was close. Once again, I was being imprisoned by my own government. On top of that, my period of detention appeared to be indeterminate, with no date certain of release. I love this country though, and the basic principles on which it is based. I was determined to do whatever I could to serve it well—on my own terms. I didn't know it at the time, but I was destined to transmogrify into the ultimate lone wolf.

The following paragraphs are intended only for those who haven't read Book One, or who want a quick refresher.

When I was working directly for President Kennedy, I think everyone knew, or at least assumed (correctly, as it happens), that I kept my personal research papers in my secure file cabinet in my office in the West Wing of the White house. Besides me, the only other entity that could open that file cabinet was the Secret Service—and then only on direct orders from the President. As long as Kennedy was president, I was secure in the confidence that he would never issue such an order. He wouldn't have to. If he had asked for them, I would have gladly turned everything I had over to him.

Johnson was completely different. Johnson would not only want those papers, he would not hesitate to use them to his personal advantage. Immediately after the news of Kennedy's assassination, I made arrangements to photocopy a number of official supporting documents and took those photocopies and all my research notes to my apartment. They weren't safe there of course, and I knew Johnson was after them because I had planted "tell-tales" on the secure file cabinet in my White House office, which had been disturbed—a sure sign that someone had opened the file cabinet. I needed to get the documents out of the country, but didn't know where I could put them if I did.

In that first meeting with Johnson after he had become President, I had accepted his offer to take a couple of weeks off—to mitigate, or at least come to terms with my grief at Jack's assassination—and I asked for 24 hours to respond to his 'generous offer' to spend that time relaxing at his ranch in Texas. I realized that I was in great danger. Both Johnson and I despised each other, so why would he want to keep me so close to him personally? I knew what he wanted. He had had my secure file cabinet searched, and he wanted me to be in a position where he could control and surveil my every move until he achieved his goal. He was determined to find and confiscate those research papers—my 'insurance documents.'

After our meeting in which he had refused my proffered resignation, I returned right away to my apartment. I needed to devise a plan and do it quickly. I had to get my papers out of my apartment, put them somewhere relatively safe, and immediately leave the country to give him the impression that I had taken them with me. The details of what I did and how I did it are thoroughly covered in Book One and are much too complicated to summarize here. Suffice it to say that I was able to put the documents in a safe deposit box in a bank in Washington, and then leave for a two-week trip in Italy.

Although the ticket that I bought from the travel agent (her name was Fiorina Moretti) was a round trip ticket to Rome, my final destination was Sardinia, where I spent two delightful weeks with her family, whose members would become life-long friends. When the opportunity came to move my documents out of the country, these wonderful (and powerful) people would be able to provide the contacts and the guidance I would need to establish a permanent, secure repository that not even the President of the United States would be able to breach.

I had just left Sardinia this morning and I already sorely missed the Moretti family. Because of my top security clearances, it had been completely illegal for me to leave the country without filling out all the necessary paperwork, and Johnson was going to rip me apart for it.

Back Channel: The Vietnam Betrayal

Chapter 1 — Return to Washington

I just couldn't concentrate and it wasn't just because I hadn't slept for a little more than 21 hours and was dead tired. I had just survived a personal meeting with an individual who, to my knowledge, had been complicit in the murder of nine people who had either gotten in his way or posed the danger of doing so. This was no ordinary thug, either. He was a thug, alright but he was also the President of the United States—Lyndon Baines Johnson. He'd be watching me like a hawk from now on. One slip—and I'm a dead man. This may sound dramatic but unless you have spent significant time around the leader of *any* large country, you have no idea of how much power they wield.

***

It was bitter cold when my flight had arrived at Washington National Airport about four hours ago (December 12, 1963). My Secret Service driver, who greeted me upon my arrival with the terse announcement that "President Johnson wants to see you right away, sir," was maneuvering our limo adroitly through the rush hour traffic on our way to the White House, as I gazed morosely through the window at the bundled-up shoppers going happily about their business.

I was scared—terrified, actually. One doesn't lightly tangle with *any* President of the United States—and particularly not this one. Lyndon Johnson could be as vicious and vindictive as anyone I have ever met and he was absolutely furious with me. I was—and still am—convinced that he was the principal organizer of the assassination of my former boss, and friend— President John F. Kennedy. There was no way I was going to be able to avoid this meeting, and I was dreading it. I thought of the sunny, warm tranquility I had left behind that morning in Sardinia, and inwardly groaned. There have been many times in my life when I wanted desperately to be back in the United States, but right now was definitely not one of them.

What a change the two and a half weeks since Kennedy's assassination had brought. Under Kennedy, the White House had become my second home. I worked there, ate there, worked out at the White House gym and pool and on a couple of occasions during the Cuban Missile Crisis, I had just plopped down on a chair in my office and slept there. I loved working for Kennedy. I

1

couldn't wait to get to work early each morning and oftentimes worked past midnight. Camelot was real and it was magical. I felt like I was at the center of the universe and working directly for the man that was making history and changing the world. Not only that, he had become a friend. I couldn't have been happier. The fact that I had essentially zero social life really didn't bother me—I frankly didn't have time for it anyway. I think I was about as content as a man could be.

Now the White House had been taken over by a malevolent man whom I detested and feared. My White House 'home' was gone. Destroyed. Turned into a hostile, alien, cold, enemy stronghold. Camelot had evaporated overnight and would never return. It filled me with bitter outrage.

My musings ended abruptly as we pulled up to the entrance to the State Floor of the White House and my driver handed my travel bag to the Marine who opened the door for me. (I was sure my bag would be thoroughly searched during my meeting with Johnson.) I wasn't worried. They would find absolutely nothing of interest. I was informed that Johnson was briefly attending a White House cocktail party for foreign correspondents and he wanted me to wait for him in the Yellow Room upstairs, in the family living quarters (the Yellow Room is directly above the oval Blue Room and is the same size and shape). I was literally going into the lion's den. I tried to mentally prepare myself for combat. The butler that met me at the entrance to the family quarters was nice, though. I recognized him as the same person who had guided my wheelchair into the Oval Office for my first meeting with President Kennedy. I couldn't remember his name so simply said, "It's good to see you again."

He smiled and replied, "It's good to see you too, sir. I'm very pleased to see that you seem to have recovered completely from your wounds." He seemed a little taken aback when he took my overcoat, and I asked him how he was doing, etc. Johnson wasn't known for treating his underlings very well. I think he was happy to be treated like an actual person again and he warmed up right away. I thought *I* needed some human warmth a lot more than he did. Actually, (while on the subject of human warmth) on a later occasion, he shared some information with me about someone rather well known who had crawled into Johnson's bed [with him in it] and stayed there for quite some time. I always chuckle a little bit when I see her on television dispensing her knowledge to the vast unwashed.

I didn't have to wait long. Johnson exploded into the room and greeted me like a long lost son, grabbing my shoulder while vigorously pumping my hand with a strong handshake. Johnson was a big guy. He was about 6'4" tall [193 cm] and early in his presidency he weighed about 220 pounds [100 kg.] He weighed a lot more later in his Presidency, and had to wear a girdle to try to hide it. Lyndon was always in a rush and those long legs made it truly hard for shorter people to keep up with him. He had outsized ears and hands, leathery skin and a booming voice which he never seemed to modulate. He was also boorish and crass and often publicly belittled and swore at his staff. (He never did it to me but he certainly yelled at me on several occasions.)

2

He had an amazing ability to almost instantly switch from bellowing in a purple-faced rage to a calm and gentle (for him) tone of voice. He was devious and a liar, and proud of it. I would *truly* trust a rattlesnake before I'd trust Lyndon Johnson. At least the rattlesnake is honest about its intentions. He motioned for me to sit on the couch while he plopped into a chair to face me. (Somehow, Johnson sitting in a Louis XIV chair seemed a little incongruous.)

"Bertie, Bertie," he said. "You've worried us all to death. Where in the world have you been— and what in the world have you been doing there?"

Why couldn't he just be honest? The Secret Service had finally found the travel agency where I had bought my ticket, and spoken to Fiorina Moretti who had sold me the round trip ticket to Rome. Fortunately for me, the little Italian shuttle airline that operated between Rome and Cagliari was too small to have the international arrangements that would permit U.S. travel agents such as Fiorina to write tickets for them. Therefore, the trail ended in Rome. Johnson was well aware that I had gone to Rome. He didn't know anything more than that, because Fiorina was not about to risk getting her parents involved by telling the Secret Service that I was staying with them.

I had rehearsed my little speech on the long flight back from Rome and launched into it effortlessly.
"Mr. President, I am sincerely regretful if I have caused you or any of your staff any consternation or worry. As you know, sir, I considered President Kennedy to be a personal friend, so news of his assassination hit me even harder that it did many of the rest of the nation's citizens. In the aftermath, I had decided to leave government service altogether, and when you informed me that you were ordering me to stay on in my position of Special Assistant to the President, I had yet another massive mental gear-change to make. I believe you sensed the extent to which my thoughts were in total disarray, and I was most grateful for your suggestion that I take a couple of weeks off to reorganize. I was particularly grateful for your generous offer for me to use your ranch in Texas as a haven in which to do so.

"As my mind was really in a bit of a jumble, I decided that what I actually wanted to do was to spend the time with a good personal friend who was a buddy of mine at Duke. He was a friend I could talk to and he always gave good advice. I tried calling him but there was no answer and on the spur of the moment, I decided to just hop in the car and go out to Des Moines to see him. I did write you a note thanking you for your generous offer, and meant to give it to the concierge when I left, but in my haste, I forgot, and left it on my desk in the apartment. I hadn't even gotten out of town when I was struck by how foolish I was being. What if my friend hadn't answered his phone because he was out of town on a trip or something?

"When I turned the car around and was driving back to my apartment, I decided that if I couldn't be with a close friend, the next best thing would be a total change of scenery— somewhere out of the country, preferably near the ocean and where the weather would be reasonably warm. I stopped at a public phone booth and picked out a travel agency at random, called them, explained to them what I had in mind and asked them to start working on possibilities. I didn't want to waste time going all the way back to the apartment to park my car, and since I was in a neighborhood that had lots of high-rise apartment buildings, I figured that I would just try to find an empty visitor's parking space in one of them, and leave my car there. So that's what I did. I took a taxi into town, went to my bank to get out some money, went to the travel agency and talked to one of the agents there about different possibilities, and finally settled on Rome. I found out that I could catch a flight out of Idlewild that very evening—and I think you know the rest, sir."

Johnson had been regarding me with a piercing stare during my little recitation, and I think he knew that a 'recitation' was exactly what it was. Everything I had told him was verifiably true—as far as it went—but what was I leaving out? All he said was, "Well, that's real interesting, Bertie. Tell me what you did once you got to Rome."

I won't bore you with the rest of the cover story I had made up and dutifully recited. It had been carefully thought out and was watertight. It's hard to hide the smell of pure bullshit however, but I didn't give a damn whether he believed me or not.

Johnson casually asked me what I was doing with my bags all this time. I told him that I didn't have a suitcase; I just had a small gym bag packed with a few changes of clothes and my shaving kit.

Johnson made a huge mistake then because he blurted out, "Do you mean to tell me that all you were carrying around is that little bag that you left downstairs?"

I just nodded and said, "Yes, sir." But Johnson realized very clearly what he had just done. Presidents do not check on the baggage of their visitors. I had no doubt that he had personally gone through it thoroughly when the Marine guard showed it to him and told him that he had found nothing. What he had just done was to confirm that he was intensely interested in the contents of the baggage that I was carrying. Of course what he was most interested in was what baggage I had carried *out* of the country but there was no possible way to check that. He was in a silent rage. The room was charged with a nearly palpable electricity from his anger. Johnson always *had* to win. Even with games like horseshoes or checkers, he enjoyed the games as long as he was winning, but would quit and walk away in a rage the first time he lost.

After chastising me severely for having left the country without filling out the appropriate forms (with my security clearances, that was a grave offense). He probably could have very justifiably stripped me of all my clearances and put me in jail but of course, if he did that, he could not possibly keep me on as Special Assistant—and he would still not have the documents he so desperately wanted. It was better to keep me under his thumb so that he could keep an eye on me. It was a good example of the type of peculiar, circular dilemma described so memorably in Joseph Heller's 1961 work, *"Catch 22."* Lyndon Johnson did *not* like to be out-maneuvered and he did *not* like to be frustrated. I was not surprised by his red face, his surliness or his screaming when he told me that whether I liked it or not, he was assigning me for temporary duty to Robert S. McNamara, (the Secretary of Defense) and that I *would* carry out the Secretary's orders as though they had been issued directly by him personally. He then calmed down slightly and asked me why I was so God-damn dead set against working in Defense Planning like the Secretary wanted me to.

"Because, sir, I consider it to be a total waste of time and effort but much more importantly, I don't want it on my conscience that I participated in causing multiple deaths and countless mutilations of fine young Americans."

"You'd better explain yourself, Bertie," he snarled.

"I've read the draft of NSAM (National Security Action Memorandum) 273[1], Mr. President. Have you approved it?"

He nodded his assent.

"Well sir, then it appears to me that far from planning to withdraw all our personnel by 1965 as President Kennedy planned, we are now prepared to significantly augment our presence and our activities in Vietnam. As you know sir, at the request of President Kennedy, I have done something that not a single one of our top military or State Department officials in Vietnam has done. Guided by a member of a prominent and respected Vietnamese family, I have visited villages all the way from the Delta to the demarcation line between North and South Vietnam. It was my guide—and friend—who did the actual speaking for us as we met with the village elders in their council huts, but through him I gathered invaluable information on what the Vietnamese *people* think, how they feel about our presence there, how they feel about our Strategic Hamlet[2] program, what they felt about then President Diem[3], what they felt about the re-unification of North and South Vietnam, and what they felt about Ho Chi Minh. It was pretty sobering. The bottom line is that the people—the "peasants"—aren't really very concerned about who is running the government, but given the choice between an American puppet government and Ho Chi Minh, they will pick 'Uncle Ho.' We may not like him, but the truth is that he is a brilliant, charismatic man that the majority of people in Vietnam—both North and South—see as a real Vietnamese patriot. If the majority of a country's population is not willing to fully support a struggle for independence or throw their support behind some other cause that the country's political and military leaders are willing to wage war for, the war has no chance of being 'won.' I'm afraid that Secretary McNamara's cautious optimism is based

---

[1] See Appendix I at www.bertiemacdocs.com.
[2] See Appendix I at www.bertiemacdocs.com.
[3] In a military-led coup on November 1, 1963, Diem had been removed from office and then assassinated along with his brother.

on overly rosy reports from the Vietnamese army generals and it certainly wouldn't surprise me to find that the *actual* situation on the ground there is quite different—and alarming. It is simply not in the Asian culture to disappoint people or tell them unpleasant things. They will always try to put the most positive spin on things that they possibly can, even if they have to stretch the truth a little. They do not want to be impolite and the bearer of bad news. But those are the only people that McNamara, General Taylor, Ambassador Lodge, etc. are talking to. I think we ought to be highly skeptical of the accuracy of the information that they are receiving."

"God damn it, Bertie, you sound just like John McCone,"[4] he growled. "Have you been talking to him on the phone, or something?"

I replied that I had not and to his next question I replied that I had not discussed my views with Secretary McNamara, either. He gave me a direct order to do so as soon as I reported to work.

I asked if I could get someone to drive me back to the apartment building where I had parked my car, to which he replied, "Sure, sure. Just get somebody to get a limo for you when you get downstairs."

As I was leaving, he stopped me and said, "You know something, Bertie? I always wondered why Jack spent so much time talking to you. You're smarter than I thought. You like to just analyze everything, don't you? Well, let me tell you something. Don't get too smart for your britches. I promise you'll regret it. And one other thing. Don't you ever, ever leave the country again without my personal approval. Never. Ever. Now you go on back home. I've got work to do."

The Marine guard at the entrance gave my little travel bag to my driver, who drove me in silence to the garage where I had left my MG. My driver insisted that he place it in the trunk for me and had the decency to blush when I told him, "Fine. Just open it up—it's not locked. The car's not locked either. Would you like to look in there, too?"

He shook his head and said, "I'm sorry, sir. I was just following orders. It's not personal, sir. Oh, and sir, I was instructed to tell you that your limo privileges remain in force but you are requested not use the service when reporting for normal duty at the Pentagon. Treasury will reimburse you for the use of your private vehicle."

I was too tired to go somewhere and try to find something to eat so I just drove back to my apartment. The apartment building was owned by the U.S. General Services Administration (GSA) and occupancy was restricted to very high ranking government employees or elected officials, diplomats, etc. The building was extremely secure and the elevator from the garage

---

[4] Director of the Central Intelligence Agency (CIA)

(which one could only enter with a personal security code) would stop only in the main lobby. In fact, the elevator had just two buttons on the control panel—a red one for emergencies, and a black one. Pressing the black one simply took you to wherever the elevator was programmed to take you, and if you got into the elevator on the garage level, it would only take you to the building's lobby. When the elevator doors opened in the lobby—about ten feet away from the desk of the 'concierge' (actually an armed Secret Service agent)—he would greet you cordially and send you on to your floor.

In light of everything that had happened since I left for Rome, and especially in light of the events of this evening, I wasn't quite sure what to expect, but I got only an, "Ah! Good evening, sir. Good to see you back. You're looking fit and tanned. I hope you had a pleasant vacation. Is there anything that you would like us to do for you? Your mail's upstairs on your desk."

My apartment had been assigned to me by President Kennedy, but its two bedrooms, 2½ baths and separate living room, dining room and study were ridiculous for a single person. Nevertheless, it now felt like home and I was happy to be back. I heated up a can of soup to appease my growling stomach and then went into the study to look at my mail. There wasn't very much—I have no family. My father was killed in a car accident and although my mother is still (barely) alive, she is in a Baltimore nursing home with terminal-stage Alzheimer's and recognizes no one.

That brings my narrative up to date.

I was profoundly puzzled by the rapidity with which Johnson had approved NSAM 273, which was so clearly counter to NSAM 263, which Kennedy had approved. It was a radical change of policy. What was so puzzling was that Secretaries Rusk and McNamara—at a bare minimum— would have had to sign off on it before Johnson's official approval. How could he have possibly persuaded them to accept something so radically different from the existing policy, as laid down in NSAM 263, and do it so incredibly fast? It usually takes many weeks—a month or more, even—to get everybody to sign off on a major policy shift like this. Then I had a thought that so stunned me that I was literally paralyzed for a few seconds. What if Johnson had *already* lined up the support of McNamara and Rusk? The implication of that was bone-chilling. I was already personally convinced that LBJ was the organizing force behind the assassination of Kennedy, but if Johnson had already lined up the support of McNamara, Rusk, and McGeorge Bundy (who wrote the draft) as well as, perhaps, some other high Administration officials, it would mean that there was a whole cabal who knew the assassination was imminent, and were complicit in it. There had to be some other explanation. I couldn't think of one at the moment but surely it would come to me.[5] I decided to clear my mind by focusing on more mundane concerns.

---

[5] Unfortunately, it never has and I've thought about it for nearly 50 years. I later found that there were quite a few others who had reluctantly come to the same conclusion.

I didn't know whether I had been followed when I drove back to the apartment but I had to assume that I had been. I also had to assume that my apartment was bugged and that I would have a 'tail' on me no matter where I went. I was pretty sure that Johnson was almost certain that I had taken my 'insurance policy' documents with me, when I went to Italy, but he was going to track me closely on the off-chance that I hadn't. Being constantly followed was no way to lead a life, and I wasn't having it. There had to be a way to get out of such constant surveillance and I was determined to figure out a way to do it. In the meantime, I would have some fun and a certain amount of satisfaction in fooling my keepers. I've always enjoyed challenges—the non-deadly ones, anyway. I undressed, unstrapped Excalibur,[6] put it on my bedside table and took a leisurely shower. I set the alarm for 5:30 a.m., which is when I normally wake up naturally, but my body was still on Italian time. I slept like a log until it rang.

McNamara usually got in to the office around 6:30 in the morning, and I used my secure phone[7] to call him. When his assistant answered, she greeted me cheerfully, but said that Secretary McNamara was going to be completely tied up for the next several days. She said that she had scheduled me to meet with Deputy Secretary Gilpatric at 8:00 Monday morning. I assured her that I would be there, hung up and thought, "Wow! What a gift! I've just gotten a three-day week-end pass." I was particularly grateful because I really needed some time to think.

Two Encounters

Delighted with the unexpected freedom, I decided I would go have a magnificent breakfast at a nearby diner that I knew of, and which had become one of my favorite places to get a casual meal. Afterwards, I'd go to my office in the West Wing to see what paperwork had accumulated during my absence. I set off feeling pretty good about things.

The diner was less crowded than I had anticipated, so I grabbed an empty seat at the counter and ordered an enormous breakfast. When it came, the guy sitting next to me said, "Good God, man! How can you eat like that and still be so trim and fit?"

I don't like talking to strangers, so barely looking at him, I just mumbled something like, "I was really hungry this morning," and turned to my breakfast. I wasn't going to get off so easily.

At least he had the decency to wait until I had finished, but as soon as I laid my fork down, he stuck out his hand and said, "Hi, I'm Peter Moore, retired Navy. How 'bout you? You in the military?"

---

[6] An extremely lethal Special Operations combat knife which Secretary McNamara had temporarily permitted me to have for a special self-protection situation. He had probably forgotten about it by now. See Book One.

[7] Issued by the White House Communications Agency to allow secure communications.

I actually was a major in the Regular Army at the time, but I didn't feel like being interrogated so I lied and said, "No, I'm just a civilian."

"You come here often? I come just about every morning because my wife, Anne, likes to sleep late but I don't recall seeing you here before."

"No, sir. I'm a pretty infrequent breakfast patron."

"Well tell me . . . aah, what did you say your name was?"

"I didn't say, sir. My name is Bertram MacFarland."

"Well, Bertram—you go by the name of Bertram?"

"Bertie, sir."

He sighed.

"Well Bertie, you're about as closed-mouthed as they come so I'll stop trying to strike up a conversation. I expect you must be in Intelligence or something. Us old retired guys enjoy meeting and talking to new people—especially young ones like you—but it looks like I've struck out this morning. I'll be seeing you around."

With that, he put some money on the counter, waved, and walked out. I noticed he had a slight limp.

I asked for another cup of coffee. For the life of me, I couldn't put my finger on it, but there was something oddly troubling about Peter Moore. His features seemed slightly Slavic, but in the melting pot of America, that meant nothing. His English was totally accentless and idiomatic American English, colloquialisms and all. However, the lack of a regional accent was common among career service members who, for twenty years or more, had been stationed on bases all over the globe. I decided that I was being paranoid. After all, *I* had sat down next to *him*—not the other way around. I paid up and left for the White House but I made a mental note that if I ever went there again for breakfast, *not* to sit at the counter but to try to find a booth or table.

I was relieved to see that my desk was piled pretty high with manila envelopes, most of which were stamped 'Secret' or 'Top Secret.' It looked like I was still on the distribution list. I grabbed the whole stack and turned it upside down, so that I could start with the earliest documents and work my way through to the present. The first two were 'old news' and went straight into the shredder. The next one was something of a shocker, though. It was a memorandum for record[8] written by John McCone, Director of the CIA, and covered a meeting in the Oval Office attended by Johnson, Secretaries Rusk, McNamara, Ball, Messrs. Bundy and McCone plus Ambassador Lodge. The subject was the South Vietnamese situation.

McCone's view of the situation was bleak. He noted a continuing level of Viet Cong activity and attacks and expressed his considerable concern over a high level of message volume on the Viet Cong military and political networks. I found one paragraph of the memo of particular interest:

> *Note*: I received in this meeting the first "President Johnson tone" as contrasted with the "Kennedy tone." Johnson definitely feels that we place too much emphasis on social reforms; he has very little tolerance for our spending so much time being "do-gooders;" and he has no tolerance whatsoever with bickering and quarrelling of the type that has gone on in South Vietnam.

I was appalled to see that the rest of the 'advisers' had a generally optimistic view of what was going on, and felt positive about the eventual outcome of the 'war.' However, the thing I found shocking was the *date* of the meeting—November 24, two days after Kennedy's assassination. I had neither been invited nor informed. I re-visited my 'cabal' thoughts of the previous evening. Could a conspiracy of the top administration officials actually be possible? Surely, not. In any case, it was clear that I was definitely 'out of the loop.' None of the other documents were of major importance so I shredded them, filed the McCone memorandum in my secure file cabinet, and went back to my apartment to reflect. It was the end of an era. Even though I remained on the daily distribution list of classified documents and reports, I was now an outsider. I was no-longer going to participate in the events that made history; I was just going to be allowed to read about them. My world was falling apart in very large chunks. I desperately wanted to be free of any further government involvement of any kind but I was trapped. What was going to happen to the rest of my life?

On my way home, I decided I needed to make some changes domestically in terms of my kitchen and pantry. Heretofore, I had eaten most of my meals in the White House and although my kitchen was thoroughly stocked with all sorts of condiments and utensils, courtesy of Helen[9] (plus a second refrigerator completely filled with white wine and Champagne—also courtesy of Helen), my capacious pantry was barren except for some cans of soup and a can or two of pork and beans. I stopped at a bookstore and bought a cookbook, and then went to a grocery store and picked up some staples. My home-cooked hot dog was delicious.

There was a public phone booth about a block and a half from the apartment and I used it to

---

[8] See Johnson Library, Meeting Notes File, Meeting with Lodge and Vietnam Advisers. Secret. Drafted by McCone on November 25. The meeting was held in the Executive Office Building. Johnson describes this meeting in *The Vantage Point*, pp. 43-44.

[9] See Book One

call Fiorina's travel agency. I was told that she had just left today for an out-of-town trip and would not be back until shortly after the New Year. I figured she was going to Sardinia to be with her parents for the holidays. Back in the apartment, I wrote a short note thanking her for introducing me to her parents and telling her how much I enjoyed them and my stay with them. I addressed it to her at the local travel agency. I then wrote a somewhat longer note to the Moretti's telling them how much I had enjoyed meeting them and the family and thanking them for their gracious hospitality. I wished them all a Merry Christmas and a wonderful New Year. I added that I truly missed them. I addressed it to their home in Sardinia and put a ton of stamps on it. I did not put my return address on either envelope.

Although it was a miserable December day—temperature around 40, patchy fog, occasional spits of rain—I needed exercise. I dressed up in warm gym clothes, unstrapped Excalibur and put it in its hiding place, and then drove out to Rock Creek Park for a good long run. Being a work day (Friday) and with such miserable weather, I had the park pretty much to myself, and once I had settled into the long loping stride that is so natural for me, my body lapsed into auto-pilot mode and left my mind completely free to think. I began to think about my forthcoming meeting on Monday with Roswell Gilpatric, the Deputy Secretary of Defense.

Gilpatric was an interesting guy. Extremely bright, he was Phi Beta Kappa when he graduated Yale in 1928. He graduated from Yale Law School in 1931. He came from a very well-connected family and he had been a friend of (the future Governor) Nelson Rockefeller since childhood. He went to work for a prestigious New York City law firm where he later became a partner. He joined the Kennedy Administration in 1961 when Kennedy appointed him as the number two man in the Defense Department. Gilpatric had been Under Secretary of the Air Force from 1951 to 1953 and Kennedy wanted to make sure that McNamara had someone on his team that was intimately familiar with the way things work in Washington. McNamara and Gilpatric quickly became so close that they would often finish each other's sentences, and McNamara would often start out a statement with, "Ros and I . . ." I truly enjoy interacting with bright people and though I wasn't sure how much negotiating leverage I had, I was looking forward to my meeting with Gilpatric on Monday.

I had been running for a little more than two hours, and was only about 15 minutes from getting back to where I had parked my car when it happened. The impact was like running into the side of a barn, and I found myself sprawled on the side of the path wondering what or who had hit me. My Army training as an Airborne Ranger, with extensive additional training in Special Ops immediately took over, and I instinctively went into a combat crouch. I wished I had Excalibur with me but I'm also very well trained to kill with my bare hands. My first job was to locate the enemy.

It wasn't hard. I heard a low moan from the other side of the path, and saw another runner lying there, with his bleeding head next to a tree trunk. It looked like both of us idiots had assumed we had the park to ourselves and had stupidly run headlong into one another because neither one of us was paying attention. I didn't seem to be hurt at all, but I was concerned about the other runner. I was hoping that the blood on his head was coming from a superficial scalp wound, as they are medically trivial but notorious for copious bleeding. I was also hoping that a superficial head wound was the only thing he had suffered, but of course, I had no idea. Quickly, but cautiously, I went to him and knelt by his side. The caution came from long training. Any time there is unexpected and violent bodily contact, never assume that the other person is your friend.

"Hey, are you OK?"

[softly and muffled] "I doan know."

"Don't try to get up. Lie still right where you are for the moment. Can you wiggle your fingers? OK. That looks good. Now try to very slowly and gently move your feet. Just do one at a time. If you feel a sharp pain, stop immediately and tell me where it hurts most. OK, that's good. Now the other one. Looks good. Now just keep lying there. I am going to gently probe your arms, legs and torso to see if I can feel anything broken. Tell me immediately if you feel a sharp pain. Are you still awake? Can you hear me?"

[Much more clearly, this time.] "Yes."

I went over him pretty thoroughly. He seemed to be intact and his muscles, though firm, were not hard. I felt a lot better after discovering that. It looked like this really was an accident. The blood was starting to clot around his scalp wound and that was a relief, since it indicated that he probably had not suffered a deep head wound. My principal concern now was for the integrity of his spinal column. If that were injured, he was in serious trouble. It was already near freezing and it would be getting dark soon. In 1963, cell phones hadn't even been thought of. It was a fifteen minute run back to the car, and I wasn't sure where I could find a public phone or a gas station. Medical help would be a long time coming. I kicked myself for my stupidity.

I asked him not to move his head, and said that I was going to put my hand on his neck, and very gently probe the bones there. I asked him to tell me immediately if anything hurt. With great relief, I felt nothing out of the ordinary and told him so. I asked if he thought he could roll over so that he was lying on his back, and said that when he did, I would help him get up. He struggled a little, but made it, and I helped him to his feet. He said he felt a bit woozy but he thought he was OK.

There was no way he was up for running, but after about five minutes on the path back to the parking lot, he felt recovered enough to take his arm from around my shoulders and continue walking without help. We chatted amicably; and we each apologized profusely to the other for being completely at fault. We exchanged names (his was Peter Boyle); occupations (he was a junior partner in a small but apparently pretty successful Washington law firm, I told him I was working with an Intelligence group in the Pentagon); and marital status (he was married, but no children yet). He expressed surprise that I was not a physician, and wanted to know how I seemed to know so well what to do when I was checking on his condition. When I told him that I had taken a bunch of pre-med courses at Duke, when I was considering going on to medical school, he laughed and told me, "You CIA guys have an answer for everything, don't you?" I think he was a little taken aback at the sharpness of my reply emphasizing that I was definitely *not* a CIA employee.

We found we had a number of interests in common. He was fascinated by mathematics (in which I had a degree); we both were passionate about protecting wilderness areas and wildlife; we both loved music—classical, jazz (we both thought Stan Kenton and Julie Christie were nothing short of fantastic); we both loved reading. For the first time in a very long while, I thought that maybe I could have a friend who wasn't put off by my inability to discuss details of my post-university past. It seemed promising, anyway. Just before we got to the parking area, where the eponymous Rock Creek flows under a small wooden bridge across the path, I told Peter that maybe we should do a little cosmetic repair. He followed me down to the creek where I untied my sweat band, and used part of it as a wash cloth and the remainder as a towel, to get the dried blood off his face and neck.. I didn't want his wife, Sally, to faint when he came in the house. When we got to the parking area, I used the pencil and pad that I always keep in the glove box to swap phone numbers, and after his strong assurances that he was OK to drive, I asked him to please call me and if I wasn't there, to please leave a message on my machine confirming that he had arrived home safely.

When I got home there was already a message on my machine. It was Sally confirming that Peter was fine but tired, and thanking me for taking such good care of him. She also invited me for dinner at their house Saturday evening of the next week. Since my return from the Soviet Union, it was the first time I had ever received an invitation to a private dinner from anyone except Jack and Bobby Kennedy, and Kenney O'Donnell. I was exhilarated. I was in such a festive mood that after returning the phone call to accept, and showering and cleaning up, I eschewed the opportunity to have the second home-cooked hot dog for the day and went to the diner for dinner.

When I got back home I decided to attack the stack of letters on my desk that had accumulated during my absence. Aside from a few minor bills, they were mostly Embassy invitations for Christmas and New Year parties. Properly vetted and eligible bachelors are difficult to find in Washington, so I get a lot of invitations to Embassy functions. I had no plans whatever for Christmas or New Year's Eve, so I saved a few invitations to look at more closely when I had the time.

A Little Chat with Ros

I was almost late for my meeting with Secretary Gilpatric. When you are in the back seat of a White House limo (which up until then had been my usual mode of travel in Washington), you tend not to pay very much attention to the route being taken to your destination, and you certainly have no need to know where people park their cars. Not knowing exactly which lane you need to be in while driving in the ferocious Washington rush-hour traffic is hazardous, to say the least, but on the bright side, there were a whole lot of drivers who got to test their cars' hooters and make sure they worked properly. Parking at the Pentagon was a nightmare. I couldn't find where they had hidden the 'Visitor's Parking' (if such even existed), and I wound up parking in an area that I think was reserved for flag-grade officers (Generals and Admirals). I figured,——'The hell with it. If I wind up getting a ticket or getting towed, I'll get Bob (McNamara) or Secretary Gilpatric to sort it out.'

It was a good thing that it was a bitter cold day, because I ran full out to get to the River Entrance to the Pentagon. I arrived in Secretary Gilpatric's outer office slightly breathless but right on time. I was in a foul mood, though. The traffic and parking problems had seriously annoyed and frustrated me, but what made me truly angry was the realization that no matter what I said, Gilpatric could simply order me to work in Defense Planning. I felt at a terrible disadvantage and as a result, I'm afraid I had an *Attitude (with a capital 'A')* when I met him. It wasn't a great way to start a meeting with Bob's *alter ego*.

I was ushered in immediately.

He greeted me warmly, as if we were old friends.

"Bertie, Bertie. Come on in and make yourself comfortable. For once, I actually get to speak to you. I don't know how many meetings we've been in together but you never spoke a word, never changed the expression on your face, never made eye contact with anyone, and then you left immediately after the meeting was over. Jack told Bob and me more than once that he absolutely treasured the one page synopsis and analysis that you would give him after those meetings. He never let anyone see them, though. Mac Bundy[10] got pretty steamed about that once, but Jack told him that he had given you his word, and he wasn't about to break it. He thought the world of you, you know."

"Thank you for saying so, sir. I know I certainly thought the world of him."

"Well, let's not dwell on it. It's painful for us both, but I truly don't understand why Lyndon doesn't want you to continue in that capacity. Just between the two of us, in my opinion, he needs you a hell of a lot more in that role than Jack ever did. What's he got against you? He

---

[10] McGeorge Bundy, the National Security Advisor.

14

sure doesn't like you—I'm sure you know that—but sometimes both Bob and I get the impression that somehow he's a little afraid of you. What's going on between you two?"

When I replied, "I'm sure I don't know, sir," I didn't mean for it to come out sounding so defiant and hostile, but it did.

He stared hard at me and said, "OK, that's it, Bertie. If you want to play hardball, we can do that, but I'll win, and you know it. I'm not stupid, you know. I know damned well you're going through all this formality and closed-mouth crap just to annoy me. Well guess what. It worked, and I'm damned annoyed, and that's a dumb way for you to start this discussion. Now how do you want to continue?"

I felt like a complete idiot and said so. "You're right of course and it *was* dumb on my part. Ros... May I call you Ros?"

"Of course. If you could call the former president and his wife by their first names, call the Attorney General 'Bobby' and my boss 'Bob', you can sure as hell call me 'Ros'. Now get on with it."

"Ros, I know the President—and incidentally, I don't call him 'Lyndon' any longer—wants me to work in Defense Planning, and I guess Bob does too, but I have to tell you that I desperately don't want to do that. I know that you can order me to, and if you do, I have no recourse. I feel like a bear backed into a corner with a gun pointing at me. Please don't pull the trigger just yet."

"Tell me why you don't want to work with us."

"Because I don't want any part of sending Americans into a war that we have no hope of winning. Since Johnson is an incredibly wily politician, I feel sure that he won't really turn up the heat on Vietnam until after next year's election, which I'm sure he'll win unless the Republicans can come up with another Eisenhower, but after that, I feel certain that he'll throw everything we've got at the North Vietnamese."

"Well, that's speculation on your part, Bertie; but I don't deny that I agree with you—and of course, I never said that."

"I appreciate your confiding in me, sir.... uh, Ros. As you know, I'm very good at keeping secrets."

"The understatement of the year. Keep going. Why are you so pessimistic about the war?"

"Well, for one thing, I've talked to the *people*. When President Kennedy sent me over there with

15

a translator, the son of a very prominent and respected Vietnamese family, we talked to the village elders in villages all the way from the Delta in the south to almost the demarcation line between North and South Vietnam in the north. As far as the villagers are concerned, they have no problem with the reunification of North and South Vietnam. All they want is to be left alone to tend their farms. After all, their experience so far with the South Vietnamese government has been a true disaster for them. As you know, the peasants (who are the vast majority of the population) are 80 to 90 percent Buddhist. When Diem took over the government of South Vietnam in the fraudulent plebiscite (Diem got more votes in the Saigon province than there were residents, for example) in 1955, he confiscated almost all of the peasants' land—particularly in the fertile Delta—and gave it to his wealthy patrons. His patrons then charged the peasants exorbitant rents to farm and live on it. On top of that, Diem was a fanatically devoted Catholic.

"In 1959, the son-of-a-bitch dedicated the entire country to the Virgin Mary. Do you know that the Catholic Church 'owned' *1,500 square kilom*eters of land and was the largest land owner in South Vietnam? Army officers and public officials were required to convert to Catholicism to gain employment or be promoted. All this is in a country that is 80 to 90 percent Buddhist, for God's sake! And who is propping up the government in South Vietnam? The U.S.—another 'Christian' nation. How can we possibly think that the South Vietnamese *people* would support armed aggression by a cabal like that against their brothers to the north? It's so unreal that honestly, sometimes I think I'm living in some sort of alternate universe. How can everyone just ignore reality?"

He looked at me intently, and then sighed and said, "Well, well. So the stone-faced Bertie can be passionate after all. Well, you've won that one, Bertie. Putting you into Defense Planning would be equivalent to Bob and me poisoning their water supply or something. My guess is that if you were assigned to the Department, within 48 hours you'd have nearly everybody in there either quitting or begging for re-assignment. So before I ask you what the hell we're going to do with you, tell me why you don't think the repercussions of withdrawing our support for South Vietnam would not lead to a Communist take-over of the entire region, including Laos, Thailand, and Cambodia to name a few. Be quick. I've got to throw you out of here in ten minutes. I've got another meeting coming up."

"I'm not suggesting that we completely withdraw our support for South Vietnam, Ros. We can train their Army; we can provide them with tanks, airplanes, equipment and all that sort of thing; we can give them money, etc., but the bottom line is that if they are not willing to sacrifice their own lives to preserve their national identity, goals and government, then I'm damned if I can see why we should sacrifice the lives of *American* men and women to do so. We can give the Viets all the help in the world but if they aren't willing to shoulder the burden themselves—with our support in every way other than putting the lives of Americans on the line—the eventual outcome is a foregone conclusion. I think we have to remember that it is only the ruling elite and their wealthy patrons who are so anxious to preserve the distinction between North and South Vietnam. *They* are the ones that have everything to lose by the re-unification of Vietnam, not the peasants who are the *people* of the country. And if that reunification happens, and the surrounding countries are not willing to take up the cudgel themselves to keep Communism out, there's not a damn thing we can do about it.

"I think we are in a war of ideology here. I think our system of government—democracy and individual freedom and free enterprise, etc.—is vastly preferable to the kind of controlled Communist governments that currently exist, and that over time, those governments will crumble under the weight of overwhelming popular discontent. But *until* that happens, it's going to be a very bumpy ride. Life is like that. But in the long term, even the Genghis Kahns of the world eventually fade from view."

He stared at me and eventually said, "I think that's overly simplistic and somewhat naïve, but then you personally are not naïve and God knows you're not simple so I'll have to think about it." He continued, "I'll be honest with you, Bertie. I don't think I like you very much but you have definitely earned my respect. I don't know *who* could control you besides Jack. I wish I could fire you but you don't work for the Department of Defense. You work directly for the President, who warned me incidentally that this might be a tough interview. He also made it very clear that you were going to stay directly under his orders in some capacity or another. That sort of limits everybody's options. I wish to hell I knew what is going on between you two. Anyway, get out of here. Bob or I will be in contact when we've decided what the next step should be. In the meantime, feel free to amuse yourself at the government's expense."

He did shake my hand when I left, though.

I was relieved to find that my little MG was still parked where I had left it. I drove home in something of a funk. I thought that Ros' parting comment about using my free time to amuse myself at the government's expense was kind of a cheap shot. Where was he when I was being tortured in Lubyanka? I decided that I didn't like *him* very much either. The more I thought about that parting shot, the angrier I became.

Christmas in Washington

When I got back home, the morning mail had just arrived, and there was yet another bundle of Embassy invitations to Christmas and New Year's Eve parties. They were from just about every country I could think of, but the ones I was most interested in were the ones from the Scandinavian, French, Italian and British Embassies. There was one from the Soviet Embassy which was personally signed by my friend, Ambassador Anatoly Dobrynin, and I thought about it for a long time before deciding not to accept. I knew I would be seated at the head table, perhaps even next to the Ambassador, and that he would provide me with a beautiful dinner companion, but I thought my appearance for the second time as a mystery guest would set too many tongues wagging and attract far too much attention to me personally. I responded with a hand-written note to be delivered to Ambassador Dobrynin personally, offering my sincerest thanks and explaining why I thought it best not to accept. I thanked him again for his previous hospitality, and sent my best wishes for a happy holiday season and a healthy and happy New Year. I also declined the invitations to both the White House Christmas party and the White House New Year's Eve gala. I didn't want to be anywhere near Lyndon Johnson if he decided to stay in Washington, rather than to go his Texas ranch for the holidays. I didn't know where he was going to be but I wasn't going to risk it.

In all, I accepted six invitations—Denmark, Sweden, Norway, England, France and Italy. On top of that, I was looking forward to having dinner at the Boyle's on Saturday. With no family and no personal friends in Washington (I had high hopes for the Boyles, though), the holiday season always tends to be pretty depressing for me. I hoped to meet some interesting people at the Embassy parties, and vowed not to repeat the experiences I had had following the last two Embassy parties I had attended. As usual, I left my responses with the concierge. I wanted everyone to feel that as far as I was concerned, life was going on as normal, and I normally left my outgoing mail with the concierge. They would find nothing strange about mail addressed to Embassies accepting invitations to parties, or a check being mailed to Brooks Brothers. The notes to the Morettis would be dropped in a public mailbox.

I spent most of the rest of the week working out, reading up about the recently formed DIA in the classified section of the Library of Congress, and reading about cooking in *Joy of Cooking*. I began to understand why it was such a popular cookbook. It is not only full of recipes—it instructs you on *how* to cook, mistakes to avoid, etc. I tried some of the simpler recipes and they mostly turned out pretty well. My pantry and my refrigerator were starting to look a lot less bare.

My first Embassy party was on Friday, and though it was enjoyable, a young lady attached herself to me like a leech within 15 minutes of my arrival, and I simply could not shake her off. She was very attractive, very intelligent, a good conversationalist, well-read on a variety of subjects, had a charming laugh—so what was not to like? Maybe I misread it, but my antennae were picking up what seemed to me to be strong signals of her wanting to establish a serious relationship. No way. She was definitely not happy when, towards the end of the evening, I gave her a hug, a peck on the cheek, wished her a wonderful Christmas, and left. I would have been happy to enjoy a casual one-night stand, but I didn't think that was all she had in mind. I was *not* going down the relationship path again.

By contrast, the dinner the next evening with Peter and Sally Boyle was a pure delight and an unmitigated success. My favorite kind of evening is having spirited, fascinating discussions on all sorts of topics with good friends, while having a great meal washed down with good wine. That's exactly the kind of evening I had with the Boyles. They both greeted me like an old friend and I felt relaxed and truly comfortable right away. Sally again thanked me profusely for having taken such good care of Peter, and Peter thanked me as well. He commented that he was absolutely sure I had some kind of medical background hidden somewhere in my past, but he and Sally both understood that they couldn't pry. We all had a drink before dinner and were chatting animatedly when we sat down to Sally's magnificent *Boef Bourguignon*. I had brought along a bottle of really good Bordeaux, and it was a perfect complement to the meal. Peter talked about some interesting cases he was working on for his law firm; Sally, a Wellesley College graduate, was teaching Art History at American University. I talked about my love of opera and a number of books that I had read recently. We all got so wrapped up in the myriad of conversational trails on which we had embarked, that when I looked at my watch and saw it was almost 1:00 in the morning, I gasped and said, "Oh, Lord! Talk about overstaying your welcome! I had no idea it was so late. I haven't had the opportunity to just talk to real people for so long that I totally lost track of time. I'm really sorry. I promise you that if you ever consent to get together again, I'll be much more observant of the time."

Sally told me not to be silly and they were enjoying themselves so much that they had no more idea of the time than I had. She said that both she and Peter truly looked forward to the next time we could all get together, and when Peter heartily affirmed the sentiment, I felt infinitely better. I drove home feeling I had made two really good friends.

I got luckier on the 23rd and 24th. Neither woman was looking for anything more than a casual good time. The astonishingly good-looking aide to the Ambassador of Italy (Sergio Fenoaltea), who came home with me on the 24th didn't have anywhere to go on Christmas Day either, so was happy to stay. I think it was the first time ever she had not spent Christmas with her family in Italy, so we both consoled each other as best we knew how. She insisted on fixing brunch the next morning, and she turned out to be a really good cook. She was less than thrilled by the 'Italian' ingredients she found in the pantry, and gave me the name and address of a grocery store in Washington that sold *authentic* Italian products. She also gave me the name of two Italian restaurants that she said served 'acceptable' Italian meals.

Brunch was wonderful and we chatted amiably until 2:00 or so. We decided to go for a stroll in the nearby park so we could stretch our legs and get a breath of fresh air, and we both welcomed the clear skies and cold air. I wasn't quite sure what to talk about, but tried to tell her—in the sketchy Italian that I had picked up in Sardinia—what a beautiful country I thought Italy was. She laughed and told me that my Italian was terrible and on top of that, I seemed to have a kind of Sardinian accent. I told her of my recent visit to Sardinia, and she asked me which hotel I had stayed in. When I told her that I had actually stayed with a Sardinian family, she became truly interested. She of course asked what family and where they lived. I told her that I didn't have the family's permission to tell her that and all that I could tell her was that they lived in a little town close to the coast south of Cagliari.

There was no reaction so I thought the subject was finished, when suddenly she gasped and said, "Oh, no! You couldn't have. No. It's not possible. He receives no one except his family."

I asked her what the hell she was talking about but it was as though she didn't hear me.

She mused, "*Perhaps* it's possible. The White House limo, the enormous apartment, the controlled elevator system . . ." She stopped, grabbed my hand, looked up to me and said, "Bertie, you must be a very, *very* important man. I doubt that even my boss, Ambassador Fenoaltea, could get an audience with Don Moretti. And you were his *house guest?* I'm suddenly a little scared of you, Bertie."

Now I was getting a little scared, too. I told her I didn't know what she was talking about, and that I wasn't going to tell her who I stayed with, and it was none of her business anyway—I was just trying to make casual conversation. I also told her that it would be a betrayal of my host's hospitality to mention his name when he had never given me permission to do so, not that I would ever have asked for it. I told her that I was starting to get seriously pissed off (and I definitely was).

She looked at me intently, and then said softly, "You really don't know who he is, do you, Bertie? He is an Italian national hero and has received our country's highest honor for his bravery in World War II when he fought against the Nazis. He is also one of the richest and most powerful men in Italy, perhaps in all of Europe. He has chosen to totally isolate himself from everyone except his family. I don't know why. He only communicates through his law firm in Rome. How could you possibly have been his house guest?"

Now I was getting really scared. I told her I didn't know what she was talking about, but if I *had* been the house guest of someone that rich and powerful and then betrayed his confidence, I didn't give myself much of a chance to be walking around for very long.

She again looked at me intently before she said, "You are quite right, Bertie. *Nobody* betrays Don Moretti and lives very long to tell of it. But you have not even spoken his name. That gives me deep respect for you. I will say nothing of our conversation, not even to my own mother. My family is from Naples. We know how to recognize a brother. Your secret—which I truly think you didn't even know *was* a secret—is completely safe with me."

I hoped so. I had no idea that Don Moretti was anything other than the very wealthy, very reclusive father of Fiorina. I assumed that he and Mama had treated me so kindly because it was his daughter who had invited me to stay with the family. I had no idea he was so powerful and such a legend. It was almost spooky somehow.

I was relieved to put my companion in a cab to go home after dinner.

I went into the office around 11:00 the next morning. Not too much had accumulated on my desk, but there were two items that really caught my attention. The first was a memorandum from McNamara to Johnson[11] dated December 21st. He had just come back from his trip to Saigon that Johnson had unexpectedly signed him up for. His analysis of the current situation there was as pessimistic as I had ever seen him admit to. The second[12] was from John McCone, Director of the CIA, which had been drafted on the 21st but delivered on the 23rd. It was just as pessimistic. I was ecstatic. Then my secure phone rang. I wondered who in the Administration was still talking to me.

It was Bob McNamara. He was curt and to the point. "Well Bertie, I suppose you know that you have totally pissed off the President of the United States."

"I'm sorry, Bob. But I don't think we ought to do anything in Vietnam other than what Jack had planned and I don't want to participate in sending Americans into a situation where some will surely die or be seriously wounded in a conflict that we cannot possibly win."

"That's not your call, Bertie. However, Ros and I agree that putting you into Defense Planning would be worse than putting a fox in the hen house. God *damn* it, Bertie! I did *not* want to have to explain that to the President. But I did and he reluctantly concurs. Bertie, I don't know what the hell is going on between you two but he's *not* going to let you go. So what do you want to do?"

"I'd like to speak to General Carroll, Bob."[13]

There was a long pause and then a sigh. He said, "Ros and I thought you were going to say that. I've got to talk to Carroll about you first. He's got to know what he's getting into, even just talking to you. You could probably be one of his best assets but you come with a lot of baggage. He's got to know that up front."

'Thanks, Bob. God, I hope the New Year is better for us all."

"Me, too. I'll be in touch."

I went to another Embassy party on Saturday. I politely eschewed the after-party opportunities so clearly outlined to me by my dinner partner.

New Year's Eve at the Swedish Embassy was a whole different deal, though.

---

[11] Johnson Library, National Security File, Vietnam Country File, Memos and Misc. Secret.
[12] Johnson Library, National Security File, Vietnam Country File, Memos and Misc. Secret.
[13] LTG. Joseph F. Carroll, the first Director of the Defense Intelligence Agency (DIA)

Chapter 2 — The Swiss Connection

Emma and Joe

I don't know what it is about winter in Washington, DC. The seemingly unending succession of gray, disagreeable, damp, gloomy, cold winter days is wearying and depressing. It was definitely *cold* on December 31, 1963—I think the *high* was below freezing, and it was supposed to drop down much lower later on. I've been in ski resorts in winter, when the temperature was well below *zero,* but somehow under those sparkling blue skies the feeling was one of exhilaration, not of cold. Washington's depressing damp cold penetrates right through to your bones, and the feeling you get is the antithesis of exhilaration. It's just miserable and dreary.

I was enjoying the comfortable warmth inside the limo taking me to the Swedish Embassy, and while the transit time from the limo to the entrance to the Embassy was mercifully brief, it still felt good to get inside.

The Embassy was full of flowers, alive with the cacophony of happy people conversing in dozens of languages, and alight with the soft glow of candles. I was relaxed and looking forward to the evening. I couldn't help contrasting my present feelings to the extreme tension and stress which I was under when I had arrived at *last* year's New Year's Eve party, at the Soviet Embassy. What a difference. My mission at the Soviet Embassy party had been to introduce myself to Soviet Ambassador Dobrynin, and inform him that Soviet KGB agents were trying to kill me, and that President Kennedy would be *personally* grateful if the Ambassador would intervene.

I started to reflect on all the things that had happened since that last New Year's Eve and then stopped myself. I was starting to get gloomy and depressed thinking of everything that had happened during those following 365 days. I took a deep breath and tried to put all those thoughts aside. The past can't be undone. All we can do is to keep moving forward as best we know how.

At the time, relations between the United States and Sweden were cordial and last month both Prime Minister Tage Erlander and Prince Bertil, Duke of Halland had come to the United States to attend the funeral of President Kennedy and offer their condolences to Mrs. Kennedy. Later in the '60's the relations between the United States and Sweden would become strained to the breaking point because of Sweden's opposition to the Vietnam War, and the relentless U.S.

bombing, particularly of Laos and Cambodia.

I shook myself out of my unhappy funk, braced up, and wandered over to the bar. Vodka is the most popular distilled spirit in Sweden, and drinking straight shots of ice-cold vodka is a common custom, but not a great idea if you want to stay reasonably sober. At official functions such as this one, I was always careful to retain a very clear head. Total abstention tends to make people avoid you, but I've found that slowly sipping a vodka martini on the rocks works well. The melting ice dilutes the vodka, and when it's entirely melted, you appear to be drinking straight vodka. Works for me, anyway.

I had just started surveying the crowd (how in the world can Sweden have so many beautiful women?) when I was approached by a young lady of exactly that description who introduced herself as Ingrid Lindstrom and asked if I were Mr. MacFarland. I responded that I was guilty as charged. She gave me a dazzling smile and said she was an assistant to Ambassador Jarring who sent his apologies for being unable to greet me personally at the moment, but who would be pleased if I would join him at the head table for dinner. (A Special Assistant to the President is considered a VIP—in Washington, anyway.) I told her that I would be honored, and I was more than a little disappointed when she excused herself, and said that she needed to get right back to the Ambassador's office. She said she had asked one of her best friends in the Embassy, an assistant to the Trade Minister, to introduce me around. Though I was sorry to see Ingrid leave, her friend (who introduced herself as Emma Dahlquist) was just as strikingly beautiful. Additionally, she had a sharp intellect, a wonderful sense of humor, and was a delightfully charming dinner companion. After dinner, when the New Year had been duly rung in and toasted and the Swedish National Anthem sung, I asked Emma if she were staying or if she would like a ride home. When we got in the limo and I asked for her address, she asked if I would like her to stay with me for the night. I told her I thought it was a terrific idea.

Emma and I got along easily and comfortably and I saw her frequently after that. There was no real romantic involvement. We were just good friends who slept together occasionally. I had been mildly surprised when she told me that Ambassador Jarring was being re-assigned and was leaving Washington January 3. Ambassadors are always being re-assigned, and I didn't think much about it, until she told me *where* he was taking up his next post. On January 25, 1964, Ambassador Gunnar Jarring took up his new post—in Moscow—as the Swedish Ambassador to the Soviet Union. That's a hell of a transition—going directly from being the Ambassador to the U.S. to being the Ambassador to its most powerful enemy. I had to wonder very much what was behind such a re-assignment.[14] Emma was distressed because Jarring had asked Ingrid (her best friend) to join his new staff in Moscow, and Ingrid had accepted.

---

[14] Although at that point there was not an outright rupture of Swedish-American relations, the storm was strongly brewing and there would not be another Swedish Ambassador to the United States until the end of the Vietnam War (in 1974) when Count Wilhelm Hans Fredrik Wachtmeister took up the post. He would remain in the post for almost 15 years.

On Monday, January 6, I was just getting ready to leave for the Pentagon gym when my security phone rang. It was General Carroll on the phone, and he was brief and to the point. He said, "Bertie, there will be an unmarked regular Air Force staff car, not a limo, that will pick you up outside your apartment building at 11:30 this morning. He will drive you to a secure location where we will have lunch and discuss things. Any questions?"

"No sir, General. I'll be outside at 11:30," I replied, and before I could add, "Thank you, sir," the line went dead. I decided to go to the White House to work out. It was much closer. While I was there, I scanned through the papers that were on my desk. Nothing really interesting. They all went into the shredder.

After the CIA-directed Bay of Pigs fiasco in 1961, Kennedy set about a complete review and overhaul of all the government's intelligence gathering services. He had fired the previous head of the CIA—Allan Dulles—and replaced him with John McCone. The military side was a mess beyond belief, however. Not only did the Department of Defense itself have an intelligence arm, every single military branch *within* the Department of Defense had its *own* intelligence gathering service. This was massively wasteful duplication of effort. Sometimes the internal agencies were working at cross purposes; nobody talked to anybody else; and each of these entities jealously and fiercely guarded its own turf. Trying to get them all coalesced under one command was going to be a mammoth task, demanding a long and successful track record of running a military intelligence operation at the highest level, as well as past demonstration of superb diplomatic skills. Kennedy decided that Joe Carroll was just the man, and in 1961 appointed him as the first Director of the newly formed Defense Intelligence Agency (DIA).

I was nervous but excited, when promptly at 11:30, an unmarked, nondescript, late model car pulled up to the entrance of the apartment building. An Air Force sergeant leaned over and rolled down the passenger side window to ask if I were Mr. MacFarland. When I confirmed that to be the case he simply said, "Hop in the back, sir," and off we went. I'd learned my lesson about not paying any attention to the route the driver was taking, and I was puzzled by the fact that the road that we were on didn't lead to any government facility that I was aware of. I was further puzzled when we turned off the main road into an attractive residential area, and I quickly lost my bearings as the driver wove us through a succession of similar-looking residential streets. Finally, we pulled up to a secluded estate entrance that was blocked by a handsome, but formidable wrought iron gate. There was no signage, no street number, nothing to tell you where you were, much less what might be behind the gate. The driver picked up a hand-held radio that had been on the seat beside him, mumbled something into it, and the huge gate silently swung open. As soon as we had cleared it, I watched out the rear window as it immediately began to close again. I froze as I spotted something that could not possibly be seen from the street. Nestled up to the impenetrable perimeter hedge-camouflaged wall was a small guard house with a heavily armed marine standing in the doorway. Anybody trying to sneak in while the gate was briefly opened wasn't going to get very far.

As we drew up to a stately Georgian-style brick house, the front door was opened, and two armed marine guards exited. One held the car door open for me, while the other observed me closely from the top of the steps. What is this place and what the hell is going on? I wondered.

I was met at the top of the steps by a three star Air Force General who introduced himself with a genial, "Hey, Bertie. I'm Joe Carroll. Good to meet you. Come on in and let's get something to eat."

I followed him into a small, but elegant dining room where two places were laid at the table. Somebody closed the door behind us as we sat down. "General Carroll", I began.

He interrupted me and said, "Let's start off being friends. Call me Joe, Bertie."

"Thank you, sir. Joe, what is this place?"

"It's a CIA safe house, and the Agency has kindly let me borrow a small piece of it for a few hours. Bertie, I'm on a pretty tight schedule so I hope you don't mind that I took the liberty of ordering lunch for the two of us. I hope you like seafood. The chef here does a wonderful bay scallop dish." He continued,
"When I got a call from Ros recounting the discussion that the two of you had, and that you had told Bob you wanted to speak to me, my first reaction was to run for the hills. You have to know that you have a very mixed reputation around here, Bertie. Jack loved you, Lyndon hates you, Bob likes you, Ros does not, Rusk[15] and McCone seem to be fairly neutral. A lot of people are scared of you and want no part of you. What made me even *consider* talking to you, though, is the fact that everyone you have ever dealt with, whether they like you or not, has real respect for you. Your reputation includes being exceptionally bright—which is good of course, but at this level of the government, there are quite a lot of exceptionally bright people running around. There's other stuff like a reputation for being fair and impartial, but the one thing that everybody gives you credit for is being unbreakably, unbendably honest. 'If Bertie said it, then that's the deal.' Not that you could never make a mistake. Obviously everyone makes mistakes now and again, but that's where the exceptionally bright part comes in. Nobody that I've talked to—and believe me, I've talked to a lot of people—could recall a specific instance in which you were mistaken. No wonder you scare people. There's something else, however."

At this point, there was a discrete knock at the door and two waiters came in bearing lunch. I remember the taste of those bay scallops to this day.

Between mouthfuls, Joe continued. "As I was going to say before we were so delightfully interrupted, you have one characteristic Bertie, which makes you uniquely valuable to me. Officially, you don't exist. It's true. As far as records go, you have never been an employee of

---

[15] Dean Rusk, Secretary of State

the U.S. Government. The only time you were ever employed in a government position, you were employed by the CIA. When the CIA swapped you for one of their other assets, they simply destroyed all your records. I personally asked John McCone to get someone to do a top to bottom search of their records, and McCone phoned me to say that the Agency has no record anywhere of you ever being one of its employees. You're an army officer in the regular army but you're not assigned to any unit, and you're not paid by the Department of the Army—you're paid by Treasury out of the president's discretionary fund. You're not in the phone book, your personal telephone line is not only unlisted, it belongs to the GSA, as does your apartment, furniture, etc. You have no family. You just don't exist. We're meeting here because I don't ever want us to be seen together, not even by my secretary and closest staff. So welcome to the DIA, Bertie. From now on, you will report only to me—and to the President of course, when he orders it. Day after tomorrow we will meet here again for lunch so that I can brief you on the arrangements that are being made for your transfer to Switzerland, and what your future duties will be. We will probably have to meet here on a few more occasions as arrangements progress. Any questions?"

"Yes, sir. Why Switzerland? I'm sure you know I speak French. Would France work?"

"I'm afraid not. Switzerland is neutral and stable; it has a freely convertible currency, and the cover company you're going to work for—Investors Overseas Services—has its headquarters there. France is not neutral. Because Vietnam was a French colony for so many years, DeGaulle is still trying to influence our policy there, and although last year Algeria became independent of France, French troops are still there, and tensions between the two nations are high. Lastly, the French Franc is not freely convertible, which would make our financial dealings with you next to impossible. Any more questions?"

"Just one. You said that a lot of people are scared of me. Why?"

"You don't form close friendships with anybody Bertie. Nobody can read you. You move in the highest circles of power. Maybe scared is a little too strong, although I think not. The very best spin I can put on it is that you make people uncomfortable. They don't want to be involved with you because they don't know how to interact with you. Oh, yes. One more thing—I don't think anyone feels in any personal danger whatsoever from you, but your exploits in Washington and in Vietnam are the stuff of legend. Just knowing that you can, and have, done things like that makes people a little shy of getting on your wrong side. Best to just leave you alone and try to stay out of your way."

"OK, well, I asked. What are my duties in the meantime? What am I supposed to be doing?"

"Whatever you want to. Just make sure that you stay out of trouble and don't get your name in the newspapers or anything. I know you've been using the Pentagon gym a lot lately, and if we happen to meet in the hall or even in the gym, there will be no sign of recognition from either of us. You are going to have the deepest, most unbreakable cover that I can imagine, because your very existence is totally deniable as far as the government is concerned. Now, I have some things to do and I believe your car is outside waiting for you. He'll pick you up at 11:30 on Wednesday."

Knowing that 'officially' you don't exist is a pretty depressing feeling. It seemed to me that I'd done more than the average bear in the service of my country, where I now didn't officially exist. I'd spent a lot of years in intensive training—language training, airborne training, Ranger training, special ops training, etc. The CIA had betrayed me to the Soviets and left me to be tortured to death by the KGB in Lubyanka, and the KGB had very nearly succeeded. I had served as an communications conduit between my government and the Soviet Union during the Cuban Missile crisis; I'd contributed heavily to getting the first nuclear test ban treaty in place (nobody else in the highest ranks of the administration had my background in advanced physics and math); I'd provided first-hand information on how the *people* of South Vietnam felt about the American presence in South Vietnam, and thereby strengthened Kennedy's decision to pull out of South Vietnam; I'd been nearly killed (in Washington) by two highly-trained Soviet KGB assassins; I'd been instrumental in getting the Pentagon's automated draftee assignment system working and then repairing it after that SOB Irwin Blasik sabotaged it; I'd had to kill—up close and personal—five people (not a pleasant thing for me to have to live with); I'd been a trusted confidant and friend of President Kennedy—and now I had been informed by the head of the DIA that my most valued quality was my lack of official existence. If I got caught and/or killed trying to carry out my assignment, absolutely no problem [for the government]. Zero mess that had to be cleaned up. Whoever I was and whatever I was trying to do, it certainly didn't involve the U.S. government. I was totally deniable, and demonstrably not in the government's employ. Although I had to give General Carroll credit for being totally and brutally honest about it, I felt sad, angry, empty, and exploited.

A Turning Point

Though I don't think I realized it at the time, in retrospect, this was the real turning point in my relationship with the power-mongers in the government. My *loyalty* to the United States remains unwavering to this day. Although I don't think that I could have verbalized it at the time, because I don't think I fully understood it then, *loyalty* and *support* are two different things. Loyalty is a beautiful, profoundly felt, almost indefinable thing. It's both intellectual and emotional, and some would add spiritual to that list. We are loyal to this country because it was founded on beliefs, principles, and values that we profoundly identify with. There have been countless American troops that have died *because* of an administration, but I think very few, if any, gave their lives for the continuing survival *of* that administration. They gave their lives for the continuing survival of their *country*. Big difference.

Support is a whole different thing. In the United States, at any rate, successive governmental administrations take on distinctly political casts. Depending on your ideology and beliefs, you may or may not lend your *support* to that particular administration's point of view. Hopefully however, your loyalty to our *country* remains steadfastly constant. You would be entirely justified to think that any reasonable citizen of this country would understand that. Heaven knows that I certainly should have. But I didn't, and I'm not using the fact that I was 'just a kid' as an excuse either. The reality was that through a quirk of fate, I had been allowed to participate in a very minor way in an administration headed by a man whose ideals and vision for the country inspired me, and motivated me so entirely that I completely identified him and his government with the country. There wasn't a particle of difference. I was embarrassed to realize how naïve I had been.

It was like having a bucket of ice cold water thrown in my face. I had to come to grips with the fact that I was now simply regarded as a tool. A valuable tool and irreplaceable in many respects but just a tool nonetheless. It would be regrettable if it got lost or broken, but nobody was going to shed any tears over it. There was just one difference. This tool had a mind of its own and was quite capable of harming the user if mishandled. I would make that painfully clear to any user that didn't realize it. All the ground rules had just changed and I couldn't possibly predict what the ramifications were going to be of this enormous paradigm shift. Camelot had been destroyed forever, but I was determined that Bertie Mac was going to rise like a phoenix from those ashes; stronger, tougher—and a whole lot wiser—than he was before.

General Carroll and I met briefly several times after the first meeting. My task was going to be to set up and run a network of DIA cells across Europe, and behind the Iron Curtain whenever that was possible. I was going to work as a Vice President in the Data Processing Division of a company called Investors Overseas Services (more familiarly known as IOS). DIA had constructed a 'legend' for me that included previous employment at IBM and Union Carbide, and I was given the names of a few retirees from those companies as being the names of my bosses there. The White House would distribute a classified memorandum announcing that the President had, on compassionate grounds, regretfully accepted my resignation so that I could care for my seriously ill mother. My official connection with the President, indeed with the entire United States government, would be officially over. The only people who would know that I had *not* been released would be McNamara, Gilpatric, Rusk, McCone, and of course General Carroll, me and the President—who refused to let me out of his control. In addition to continuing my army pay, I would receive a salary from IOS, plus DIA would deposit a very large amount of cash in my name in an account at UBS in Geneva for my mission expenses. Joe told me that in Europe, it was common for people to ask for a banking reference if they were contemplating doing business with you. The amount to be deposited to my account would definitely qualify me to have a personal account manager at UBS who could be called on to verify that I was a substantial client of theirs.

Joe told me that I could keep my MG if I wanted to but that I was to purchase (for cash, which wasn't at all uncommon in Europe in those days) a large Mercedes as soon as possible after my arrival in Geneva. It was important to be *seen* as a substantial citizen. He told me that it would make a lot more sense for me to sell my current MG and buy a new one when I got to Geneva as the dealer there would deal with all the registration and license plate formalities. (It was excellent advice, and I followed it.) He said that they had located a house for me that met the requirements of being both luxurious and isolated. He said that the only unfortunate part was that it was located nearer to Lausanne than Geneva, but reminded me that there was no speed limit on the Autoroute (Autoroutes are major, limited access divided highways with a minimum two lanes in each direction, similar to the best of our Interstates). I asked if my security clearances would still remain in place, and was told that as Special Assistant to the President it was mandatory for them to stay in place. I asked how I was supposed to communicate.

"The CIA has a safe house in Geneva. You will have a small office there. Any classified material you are copied on will be left on your desk. If there are communications for you personally, you will receive a phone call purporting to be from the American Express[16] office in Geneva informing you that you have a package waiting for you at their office. If you are asked when you would like to pick it up, the communication is high priority—probably from me. If you are told that you have a *large* package waiting for you, the communication is ultra-urgent and will be from the President, McNamara, Rusk or McCone. Drop whatever you're doing and get to the safe house immediately."

"How do I reply to a secure communication?"

"You'll dictate your reply to one of the communications staff at the safe house. You are authorized to personally set the secrecy level. God knows you've read enough communications to be able to judge what secrecy level your communication should receive."

"When am I leaving, Joe? I can't stand not working. It's driving me nuts."

"We're doing the best we can. We've got everything ready on our side but we're still waiting on the Swiss to issue you a work permit. Not even the United States Government can make the Swiss hurry up. We think you *should* be able to leave on the 29th meaning that you will arrive in Geneva about 8:00 a.m. local time on the 30th. I'll try to let you know a couple of days beforehand. Don't try to pack everything, just take what you think you'll need for the first week or so. We'll take whatever personal effects you leave in your apartment, and put them on the next military transport plane that's going to Europe. You'll be met at the airport in Geneva by a

---

[16] In those days, long before cell phones, personal computers, email, etc., it was common practice for American travelers to give their friends an itinerary so that they could receive mail or telegrams at the nearest appropriate American Express office. American Express at the time was probably the largest travel agency in the world and American Express Traveler's Checks were accepted almost everywhere in the world as being the equivalent of cash. Amex issued the world's first international credit card in 1950 and by 1964 the cards were accepted by every major merchant in Europe (as well as all over the United States, of course).

driver from the CIA who will take you to the safe house and acquaint you with procedures. You'll probably want to stay overnight there."

"I think that's about it, Bertie. God knows when or even if we'll see each other again but as the saying goes—we'll be in touch. Oh yes, one last thing. On your way out of the apartment to the car that I'll send to take you to the airport, leave your White House and Pentagon passes with the concierge. The next time you need to visit either of those buildings, you'll be issued the appropriate temporary passes. Your apartment and your White House office will be re-assigned."

I knew that they would be of course, but it was nonetheless hard to hear it said. Joe looked at me very carefully. "You volunteered for it, Bertie. You asked to speak to me, not the other way around."

"Of course you're absolutely right, sir, and I'm grateful for the assignment. It's just that the reality, the finality, of taking this on, brings home just how entirely I've cut myself off and isolated myself from everything I've ever known. I no longer have any *personal* support system whatsoever. I am now truly 'out there' in the cold. I'll be honest with you, Joe. I'm scared. Also, I'm really, really tired of being lonely all the time, and I think that part's about to get even worse. Anyway, again, I'm grateful for the assignment. I give you my word, I'll do my best. It's just such a shame that this assignment is the best of the very few bad options that I had to choose from."

He shook his head. "Bertie, I wish I knew why the President hates you so much."

"In fact Joe, you don't want to know."

"OK, but why do you say that you have no personal support system? If you don't do something really egregious, I'll support you."

"Yeah? Would you seriously challenge Bob McNamara or the President on my behalf?"

"Well . . ., well . . ., hrrumph. I see what you mean."

"If I screw up, there's nowhere to turn to for help, Joe. The other side sure won't provide it. They'll kill me—probably as painfully as possible. If I can escape that, at least temporarily, my own government will turn its head, withdraw its support and leave me as food for the wolves. Don't try to deny it Joe, you know it's true. You're not about to ever risk damaging your career on my behalf—nor is anyone else. I'd be a fool not to have learned from the past, and I'm no fool. I've learned my lesson very well indeed."

"Well . . ., Good luck, Bertie." He stood up and left.

I thought I'd go home and have a good, stiff drink.

Geneva

I did, but it didn't help. The enormity of the task before me was overwhelming. How does one go about setting up a spy network? The CIA and their counterparts in other countries had been doing it for years but none of those entities seemed to be giving out any handbooks on methodology. The more I thought about it, the more I became convinced that I was simply being set up to fail. A second, but far more subtle, betrayal and abandonment by my own government. Johnson was determined to get me one way or the other and do it in such a way that he was entirely removed from the actual event. He was in no rush. So what if it took a year? Maybe even two? The outcome was inevitable. I think Johnson had come to the conclusion that in the final analysis, whatever research notes I had really didn't matter. He would figure that first of all, as President, he could probably make sure that anything I attempted to reveal would be quashed before it ever saw the light of day, and secondly, there would be no way that I could verify that any assertions which I might make were true. But there were a few facts that Johnson was unaware of.

The government kept meticulous records of any photocopies of documents which were classified as Secret or higher. Lengthy request forms had to be filled out, and then independently authorized for any such copies to be made. While commercial photocopying centers existed, they were few and far between. Photocopy machines were rare, and they were extremely expensive, and only trained employees were permitted to operate them. It would be impossible to simply slip some top secret documents into your briefcase and zip down to the local copy shop to run off some duplicates. I'm sure that Johnson had verified that I had *never* requested a photocopy be made of *any* classified document. I think he was starting to feel pretty confident.

That was a mistake. Yes, my research notes were hand-written, and they contained no opinions whatsoever. They just contained what I considered to be relevant, or simply interesting information, and the source of that information was carefully documented. To a large extent those sources were not classified, but they were very, very credible. Some *were* classified however, and I had been able to photocopy them, courtesy of a good friend in the Pentagon, who was a high enough official that his office had its own, dedicated Xerox machine. I definitely *did* have the documents Johnson was sure that I couldn't *possibly* have in my possession. In fact, I had a whole lot more.

How I was going to get those documents out of their safe deposit box in a Washington, DC bank and into Switzerland was another matter.

I started the process of winding down my affairs in Washington. I sold my MG to a dealership, closed out my checking account, closed my Brooks Brothers account, etc. I called our family lawyer in Baltimore to see how my mother was doing. He told me that sadly, there was no change , except that she was steadily growing weaker. He didn't expect her to survive for much longer. I told him of my transfer and promised that I would contact him immediately once I had an address and/or phone number where he could reach me. I hung up disconsolately. What a grotesque killer Alzheimer's is.

I used my limo privileges to go back and forth to my office in the West Wing, and paid rather desultory attention to my classified mail. On the 23rd, I was surprised to see a memo of a meeting that McNamara had had with the Joint Chiefs the previous day. The contents were astonishing. It proposed that the U.S. Military assume complete control of the war in Vietnam, that the U.S. commence large scale bombing of key targets in North Vietnam, augment U.S. forces in South Vietnam, and proposed that the U.S. commit American troops 'in direct actions against North Vietnam.' I was outraged and shocked. Completely gone was the Kennedy position of 'we will provide the South Vietnamese with all the support, training, equipment, etc. that is necessary—but in the final analysis, it is their war to fight.' This memo said that the Joint Chiefs wanted to assume control of the war, *and* that they wanted to send American combat troops against the North Vietnamese. That meant that Americans were not only going to assume responsibility for the protection of South Vietnam, Americans were going to *invade* North Vietnam! I was beginning to think that McNamara was becoming unglued. Maybe that *StaComb* stuff he used to slick back his hair was eating away his brain.

I had invited Emma and Peter and Sally Boyle out to dinner Friday evening, at a new restaurant that had gotten rave reviews in the newspapers. I had previously introduced Emma to the Boyles, and we all dined with the cheerful camaraderie and banter of good friends. We were having a cognac after a truly marvelous meal when I finally broke the news of my 'transfer' to Switzerland. Emma was particularly upset. Her best friend in the Swedish Embassy, Ingrid Lindstrom, had just followed Ambassador Jarring to Moscow, where he would take up his new post as the Swedish ambassador to the Soviet Union. Now she was losing me, too. Everyone wanted to know how to stay in touch, and I told them I didn't have a permanent address yet, but would write or call them just as soon as I did. Emma came home with me and cried the whole weekend.

On Monday, I finally got the call I was waiting for. I was leaving for Geneva Wednesday evening. I went to my office Wednesday morning just to take one last look around, and was surprised to learn that the day before; the CIA had gotten an intimation of an imminent coup in South Vietnam. Surely not, I thought. Big Minh has been in power for less than three months. I would later learn that Nguyễn Khánh had bloodlessly deposed Big Minh by the time I arrived in Geneva early Thursday morning. It was unclear what the consequences of the coup were going to be.

A little background on Switzerland. It is an amazing country. The entire population of the country was something like 5.8 million in 1964—about one third of the then population of New York State, and more than two million souls *less than* the population of *just the Delta region* of South Vietnam. Switzerland is entirely land-locked and shares its borders with no less than five other countries: Germany to the north, France to the west, Italy to the south, and Lichtenstein and Austria to the east. It has four national languages—German, French, Italian and Romansh. The last one, Romansh, is the only 'native' language of Switzerland. It originated from the occupation of the Romans when they defeated the native Helvetii tribe around 58 BC. Today, it is probably spoken by no more than 30,000 people as their main language.

In Switzerland, all school children must learn a language other than their mother tongue, so everybody is at least bi-lingual, and the more educated classes will generally speak German, French, Italian, and English. It is one of the wealthiest countries in the world; its ETH University is ranked #1 in the world; its products such as high-grade steel, watches, chocolate, etc. are rated among the best—if not *the* best—in the world, and the list of superlatives goes on and on. Of course in addition to all that, the scenery is absolutely breathtaking. It truly is an amazing country, and I quickly grew to love it and consider it home.

It was grey and cold when I arrived in Geneva, and I was glad to get into the warmth of another spectacularly beautiful safe house. (The CIA takes good care of itself.) My reception there was far from warm, however. Although nothing was said directly, it was very clear that I definitely was *not* a welcome guest. It was a miserable way to start out my first day in a new country.

My driver and I had just entered the elegant reception room when he inquired rather curtly if I wanted to take a nap or wash up, or something. I figured I'd better get things straight from the start and put down my suitcase (nobody was going to carry my suitcase for me here, boy). I looked him in the eye and said,

"Look, you've made it abundantly clear that I'm not welcome here. I'm sorry that's the case but I'm not going to let it affect me or what I have to do. I'll get out as quickly as I can, but I've got some work to do first. I need to know where I am and how to get here again if I need to. I know what the call signals are if you contact me, but I also need to know how to contact you. If I'm in trouble and need to get in here in a hurry, I need to know how to do that. I need to know the address and telephone number of the house that my agency has acquired for me. I need to know what security arrangements there are there, if any. I need to know if a rather large sum of money has been deposited in my name at UBS, and the name of my personal banking contact. I need to know the name and address of a Mercedes dealer here, because I've got to have some transportation of my own. I need a street map of Geneva, a street map of the nearest town to my house, and a road map of Switzerland. And damn it, if you want me out of here so badly, you'd better start getting all of that together for me *right now!* Look, you need to remember something. In the final analysis, we're all working for the same boss—the people of the United States. Like you, I'm just an employee trying to do my job. You and your buddies can take your

Attitude and shove it right up your ass. I'm staying here until I get what I need, so if you want me out, get busy! You got that straight?"

An older gentleman who had been sitting in one of the comfortable leather chairs reading a newspaper stood up and strolled over and stared at me intently. Finally he said, "That was a nice little speech Bertie. They said you were good." He extended his hand.

I shook it and said, "Thank you, Mr. Martin. I hope we can get along." He couldn't quite hide the shock, and the driver looked stunned.

"Christ!" he said. "They would have *never* given you my name! You really *are* good—*very* good. Do you want to wash up, take a nap, would you like some breakfast or did you eat on the plane?"

I told him that I *would* like to wash up, shave, and change my clothes, and that some breakfast would be much appreciated. I asked if my new house was ready for occupancy—heat turned on, phone, electricity and water working, some food in the house, etc.

He turned to the driver and raised his eyebrows.

The driver looked down at his feet and just shook his head 'No'.

Martin growled, "Well you God-damn well get somebody to take care of that *right now!* When Mr. MacFarland gets there this afternoon for his initial inspection, I want that house warm, clean, in perfect operating order, food in the pantry, food in the fridge, wine in the wine cellar, some good scotch whiskey, bourbon, gin and vodka at the bar. Make sure that he's got a complete set of nice tableware, glasses, pots, pans, whatever. Make sure all the beds are made with good linen sheets, with nice comforters on top. Put Yolande in charge. She'll know what to do. And no more dirty tricks, God-damn it! You'll treat Mr. MacFarland as my personal guest. You're assigned to him for as long as he needs you. Now, grab his bag and show him to his room. Make sure he's got everything he needs in there." He turned to me and said, "Sorry, Bertie. Looks like you would have had a nasty surprise and it's probably my fault. I think the staff was well aware that I wasn't too happy about the prospect of baby-sitting someone from another agency. I suppose they took it on themselves to demonstrate my displeasure. So I think I owe you an apology. We'll get along just fine, you and me. When you're ready, come on back here and we'll have breakfast and chat."

As I was following the driver, I turned around and asked, "What's the status of the coup?"

"Done," he answered. "Khánh's in power and Big Minh's under house arrest. No bloodshed as far as we know at the moment. We'll talk more over breakfast."

34

My banker, Monsieur Michaud, was a pleasant, rotund man in his late forties, who greeted me obsequiously. He told me that the bank was honored to have such a distinguished client, and that I could absolutely depend on him to assist me in any way he could. He said they had received $250,000 from 'my' account in the United States, and that 'my' bank had also conveyed 'my' instructions to ensure that there was always a minimum of $100,000 in the UBS account. When that lower limit was getting near, he was to notify them, and they would cable transfer sufficient funds to restore the account to $250,000. (The exchange rate at the time was 4.33 SF to the dollar—meaning that I had well over a million SF.) The implication, however, was that I had essentially unlimited funds in the United States. I could understand why he was impressed. I certainly was. He said that he had taken the liberty of opening a Swiss Franc account in my name, and asked if I would like some of the dollars converted into Swiss Francs and placed in that account. I told him to convert sufficient dollars such that I had SF 500,000 in the new account.

My reception at the Mercedes dealership was just as cordial when it became clear that I was prepared to immediately purchase one of their top-of-the-line sedans. I asked them to have it ready for me by early afternoon. While I was signing all the purchase documents, the manager called my bank at my request. I asked M. Michaud if he would please make the arrangements for payment, and handed the phone to the now beaming manager.

I left, and repeated the scene at the MG dealership.

Back at the safe house, I phoned the Geneva headquarters of IOS, and was told that Mr. Cornfeld could meet me Monday morning at 10:00. There didn't seem to be much more to do other than thank my host and go see my new house.

Martin shook my hand warmly, apologized again, and handed me a bulky, sealed envelope. He told me that all my maps were inside, plus instructions for emergency and non-emergency contact. He asked me to memorize all the contact information and then burn the written instructions. He gave me his personal phone number, and told me to call him if I had any problems with the house. He also invited me to call him from time to time to get together for lunch or dinner. We could never be seen together in public, of course, but he assured me that the safe house had an excellent chef. I left with two of his employees to go pick up the cars. One of them drove the Mercedes, and I slipped into the more familiar seat of my new MG and followed the other two cars to my new house.

In 1964, the speed limit on almost all U.S. highways was 55 miles per hour. Most people exceeded it but fines and penalties could be severe if you were caught exceeding the speed limit by more than 10 mph, and very few people made a practice of doing it. It was liberating to cruise along the Autoroute at 85 mph, and I was starting to think, 'I'm really going to enjoy living in this country.' I was kind of disappointed when I found it only took about 15 minutes to cover the 22 miles between Geneva and the Autoroute exit for Aubonne.

We wound our way slowly through the village, and exited the west side of the village on a small, two lane country road bordered by farmland and pastures on either side. Ever since we had exited the Autoroute, the road had been climbing fairly steeply as we approached Aubonne and the Jura Mountains. The road we were on was perfectly clear and dry, but patches of snow started appearing on both sides. The patches got bigger and bigger as we climbed, until finally the entire ground on both sides of the road was covered with a thin layer of snow. Unexpectedly, we turned left onto an unpaved road that looked like it was the driveway to a distant old farmhouse. My heart sank. I didn't want to live in some old drafty farmhouse surrounded by barns that probably stank of ancient cow manure.

Trouble Follows Me Home

Abruptly, we turned left again, this time onto a broad, paved driveway going downhill. I gasped at what I was seeing though the windscreen of the MG. Stretched out far below me was Lac Leman (sometimes called Lake of Geneva), and in the distance on the other side of the lake were the snow-covered Alps, and the really high peak *had* to be Mont Blanc—almost three miles high. It was absolutely stunningly, breathtakingly beautiful. The house at the end of the driveway was something of a surprise, however. From my vantage point, it looked like a large concrete blockhouse. The area in front of its (attached) garage was filled with workmen's trucks, but there was a little one-lane road or driveway or something that turned off to the right, and we parked in that.

I was puzzled as I negotiated my way to the front door through the maze of small trucks. Why would anyone build a house that looked like a concrete blockhouse on a site that had such incredible views? I decided that maybe the 'front door' was more of an 'entrance door' and that there would be windows on the other side from which one could see at least a part of the spectacular view I had seen when driving down the driveway. I sure hoped so.

Before I got to it, the 'front' door was opened by a more than pretty young lady who greeted me with, "*Ah bonjour, Monsieur MacFarland! Je suis Yolande. Bienvenue*".

I entered a very large and open vestibule, and was absolutely speechless. There weren't any *windows* at the 'back' of the house. The *whole wall* consisted of floor-to-ceiling huge glass panels. The sense of spatial continuity was unbelievable. It was almost as though the wall didn't exist and there was an uninterrupted transition between the inside of the house and the beauty of the outdoors. I wish I knew how to better describe it. It wasn't quite like being inside and outside at the same time. It was like there was no *difference* between inside and outside— they were a smooth continuum.

As I wandered past the massive, circular, raised fireplace, with an enormous, round brass hood suspended above it, and entered the living/dining room, I was just amazed by the sense of space. The room itself was about eight meters (approx. 26 feet.) wide, and some 25 meters (approx. 82 feet.) long. The entire length of the house faced the lake and the Alps. To add to the miraculous feeling of space, both side walls were glass as well. The floors were of semi-glazed fire-brick, the 'wallpaper' was made of burlap, and the ceiling was done in narrow strips of knotty pine.

Yolande took me on a tour of the house, which turned out to be on five levels. We went up the steps about half a story, and to the left there was an arm that jutted out over whatever part of the house was underneath it, plus three bedrooms, a living room, and two baths. The master living area, which was directly above the living/dining area, was another half story up. It consisted of just two rooms—a library/lounge with bookshelves floor to ceiling on two walls, and a massive bedroom/sitting room. It also had one and a half baths, which were huge The bedroom was slightly narrower than the living/dining room directly underneath it, to accommodate a long, broad, concrete balcony, the rail of which was a concrete platform about a meter wide [one meter is just a bit more than a yard], which had its own far side rail a few inches high. It was clearly designed for sunbathing. Yolande demonstrated how the glass panels worked. Every other panel was actually a sliding glass door, which could be opened to slide in front of the fixed panel beside it. If you opened them all, half of that enormous wall was completely open to the world outside.

We proceeded downstairs, past the guest level and the main level, to the next half level, where the stairs ended at what I suppose I would call the 'club' level. Although it was directly underneath the guest level, it wasn't quite as wide. The natural slope of the land, which would terminate at the lake's edge four or five miles downhill, meant that the lower level rooms would have to be partially excavated into the uphill side of the house. Nonetheless, the room was very large, dominated in the center by a competition-sized billiard table. Leather couches and chairs lined the side walls, and there was a massive stereo system against the back wall. A gorgeous floor-to-ceiling modern tapestry with an intriguing abstract design hung on the far wall towards the back of the room. It added some much needed warmth and color, and made the room seem more intimate and human somehow. The lake-side wall had a door which led out to a large, pleasant patio which was currently covered by snow.

The room's only other door led down a few steps to what looked like the 'business' part of the house. On the right, at the bottom of the stairs, a large, unidentifiable piece of machinery, dominated by a big electric motor, hummed away softly. Behind the motor was a big, vertical, galvanized tank with all sorts of pipes and valves emanating from it. Directly across the small room was another door, which opened to reveal a furnace, air handler, and massive fuel tank.

To the left of the stairs [the uphill side], a door opened into a small area which would become one of my favorite parts of the house. Curiously, the floor was made of raised wooden slats about half an inch apart. On the immediate left was a small room with a sink and toilet. Past that room, there was another room that only had a plastic curtain for a 'door' and it was a really strange room. Half of it was an empty, man-sized, fairly deep basin. It wasn't long enough to be a bath tub but it was much deeper. It had a single, fire-hose size faucet. Right next to it was a small, but normal shower. But the most wonderful room was behind a wooden door with a wooden handle—directly across the slatted wooden floor from the toilet room and the strange shower and basin combination.

Inside *that* room was an absolutely gorgeous sauna. I thought I'd died and gone to heaven.

We weren't quite through, though. There was one more door on that level. It was just past the motor and tank apparatus. Yolande pushed a dimmer-type light switch and beckoned me to come in. The first thing that hit me was the heat of the air flowing through the door. Then I saw it. One of the biggest indoor swimming pools I have ever seen in a private residence. It had its own furnace with two thermostats—one for the air temperature, and the other for the water temperature. The long dimension, of course, faced the lake and the mountains, and the walls had the same fixed panel/sliding door configuration as the upper floors. The whole pool-room was pushed well further out than the lake-facing walls of the living room and the master bedroom, and the lawn outside the living room upstairs was on its roof. Yolande dimmed the main lights and flicked on the underwater lights lining the side of the pool. I'd never seen anything like it.

It was starting to get dark outside as Yolande led me back up to the main level, and showed me the kitchen, which was parallel to the living/dining room, but less than half of its length. It looked out on the large concrete parking area at the end of the driveway, which now contained just my two cars and Yolande's car. The keys to both my cars were on the kitchen counter. I noted that the land sloped up so sharply that it was impossible to see any part of the large farmhouse and barns which I'd seen earlier. Joe had told me that he wanted to find a place for me that was both luxurious and isolated. I don't think he could have done a better job.

Yolande said, "Well, I think that's about it, Mr. MacFarland. Do you like it?"

"First of all, call me Bertie. Secondly, 'Yes' but 'like' doesn't even come close. This place is absolutely fantastic. Did you pick out the furniture? Because I think it's great. I love the clean lines and the uncluttered space."

"*Merci!* It pleases me very much to hear you say that. Yes, I've been working on it for over a month. It is very difficult to try to choose for someone that you don't know. I've saved all the receipts, however, so anything you don't like can be taken back without a problem. But look, you must be very tired and hungry. I know a wonderful little restaurant near here that serves delicious fondue. Would you like me to take you there? It's not far."

"I'd love it if it's not too much trouble. I'm ravenous."

"Well, let's go then, Bertie. We'll take my car."

She was right on both accounts. It wasn't very far, and the fondue was delicious. Nobody makes fondue like the Swiss. We were finishing up dinner when it struck me. "Oh, Lord!" I groaned. "Yolande, I've got a serious problem. Tell me what to do."

She looked horror-stricken. "What is it? What is it? Are you sick? What can I do?"

"Yolande, I've got a bank account with stacks and stacks of Swiss Francs in it, but I don't have a single centime of cash on me. I've got lots of dollars, though. Do you think they would take dollars?"

She started to laugh and couldn't stop.

Finally she regained enough control to say, "Let me catch my breath and wipe my eyes first. Bertie, Bertie. Don't worry. I've got plenty of cash. Actually, I'm quite pleased because I'm going to insist that you repay the loan personally on another occasion. That way I know I'll get to see you again at least once. Incidentally, there's still one more feature to the house that I haven't shown you yet. It's getting late and I live in Geneva. Shall I come back in the morning?"

"You're more than welcome to stay at the house, if you'd like. Lord knows we have enough bedrooms."

"I like the one on the top floor best."

I was tired but I wasn't *that* tired.

I awoke to the wonderfully delicious smell of bacon being cooked. The bedroom was flooded with sunshine. I simply could not believe the view. It was truly overwhelming. I was jolted out of my absent-minded absorption by Yolande wanting to know if I were ready to come down, because breakfast was nearly ready. I threw on jeans and a T-shirt and went running downstairs.

The one remaining feature of the house that I hadn't yet seen was intriguing to say the least. After breakfast, Yolande led me downstairs to the 'club' level. She went over to the tapestry and pulled it back to reveal—a door. I thought, *Surely that's not possible. It's far too near the back wall* (which was deeply cut into the uphill slope) *not to have solid earth behind it.* The door looked very heavy and it was double locked, but when Yolande opened it and flipped a light switch, I was looking into a brightly-lit pedestrian tunnel that was maybe 30 meters long.

"Yolande, where the hell does this go?"

"Did you see the house at the end of the small driveway where you parked yesterday afternoon?"

"Yes, but to be honest, I'd completely forgotten about it. What is it?"

"Well, the former owner used it as a guest house. I know that you refer to the level just above us as the 'guest level,' but the former owner housed his servants there, so they would be on instant call. He felt that guests should have more privacy, have larger rooms, their own outdoor patio, their own kitchen, etc. However, he didn't want them to have to walk through snow or inclement weather to get to the main house, so he had this tunnel built to connect the two houses. There's an intercom system between the two houses to make communications easier, and since the guest house connects at this level, it's easy for the occupants to come over and use the pool, the sauna, the billiard table, etc. without disturbing anyone in the main house. It's quite thoughtful, don't you think?"

"Honestly, I don't know what to think. It's a bit much to take in."

"Well, come along and take a look. It doesn't have any furniture in it at the moment, and I think all the rooms probably need to be repainted. But we can worry about that later. Come on, Bertie."

I followed, but groaned inwardly. *We*? Shades of Helen.[17] I didn't think so. At least not now anyway.

The so-called 'guest house' was a charming and relatively spacious little house. We entered on the basement level which, besides housing the furnace on the uphill side, had a pleasant sitting room that led to an outside patio, a full bath, and another room, which was probably intended to be a bedroom, but judging by the colorful daubs of paint which speckled one of the walls, looked like it had previously been used as an artist's workshop. As in the main house, glass panels formed the downhill wall. The upstairs area was comprised of a small entry foyer, a kitchen, a living/dining room and two bedrooms, plus two and a half baths. There was also a balcony running the entire length of the house. Hell of a guest house.

When we went back to the main house, Yolande carefully locked the guest house door to the tunnel then did the same to the main house door to the tunnel. I asked her why.

"There are motion detector sensors all around the main house and the guest house. You can set them to be silent, as they are now, or set them to sound an interior alarm, or to sound both an interior and an exterior alarm. There's a master control switch for the guest house behind the panel next to the door to the guest house furnace room, but it can be over-ridden by the master

---

[17]   See Book One.

control in the main house, which is upstairs in your bathroom. Come, I'll show you."

It was behind one of the mirrors over the one of the sinks. I had assumed that if there were anything at all behind the mirrors, it was just the standard medicine cabinet. Nothing was standard in that house.

Yolande told me that there was a clever little switch on top of the mirror, but that she was too short to reach it. She asked me to give her a boost up. As soon as I put my arms around her waist to do so, she turned around and kissed me deeply. Well, you know how that wound up.

Afterwards, she said, "Maybe if I just stand on my tippy-toes . . ." She had no problem whatever reaching it. She left around 2:00 p.m., humming happily as she closed the entrance door.

I went outside to the MG, and pulled from its hiding place under the passenger side floor mat, the manila envelope Martin had given me. I brought it inside and studied the contact instructions carefully. Back in those days, I had a well-developed 'photographic memory.' It was easy for me to look at a sheet of paper for only a few seconds before being able to throw it away, close my eyes, and see it just as clearly as if I were looking at the original. I can still do it some, but back then, it was perfect. Following instructions, I burned the sheet, and then flushed the ashes down the toilet.

The next thing I did was to sit down with the maps (there were a whole lot more than the ones I'd asked for) to try to figure out just exactly where this house was located. It wasn't easy as the scales of the maps seemed to be either too big or too small. I finally found Aubonne on a fairly large-scale map and began to understand why I had such spectacular views. Lac Léman (or Lake of Geneva as it is usually called in English) is a big lake—one of the biggest in Western Europe. It's about 45 miles long and nearly 8 miles across at its widest point. It's shaped in a gentle arc, and Aubonne is situated very near the apex of the arc. That explained why I could see both the lights of Geneva and Lausanne at night.

It was getting too late to do a lot of sightseeing, and I needed to find a bank to get some cash. Although Lausanne was considerably closer than Geneva, I had a map of Geneva, and I didn't want to get lost in Lausanne, so I went back through Aubonne, down to the Autoroute, and headed towards Geneva. With a sense of incredible freedom, I accelerated through the gears until I reached 100 mph, and though the tachometer was getting near the redline, it wasn't there yet. I felt free as a bird. It gradually dawned on me that I was concentrating so hard on driving that I wasn't seeing anything except the road in front of me. That hardly qualifies as sightseeing, so I got off at the next exit, the exit for Nyon.

Nyon was tiny but charming. I found a UBS, but there was no place to park. The tiny parking lot at the train station, about a block and a half away, was full. I finally found a public parking lot with lots of open parking spaces, and retraced my route back to the UBS office, where I asked the teller for SF 10,000 "...nine 1,000 franc notes, and ten 100 franc notes, please." I showed him my newly minted UBS plastic card, with my account number embossed on it. I also gave the teller one of the many business cards that Monsieur Michaud had given me. Today of course, he would have simply typed my account number into his computer workstation and immediately verified my bank balance. Things didn't happen that way in 1964. He courteously asked me if I would wait for a moment while he phoned Monsieur Michaud, whom he knew well. After two or three minutes he came back, positively beaming. He apologized for the wait, said that Monsieur Michaud sent his respectful greetings, and then asked if he could introduce me to 'his superior.' I still hadn't gotten my money yet, so I thought I'd better agree. The branch manager came over, leaned across the counter (there were no grills, no bullet-proof glass—just an open counter), shook my hand, gave me his card, and told me that if there was anything in the future that his branch could do for me, to let him know personally.

Finally, they counted out my money. I was taken aback by the size of the banknotes. The thousand franc notes were about 9" by 5" and the 100 franc notes were around 7½" by 4". I've never used a wallet. I just shove the notes in my left pants pocket, and the change in the right, but the 1,000 franc notes were too bulky. I stuffed them in my jacket pocket, and set off to see Nyon. It was a tiny little town. I think the population was about 8,000, and it was charming and lovely. Parts of it had obviously been around for a long time, as there were Roman ruins scattered here and there, and most of the roads were extremely narrow one-way streets. It had a small castle [well, small for a castle] overlooking the lake below; lots of attractive shops; some interesting cafés and restaurants; a port filled with private boats—the vast majority of which were sailboats; and a landing wharf for the picturesque large paddle boats that ply the length and breadth of the lake, etc. I also discovered that people greet each other on the streets; it doesn't matter if you're a stranger. People nod and smile, make eye contact, say 'Bonjour.' What a difference from Washington. I chose a little restaurant at random, and had a wonderful meal before I drove back to the house.

I was puzzled when I got to the top of my driveway and saw a dim light on in the kitchen. I didn't remember leaving any lights on, though I wished I had because the house was now quite dark. I should have at least turned on the lights on either side of the entrance door. Maybe Yolande had turned on the light in the kitchen this morning when she was making breakfast, and just forgot to turn it off. I froze. There was another possible explanation. I slowly extracted Excalibur from its sheath, switched off my headlights, turned into the top of the driveway, stopped, and killed the engine. I silently opened my door, and coasted down the drive using the emergency brake to slow my descent, because emergency brakes don't activate the rear brake lights. At the bottom, I turned the MG so it was blocking the driveway, and quickly slid out through the open door. I was wearing dark clothes, but the moon was shining brightly. I carefully edged around the side of the house, and looked through one of the glass panels. It was pitch black in the living/dining room except for the dim light coming through the kitchen door. I backed up enough to see that there were no lights on upstairs, and then retraced my steps and walked down the narrow driveway towards the guest house.

It too, was totally dark.

I went back to the entrance door. Just because the house was dark inside, that didn't mean it was empty. The entry door had two locks. The top one was double-sided, so you would have to lock or unlock it with a key, whether you were outside or inside the house. It had a special key. I think the previous owner only used it when he and his family were going to be away for a long trip or something. The bottom one was the more typical lock—keyed on the outside, but with a turn bolt on the inside. I paused, and deeply meditated for a moment to make mental preparations for combat, then silently tried the top lock. It wasn't locked. Good. I certainly hadn't locked it when I left. It was only the bottom lock that was securing the door. I took a deep breath, quietly unlocked the door, and violently threw it aside while I flattened myself against the outside wall, just beside the door. The door hit the rubber bumper, which prevented the door from being opened too far, and started to swing back. I slipped into the house and flattened myself against the inside wall just before the door clicked shut. I silently turned the deadbolt latch to lock the door, and waited a full two minutes before I moved. The house was dead quiet. Keeping one eye shut to preserve its dark adaptation, I peered around the kitchen door. It was just a small counter light over the prep area, that Yolande could have easily left on this morning. I went past the kitchen entrance to the living/dining room and used the main switch panel to throw on every light in the room. Nothing. I ran over to the glass wall and cupped my hands against my face so that I could see outside. Nothing. I checked every room in the house, including the sauna—nothing.

I put Excalibur back in its sheath.

As my heart rate slowed down, I went over to the bar, fixed myself a scotch on the rocks, and sat down at the dining room table to think. I glanced at the maps I had left scattered around the table, along with the information sheet with my address and phone number on it. Something seemed vaguely wrong. But what? Then I realized. When I had been looking at these maps before I left, I had been sitting in this very same chair, and although the maps had been scattered around me, the focal point of that scatter had been this chair. Now they were all slightly displaced to my left.

Someone had stood just beside this chair and examined them.

The clincher was that when I had pulled the stack of maps out of the envelope, I knew that the one map that I wasn't going to use today was the large-scale road map of the whole country. I had put it down first, and then started looking at the rest of the maps in no particular order. The one constant was that the big map stayed put, with the others scattered over it. Now it was no longer on the bottom.

Somebody had definitely been in here. And they had a key.

Thank God I'd memorized all the contact information for the safe house and then burned the paper and flushed it. Was that what they were after? Much more importantly, *who* was looking for something, and *why?* The house hadn't been broken into so where did they get the key? Yolande had told me that the locks on all the doors were very special and almost impossible to pick. Whoever it was apparently wasn't looking for me personally; otherwise he [she?] would have waited for me to get back. What did I have that they wanted? The safe house contact info? How could they have known that I had it? It gave me the chills to realize that I had left it outside in the MG where it was totally unprotected, but oddly, that's one advantage of leaving your car unlocked. The (fairly reasonable) assumption is, that no one, particularly not a professional, is going to leave something valuable hidden in a car that's totally unlocked.

I went outside, moved the MG down to the parking area outside the 'front' door and left it unlocked . You can't really lock a convertible, anyway. All anyone has to do is just cut through the top. It made me think about the entry door lock precautions. With as much glass as this house had, if you wanted to get in, all you needed was a really big rock.

Nowhere to Turn

I reflected that sadly, there was absolutely no one that I could turn to for help or advice. By accepting this assignment I had well and truly put myself 'out there' and I'd better learn to deal with it. I'd also better assume that my phone was tapped, too. On the subject of phones, I really needed to hear a friendly voice so I thought I would try calling Emma—and Peter and Sally as well. It was a little after 10:00 p.m. my time, which meant that it would only be a little after 4:00 in the afternoon in Washington, but it is not at all uncommon for folks in Washington to leave the office for a 'late afternoon meeting' on Friday afternoons. I thought I'd give it a shot, anyway. In any case, I would probably have to wait twenty minutes or so for the international operator to place the call (no direct international dialing in those days).

I tried Peter and Sally first. Sally was there, and I told her all about this fabulous house I was living in and about my visit to Nyon, and how you could drive 100 mph on the Autoroute without worry, etc. She was excited, said that she was sorry that Peter wasn't home but he was working on a big case, and was working late almost every day. She said that she and Peter were going to try to plan a vacation to Switzerland in the summer, and I told her that I had more bedrooms than I could count, and they would be more than welcome to stay at the house if they would like.

Emma was delighted to get my call, and was overwhelmed by my description of the house etc. She then shocked me by saying that she had applied for a transfer to Sweden's embassy in Switzerland. I had very mixed feelings about that. I said I thought that would be great if she could swing it, but that Berne wasn't all that close to Geneva. She replied that she knew, because she'd been studying the maps (I closed my eyes and inwardly groaned), but Berne was a lot closer to Geneva than Washington.

Before I went to bed, I stood at the bedroom window with all the bedroom lights turned off and just looked at the nighttime panorama of distant lights. It was kind of like toyland. Geneva to my right, Lausanne to my left, Morges, Rolle, Nyon on my side of the lake with the lights of Evian, Thonon, and smaller French villages on the other side (the Franco-Swiss border runs through the middle of the lake).

Finally, I went into the bathroom and turned the motion detectors on in both houses, and set the alarm volume to low. Even though I sleep very soundly, I'm trained to wake instantly if I hear an unusual noise. I've had people ask me how that's possible and I point out to them that your ears don't stop working just because you're asleep. The brain simply filters out anything that it doesn't consider to be important. My brain is trained to interpret *any* strange sound as important.

The next day, I got a real education in how Swiss tradesmen worked. It was Saturday, Feb. 1, and the first thing I learned, was that few of them work on a Saturday. When I finally got hold of a locksmith, and told him that I wanted all the locks in my house changed, he wanted to know how many locks. I told him ten altogether, but three of them had to have a different master key (it's useless to have a double lock if one key will open both locks). He whistled and told me that would be a lot of work, and he would probably have to have a helper. I told him that was fine, and asked when he could get started. I expected him to say that he could get to the house in two to three hours. I about fell over when he said that the first timeslot he had available would be at 10:00 on the 13th but that he wasn't sure he could finish in one day. I explained to him that it was urgent, but it made absolutely no difference. I thanked him politely and said that I would try to find someone less busy. He bade me 'Good day' politely.

I only got two other locksmiths to even *answer* the phone, and their time schedules were even worse. Resignedly, I called back the first locksmith, who told me that he had received other calls in the interim, and that now the first time he could make it would be on Monday, the 17th at 9:00 in the morning. I told him that I would see him then. I also told him I wanted some very special locks, and described them to him. He sighed, and told me that such locks were rare and very expensive. They were all custom-made. I would have to give him a 2,000 franc deposit, and he could not guarantee when they would arrive. I gave him M. Michaud's telephone number.

I found a hardware store that duplicated keys, and bought four copies of the regular house key, plus three copies of the special tunnel and entrance door key. I also bought a hammer and a metal file. Back at the house I inserted the appropriate keys in their locks, turned them about a quarter turn, and hammered them in to make the locks useless. I then used the hammer to break off the bow of the key (the bow is the part of the key that you grasp to turn the key), and filed whatever was still sticking out flush with the surface of the lock. The locks were totally ruined and useless, but that was the plan. The locksmith would probably have to drill them out or something, but in the meantime, *nobody* was going to open those doors. That left just one door unsecured. The main entry door. I thought long and hard about that one, and then drove back down to Morges where I had found the hardware shop. I bought some springs, and some very thin nylon fishing line, plus two other common hardware items. I then went to a large grocery store and bought several items that are commonly sold in any medium-sized grocery store. I searched around and finally found a record store. For those readers who do not pre-date the iPod generation, records were plastic discs that had music recorded on them. I bought some Frank Sinatra, Ella Fitzgerald, June Christie and Édith Piaf albums, some classical music and opera albums, and stowed them, plus my grocery and hardware purchases, in the trunk of the MG. I locked it, found a great little restaurant, and after an enjoyable meal, went happily home.

I fell asleep on the leather couch in the club room listening to the music.

The next morning after a swim, a sauna, and some breakfast, (God, what luxury), I set to work on my little intrusion protection device. It was an interim measure, but would serve until the damn locksmith replaced the locks. It took me a while to get the tension on the thin nylon fishing line adjusted just right. However, if you knew what you were doing, after you had unlocked the entry door, you had just enough room to stick your hand through the partly opened door and unhook the nearly invisible nylon line, thereby disarming the device. If you just pushed the door open without disarming the device, you were going to die a particularly painful and inescapable death.

I spent the rest of the day exploring the perimeter of the property, which had a chain link fence (overgrown with weeds and vines) running around much of it. I suppose it was put there just to be a perimeter marker. It certainly wasn't going to keep anybody out. I walked up to the farmhouse and met the farmer and his wife and their two sons, plus their Bernese Mountain dog. The barns were occupied by their cows, which they raised both for milk and for meat.

I went back down to the house, exercised, fixed a light supper, listened to some music, and sacked out. I was looking forward to my meeting with IOS in the morning.

Chapter 3 — IOS and the DIA

I walked into the main office of Investors Overseas Services at 119 rue de Lausanne in Geneva just before 10:00 a.m. on Monday, and immediately sensed that IOS was far from the typical buttoned-down American investment company. For starters, the woman behind the reception desk looked like she was getting ready for the Miss Universe contest, and would probably win. When I told her that I had a 10:00 a.m. appointment with Mr. Cornfeld, she gave me a dazzling smile and stood up to shake my hand. I think she stood up because she wanted me to get the full view. I got it alright. I tried not to stare and concentrated on trying to quell my immediate physical reaction. I think the miniskirt craze had been started by Mary Quant in London a year or so earlier, and while it hadn't yet caught on much in the U.S., it had clearly spread to Switzerland, or at least to here anyway. Her miniskirt looked great with the knee-level leather boots she was wearing. She shook my hand, said that she wasn't sure if Mr. Cornfeld had arrived yet, but to please take a seat and she would ask Mr. Cornfeld's assistant to take me up to his private reception area.

I sat down and tried to occupy my mind by recalling the little bit that I knew about Bernie Cornfeld. Bernie had been born in Istanbul, Turkey in 1927 to a Romanian-Jewish actor father, and a Russian-Jewish mother. The family moved to Brooklyn, NY when Bernie was four, and his father died two years later. Money was scarce—this was the middle of The Great Depression—and Bernie worked after school each day in fruit stores and as a delivery boy. He was a natural salesman and entrepreneur.

He graduated from Brooklyn College, and later obtained a Master's in social work from the School of Social Work at Columbia College. He initially worked as a social worker, but then switched to selling mutual funds for a small American investment firm. In 1955, while on vacation in Paris, he learned that there were about 3½ million American servicemen stationed in Europe and when he returned to his job in the U.S. he begged the firm's owner to let him sell mutual funds in Europe. The owner refused, and Bernie quit, took his savings of a few hundred dollars, returned to Europe and founded IOS. It took real *chutzpa* to make that move from Brooklyn to Europe. He spent most of his money to buy an old Chrysler convertible to get around in, and which on many occasions doubled as his hotel room. Initially, he sold only American mutual funds but in 1962, he launched his own fund—the "Fund of Funds" which was a mutual fund that only invested in other mutual funds—some of them IOS mutual funds. In only seven short years, IOS—and Bernie—had become fabulously successful and very wealthy.

I hadn't been sitting in the reception area for more than three minutes before Bernie's assistant arrived. I know for a fact that I had never seen that many pretty women in three minutes in my life. They weren't all as stunningly beautiful as the receptionist, but they were stunningly attractive. They all seemed to be scurrying here and there very purposefully but all of them gave me a bright smile as they passed. There were plenty of guys that passed through as well, and they too were walking briskly with a business-like intensity. Most of them either smiled or nodded as they passed by. IOS was starting to look like a super company to work for.

Bernie's assistant was a charming, middle-aged woman who greeted me cordially, and led me to the elevator to go up to Bernie's office on the top floor. She apologized that Bernie hadn't made it to the office yet, and told me that punctuality was not Mr. Cornfeld's strongest suit. She told me that my direct boss, Mr. Friedman, *had* already arrived, however, and perhaps the two of us could get acquainted while waiting for Mr. Cornfeld. She opened the door to Bernie's office and led me in. It was all I could do to keep a straight face. That whole huge office had its walls covered with bright red silk. I'd never been in a French whore-house before but I was pretty sure that this was what they must look like on the inside.

She was watching me closely with a sort of half-smile on her lips, and said, "It really is quite *avant-garde*, don't you think?"

"Yes ma'am. Definitely," I replied.

She laughed and said, "You'll do well here, Mr. MacFarland. Let me introduce you to Mr. Friedman."

We got along well from the beginning. Kent's background was also in mathematics, and he had a strong computer background, so we had lots to talk about. He told me that I was the first person ever to work for him that he hadn't personally interviewed, but Bernie had called him some six weeks ago and said that he had been contacted by one of his best friends in New York, who told him that if he moved quickly, he could probably get me to come to work at IOS.

He told Bernie of my background at IBM and Union Carbide, and Bernie had simply responded, "He's hired. We're growing fast and our data processing operations are desperate for good people. Hondle [Jewish for 'bargain'] him a little bit on the salary if you can but don't lose him. Tell him we'll pay all expenses to get him and his family and furniture and pets over here. Bachelor? Seriously? God, he's going to love working for IOS. Get his ass over here as quick as you can."

Kent and I were chatting animatedly when the door burst open and Bernie came in like a whirlwind. He wasn't very tall, maybe five foot six inches, or so, and although I think the term 'overweight' might be a little strong, he was definitely chubby. He was balding, and his sideburns descended down to a short beard which joined his moustache. Although I've seen him in a furious rage, he was generally in a gentle, good mood with a smile on his face.

48

He rushed over and clapped both of us on the back, and turning to Kent, said, "K-, K-, Kent, h-, h-, how're you doing?" Turning to me he said, "Buh-, Buh, Bertie, g-, g-, good to meet you!" Bernie had a stammer—and that's the last time I will try to duplicate it in writing. The funny thing is that after you got to know him, you literally didn't hear it any more. It wasn't that it wasn't there—you just didn't hear it. I've seen him give speeches to international banker's conventions and watched their reactions as they first heard him speak. No matter what those initial reactions were, by the end of the speech they were spell-bound and he often got a standing ovation. Bernie was a bright guy with novel ideas, and you ignored them, and him, at your own risk.

He went around and sat behind his desk and took up a huge stack of those square, pink '*While you were out*' telephone notes, and sorted through them rapidly. Most of them went straight into the trash can. He fixed me with one of his cherubic gazes and told me he was happy that I had decided to join IOS, and that his friend in New York couldn't stop raving about how talented I was. He said that Kent's team was beginning to buckle under their ever-increasing work load, and that so much of their business was coming from France, Germany, Italy and the UK that they had decided to set up back-office operations in those four countries—for starters, at least. My job was going to be to spend as much time as I needed with Kent and the other administrative teams to gain a thorough knowledge of all back-office operations, and then go set them up regionally.

He smiled and stood up to shake our hands, and then added, "We're having a dinner party at *Bella Vista* Saturday evening. Try to make it if you can. It will give you the opportunity to meet a lot more of the staff."

I asked him about dress, black tie, business wear, etc. and he just laughed and told me to wear whatever I was comfortable in. Jeans, if I liked. I knew right then that I'd found the business home of my dreams.

The working environment at IOS was extraordinary, the likes of which I haven't seen before or since. Most of the administrative employees were Brits, and for most of them, it was the first time they had ever been outside their native country (for some, it was the first time they had been very far away from their village). IOS paid quite well, so not only were they working in an exotic atmosphere, most of them were making more money than they had ever thought possible. Also, IOS itself was becoming somewhat legendary with its phenomenal growth. It was being written up in periodicals such as *Time* magazine and the *Economist* as well as newspapers such as *The New York Times,* the *Wall Street Journal,* the *Financial Times* and their counterparts all over Europe. Bernie gave IOS a sort of Hollywood star aura, so being an IOS employee provided lots of reflected glory. On top of that, to add to the adrenaline rush, most employees in Geneva were working there illegally because they didn't have Swiss work permits, and thus were subject to stiff fines, plus deportation if they got caught.

I'll never forget one afternoon when suddenly there were the sounds of multiple police sirens outside the building where I was working. Through the office windows we could see maybe a dozen or so Swiss police cars pulling up just outside. Instant panic. Guys were running up and down the halls yelling, "Raid! Raid!" and I've never seen a building empty out through its back door so quickly in my life.

Having a valid work permit, I wasn't concerned, and went downstairs to see what was going on. I discovered that there had been a horrific traffic accident in the street outside our building. Back upstairs, I found one of the supervisors, hurriedly trying to restore some order to desks and hide the evidence of money orders received from countries which had blocked currencies, etc. I told him what had happened. His face was a real study as it first paled with relief, and then reddened with rage as he went pounding down the stairs of the back exit. Three or four months earlier, an entrepreneurial Swiss had opened an ersatz English pub not more than a block away, and it was happily jammed when the supervisor threw the doors open and bellowed, "It were a bloody traffic accident, weren't it? You lot better be back at your desks within the next ten minutes or I'll be knowing why not."

But for most of the foreign employees—and most of the Swiss ones as well—IOS was sort of a mini-Camelot. They were excited to be working there; they believed deeply in their charismatic leader; it was clear that he really *was* changing the financial world in total defiance of the rigid rules of the established financial community. They were probably working harder than they ever had in their life but they loved it. They were part of an organization that was changing the world. They were not only seeing history made, they were participating in it; and never in their young lives had they ever imagined such a thing. There was no such thing as 'working hours.' You came in as soon as you could get there, and you worked until you nearly dropped. You kept doing it day after day because you *couldn't wait to get to work.* Obviously, nobody outside the company could even *conceive* of that kind of mind-set, but your co-workers could of course, and the bonding was complete. IOS had initiated the amazingly successful *Fund of Funds,* but as far as the employees were concerned, they belonged to the *Club of Clubs.*

I entered whole-heartedly into the fray. The 'back office' system of IOS was its most unglamorous system but it was the glue that kept everything together. The client's money had to be accounted for, directed to the client's choice of fund, and an accounting system set up to show the client each month how his investment was faring. Company bank accounts had to be balanced, money had to be transferred to the investment firms, sales records had to be scrupulously recorded, salesmen and their multiple levels of supervisors had to be paid their commissions, administrative staff had to be paid their salaries, and the company's books had to be kept. It was a massive undertaking. It would have been nice if I had had a business or accounting degree, or something. My background in quantum mechanics and pure [as opposed to applied] mathematics was no help at all. I had to wonder if this was simply icing on the cake of being set up to fail.

I decided then and there that failure wasn't going to happen. I'm bright, I'm proud, I'm combative—very combative . I'm a quick study and I'm tenacious as hell. I absolutely haunted the IOS administrative offices for the next three months. The computer work was done at night and I'd stay on from 8:00 p.m. until 7:00 a.m. when it was finished, then shave and shower, and dictate my notes to my secretary when she came in at 8:00. Both Kent and Bernie called from time to time to tell me to slow down. They weren't worried about me so much as they were afraid I was going to kill my staff. I assured them we would all survive.

That first Saturday night dinner party at *Bella Vista* was a real eye-opener. Bernie had said to just show up in whatever clothes I was comfortable in, so I took him at his word, and showed up in a black turtle-neck sweater, blue jeans and loafers. *Bella Vista* itself was an incredible corporate 'facility.' Not more than five or six kilometers from the very center of Geneva, it was an enormous, lake-side stone mansion which served simultaneously as IOS' guest house, training center, conference center, banquet hall and discothèque. Switzerland is a small country but a very wealthy one. Mansions which occupy large private areas near the center of one of its major cities, and which additionally are lake-side or have magnificent mountain views (*Bella Vista* had both), are exquisitely and painfully expensive.

I showed my IOS identification badge to the receptionist, who was flanked by two rather serious-looking large men in black suits. She greeted me cheerily by name, and summoned one of the multitude of waiters who were running around carrying *hors-d' oeuvres*, glasses of champagne, and other similar goodies, and asked him to escort me to the bar. It was an open bar, and getting very heavy use. I decided I'd just stick with white wine for the moment, and look around.

The party was apparently limited to top and middle level executives, and I waved to Kent and a number of other people I'd met. One was a young fellow I'd met just a few days before who ran one of the many administrative processing departments, and who was all excited because his wife had just delivered their first baby. As I approached him, I thought, Wow. *That is one good looking wife.* She also looked pretty thin and in remarkably good shape for a woman who had delivered an eight-pound baby two days before.

I walked up and clapped him on the back and said, "Nelson, good to see you! Introduce me to your gorgeous wife!"

While she smiled up at me appreciatively, Nelson looked a little sheepish and replied, "Well, ah, actually Mr. MacFarland, this isn't me wife. Me wife's home looking after the baby. This party is for employees only, you see."

I mumbled something stupid like, "Oh! Of course you're right. I knew that, but it totally slipped my mind. Well, have fun, you two." I was learning a lot about Bernie's management style.

Somehow, maybe thirty minutes later as we moved into the dining room, I had not one but two young ladies who had barnacled on to me, and neither one seemed concerned that the other was there. I was definitely moving into uncharted waters—for me at least. Pity that the MG seated only two. Maybe one of them would be willing to scrunch in onto the little bench behind the seats. What the hell. The night was young.

Dinner was magnificent. During my time with IOS, I'm sure I had either lunch or dinner at *Bella Vista* at least 50 times, and the level of excellence never faltered once. Bernie truly went to extraordinary lengths to establish the reputation of IOS as a world-class company. He was prescient in realizing that the world-class talent that he was hiring would promulgate that message to their peers if a seamlessly discrete but opulent life-style pervaded the business culture of IOS.

During dinner I met one of the lawyers that worked in the IOS legal department and we struck up an instant friendship. We had a chance to introduce ourselves and talk more after dinner, and the more we talked the more we enjoyed each other's company. His name was Pierre Lambert, and he'd graduated with honors from the Law School at the University of Geneva, and had spent a year at Harvard Law School under the ongoing professor and student exchange program between the two schools. He was a couple of years older than I, around six feet tall, fit, handsome, wore round glasses with thin horn rims (which sounds incongruous, but on him they looked good), and had an easy laugh. He was a bachelor as well and promised to show me around Geneva and introduce me to some of his friends. He confided that he had recently turned in his resignation to IOS because he and three other local lawyers were setting up their own law firm in Geneva. I promised I would become one of his first customers, because I wanted to set up a Swiss administrative holding company. Holding companies simply hold shares of other companies. I had the feeling that when things started to really move on the DIA front, I was going to need to set up shell companies in several countries in order to funnel money to my 'recruits.' We exchanged both work and private phone numbers before leaving for the evening.

I semi-regularly went to the safe house in Geneva and worked though the piles of classified documents that had accumulated on the desk in my tiny little office. Vietnam was a continuing mess but Johnson, McNamara and, above all, McGeorge Bundy were becoming increasingly hawkish. I thought it was a recipe for total disaster but there wasn't a thing I could do about it. I was heartened, however, by occasional reports from the DIA that shared my point of view. In a subtle way I was beginning to separate myself from the ongoing debacle in Vietnam. Clearly, my 'area of operation' for the foreseeable future was going to be Western Europe, the Soviet Union, and other countries behind the 'Iron Curtain.' I felt relieved somehow.

Finally, the locks on the doors of my house got changed. Pierre introduced me to several of his friends and the (non-IOS) Geneva night-life. He and I and his friends (plus our companions), began sharing some wonderful weekends at the house, and it seemed as though I was beginning to be tentatively welcomed as a new but untested potential member of Geneva society. (Reasonably full acceptance for a foreigner can easily take 40 years or so. The Swiss are cautious.) In any case, I was able to join a couple of Geneva's most desirable disco clubs—The Griffiin's and Regine's—and even though I was working 18-hour days five to six days a week, I was beginning to feel really happy.

The situation in Vietnam was steadily deteriorating, but nobody seemed to have a workable plan to turn it around. In late February, U.S. helicopters spotted a large group of Viet Cong fighters assembling in a forest glade near Long Dinh. They notified General Khanh (Commander of the South Vietnamese Army), who immediately rushed 3,000 heavy infantry forces there using armored personnel carriers. They encircled the entire battalion of Viet Cong fighters, but during the eight hour battle that ensued, Khanh's troops avoided any direct contact with the Viet Cong, calling in air and artillery strikes instead. As a result, the entire Viet Cong battalion was able to slip through gaps in the line, and used sniper fire to cover their retreat across the river. Khanh fired five of his division commanders for incompetence, but it was a humiliating and cowardly performance by the South Vietnamese Army.

Around the middle of May, I spent the entire week with Kent and his top administrative staff going over my plans to establish the first 'satellite' processing facility in Italy. There were several reasons for choosing Italy. Although we had a large volume of orders flowing in from Italy, it was far less than half of what was flowing in from either Germany or the UK. I wanted to set up the first operation in a relatively low volume country to minimize the impact of the inevitable teething pains. Additionally, our top sales people in both Germany and the UK were control freaks. They wanted absolutely everything that occurred in 'their' country to be controlled by them. I wanted to be able to demonstrate a smoothly running operation in another country, to help convince them that the back office operations were better left in the hands of the Geneva staff.

Kent agreed with the strategy but was skeptical about how I was going to put it together. He said, "God only knows how you're going to pull this off, Bertie—but give it your best shot."

Benevento a Roma

I booked a small suite in a major hotel on the Via Veneto in Rome for a month, and put an ad in what is now the *International Herald Tribune*. I think at the time it was still called *The Paris Herald Tribune*. It was read by every ex-pat in Europe, and its want ads were assiduously perused by anyone wanting a top job with an American company. I gave my name and the hotel's telephone number and address. I have to admit here that IOS had a little problem with its Italian operation. The Italian Lira was not a freely convertible currency and Italians could only invest in Lira-denominated securities, which in general offered pathetic returns. As always, for the very rich, this restriction wasn't a problem because they had huge assets in

Swiss banks, American banks, etc., but it was a real problem for the rich Italian doctor, dentist, lawyer, etc. Now that IOS—and Bernie—are no more, I can confess that IOS participated in smuggling huge amounts of Lira out of Italy.

Bernie's philosophy was, "It's their money, God damn it! Why should the government be able to tell them where they can invest it or spend it?"

The Italian government was well aware of IOS' successful efforts to help their clients circumvent the monetary regulations, but due to extensive palm greasing, made little serious effort to prevent it. Nonetheless, I deemed it best not to openly advertise my IOS affiliation while in town trying to hire an administrative manager for the country.

I had another small problem. Although I had twice transited through the airport in Rome, I had never actually been in the city. I didn't speak enough Italian to read the ads for commercial office space, and I was scared to death that if somehow I happened on some space that seemed acceptable, I might sign a lease only to find out that the space in question was smack in the middle of the red light district. I knew who to call though.

My flight to Rome was uneventful enough, but the taxi ride into town was hair-raising. It was my first introduction to the Italian attitude towards traffic, and driving in general. First of all, there is the *machismo* of the driver, which is often demonstrated by such things as an outraged refusal to let anyone merge into 'his' lane ahead of him. The righteous indignation engendered by any such brazen attempt is demonstrated by the driver leaning halfway out of his window and waving his free arm, which is also simultaneously engaged in making continuous rude gestures. Meanwhile, the 'steering arm' frequently leaves its post to pound on the horn button. All this is accompanied by a cacophony of full-throated dialogue by both parties—which I was happy not to understand.

I have no idea why Italian road officials bother painting lane lines on the road. Absolutely no one pays them the slightest bit of mind. If the driver feels that he can fit his car between two other cars, that's what's going to happen, and the hell with the lines painted on the street. I thought traffic was chaotic in Washington, DC on the afternoon of Kennedy's assassination, and it was. It couldn't hold a candle to everyday traffic in Rome, however. I was profoundly grateful to arrive at the hotel in one sweaty piece.

It's wonderful to explore a new country. Almost every minute is a learning experience. I wasn't going to have any financial limitations on exploring because all the hotel bills were going to be sent to one of IOS's numbered accounts in Geneva, and my American Express card, backed by the same bank account, was issued to one of IOS's myriad Swiss companies. My 'modest' hotel suite was nearly the size of my apartment in Washington, and there was a lovely bouquet of freshly cut flowers on the dining room table, along with a bottle of excellent champagne in a bucket of ice—all 'Compliments of the Management.'

When I checked in, the desk clerk had given me an envelope, which I now opened to find a message from my secretary, asking that I call. When I did so, Marianne informed me, rather grumpily I thought, that she had received a call from a Mademoiselle Emma Dahlquist, who wished to inform me that the Swedish Embassy had approved her request for a transfer to the Embassy in Berne, and that she would take up her new post around the middle of June. Mademoiselle Dahlquist had also requested that I call her at home in Washington. When Marianne inquired if I needed her number, and when I replied that I did not, I think there was a distinct iciness in her voice as she asked me if there were anything I needed her to do before she left for the day.

Emma and I were fairly good friends, but as far as I was concerned, that was all there was to it. I wasn't at all happy about her following me to Switzerland, but there was clearly nothing I could do about it. I didn't want to hurt her feelings, but I thought it might be best to wait a couple of days before returning her call.

I thought long and hard about the next phone call that I made. When it was answered I was sure that I recognized the voice of the maid that was the nanny for Don Moretti's grandchildren and I greeted her with, "Buonasera, Elisabetta. It's Bertie. May I speak to Don Moretti?"

There was a long pause and then, "Signore Bertie? Signore Bertie?" All I could hear after that was Elisabetta screeching and calling for Don Moretti and yelling, "Signore Bertie! Signore Bertie!"

It was a real relief to hear Don Moretti's calm, authoritative voice on the phone greeting me warmly. "Bertie, is it really you? What a pleasure to hear from you. How are you?"

"Don Moretti, my most respectful personal greetings to you and Mamma Moretti. Thank you for taking my call. Are you both well? How are Gino and Carmela and the girls?"

"You are kind to ask and the entire family is very well. The entire family also misses you very much. You are a frequent subject of our conversation. I know you must be very busy in Washington but I hope that you will find some time to visit with us again in the near future. I thank you for the kind letter that you sent us and I want you to know that you will always be welcome in my house. Gino says that the villagers of the many towns that you visited often ask about you as well. And Bertie, please know that I will *always* take your calls. No questions asked. Now tell me why you have honored me with this call."

"I'm in Rome, sir and I really need some business advice."

The change was instantaneous. I could hear it in his voice. This veteran warrior was on full alert. His immediate question was whether or not I could speak freely. I confirmed that I could, and he quickly asked me which one of his two granddaughters I thought was prettiest.

I told him that I couldn't possibly decide between Melisa and Isadora.

He breathed a sigh of relief. It's an old but very effective spy's trick. If I had given him one of his granddaughter's names incorrectly, my phone call was being listened to but there was no immediate threat, I was just uncomfortable and suspicious. Two false names and I was in imminent danger. I don't know how he knew all this stuff but given his status as an iconic World War II Italian hero and reputation for being one of the richest (and most reclusive) men in Italy, I wasn't totally surprised—just totally impressed.

He said it was best to talk business personally rather than over the phone, and suggested that I come visit for a long week-end. I readily agreed, but was surprised when he 'suggested' that I take the tourist bus from Rome to Civitavecchia tomorrow morning at 8:00 a.m., and to get off at the central bus station when it arrived there at around 10:00 a.m.. He said that there would be a young man holding a sign that said 'Roberto Scarlatti' and to just go up to him and say in English, "I'm Robert." He told me that the driver would take me to the small, private airport in Civitavecchia and put me on a two engine prop aircraft. He gave me the tail numbers of the aircraft. He said that the plane was small but it was very fast and capable of landing on water. He told me that Gino would pick me up and bring me to the house. He added that the whole household would be delighted to see me.

Without giving me an opportunity to respond, our connection was broken.

Although I knew that I would thoroughly enjoy seeing the Moretti family again, I confess that I was a little miffed by the almost peremptory summons of Don Moretti. If I didn't want to keep him as a friend, I could just ignore his instructions, but I *did* want to keep him as a friend and moreover, I had the distinct impression that ignoring Don Moretti under *any* circumstances was probably not a good idea. I was on the bus at 8:00 the next morning.

I was greeted as the long-lost son at the Moretti estate. 'Mamma' was hugging and kissing me while crying and poking me and telling me I was far too thin, and who was looking after me and who was feeding me, etc. Don Moretti greeted me warmly from his wheelchair, shook my hand firmly and told me how pleased he was to see me. Gino hugged me (I was slowly beginning to understand that outside the United States, it was perfectly acceptable for men to hug other men as a greeting), Carmela hugged me and kissed me on the cheek, even the two girls hugged my legs and turned their faces up for a kiss. Elisabetta had been standing discretely in the background but at a nod from 'Mamma', she came running to give me a hug and a tear-stained kiss on the cheek and I felt totally at home. For the hundredth time I wondered why I had ever left this welcoming sanctuary and for the hundredth time, I sadly answered my own question.

After a stupendous 'lunch', Don Moretti announced that he and I needed to discuss some business together and the rest of the family immediately melted away. When we were alone, he said, "Tell me Bertie, my son, are you safe?" I was so thunderstruck that I was speechless. Had he really referred to me as his son? He smiled sadly and said, "I wish you were the son I never had. I hope that one day you will come to live with us as part of the family, but I know that will never happen. You have given yourself a mission in life and you will follow the path that you have laid out for yourself. I regret it but I respect you for it. Now tell me about your business problem."

I was truly taken aback. I hardly knew how to respond. I started, "Don Moretti . . .."

He interrupted me and said, "When we are alone together, just you and I, you may address me as Umberto." (Umberto was *not* the name he gave me but it is the one I'm going to use.)

Again, I was stunned. Even his own son-in-law—Gino—addressed him as Don Moretti. I don't think my voice was as steady as it might have been when I told him how deeply honored I was but there was no mistaking my sincerity.

It took about two hours but I told him everything—absolutely everything. Lubyanka; my relationship with Kennedy; my suspicion of Johnson as being the organizer of Kennedy's assassination; Johnson's hatred of me and refusal to let me resign; my 'insurance documents'; my wrangling of a job with the DIA to set up a European military intelligence-gathering operation; the cover position with IOS to explain my constant travel—everything.

He listened quietly the whole time, only now and then interjecting a quiet question for clarification, and when I was finally finished he sighed deeply, "Ah, Bertie, Bertie. It's even worse than I had feared. You are *not* safe, but the danger does not come from some criminal element. It comes from the President of the United States. Few people can survive the wrath of an enemy with such enormous power. However, if anyone could, it would be you. I don't know how or even if I *can* help but I will think about it. You know that of course, you always have a safe haven here if you need it.

"Now on setting up an office for IOS in Rome, I think I can definitely be of help. That Cornfeld fellow is a scoundrel and a rogue, but I have to admire his brazen challenge to the world financial community. He will fail in the end, of course, but you should have some fun times before that happens. Take my advice though Bertie, do *not* invest in the IOS stock. You will lose every penny you invested.

"About the office, I'm going to give you a note to the head of my law firm in Rome. I will tell him that he is to make an introduction for you to the head of the [name withheld, but one of the largest oil companies in the world] oil company in Rome." I'll use the name 'Petro Oil Company.' [Lord, I hope there's not a *real* company named Petro Oil Company.] He said that they had very nice offices in a high-rise building located not far from Rome's Fiumicino airport, but that they were moving a significant portion of their operations to Saudi Arabia, and that they were looking to sub-let the vacant space. He told me that he was also going to tell the head of the law firm that *any* request that I made of the firm should be considered a request made by him personally.

He smiled as he told me that Rome, like any large city, is rather 'clubby' and it always helps to have someone open doors for you. "Now I'm getting to be an old man, and my leg is starting to hurt, so I'm going to go upstairs and take a nap. Come over and give me a kiss on the cheek." I hoped he didn't see the tears in my eyes when I did so.

I was depressed when I boarded Don Moretti's plane late Monday morning. Although absolutely nothing had been said, it was clear to the rest of the family, and to the servants (to this day I don't know how many servants lived in that house but there must have been at least a dozen), that something had changed between him and me. If possible, I felt that I was loved and trusted even more than previously. I hated to leave. This really felt like my home and my family.

We landed at the private section of Rome's airport and as the door opened and the steps lowered, a limo pulled up to the base of the stairs, and a liveried driver rushed around the car to open the door for me. I hesitated as I started to enter. There was another passenger in the back seat. I relaxed and got in when he introduced himself and greeted me by name. We shook hands and I gave him the note from Don Moretti which he read carefully. He asked if he could keep it and when I replied, "Of course," he said that he would shred it personally when he returned to the office. He told me that of course he would make the introduction to the president of the oil company, and was at my complete disposal to assist me in any negotiations. Although he was too discrete to ask, I told him what I was trying to accomplish in acquiring office space for IOS.

He said that there might well be interest on the part of the oil company to sublet some of their space, and added in a questioning tone of voice, "So, IOS is your employer?"

I hesitated before responding, "Well, one of them anyway."

He laughed and said, "I thought so. It would be most unusual for our mutual friend to express so much respect for just an ordinary businessman. You are clearly not an ordinary man in any way whatever, and I deem it a privilege to know you."

As we approached my hotel, he said, "Let me come in with you for a moment, I want to introduce you to the manager. He is a friend of mine." I told him that I had already met the manager, and he smiled and said, "Yes, I'm sure. But please permit me anyway."

The moment he entered the hotel lobby, there was a look of surprise by the staff behind the desk, and one of them immediately disappeared into the offices behind, re-emerging almost immediately with the beaming hotel manager who rushed over to greet his friend. I was then re-introduced to the hotel's manager, Enrico, as 'a highly valued client of the law firm and a personal friend.'

The hotel manager bowed his head to me and said, "Ah, Mr. MacFarland. If we had only known! But please allow me to express the hotel's pleasure at having such an honored guest. We have a much nicer suite which has become available just this morning." When I hesitated, he said, "Please allow me. We can have your personal effects transferred immediately."

I thanked him and told him that I found my present suite quite acceptable but if he thought the newly available suite would be more suitable I would be honored to accept. He clapped his hands and hotel employees appeared from everywhere while he barked instructions so rapidly that I found it impossible to understand his Italian.

In the meantime, the director of the law firm shook my hand, gave me his personal card and said in a low voice, "You handled that perfectly, Mr. MacFarland. He would have been insulted if you had refused his offer. We will work well together. Our mutual friend is an unfailingly accurate judge of character."

Enrico led me respectfully over to the desk manager and informed him that I was an honored guest of the hotel, and was to be shown every courtesy. Should I require it, one of the hotel's limos was to be continuously at my disposal. He then asked if he could personally escort me to my new lodgings.

He led me past the elevators, and used a small, curiously shaped key to open a door marked 'Private,' which opened into a charming mini-lobby, tastefully furnished with couches, comfortable armchairs, reading lamps, coffee tables, telephones, etc. Little gilded boxes were on every table with call buttons for the valet, waiter, and maid. I followed him around a corner to a massive door, whose elaborate gilding could not quite mask the fact that it was bullet-proof.

Again he used the small, brass-colored key to unlock the door. It revealed a luxurious elevator cab with one button. He pressed it, and while the elevator was gliding silently upward, Enrico informed me that it only stopped on the top floor of the hotel, and that none of the regular elevators in the hotel could access that floor, even though their top buttons were labeled 'Penthouse.' I was surprised when we arrived at the elevator's only stop, and the heavy door opened to reveal a small, metal lobby that could accommodate probably no more than ten people.

As soon as Enrico and I had exited, the elevator quickly slid shut. *Pressure sensitive elevator floor*, I guessed. *Unless everyone's out, the door won't close, and even if everybody gets back in the elevator, it won't move. Nothing is going to happen, and nothing is going to work unless everybody gets out of the elevator, and then they will then be enclosed in a small metal lobby where walls, ceiling, floor and the two metal doors are all but impenetrable. The key to the elevator door won't work anymore.*

Enrico had been observing me carefully as I looked around, and carefully examined this sterile, metal elevator 'lounge.' 'Cage' would probably be a more appropriate term.

"Ah, yes, I was sure of it, sir," he announced enigmatically. "You are one of the very few who have ever seen this sort of security level. Your suite is this one, to the right of the elevator," and he gave me a small, intricately shaped, silver-colored key. "As you know, once you have opened the door to your own suite, all the security provisions are re-set and everything will function normally. Incidentally sir, if you wish to exit the hotel more privately, just press the black button in the elevator twice in quick succession; the elevator will take you down to the kitchen level. If you will use the internal phone to call us before you exit your suite, I will personally ensure that you are met with highly trained security personnel at the kitchen exit. Our limousines are bullet-proof, sir. Be assured that your security is our very highest priority, sir. I will engage our police and national security agents to supplement our efforts, should that be necessary."

I about had a heart attack. I said nothing. There had to be recording devices all over this 'lobby.' I just gave him a conspiratorial smile, took the silver key, and opened the door.

I won't even try to describe the size of it. It was really two suites. A master suite plus another, smaller suite with its own set of bedrooms, living room, kitchen, etc. I suppose that was for the entourage that world leaders, major entertainment figures, etc. always have surrounding them. Who the hell did he think I was anyway? It was embarrassing and I felt like a fraud. I reminded myself that this was something which I had definitely never asked for, so I smiled at Enrico, told him it was magnificent, and that while I didn't really need such luxurious lodgings, I would certainly enjoy them and I was extremely grateful for his thoughtful generosity. As he left, he pointed out that the silver phones connected directly to the front desk, and to please call the moment I needed something. I wandered around a little bit just to see what the suite contained. I had thought that my original suite was a bit much but this was way over the top. I found the excessive opulence distasteful and claustrophobic.

I had just changed into my usual attire—black turtle-neck sweater, jeans and loafers—when the phone rang. It was the head of the oil company, who said that he understood I might have an interest in sub-leasing some of the office space, and asked if I would like to come see the vacant space sometime tomorrow. I suggested 10:00 a.m. and he said that he would send the company car for me.

I left to try to find a simple *trattoria* for a light meal.

Paul Hawkins, the American who headed up Petro Oil Company Italia, was a tall, spare man in his mid-forties, with the hassled air of being at the absolute limit of keeping up with the myriad tasks that faced him. The office space was just what I was looking for, however. Even though Petro did not own the building, it had been built especially for them and to their specifications. It was, therefore, a typical American midrise building with glass curtain-wall construction and minimal interior support columns. In contrast to typical, fixed floor plan Italian office buildings, where every wall is load-bearing and therefore very difficult to move, the only thing you couldn't touch in this building were those support columns, otherwise you could place the modular walls anywhere you wanted them, and later change them at a moment's notice.

The other really nice thing was that Petro had a huge dollar income from its worldwide operations and in the case of Petro Italia, they had to convert a significant amount of those dollars into Lira to pay their local operating expenses and their Italian employees. Even though the Italian banks were exchanging the world's most valued currency [the U.S. dollar] for one of the world's least valued currency [the Italian Lira], they still took a healthy cut for making the conversion. It was one of the reasons that Petro was transferring a good portion of its non-U.S. operations to Saudi Arabia.

What was great for both Petro and IOS was that IOS Italy had huge Lira income that had to be converted to dollars for investment. Swiss banks were happy to do the conversion (also taking a healthy cut), but IOS had to get the Lira to Switzerland first. That meant smuggling—which was risky at best. I know that on one occasion they had actually used mules with suitcases full of Lira strapped to their backs, and had a guide lead the mule train over the Alps, using little-known trails. Now we could forget about all that. The only thing we would have to move out of Rome every evening was processed paperwork, and the airport was just minutes away. It was a transaction made in heaven. Banks in both countries would lose their conversion fees, and the Italian government would lose a large monthly contribution to its ever-growing dollar reserves, but it was a perfectly legal transaction. Paul and I were both smiling as I left.

The next problem was to find someone to run the Italian operation. I'm a big believer in hiring from the top down. My objective was to find someone that I believed in and respected and who would need minimal supervision from me. I would take him to Geneva so that he could learn what was required, negotiate a salary, give him a budget—and turn him loose. It was important that his employees were loyal to *him,* and that they understood that he had the total support of Geneva. Hanky-panky and attempts at power plays would be simply non-starters.

I was appalled at the huge number of responses the *Tribune* ad had produced. Most of them were dead serious, too. Some were fluff, some looked like they came from some department of the Italian government trying to identify the advertiser, but most of them were really good. Winnowing out the ones that I wanted to look at again was a tedious task. I got the hotel to get me a stenographer/typist because I believe that if someone takes the time and effort to collect all their personal information and send it to you, they at least deserve the courtesy of a written response. Remember, all this was taking place before the days of the personal computer and photocopying mills. Everything had to be hand-typed. You could get things like diplomas and personal references photocopied but it was expensive. My feeling was that to simply not respond to all that effort would be egregiously rude.

The young lady [let's call her Adriana], that the hotel supplied, had amazing capabilities. She took dictation and typed at blinding speeds. She told me later that she almost turned around and left, when I opened the door to that intimidating metal elevator lobby. Additionally, my stupid, gigantic suite would frighten anybody, and on top of that, she was going to be alone with me. I think the only thing that kept her was the fact that she was going to be able to use the revolutionary new IBM Selectric typewriter. She was fascinated by it; and simply because IBM could not keep up with the demand within the United States, there were *very* few of them outside the United States. I think she was reassured when I unceremoniously dumped a stack of 'rejects' on her desk and dictated a courteous letter thanking the addressee for their application and complimenting them on their accomplishments but informing them that we were pursuing other candidates that we felt better met our particular requirements. I gave her a stack of hotel stationary and large envelopes and told her to sign the cover letters with an undecipherable signature and to include all of the originally submitted documents. At least it wouldn't be a total waste for the candidates.

It took several days but Adriana gradually felt comfortable that this was a real job, she wasn't going to get raped, and that I was a reasonably decent human being. I used the downstairs private lobby to conduct interviews, and if the interviewee were Italian (most were), I asked her to be present in case translation was needed. Back upstairs after the interview, I would ask Adriana for her impressions of the candidate and she proved remarkably insightful. Women are really good about picking up things about men that men miss. She got so much 'into it' that she suggested that she, not me, open the incoming mail because I was always interrupting her to ask for translations of Italian reference letters, questions about diplomas, awards, etc. She became the iron-lady gate-keeper. Nobody with questionable documents was going to get by her steely eye.

Disappointingly however, I/we hadn't yet found a single person that I/we felt to be suitable for the job. It had been over two weeks of non-stop reading of resumes and interviewing, and I was starting to get fairly anxious. It was great to have found wonderful, flexible office space within a ten minute drive to the airport, a totally serendipitous solution to the Lira to dollar conversion problem, but if I couldn't find somebody to run the Italian operation, all was for naught.

Then we got Sergio's application. Sergio was—at the time anyway—the youngest person to ever receive the extremely difficult-to-get title or diploma or whatever to be a *dirigente commerciale*. I was startled to hear Adriana squeal with delight when she opened his letter.

She told me, "I think we have found him. If you permit, I will call right away to set up an interview. His credentials are impeccable. If he hadn't included a photocopy of his diploma, I would think him a fraud."

I told her to please call right away.

Sergio was a hoot. Physically, he reminded me of Bernie. They were both about the same height and weight but Sergio had a full head of black hair and no beard or moustache. He had the same sort of jolly, Santa Clause-like demeanor, though. Astoundingly, he had just walked away from a job that most Italian financial directors would have given their right—whatever—for. In those days all large American companies appointed an American to run their country operations overseas. But this was not just any large American corporation; it was one of the largest automobile manufacturers in the world. Dorf Italia (not its real name of course), with its unlimited resources had hired Sergio to be its financial director, and everything went swimmingly well until it was time to file their corporate tax return. Sergio requested a meeting with the president of Dorf Italia, and came into his office with two large sets of documents.

"This one," he explained, "is the one we will file. This other one is what we really owe. I think we can negotiate a final bill that is a little bit less than half of the difference."

Sergio was dumbfounded when the president arose from his chair and declared with righteous indignation, "Mr. Laspetti. We are the Dorf Motor Corporation. We pay our just taxes. I rely on you to ensure that this tax return," he pointed to the second document, "has been prepared using every possible tax provision available to us such that we do not pay one more tax dollar than we have to, but if you are confident that you have already done that, then that is the tax return that we will file." End of conversation.

Sergio said he tried to explain that in Italy, that's simply not the way things were done, but to no avail, so he filed the full return. As expected, some two weeks later, the regional representative of the Italian tax authorities made an outraged phone call to Sergio and demanded to see the president right away. That afternoon, with Sergio trailing behind, he marched into the president's office, took the entire return and threw it onto the president's desk, told the president that the return was unacceptable and that he had better have an acceptable return in his hands within three days or he was going to impose a heavy penalty for late filing. He then marched out again. Finally, Sergio got to explain.

"Sir, in Italy, the government just assumes that everybody is going to try to cheat on their taxes, and they rely on their regional representatives to try to bargain up the tax amount due. The salary of a tax representative wouldn't support a sparrow, but it is one of the most sought after jobs in the government. A lot of money changes hands to procure one of these jobs. Why? Because the tax representative gets a percentage of the difference between the tax amount filed and the amount of tax finally agreed to. In the case of a large corporation where the tax bill is in the tens of millions of dollars, that small percentage adds up to a lot of money for the representative. Now Dorf Italia is in a terrible bargaining position because the tax representative knows exactly what the real tax liability is. The bottom line is that the corporation will wind up paying millions more than it would have otherwise had to. Sir, this is now your problem, not mine. I refuse to work for a company that refuses to even listen to my advice. I quit."

Then he just turned and walked out. Their loss, our gain. On top of that, Sergio built a top notch organization for IOS in Italy and was a superb manager.

Pierre in Washington

It was good to be back in Geneva. Geneva in the summertime is a truly glorious city. It is filled with tourists and bustling with activity and color, and it is spectacularly beautiful. For example, just over the Pont du Mont Blanc in the *Jardin Anglais,* there are numerous park benches where you can bask in the sun, marvel at the bluest of clear blue skies that you have ever seen, gaze at the sparkling lake filled with colorful sail boats. Occasionally, you will see one of the very large, iconic paddlewheel lake transit ships, government owned-and-operated ships running regular routes and transporting passengers to lake-side cities all along the 43 mile length of the lake. You can watch the nearby, spectacular *jet d'eau,* which is one of the largest water fountains in the world (it reaches a height of nearly 460 feet [140 meters]), and see the eternally snow-covered peak of Mont Blanc in the distance. It truly is idyllic.

I called my lawyer friend, Pierre Lambert, to tell him I was back in town, and asked if he would like to come over to the house over the weekend so that we could catch up. It turned out to be a much more interesting weekend than I had planned on.

Pierre showed up around noon on Saturday, bringing gifts and goodies for a picnic, and over lunch, told me that his newly formed law firm was doing much better than he had even hoped, and that he was swamped with work. He said that he had gotten a substantial number of clients in the United States, and that the network he had formed with fellow law students when he was doing his exchange year at Harvard Law School was really paying off. The majority of his fellow students were now working for law firms all throughout the States, and many had clients that wanted to know about setting up Swiss holding companies; setting up Swiss bank accounts; how the famed Swiss banking secrecy laws worked, etc. He said that he had already given a seminar for a law firm in New York, and one in Chicago, and was leaving next week to give one in Washington.

Bells in my head began to jingle loudly. I asked Pierre if he would do me a favor and get my bag with documents in it out of my safe deposit box in the Washington bank, and close the account. He said that he would be happy to do so and would get a notarized document drawn up which would give him the power of attorney to act for me in this matter. All I would need to do was to come by his office Monday afternoon, sign it and give him the key to the box. I said I would also give him the phone numbers for Peter and Sally Boyle, who would probably love to invite him to dinner.

I was impressed by his new office. It was on the third floor of a well-known building in the heart of Geneva with a prestigious address, and had a beautifully designed reception area which struck just the right note of 'establishment, discretion and solidity.' The chairs and couches were all in leather that gave the appearance that it had been lovingly cared for over many years. Good 18th century art on the wall, a cordial, no-nonsense receptionist who was probably in her mid to late forties—it literally reeked of 'Geneva establishment.' When Pierre came in to lead me to his office, one of the first things he did was to introduce me to the receptionist, Madame DuVal and tell her that I was a personal friend as well as a valued client. What a smart man. He accomplished two things with that single introduction. First, that he would find it appropriate to introduce me to his receptionist signaled his respect for her and informed me that she was the firm's gate-keeper. Secondly it told her that if I was not able to get him on his private line at the office, I could call her, and she would make sure that he knew that I was trying to reach him. We went through the same routine with his secretary.

I signed the papers, gave him my safe deposit key, told him that he might want to look up Peter Boyle, and gave him the name of the law firm where he practiced. He said that he knew a couple of lawyers who worked there, and that it was a first-class firm. I also gave him the home phone number and told him about Sally, who was teaching Art History at American University. He told me that he was leaving the next day and that his time in Washington was all pretty much scheduled, but that he would at least try to find the time to call and give them my regards. He said he would pick up my bag on his way to the airport on Friday afternoon.

I was pleasantly surprised to hear Pierre's voice when I answered my phone late Thursday night.

"Bertie, something strange is going on."

"What do you mean?"

"I called Peter's law firm. They've never heard of him. I called the home number and got a recorded message saying that the number had been disconnected and no further information was available. I called the Art History Department at American University. They've never heard of Sally Boyle. It's a little creepy, Bertie."

I was aghast. What in the world was going on? Then a thought hit me. Oh, no. Surely not. I paused and said, "Jesus, Pierre! I just don't know what to say. Will you be too tired to come over to the house Saturday afternoon? Just the two of us. I promise you a fabulous dinner."

"OK, Bertie, I'll be there. But you've got some explaining to do."

I had been reading in bed. I turned the light out and went out onto the balcony outside the bedroom to think. I was stunned by what Pierre had just told me. The enormity of the implications washed over me like a wave of cold acid. My assumption that Johnson was not concerned about my research documents was totally wrong. He was after them with all the force he could muster. Don Moretti had warned me about the wrath of such a powerful person. As always, he was spot on.

I had to admit, thinking back on it, that Johnson's plan was quite clever. So much so in fact, it made me wonder who devised it. Those kinds of dirty tricks are usually the purview of the intelligence agencies. Was McCone gunning for me? Might my own boss, Joe Carroll be in on this? All things considered, I thought it more probable that it was a CIA and not a DIA operation. Peter—or whoever he was—wasn't physically hard enough to be career military. Although the military certainly was not bereft of female members, they are especially proud of their role in the military and even if they don't mean to talk about it, it almost invariably slips out. That's too big a risk to take. CIA made a lot more sense—they're taught from day one to conceal their role as a CIA agent. Thinking about it, my guess was that McCone himself had no knowledge whatever of the operation. He was keenly aware of what his predecessor had let happen to me in Lubyanka, and I don't think he would have given his approval for the operation.

I guess they had folded the operation soon after Carroll had agreed to let me work for the DIA. I presume that the previous plan was for Peter and Sally to become such close friends that I would feel comfortable sharing confidences with them. With me out of the country, however, that was no longer a viable plan. That by no means meant they were going to quit, though. They were just going to shift gears. They had already made a 'house call' soon after my arrival.

Late the next morning, I drove down to Morges and bought the makings for a fabulous dinner. I put everything in the trunk of the MG and drove to a small hotel near the center of town. They had a public phone booth in the lobby. I called Pierre and asked him if he would please put the package he had brought back for me in the law firm's safe before coming over. He wasn't too happy about it but grudgingly acquiesced.

He was in a foul mood when he arrived. He said that some jerk who had been tailgating him ever since he left Aubonne failed to see his left turn signal and ran into the back of his car, when he slowed down to turn onto the dirt road that led to the farmer's house and my driveway. He said that there wasn't much damage; at the last moment, the other driver had slammed on the brakes, so the contact was little more than a mild bump, and the repair wouldn't amount to much. The other driver had taken full responsibility, written a note to confirm it, had shown Pierre his driving license and insurance card, etc., all of which Pierre had duly recorded. He said the guy was really strange. He had insisted that Pierre open his trunk 'so that they could make sure there was no hidden damage.'

I had set up a table and two chairs on the lawn outside the living room. It took me almost two hours to tell Pierre everything—just as I had confided to Don Moretti.

Pierre was a little ashen-faced when I finished. "So among other things, you're telling me that the President of the United States very badly wants what is now sitting in the safe of my law firm."

"I'm afraid so. But look on the bright side. He doesn't know it's there."

"What about that little fender-bender I just had? After the accident and his verbal acceptance of responsibility, what was the first thing he wanted to do? Look in my trunk."

"So at that point, he hadn't yet shown you his driving license and insurance card?"

"Well . . ., let's see. No I guess he hadn't."

"I didn't think so. They're shooting in the dark. You got hit just because they assumed, rightly I think, that the farmer doesn't have too many visitors who drive Alpha Romeos. Did the guy who hit you ask to see your ID at all?"

"No, he just wrote down my license plate number."

"Feel better, now?"

A great dinner, plenty of wine, and the ability to talk freely made us both feel a lot better. Pierre admitted to me that not only he, but several of his friends, had a vague sense that there was something 'hidden' about me. Not dishonest, not something bad or to be ashamed of—just a sense that was more to Bertie than met the eye. He said that he felt truly relieved and that he no longer had any reservations whatsoever about our friendship. He also said that if the question ever arose with any of his friends, he would have no problem telling them that he couldn't talk about it because of our client-attorney relationship, but that if he could, they would be very favorably impressed. Having that kind of endorsement from a prominent member of the Geneva aristocracy was rare for a non-Swiss.

He slept over because we really had gone through a significant amount of wine, but the next morning, just after he left, I got a call from Emma. We had spoken a number of times when I was in Rome but she was cross with me because she had just called me at the hotel in Rome to inform me that she was now in Berne, only to be informed that I had checked out some two weeks ago.

I sincerely apologized and tried to excuse myself with the honest fact that there was a truly daunting amount of work that had piled up for me during my long absence, and that I was only just now getting it all cleared up. She told me how interesting she thought Berne was, and all about her new apartment and how difficult she found it to understand 'Swiss-German.'[18] She told me that her best friend, Ingrid Lindstrom—who was working in the Swedish Embassy in Moscow—was coming to Berne on vacation, and she wanted to know if they could both come and spend a week with me starting next Saturday.

Actually, I thought it might be fun. I'd only met Ingrid briefly at the Swedish Embassy's New Year's Eve party, but she seemed very nice and she was classically beautiful. I told Emma that I would enjoy that very much, but that I couldn't promise that I could take an entire week off from work, but that I was sure that I could spend most of it with them. I told her that I had an extra car that they could use to explore the surrounding countryside, and that I would be happy to introduce Ingrid to some of my best (male) friends. She laughed with excitement and said she couldn't wait.

Thank heaven that we had no idea of the horror that lay before us.

---

[18] Each of the 26 Swiss Cantons (a Canton is roughly equivalent to a State in the U.S.) has its own native dialect. Although the residents of the German-speaking, French-speaking and Italian-speaking Cantons can converse perfectly well in 'standard' German, French or Italian, it is more natural for them to speak to their neighbors, shop-keepers, etc. in the local dialect. Each dialect has its own vocabulary, accent and sentence structure. I used to have a very good friend who was a pretty high-ranking Soviet (later Russian) spy who was fairly fluent in an astounding 26 languages tell me that one morning when he was taking one of the Swiss paddleboat ferries across the lake, he was standing outside near the bow while two men were talking earnestly to each other next to him. As fluent as he was in German, he told me that he could not understand a word of it. They were speaking 'Zurchicoise,' the dialect of the Canton of Zurich—which at the time had a population of around 800,000.

Chapter 4 — Johnson Starts the War

Swedish Delight

Pierre and I met them at the train station in Lausanne the next Saturday morning. We saw them before they saw us. They were hard to miss. Two tall, slender, spectacular women with swaying long blonde hair, sparkling blue eyes, knock-your-socks-off figures, in their mid-twenties, obviously happy, smiling at everyone—I mean really, they were absolutely sensational and they clearly enjoyed the stir that they were causing. I told Pierre that his mouth was agape, and that it was unbecoming.

Emma spotted me, dropped her bag and came running with outstretched arms, with Ingrid right behind her. She literally jumped into my arms and Ingrid wrapped her arm around my neck and kissed me on the cheek. People stared. I felt like a rock star or something. Gently lowering Emma to her feet, I turned to Pierre, whose jaw was back in place but distorted by an idiot grin, and made the introductions. I hadn't been too sure about this visit, but I was starting to feel a whole lot better about it now. We retrieved their bags, nicked into the Mercedes just as the police officer was getting his book out to start writing us up for a violation of the fifteen-minute parking restriction, and headed home. Driving to the train station was the first time I had driven the Mercedes since I bought it. It was luxurious and I liked the leather smell, but I missed the instant responsiveness of the MG.

The girls loved the house, and were overwhelmed by the views. We opened up all the glass panels in the living/dining room, so that fifty percent of the side walls and lake-view wall 'didn't exist.' Not only was the fresh, cool air sublime, we had the occasional bird whizzing through from one side to the other. I don't think I will ever forget that beautiful sunlit afternoon. Over a lunch with local wine, cheese, *viande séchée du Valais*, and other Swiss goodies, we all chattered away happily, totally contented and without a care in the world.

Ingrid had found Moscow fascinating and welcomed the opportunity to practice her Russian, but was frustrated by the fact that there was no way to meet and talk to ordinary citizens. Diplomats and their staffs were allowed to mingle freely within the Embassy circuit, but all travel inside the Soviet Union, as well as contacts with individuals outside the international Embassy community in Moscow, was strictly controlled. I observed to Ingrid that that sounded pretty limiting for a private social life, and she agreed, but said she *had* made one Russian friend. He was the military attaché to the Soviet Foreign Minister, Andrei Gromyko.

Emma said that she had not even really started to work yet, as she was constantly going to orientation classes for new employees of the Swedish Embassy in Bern, but aside from her problems with the local German dialect, she could tell that she was going to love Switzerland. She gave me a dazzling smile and added, "*and* it's so nice to know that you're less than two hours away, Bertie." I smiled right back at her.

She also told me she thought Peter and Sally had moved, or something, because she had tried to call them at home on a couple of occasions and just got a recording saying the phone was disconnected. She said she felt a little hurt that they hadn't called, or at least sent a note with their new address. I told her I had learned they had moved as well, and I was also a bit hurt that they hadn't contacted me either. I opined it must have been a family emergency or something.

Of course I knew what was coming so I was pretty much prepared for it when Emma asked, "Well Bertie, tell us. What is the Special Assistant to the President doing these days?"

I told them I really couldn't say too much, but I was willing to tell them as much as I could if they would swear not to repeat it—not to anyone. Everyone duly swore, and I explained that I was doing some undercover work involving certain European organizations that would necessitate a lot of travel around Europe. It might look strange if I were doing all that traveling without having any apparent reason to do so, and so it had been arranged with IOS for them to give me a position working as their Vice President for International Operations. I told them I really couldn't say a lot more, but it was a complex assignment and I expected it would take me at least a year, maybe even two, to complete. I also told them they were the only three people on this side of the Atlantic who knew I was Special Assistant to the President, and to please not divulge it to anyone.

Things worked pretty much as I had hoped. Pierre of course knew the whole story—I had held nothing back from him—but the girls were now co-conspirators in some sort of ultra-high level skullduggery, and it seemed pretty clear that they were both sure they were actually talking to a real live spy. It was special and exciting, and they had to keep a secret. Neat stuff. We decided that we were all a little bit tired and that it might be a good idea to take a short nap to rest up before we drove into Geneva for dinner and dancing at the Griffin's Club. It was a pretty tiring nap.

We had a wonderful evening, and both Emma and Ingrid turned out to be great dancers. With those beautiful figures, the swishing long blonde hair, the brilliant smiles, the suggestive moves, etc., Pierre and I were probably the most envied guys there. However, Emma and Ingrid received more than a few scathing looks from the females guests in the club.

At one point, when Pierre and I were sitting alone while the girls were 'freshening up,' he said that as we had discussed, he had called his banker on Monday and informed him that he wanted to open an account immediately in the law firm's name for an important client, but it

BACK CHANNEL: THE VIETNAM BETRAYAL

would be several days—perhaps a week or so—before it was funded. In the meantime, the client had some very important documents that he wanted to place in the safe deposit box for the account. He had asked his bank to send an armed courier to pick up the documents. Pierre's standing in the community was such that his bank dispatched a Brinks-type armored van to pick up my package. It was now safely ensconced in a safe deposit vault in his bank, to which he alone had the key. He asked me if I wanted it.

I told him, "God, no! But I want to sit down with you next week and draw up some documents with guidelines which will require you to release those documents to the press if I or any of the people on a list that I will give you die a 'suspicious' death."

Before we could talk any more, the girls came back more radiant than ever. We danced until three o'clock in the morning.

We were all a little hung over when we drifted into the dining room the next morning. Emma made coffee for everybody while we sat around making contented, but rather desultory and somewhat disconnected small-talk. I think it was Ingrid who suggested that we all needed was a good sauna and a swim. That sounded fine to Pierre and me, and we all trooped downstairs and turned the sauna heaters on. I felt pretty proud of myself because I had actually found a pharmacy that sold eucalyptus oil, and though I had used the sauna on several occasions, and enjoyed it immensely, I really wasn't sure what one of the things I found in it was supposed to do.

Obviously the wooden bucket was for putting water and eucalyptus oil in to splash over the rocks that the heaters heated up. I quickly learned to use the eucalyptus oil very sparingly indeed, but I had no idea what the sort of birch whiskbroom was supposed to be used for. The big tub thing next to the shower outside was also a puzzle. My usual routine was to heat up the rocks, pour the water and oil combination over them, lie down on the top bench and parboil in the steam until it got really, really uncomfortable and then go jump in the pool. I found out that wasn't even close to what you were supposed to do.

It took about 30 minutes to get the rocks up to temperature, and in the meantime, we opened all the sliding glass panels around the pool and had a leisurely swim. One of us would get out occasionally to check the temperature in the sauna, and when it finally got to 185 degrees Fahrenheit, Emma and Ingrid led us into the small enclosed area outside the sauna.

Emma jumped into that strange tub just across from the sauna and twisted something on the drain, then hopped out and turned on the fire-hose faucet. It was amazing how quickly the tub filled. She turned the water off when the tub was about three-quarters full. The water supply for the house was pumped up from a deep underground mountain aquifer and was incredibly pure but icy cold. Emma and Ingrid obviously knew what they were doing but Pierre and I had no idea. I just hoped that part of the ritual did *not* include jumping into that icy cold tub. It did.

Both the upper and lower shelves, or platforms, or whatever you call them, comfortably accommodated two adults lying side by side. Nonetheless, everyone stood until the water/eucalyptus mix had been poured over the rocks. After the initial burst of steam had subsided, we all lay down and let our bodies absorb the intense heat. As I found out over the years of using the sauna, the body can welcome an enormous amount of heat during quite an extended time, but conditioning it to do so requires the training of taking regular saunas over a considerable period. After about 15 minutes, Pierre and I were getting really uncomfortable, but Ingrid and Emma were quietly luxuriating.

However, when I told Emma that I thought Pierre and I needed to cool off, she was immediately solicitous and led us both outside. It turned out that the shower, which only had a cold water faucet, was for getting the sweat off your body and that after showering, you were supposed to jump into that tub of icy water, immerse yourself, head and all—as a matter of fact *particularly* your head—until the cold became unbearable, and then stand up, manipulate the drain switch so that about half the water drained out, then close it and refill the tub to the three-quarters level. That was a courtesy for the next user so he/she would find the tub good and icy cold. Then you get back in the sauna. I thought it was the most masochistic procedure that I could imagine. Pierre and I did it anyway.

Icy cold water has a pronounced effect on both the male and female body. Both get 'goose bumps' but they are more visible on the smooth female skin. Women's nipples get rock hard which is actually pretty sexy. Men's bodies have a different reaction. Penis and testicles shrink to a length and size more normally found on small boys. Fifty percent of our group didn't think it was hilarious. Pierre and I also found out what the birch 'whisk broom' was for. After you get really hot, the girls whack you all over with it and then you're supposed to do the same thing to them. If you don't have anybody with you in the sauna, you're supposed to do it to yourself! Who invented this stuff?

I have to admit though, that after a total of three of these cycles, I felt absolutely fantastic and full of energy. I'd never felt such a pleasant tingling in my skin. I felt alive all over. I felt wonderful. I couldn't believe that less than two hours ago, I had been feeling a bit dull and lethargic. Now, my batteries were not only recharged, they were supercharged. We all felt the same way, and for the next half hour or so the swimming pool got some very intensive use. It helped drain some of the excess energy off, but it didn't attenuate the fact that everyone was absolutely ravenous. We went to a wonderful lakeside restaurant that I had discovered in Nyon, which specialized in *omble chevalier* ('noble knight').

Omble is a fairly large fish [2 – 5 pounds] which is found in very few lakes in the world. It lives at great depth in glacier-carved lakes and is extremely difficult to catch. I used to sit, fascinated, on the lake-side park benches to watch the extraordinary technique the fishermen used to catch them. They used small, open boats, powered by a tiny outboard motor, and equipped with a big spool of thin copper wire mounted on each gunwale. At the end of the wire was a small, three-barbed *baitless* grappling hook. Because the boat was constantly moving, albeit very slowly, the lake was so deep that the fisherman would have to pay out a hundred yards or more of copper line before getting the hook to the depth he thought appropriate. Then, as the boat was crawling forward he would alternately grasp each line between thumb and forefinger, and yank it violently if he thought he felt something. How anyone could possibly sense through that much line that the hook had encountered something was totally beyond me. If a fisherman caught three fish in a day, it was a really good day. Needless to say, omble is a very expensive fish. Prepared *au court bouillon,* its delicate but complex flavor is exquisitely delicious. We diminished the restaurant's precious supply by two memorable fish.

It was a wonderful week , marred only by the fact that neither Pierre nor I could be totally absent from work. In my case, I grudgingly agreed to use the Mercedes to go to work so that the girls could tool around in the MG with the top down. Although the four of us were always together after working hours, both Pierre and I did as much as possible to sneak away early. I don't know what excuses he used with his secretary, but mine did everything but roll her eyes.

One afternoon, when Emma and Pierre had gone into Aubonne to pick up some bread and cheese, I was idly talking to Ingrid about the Soviet Union and asked her, "How is Chairman Khrushchev doing? How is he perceived by the ordinary citizen?"

She responded that she frankly didn't know because it was impossible for her to talk with ordinary citizens. Then she blithely dropped a bombshell. "Alexey (her friend who was the military attaché to Andrei Gromyko) told me that he overheard Secretary Gromyko talking to someone, and agreeing that Khrushchev wouldn't last through the autumn. But it's probably just political gossip, or maybe Alexey was making it up to try to impress me with what an important position he has. Anyway, do you think Johnson will win the election in November?"

I tried not to appear thunderstruck and responded casually. "Oh, I feel almost positive that he will. Incidentally, did Alexey say if anybody's name was mentioned as a replacement for Khrushchev?"

She thought for a moment and then shook her head. "I don't think so," she said. "He might have said something about Brezhnev or Kosygin. I don't really remember. We were at an Embassy party and frankly, I wasn't paying much attention. I'm much more interested in people than politics."

I felt like somebody had just given me lifetime box-seat tickets to the Metropolitan Opera. In this cold war atmosphere between Washington and the Kremlin, both sides were doing everything possible to penetrate the upper reaches of the other side's administration, and gather information on their strengths, weaknesses and future plans.

After the end of the Cuban Missile Crisis, the two Soviet Generals with whom I had been dealing, had broken off all further contact. They weren't traitors—they were patriots of the highest order, and were willing to sacrifice their lives for the good of the Soviet Union. They had accomplished their objectives, and having done so, slammed the information door tightly shut.

U.S. intelligence agencies continued to have low-level informants scattered throughout the Soviet military (as the Soviets did in ours), but no U.S. intelligence agency had come anywhere near to having a pipeline into the upper reaches of the Kremlin. The news that I was going to give Washington of the possible coming coup was priceless.

The next morning, I went straight to the safe house and sent an encrypted top priority 'Eyes Only' telegram to General Carroll, summarizing my conversation with Ingrid. I mentioned only that a 'reliable source' had close contact with the military attaché to Andrei Gromyko, who had been present at a meeting where this discussion took place informally and privately after the formal meeting was over. It was not intended to be overheard.

The dreaded Friday finally came. Both Emma and Ingrid were due to catch an early morning Saturday train back to Bern. Ingrid had to get back to Moscow on Sunday, in order to be at work bright and early Monday morning, but after a conference with Ingrid, Emma pleaded with me to let her stay until Sunday afternoon. Ingrid assured me that she wouldn't mind. I said I would be delighted. I also said that I had an urgent matter to attend to in Geneva, but would be back by noon at the latest.

I had gotten a telephone call from 'American Express' telling me that I had a package waiting for me at their office.

Carroll's cable was extremely congratulatory. He said the information had been distributed immediately to 'higher authorities'. That meant McNamara for sure, but since he had used the plural, it meant at least Rusk and probably Johnson. Johnson would welcome the information, but would be pissed that it came from me. Too bad. Carroll said that it was impressive that I had been able to establish a channel into the highest reaches of the Kremlin in such a short time, and to 'keep up the good work.' He added that any requests that I might make in the future for additional resources would receive his 'immediate attention.'

Martin, who of course read all my classified mail and made no secret about it said, "Bertie, as I told you the day you arrived, the Agency told me that you were good. I won't deny that I was shocked when you addressed me by my real name rather than by my work name. I have no idea how you got it but you sure got my attention. Now I find that you've apparently gotten a channel into the upper reaches of the Kremlin, and you've been here, what, five months? I'd offer you a job but you are already on a first name basis with my boss's boss's boss—the Director of the Agency. Just between us girls however, I know that despite what the official internal memorandum said about your release, you are in fact still a Special Assistant to the President. So now we're kind of even, Bertie. You know my name and I know your position. I'm not bad at what I do, either. Let me know if you need anything, you old horse's ass. Grudging congratulations."[19]

I drove back home feeling pretty chuffed with myself.

We spent the rest of the afternoon and evening just swimming, sunbathing, picnicking out on the lawn, listening to music, thoroughly enjoying each other's company and talking into the early hours of the morning.

There were lots of hugs and kisses and tears when we put Ingrid on the train in Lausanne the next morning. Pierre drove glumly back to Geneva and Emma and I drove back to the house. We had a sauna, then a swim, and took a long walk together. Emma told me that Ingrid was truly smitten by Pierre, and since the four of us all got along so well together, she wouldn't be surprised if Ingrid didn't also ask to be transferred to Berne. As I was inwardly groaning, she added that she knew there were no openings in Berne, and that in fact, there were no current openings anywhere in Western Europe. In her opinion, Ingrid was going to be stuck in Moscow for the foreseeable future. As we were scratching around in the kitchen to see what we could cobble together for dinner (neither one of us wanted to go out to eat), Emma discovered that we had no bread, and I went into Aubonne to get a loaf.

Death in the afternoon

As soon as I turned onto the dirt road on my way home, I saw something that raised a red flag. An old, beat-up car was pulled off the road. The farmer at the end of the road had more junk cars and farm equipment than I could count, so I knew I was probably over-reacting, but with my background and training, *anything* out of the ordinary gets my adrenaline going. I pulled up behind it, noted the license plate number, and tried to open the doors. The car was locked. The farmer would *never* lock his car doors.

Thoroughly puzzled, I walked through the field that ran beside my house, until I could get close enough to see the front of the house. What I saw was chilling. Somebody was fiddling around with the new locks on my front door.

While I was running back to the car, I was thinking, "Where the hell is Emma?"

---

[19] On October 14, 1964 Nikita Khrushchev was ousted as First Secretary of the Central Committee of the Communist Party of the Soviet Union (CPSU). Leonid Brezhnev replaced Khrushchev as First Secretary and Alexei Kosygin replaced him as Chairman of the Council of Ministers. The CPSU became the Union of Soviet Socialist Republics (USSR).

I pulled Excalibur out of its sheath, grabbed the roll of duct tape out of the glove box, and ran silently down the hill through the field. When I was on the same level as the front door, I started moving towards the house. As I did so, it was all I could do to keep from gasping. The person who was fiddling with my new locks was a *woman*. She had an open tool kit beside her, and was so intent on what she was doing that she didn't hear me until it was too late.

I used my hand to chop her so violently on the back of the neck that she collapsed without a sound. I used the duct tape to tape her elbows together behind her back and also taped her wrists and ankles. I turned her over to tape her mouth shut and got the shock of my life.

It was Sally Boyle. Unbelievable! I was putting multiple layers of tape over her mouth and around her entire head when I heard what sounded like a woman's choking scream.

I ran down the hill to the pool level and looked in. Some old bastard was kneeling by the pool, and was screaming at Emma in a language that I didn't understand. Emma was in the pool, tied up with nylon rope, and this bastard had her hair in his hand. He would pull her head out of the water, scream at her and when he didn't get the response he was looking for, pushed her head under the water and held it there.

Excalibur didn't quite sever his head from his body, but nearly. I gently pulled Emma out of the pool and when she recognized me, she fainted dead away. I checked her pulse and her airways. The pulse was a little weak but it was steady and her airways seemed clear. I didn't want her to wake up and see all the blood, so I carried her into the downstairs music/billiards room, put her on the couch and covered her with towels.

I went back to take a look at the guy I had just killed. His carotid artery was pumping blood all over the deck of my pool so I dragged him outside and turned him over. I was stupefied. I thought, *My God! What the hell is going on here? This guy is the old guy I met when I was having breakfast in the diner in Washington! What was his name? Peter something. Peter Moore. Well I guess Sally likes guys named Peter, and I'm going to drag her down here and get some answers.*

I went up the hill to the front door, and found Sally awake and flopping about like a fish out of water. Her eyes grew wide when she saw me, but I just grabbed her by the hair and pulled her unceremoniously down the hill (that must have hurt), and put her next to Peter Moore. They obviously knew each other, as they had arrived in the same car, but I could never have anticipated her reaction when she saw him lying there with his half severed neck. She writhed around as if in agony, and tears streamed down her face.

My main concern was Emma, and I went back inside and gently stroked her face and her limbs until she woke up with a convulsive gasp and a look of horror.

I took her into my arms and murmured, "Everything's OK. Everything's OK. You just had a little accident but you're completely OK. You're not hurt, just a little scared. Don't worry. I'm here. I'll take care of you and protect you. You're completely safe."

She smiled and relaxed a little, and I gently lifted her and walked upstairs and put her in my bed. I tucked her in, and covered her with the duvet.

I took Excalibur back out of its sheath, and unscrewed the cap at the end of the haft. Excalibur was a pretty neat weapon. In addition to its incredible sharpness and the lethalness of the backwards-facing hooks on the top, you could put a lot of stuff into the hollow haft. The inside of the cap of the haft had a little compass embedded in it, and I had packed quite a few small items into the haft itself. The most important one was a cyanide pill, next down was my 'sewing kit' for wounds, then some matches, then two pain pills—and there was a lot more under that. The pain pills were very strong so I cut one in half and gave it to Emma, along with some water to wash it down. Emma was shivering under the duvet even though it was warm that late afternoon. I told her the pill would make her feel better and I stroked and comforted her for about 15 minutes until she went to sleep.

Then I got down to business. I called the emergency line at the safe house (yes, my phone was tapped but it was tapped by the CIA, and I was calling the CIA, so the hell with it). The voice at the other end simply said, "Yes."

I said I had a critical situation and needed help, and that I wanted to speak to Martin. There was a barely stifled gasp—one did *not* use Martin's name, and particularly not on an unsecured, albeit tapped, telephone line.

The next thing I heard was Martin's voice saying, "Hang up. I'll call you right back. We can jam from this end."

I hung up and the phone rang immediately although his voice sounded a little hollow. After my, "Martin?" without responding he said:

"Answer my questions with 'Yes,' 'No,' or 'Maybe.' Do not use any other responses. Do you understand?"

"Yes."

"Are you in immediate danger?"

"No."

"Are there 'hostiles' around you?"

"No."

"Do you feel that you can speak safely?"

"Yes."

"Then tell me what the hell is going on."

"I've killed one person and I'm probably going to kill the other one. I need a meat wagon out here pronto. I need a good medic for my girlfriend, and a vehicle to get her to a hospital if that's necessary. I need a clean-up crew. I need a vehicle that can tow away a car, and I need them *now*! Dark, no flashing lights."

"Noted. ETA (expected time of arrival) 25 minutes." Click. The conversation was unceremoniously terminated.

I went back into the bedroom to check on Emma. Her pulse was slow but strong, which is normal for a sleeping person. Her breathing was normal and unobstructed. I felt her hands and feet and they were warm.

I went downstairs to talk to Sally. I found her lying almost on top of the old guy. She wasn't flopping around anymore, but she was sobbing softly. I pushed her roughly over onto her back and said,
"Well, well, my old friend Sally. Such a pleasure to see you again. And accompanied by your husband Peter, no less. He seems to have aged dramatically since the last time I saw him. I would hardly recognize him as your husband. He looks like a guy that I met in a diner in Washington, but that surely can't be. How could you and he have possibly met? So tell me what you and your remarkably aged husband have been up to. Ah, of course. I forgot that you really can't talk very well with all that duct tape over your mouth, so I'll tell you what I'm going to do. I'm going to cut a slit in it so you can speak. Now it's starting to get a little dark and my knife is exceptionally sharp so I'll try not to cut your lips, but, you know how it is, you try your best but you really can't promise."

I pulled my handkerchief out of my back pocket, dangled it in front of her and said, "Now Sally, just a moment, I'm going to find a nice rock that's just the right size, and wrap it in my handkerchief here."

There were lots of rocks at the edge of the farmer's field. I found a suitable one, and returned and continued my monologue with Sally. "I do wish my handkerchief were cleaner, but it's the only one I've got for the moment. Now let me tell you something. When I cut the tape so you

78

can speak, if you start to scream, I'm going to jam this handkerchief-wrapped rock into your mouth, and tape your mouth back up. I may have to break a few teeth to get it in there. This rock does seem to be a little large but it was the best I could do on the spur of the moment. Now Sally, it's up to you. Do you want to talk to me? I've got a whole posse of your CIA buddies coming to pick you up, so you can wait and talk to your colleagues if you'd like. Your choice, Sally. Shake your head 'No' if you want to wait, nod your head 'Yes' if you want to talk to me."

She nodded her head 'Yes.'

I truly didn't mean to, but I sliced off a good bit of her lower lip when I cut a mouth opening for her. It was bleeding profusely when she tried, in vain, to spit on me. This was one tough cookie. I was astonished when she spoke to me in Russian. The language was filled with invective and was pretty salty to boot. She told me that the old guy's name was not Peter Moore, it was Petr Morozov, and he was her father.

I told her that frankly, I thought he was a bit old to be working for the Agency and that she was lying.

She said that because of his interrogation experience at Lubyanka, the 'wet works' department at the Agency used him for particularly difficult interrogation cases.

I presumed he was there to interrogate me. I was the tough case. There was such outraged power behind the stroke that this time, the decapitation was complete. I don't think she felt a thing.

I did though. I was seething with rage. Had I known, I would have made sure that her father died a very different death. I was still standing over them, shaking with anger when the safe-house team moved down the hill.

Martin signaled the others to stop, approached to within about five yards, and gently spoke, "OK, Bertie. It's over now. Now either put your damned knife down or put it back in its sheath, because I'm not going to talk to you while you're still holding that thing. Snap out of it, Bertie! It's over. It's not the first time you've killed and I'm sure it won't be the last. Listen to me and put that damn knife away!"

What he was saying finally got through to me. I think I'd been in some sort of enraged trance. I looked at Martin, apologized, wiped off Excalibur on the grass first and then on my handkerchief (minus rock) and put it back in its sheath. "Sorry, Martin, I said. "There was a little bit of a personal connection here. The old guy's an ex-interrogator at Lubyanka. The girl's his daughter. I'm pretty sure she's one of your crowd." I extended my hand.

He looked at it and said, "I sincerely appreciate the gesture, but I think I'll pass if you don't mind. You might want to look at your hand. Let's go inside and talk. Show the cleaning crew here where they need to work, and let's get our doctor to look at your girlfriend."

I showed the cleaning crew the blood-soaked deck floor of the swimming pool, and led Martin and the doctor upstairs where Emma was sleeping soundly. I showed the doctor the remaining half of the pain pill that I had given to Emma. He said, "I don't know where you got that but it's totally illegal. It's powerful stuff and it's hard to tell what the reaction is going to be. That's why it's illegal. In general, if you are in severe pain it will cut the pain a lot but leave you alert. If you aren't in severe pain, it will just knock you out, and from all reports, pretty pleasurably. It's a powerful opiate derivative."

He said Emma would probably wake up around midnight. He checked her vital signs, listened to her heartbeat, took her blood pressure, etc. and said she was fine. He said, "When she wakes up give her this pill that I'm putting on your bedside table. She's probably going to be pretty distraught and the pill will put her back to sleep again plus when she wakes up in the morning, she ought to have very little memory of what happened to her. The clinical trials aren't finished yet but in four or five years I think it will be commonly administered to patients who are going to be operated on so they don't have much residual memory of the pain."

I thanked him and he left. Martin and I moved into the library.

As I started to sit down, he said, "Bertie, would you do me a favor? Go wash your hands and change your shirt. You've got blood all over you."

I stared at myself in the bathroom mirror. I had blood all over me—my face, my hair, my shirt, my arms and hands—just everywhere. I felt miserable and drained and sad and dirty inside, somehow. Movies are always showing gangsters that mow down their rivals without any apparent remorse, and maybe there are people who are actually like that. I'm not one of them. Disconsolately, I set about trying to clean myself up a little bit.

When I came back and sat down he asked gently, "Tell me what happened, Bertie."

I told him the whole story and he commented, "You're a little too quick to use lethal force, Bertie. You didn't absolutely have to kill either of them—especially not 'Sally'—whoever she is. That was pretty gratuitous. You need to try to quell those Lubyanka demons, Bertie, they're clouding your judgment. You keep on like this and you're going to find yourself in some real trouble one day. Fortunately for you, today isn't that day. We've been suspicious of 'Sally' and her young friend 'Peter' for quite some time. We suspected both of them as being double agents. We had our suspicions confirmed only recently. We fed Sally some totally bogus information about our secret development of a new class of nuclear submarine—we dubbed it the 'Q' Class. Sure enough, within two weeks, we had one of our assets in the Soviet Navy inform us that top Navy brass was urgently seeking information on the new Q Class submarine. So we would have killed her anyway, but we might have been able to determine who she was reporting to, and more about whatever network she was operating within. Except for the fact that her young friend is still out there somewhere—and we'll get him and get the information we want from him—I'd be very angry with you Bertie."

I thought about it before agreeing. "Martin, sadly, I think maybe you're right about my hair-trigger willingness to kill, but after-action analysis, correct though it may be, is done in the calmness begat by safety. In the heat of battle, you do what your training has taught you to do, or you're going to die. I guess in the case of the old guy I was being over-protective of Emma, and killing Sally was pure outrage at the KGB, but you're right and—to the extent that I can—I'll try to be more careful in the future. But Martin, I have to tell you that I think you are being shockingly casual about why those two people were here in the first place. If what Sally told me is true, her father was a temp hire from your 'wet-works' department, but Sally had to be full-time with the Agency, and apparently so was her 'husband'. Those are *your* guys, Martin. *Somebody* got them to come after me and it had to be somebody in the Agency that authorized it. If McCone has authorized this, I'm in huge trouble. It'll be tough to fight the entire Agency, but I will if I have to."

He suddenly stood up, and in one smooth motion, I snatched Excalibur from its sheath and lunged at him, knocking him back on the sofa with me on top of him and Excalibur at his throat. His eyes went wide with terror, and I could feel him trembling underneath me.

"So that's the way it's going to be, huh? Johnson's told McCone to do whatever's necessary to get my research papers. Well let me tell you what's going to happen before I kill you. You're going to pick up that phone on my desk and call headquarters in Washington. You're going to tell them that I—and you'll use whatever codename you bastards have assigned me—am holding a knife to your throat, and that I want to be patched through to John McCone immediately. When McCone comes on the line, you're going to tell him that I am right behind you with a knife to your throat, and that I've already killed two people tonight, so you have every reason to believe that I am very serious.

"You're going to tell him that he can tell Johnson that my research papers are now in a Swiss safe deposit box, the key to which is held by a Swiss law firm. You're going to tell him that if I, or anyone else on a list that I have filed with the law firm, die a suspicious death, their instructions are to immediately send photocopies of all the documents with the supporting documentation that accompanies them, to every major newspaper in Europe and in the United States. If I get written confirmation within three hours that he has followed my instructions and has immediately and permanently called off the dogs, you live. Otherwise, game on. Got that? Now get up slowly and get over there to the phone."

He was shaking when he got up and I used my left hand to grab his left wrist and poke it into his waistband, like he was tucking in the back of his shirt. The difference was that I kept my fingers behind his wrist and my thumb on the outside of his belt so that his hand was pinned behind his belt and there was no way that he could run. I said, "If you try to move that hand Martin, I'll either cut it off or slit your throat. You got that?"

He nodded his head.

I continued, "Martin, I have to tell you, I really liked you. I really trusted you. I wanted us to be good friends. It just goes to show that trusting anybody in this business is a sign of severe mental incompetence. I know that now, but I'm still disappointed."

He held up his right hand and pointed to Excalibur. I was puzzled. "What do you want, Martin? I'm not letting you go."

He mumbled one word, "Speak." I thought about it a moment and said, "Ah, You want to speak but you're afraid that if you do, Excalibur is going to cut off your Adam's apple. Is that correct? Hold up two fingers on your right hand if it is."

He held up two fingers and I moved Excalibur slightly away from his throat. I told him to say his piece.

He said, "Bertie, I've got to sit down. I'm 62 years old, and I've never been this scared in my life, I'm afraid that I'm going to pass out or that my legs just won't hold me. Please let me sit down and talk to you. I swear by all that's holy that I'm not your enemy."

I took a deep breath and said, "Martin, I'm young, strong, very well trained, and extremely good with this knife. I'll kill you in a heartbeat if you try to screw around. Take your right hand and jam it into your waistband behind you and sit down in my desk chair here."

He sat. He said, "Bertie, when I'm deep in thought, I tend to pace back and forth while I'm thinking and talking. Ask anybody that knows me. Unless I'm in a conference room or something where I can't do it, I always pace back and forth when I'm confronted with a knotty problem and need to think. I just think better on my feet. It's been a habit from childhood. What you told me about your suspicions that McCone was sanctioning all this was shocking, and since I thought I was with a trusted friend, I never thought twice about getting up to walk around the room and think about what you told me. It was just a natural reaction. I *am* your friend, Bertie and I'm going to get up now and I'm going to go the bathroom and take a much needed pee and get a glass of water."

I stepped back a pace and he freed his hands, and used them on the arms of the chair to get shakily to his feet. I moved back some more, and he started walking but I thought he was going to fall.

82

I put Excalibur back in its sheath and said, "Martin, use my shoulder to steady yourself until you kind of get your breath back."

He straightened up and said, "Thank you, Bertie. I think I can make it on my own."

He really impressed me. That was one courageous, tough man. I called after him, "I'm sorry, Martin." He just raised his hand and waved.

I went in to check on Emma while he was in the bathroom. She was still sleeping soundly, but she had partially pushed the duvet off her. That was a good sign. It meant her normal circulation was returning. I kissed her gently on the cheek and her lips curved into a small, contented smile. She would be waking up soon. Martin and I needed to finish up. I heard the toilet flush and Martin emerged looking much stronger.

"Before I forget, your blood-stained shirt is on the floor, and some blood splashed up on the mirror when you were cleaning up. My cleaning crew is long gone but, you'd better do something about it before Emma gets up. She'll freak out."

"Thanks. I never would have thought of it. I'll take care of it."

"I've been thinking about what you told me. You've certainly cleared up the mystery of why Johnson hates you so much. You seem to have put him in a position now where it's in his best interests to *protect* you rather than get your documents and kill you. But of course, he doesn't know that yet. Those must be *some* documents, but I assure you that I don't want to know about them, or even hear about them. Now logic would tell us that Johnson got one of his cronies—and he's got plenty of them—to contact somebody fairly high up in the Agency about this. You may not like him, but Johnson's no fool. He would never have made the contact directly. But to be fair Bertie, our man could have simply been told that a 'high Administration official' had reason to believe that you are in possession of some government documents that don't belong to you, and it is a matter of national security that they be recovered. It is believed that you have hidden these documents somewhere and the Agency is tasked with getting someone into your confidence. Perhaps they could get you drunk or get you to brag about it or something. That's not necessarily a sinister task, Bertie."

"That's true, Martin, but when your 'wet works' department sends somebody to torture me to get the information they're after, it's hard for me to be off-handedly detached and coolly analytical about it. I *do* take it personally. Besides that, there are two other things that trouble me. Somebody in your agency picked *those particular two people* to try to get information from me. Why? You said that the Agency has been suspicious of both of them for some time. So why pick *them*? I think it's quite possible that they were told to get the documents at any cost because their supervisor was sure that my documents contained information extremely damaging to a 'high administration official' and if those documents, or at least a copy of them could be gotten to the Kremlin, it would provide invaluable blackmail material. I don't know how many levels of supervisors this request filtered down through, but I think one of those supervisors is a mole, Martin.

"The second thing that bothers me is that they were going way beyond any attempt to worm their way into my confidence. They were clearly prepared to use deadly force. It looks like 'Peter' must have been idly wandering around the house when he discovered Emma in the pool, with wide open sliding glass doors. I'm sure he regarded her unexpected presence as a godsend. If they could immobilize me, and force me to watch them torturing her, I might well have broken. Then they would have simply killed us both, and tried to arrange our bodies to look like a murder/suicide. After I bound up Sally, I looked at that open toolkit she had beside her. Lying on top was a .357 magnum pistol. The safety was off. I don't know what she intended to do with it, but I'm glad I didn't find out the hard way. I kept it, incidentally. It may come in handy sometime. It's also easy to throw away—the serial number has been professionally filed off."

Martin sighed and sat down. "Unfortunately, what you say seems to make sense, Bertie. Maybe your assassination of Sally wasn't so gratuitous after all. One thing's for sure. Your mole hypothesis puts all this way beyond my pay grade. I'll write it up and send it to Washington and let them deal with it. Now it's close to midnight and this has been an exhausting day for me. Go look after Emma. I'll call you in the morning."

As he was leaving, I said, "Martin, I can't tell you how sorry I am about what happened tonight. I hope I haven't totally ruined the chance of our ever becoming good friends."

He put his hand on my shoulder and said, "Bertie, there are very few advantages to old age, but one of them is that you learn that any truly long-lasting friendship will have to undergo a 'trial by fire' at some stage. We just had ours. Good night, my friend. I'll call you in the morning."

I went into the bathroom, put my blood-stained shirt in the laundry hamper, and covered it with towels, and wiped off every trace of blood that I could find. Back in the bedroom, I turned on a soft light, and moved a chair beside Emma's side of the bed. She didn't fully awaken until around 12:45 a.m., but when she did, it was with a scream of horror. I hugged her, stroked her hair, kissed her on the cheek and neck, told her she was OK, I was with her, murmured that she'd had a bad dream, etc. until she finally calmed down and relaxed.

She said she'd had this awful dream and some horrible man kept screaming at her and pushing her head under water. She then looked around and asked, "Bertie, how did I get into bed? The last I remember I was swimming in the pool, waiting for you to get back with the bread."

I told her that when I got home, I found her on the deck of the pool and that apparently she had slipped and hit her head. I said I had carried her upstairs, put her into bed, and called a doctor.

(In those days, in Switzerland at least, doctors still made house calls.) He'd examined her—she blushed, probably because she was still naked—and given her a pill to relax her and put her to sleep. He'd left me another one for her to take after we'd talked. I told her that he'd said she'd be fine by the morning. Sweet gal that she was, she hugged me and kissed me and thanked me for taking such good care of her, and then said she needed to go pee and wash up.

She said, "God, I must look a fright."

The next day was difficult, to say the least. I tried really hard to be bright and cheery, but I must not have been very good at it, because she told me on a couple of occasions that I seemed unusually quiet and a little 'down.'

I put her on the train back to Bern with a mixture of sadness, hopelessness and anger. Why, God damn it, did death have to follow me wherever I went? And what kind of monster was I turning into? I'd brutally killed two people the previous day, and just about killed a friend.

I used the pay phone at the train station to call Pierre to see if he were free for dinner, but of course he had a date. I went back to the house to brood. It seemed terribly empty, and I felt terribly alone.

Before I left for the office the next morning, I called the non-emergency (but unlisted) number of the safe house, and asked if I could speak to Martin, using his work name. (Throughout the remainder of this narrative, I will refer many times to 'Martin' but in reality, I never again used his real name except when he and I were alone. I suppose I could make up a work name for him but why bother? 'Martin' wasn't his real name anyway.)

The telephone receptionist asked who was calling and I responded, "This is not a secure line so just put him on. He'll recognize my voice."

In response to his tenuous 'Hello' I responded, "You free for lunch?"

He told me that unfortunately he was not, that he had had a very busy weekend and was still preparing a report for his boss, and thought it would take the rest of the day. He then said, "I hear you have had a rather busy weekend yourself. Have you reported to *your* boss?"

I was aghast. I'd gotten so used to thinking of myself as totally cut off from the administration, that it had never even *occurred* to me to file a report with General Carroll. I replied that I hadn't gotten around to it yet but I'd try to get to it later on today.

He sighed and said, "I think that when God was designing travelling salesmen, for example, he wanted to create something which would be vitally necessary for the well-being of a corporation but, being in a playful mood that day, ensured that they would be genetically irresponsible. You may have missed your calling. It's not my place to say of course, but reporting in to your boss might be something you'd want to consider. Oh, and I'm free for lunch tomorrow if you'd like."

I left work a little early and drove to the safe house. I had hoped to see Martin but he was out to a meeting somewhere, so I just continued on to my little office. There was a huge pile of classified material to go through, but I wanted to get a cable off to General Carroll first. The problem was that I didn't know what to say. I wanted to tell him about the deaths of Peter and Sally and I wanted to make sure he heard it from me first. It was really an Agency matter though and I wasn't sure if I would be breaching security protocol to inform him of the Agency connections of both Peter and Sally. On top of that he had no knowledge of my research papers and the fact that Johnson was seeking them and I certainly didn't want to put all that information in a cable.

Finally, I settled on, "Regret to inform you of my necessity to use lethal force at my residence against two intruders seeking information. Situation is now completely sanitized. Further details available from Director, GPO."[20] I would leave it up to John McCone to determine how much information to pass along. I then sat down to attack the pile of documents on my desk.

As usual, most of them concerned Vietnam and the deteriorating situation there. Even though—finally—there was general acceptance of the fact that the South Vietnamese people would not fight, and resented the American presence in their country, the Administration's belief in the "domino theory" was unshakeable. If South Vietnam should fall to the communists, then all of the surrounding countries in Southeast Asia—Laos, Cambodia, Thailand, Burma, Malaysia and even perhaps Indonesia—would fall under communist domination as well, or at least so the theory went. Southeast Asia would be dominated by the Chinese communists, and this massive communist influence and control, when combined with that of the Soviet Union, would pose an existential threat to the United States, its European Allies and the remainder of the free world.

France's DeGaulle had repeatedly made the point that, while he agreed whole-heartedly with the goal of keeping South Vietnam out of Communist control, it could not be done by waging war. As France had found at Dien Bien Phu and in Algeria, even though you control a country militarily, if the people aren't with you, you will lose it. DeGaulle favored a massive diplomatic effort with a conference including Russia, China, North Vietnam, South Vietnam, France and the United States to declare South Vietnam a neutral country, and to extract guarantees from each of the participants that such neutrality would be assiduously respected. The United States would withdraw from South Vietnam, and the UN would send in observers to ensure that all nations respected their guarantees. The United States had rejected this proposal out-of-hand

---

[20] The CIA Headquarters building in Langley, Virginia originally had a sign posted at the entrance gates identifying it as the Government Printing Office (GPO). After even the Washington tour busses would point the building out as being the new headquarters of the CIA, the CIA bowed to reality and changed the sign.

saying that regardless of what North Vietnam promised, they could not be trusted, and would continue to seek the reunification of Vietnam.

President Khanh was having a terrible time trying to lead the country. Trained as a soldier, not a politician, he relied heavily on Ambassador Lodge not only for liaison with Washington, but for advice on how to set up and manage his own administration. Unfortunately, Lodge was not strong on administration. Khanh had problems with his Army as well. Other Generals were envious of his power and there was always a real risk that he could be overthrown and/or assassinated, meaning that the whole development process would have to start all over again. In addition, the Vietnamese Army was growing increasingly restive. There was a pervasive feeling that the Army needed to do *something*. Sending troops across the 17th parallel would mean war, but surely there could be a 'surgical' bombing of a steel mill or something. The North Vietnamese Army was well-equipped however (by both the Chinese and the Soviets) and their air defenses were strong. The North Vietnamese had already shot several South Vietnamese reconnaissance planes out of the air.

Given that the French had ruled Vietnam from 1887 to 1954, almost all the higher ranking officers in the South Vietnamese Army had dual French/Vietnamese citizenship, and most of them owned vacation villas in France. DeGaulle's push for neutrality found favor with many of the Generals, further complicating Khanh's ability to persuade them that the U.S. predilection for war was the reasonable path to counteract North Vietnamese aggression.

Khanh also faced constant bickering between the powerful minority Catholics and the Buddhists. On the civilian side, almost all of the middle and upper level managers, executives and professionals were Catholic. France is, after all (or at least was at the time), a Catholic country, and therefore Vietnam's schools were taught almost exclusively by French priests and nuns. Although the vast majority of the population in South Vietnam was Buddhist, most of them were uneducated peasant farmers. Their leaders, however, were extremely well educated and well aware of the latent power of the peasants. The constant power struggle between the two sides was both wearing and dangerous. Khanh was caught in the middle.

In South Vietnam, the night belonged to the Viet Cong ("VC"). In quite a lot of the fertile Delta region, the VC ruled by day as well. The North vehemently denied having anything to do with the VC. They claimed that the VC was made up entirely of South Vietnamese peasants revolting against the corrupt, puppet South Vietnamese government. In reality, many (perhaps the majority) of the VC troops, had indeed been recruited in South Vietnam, but their leaders were either North Vietnamese or South Vietnamese who had received extensive military training in the North. For the most part, military supplies were furnished to the VC from the North, via the infamous Ho Chi Minh Trail. Frankly, South Vietnam was a total, non-functioning mess, and Johnson and all his top Administration officials were painfully aware of it.

Huge meetings were held in the White House on a nearly bi-weekly basis. They envisioned all kinds of 'fixes' for the provincial governments and the South Vietnamese Army, but there were two constants that ran through every one of these meetings: 1) the need for a Congressional resolution to authorize the use of U.S. military force against North Vietnam, if that became necessary after all diplomatic efforts had failed, and 2) the need for some shocking incident that the South Vietnamese army could respond to. Although it was generally conceded that North Vietnam was not planning such an incident, everyone agreed that South Vietnam needed to carry out some strong action which would put pressure on Hanoi and lift morale in the South.

Getting a Congressional resolution for more funds for Vietnam was not going to be easy. Many in Congress felt that more consideration ought to be given to the strong diplomatic route that DeGaulle was pushing (and which the editors of the influential *New York Times* supported). It was not unknown in Congress that the South Vietnamese people were not willing to wage war, and that even the South Vietnamese Army was not completely behind going to war with the North. Many in Congress felt that if the Army couldn't control the Viet Cong in their own country, it was improbable that the Army was going to be very effective against the well-trained North. If the South Vietnamese Army was neither willing nor capable of defending itself, why should the United States intervene? The likelihood that Congress was going to give Johnson a blank check was extremely low, and all the discretionary and contingency funds that he could draw on without further Congressional approval were nearly exhausted. He could always go to Congress asking for additional funds, but the amount of the requested additional appropriation, as well as its purpose, would have to be narrowly and strictly defined. Johnson found himself between a rock and a very hard place that July, 1964.

I drove home with an uneasy sense of foreboding.

Martin and I had lunch the next day. I told him about my cable to Carroll (knowing Martin, he had probably already read it). He laughed about the part mentioning that further details were available from the Director of the GPO, but told me that he thought it was quite proper that it should be McCone's decision on how much information to share. He said that he had filed a very lengthy report detailing all of the events of the afternoon and evening, except the part that was private between the two of us. He said that he had already gotten some feedback, and that apparently, my speculation about a mole was being taken very seriously. He said that they had redoubled their efforts to track down the person I knew as Peter Boyle, and that he personally was surprised that they hadn't yet succeeded.

I was surprised, too. The Agency has a lot of resources. I asked him if he would take the tap off my line. He knew everything anyway, and it would be nice to have a little privacy. He promised that he would, and that he would also provide me with a voice encryption device—a 'scrambler' so that I could make secure calls to the safe house.

For me, the rest of July was pretty quiet. Sergio was doing a wonderful job in putting together and managing the operations for IOS Italia, and while there were the inevitable glitches, overall he was doing a magnificent job. The load on Geneva operations wasn't falling all that much, because IOS was growing at a phenomenal rate, but sufficient load was being drained off such that IOS was not compelled to add more employees in Geneva. I figured that within a few months, the concept of regional operations would be very successfully proven and that I could begin another one. These legitimate regional operations were going to provide me with the perfect cover for setting up intelligence-gathering cells. But for starters, I was going to have to try to figure out how to use the beachhead that I had established in Italy as a basis for establishing a cell there.

Vietnam and the Truth

Here, I'm going to jump ahead a few days to cover those tragically eventful incidents that occurred on August 2nd and 4th, 1964. Outside of Washington and Vietnam, the lives of very few people would be immediately affected, but as the ominous tempo of the drumbeat of war increased to a frenzied crescendo in those early days of August; the slow, opening notes of the tragic opera that was to follow could be clearly heard in the distance. If one cared to listen.

It's nearly impossible to describe how difficult it is for me to write about all this. Literally, I write maybe two sentences and have to stop and walk around the room, go pet my dog (the world's sweetest Golden Retriever), fill the bird feeder—anything to stop these memories flooding in. This stuff has been buried in my head for fifty years, and pulling it out and reliving it is amazingly painful. I keep having to remember that nobody forced me to write these memoirs; it was my decision to do so, and I need to mentally gird up my loins and get on with it. I also have to face the fact that the rest of the chapter is going to be much more difficult. How bad do you feel when you have personally just killed two human beings? How horrible do you feel when you discover that you are helpless to stop your country from embarking on a completely fraudulent war that would cause the death of over two *million* human beings?

I am going to summarize the events that transpired during those early August days. They would change history (as all wars do), and cost over two million human lives. The United States would lose nearly 58,000 of its finest young men and women, and an additional 303,000 would bear the physical and emotional scars of the Vietnam War for the rest of their lives. Countless others would have their lives ruined by emotional trauma, and yet others would have their lives wrecked by unshakeable drug addiction. The ultimate tragedy and unspeakable outrage is that the Vietnam War was rushed into and justified by Lyndon Johnson based on *an event that never happened*. He wanted the war, and wasn't going to be bothered by getting his facts straight. Sound familiar?

On August 2, a United States destroyer, the *Maddox*, specially equipped to gather signal and electronic intelligence, was patrolling off the North Vietnam shore (well inside North Vietnam's territorial waters) when, at about 1:00 p.m., it intercepted a message sent by the North Vietnam Navy (NVN) to three of its torpedo equipped patrol boats, directing them to attack the 'enemy.' Although the *Maddox* turned and steamed out into open waters, the NVN ships were much faster, and were inexorably closing the gap. The *Maddox* requested air support from the aircraft carrier *Ticonderoga,* which was about 280 miles southeast. Four F-8E crusaders, already aloft, were vectored towards the *Maddox.* As the patrol torpedo boats approached, the *Maddox* fired off three warning shots which were ignored by the NVN.

The battle began in earnest when, about 15 minutes later, the four jets arrived and strafed all three patrol boats, leaving one dead in the water and the other two badly damaged. The *Maddox* was untouched except for a single bullet hole from a machine gun round.

In his definitive study[21] the NSA's in-house historian R.J. Hanyok writes:

In Washington, the reaction to the attack was relatively subdued. Since no Americans had been hurt, President Johnson wanted the event downplayed, while a stern note of protest was sent to the North Vietnamese. (Ironically, this message was the first diplomatic note ever sent to the North Vietnamese). The president had said "we would not 'run away;' yet we were not going to be 'provocative.' However Hanoi was going to be informed in no [*sic*] unambiguous terms that any more unprovoked actions would entail 'grave consequences.'"

It seemed to me that there were a few things wrong with this. First of all, cruising well within the North's territorial waters could hardly be construed as other than provocative. Secondly, Johnson said that we were attacked 'on the high seas in international waters.' That's true but only because we *were* 'running away.' Lastly, Johnson claimed that the NVN fired first. That's not true. The 'warning' shots from the *Maddox* were the first shots fired.

August 3rd was uneventful, although the *Maddox* resumed her patrol—again, well inside the North's territorial waters. In addition she was accompanied by a second intelligence-collecting destroyer, the *Turner Joy.*

All hell broke loose on the 4th.

At about 4:30 p.m. on the 4th, the American listening post at Phu Bai, in South Vietnam intercepted a NVN message to three of its ships 'to make ready for military operations the night of August 4.' Although the message made no reference to what kind of military action, the personnel at the Phu Bai station seemed to interpret it as an NVN order to attack the *Maddox* and the *Turner Joy.* Both ships were so informed. At this point the two ships were about 80 –

---

[21] Robert J. Hanyok, *Skunks, Bogies, Silent Hounds and the Flying Fish: The Gulf of Tonkin Mystery, 2-4 August 1964,* published in NSA's Top Secret internal publication the *Cryptologic Quarterly* in the Winter 2000/Spring 2001 edition. Now declassified and available in pdf format on the web.

85 miles off the coast. A couple of facts need to be interjected here. One is that the *Maddox's* long range air search radar was malfunctioning, and the fire control radar on the *Turner Joy* was out of action completely. The second is that there was rather freakish weather accompanied by high winds such that the normally tranquil Gulf of Tonkin was experiencing heavy swells of up to 6 feet.

At about 8:00 p.m., the *Maddox's* radar picked up two 'skunks' (surface contacts) and three 'bogies' (air contacts). The skunks were about 45 miles away. The bogies mysteriously disappeared. The carrier *Ticonderoga* dispatched the four aircraft that were already aloft, and scrambled four more to aid the *Maddox* and the *Turner Joy*. At this point total chaos ensued. The radars on both ships were picking up bunches of skunks (though not necessarily in the same place) and the ships themselves were performing high speed evasive maneuvers. When the aircraft arrived, they were directed to attack the skunks, but they could find nothing, and no enemy ships at all appeared on the aircraft radars.

James Stockdale, one of the Navy pilots at the scene, who said he had 'the best seat in the house from which to detect boats' saw nothing. Hanyok states that Stockdale later wrote that he saw nothing, "No boats, no boat wakes, no ricochets off boats, no boat impacts, no torpedo wakes— nothing but black sea and American firepower." After two hours of frantic action (they were turning so drastically that some of the sonar signals were bouncing back from their own rudders) with the *Turner Joy* alone madly firing off more than 300 rounds at swarms of 'attacking ships,' it finally began to dawn on Captain Herrick that it was curious that the skunks found on radar would suddenly disappear and that there was no evidence of even a single round of enemy fire directed towards his vessels. In addition, the radars of the support aircraft detected nothing no matter where they were sent and that the flares they dropped over 'the enemy ships' illuminated nothing but empty ocean. In fact, as Hanyok reports:

> *It is not simply that there is a different story as to what happened; it is that **no***
> ***attack** happened that night. [...] In truth, Hanoi's navy was engaged in nothing*
> *that night but the salvage of two of the boats damaged on August 2.*

The *salvage operation* was the 'military action' referred to in the intercept of the NVN message. Washington was following all this closely as it was going on, and they were convinced, as Captain Herrick was, that both American ships were under attack. However, just hours after the incident, Herrick radioed the Navy Commander-in-Chief, Pacific, Admiral Sharp, telling him that he was doubtful of many aspects of the 'attack.'

Indeed, he should have been. One of the most valuable things that the Navy learned from the August 2 attack was the signal chatter and electronic activity that preceded it. The *Maddox* had been continuously tracked by NVN radar and there was a steady flow of communications between NVN stations giving updates on her current position. None of this activity occurred on August 4th—all the NVN was doing was trying to salvage their ships that had been damaged in the August 2 incident. What Washington jumped on however was an intercept of an NVN 'after battle' report, saying that they had lost two ships. The message was *not dated* and it did not carry a high priority rating. It turned out to simply be a re-transmission of the August 2ⁿᵈ after-battle report.

Although many in the Administration were having serious doubts as more information began to come in, Johnson was having none of it. Within three hours after the 'attack' Johnson gave orders for four NVN naval bases and an oil storage facility to be bombed the next day—August 5th.

On August 10th, Congress not only gave Johnson a blank check for military action in Vietnam, it set the precedent for a President to wage war without a formal declaration of war. It also set a precedent for the NSA to conceal from public view any information that it feels might cast the agency in an unfavorable light.

George Mason University's *History News Network* commented immediately after Honyak's study was released in 2005:

> Mr. Hanyok's findings were published nearly five years ago in a classified in-house journal, and starting in 2002, he and other government historians argued that it should be made public. *But their effort was rebuffed by higher-level agency policymakers, who by the next year, were fearful that it might prompt uncomfortable comparisons with the flawed intelligence used to justify the war in Iraq, according to an intelligence official familiar with some internal discussions of the matter.* [Italics added.]

And so began the Vietnam War, one of the most ruinous wars in our history. This headlong rush into war was based entirely on an event *that never happened.* Even at the moment Johnson was giving orders to bomb North Vietnam, there was considerable doubt among his own advisors as to what had actually transpired. No U.S. personnel had received so much as a scratch; no ship had been damaged; the warplanes dispatched from the *Ticonderoga* could find nothing visually and nothing on their radar; Captain Herrick had already expressed his doubt and confusion, so why in the world would the President of the United States and the Commander-in-Chief of all its military lead his nation into war without gravely and painstakingly assuring himself that our Navy ships had indeed been attacked, and that war was the *only* course of action left to take?

The only person who could answer that of course is Johnson himself. Perhaps he felt that the North Vietnamese were preparing to immediately invade South Vietnam. The massive preparatory troop and equipment movements which would have been necessary—along with hugely increased volumes of message traffic—were nowhere in evidence, however. There was simply *no* credible immediate military threat.

There *were* other non-military considerations which were of great interest to Johnson. It was an election year and his opponent, Barry Goldwater, was accusing Johnson of being weak and ineffective in dealing with North Vietnam. In addition, the South Vietnamese military had grave doubts as to whether or not the U.S. was a reliable and committed ally, and there was increasing consideration of DeGaulle's insistence on trying the diplomatic route to find a solution. Going to war with a congressional blank check was a wonderful way to wipe out all these annoyances. The Gulf of Tonkin non-event was almost miraculously convenient.

Perhaps the families and friends of the 12.7 *million* people who were either killed or wounded in that war might describe it differently.

As for Johnson himself, he would have done well to remember Winston Churchill's observation:

> Never, never, never believe any war will be smooth and easy, or that anyone who embarks on the strange voyage can measure the tides and hurricanes he will encounter. The statesman who yields to war fever must realize that once the signal is given, he is no longer the master of policy, but the slave of unforeseeable and uncontrollable events.

Chapter 5 — Geneva, Paris and Laos

CERN and the Bomb

I was very much looking forward to another party at *Bella Vista* on Saturday, August 1st to celebrate Swiss Independence Day. It was way back in 1291 when the Swiss gained their independence from the Habsburgs, when both parties signed the Grütli Pact. I don't think anybody really knows now what the exact date was in August, 1291 but in the intervening years, August 1st has become the official date.

In any case the party at *Bella Vista* was fantastic. Although there was no formal dinner this time, the dozen or so tables groaned with all sorts of food. By now, I was acquainted with scores of IOS employees, and I greatly enjoyed moving between the little groups which would briefly form and then evaporate.

As I was coming off the dance floor in the surprisingly firm grasp of my delicate-looking dance partner, I was hailed by one of my friends who yelled at me, "Hey Bertie, come over and join us for a moment." When I did, he turned to the rather short, slender and somewhat Asiatic-looking person on his right and said, "Bertie, meet Mike Chen. He works over at CERN and you're probably the only person here that he can talk shop to."

I was delighted. CERN, the European Organization for Nuclear Research (originally the *Conseil Européenne pour la Recherche Nucléaire*) was by far and away the leading organization for fundamental particle physics outside the United States. It had been formed by twelve European countries in 1954 and now, 10 years later, it was producing a constant stream of discoveries from the operation of its accelerator ring. I'd been dying to go out there and visit, but although the facility is not guarded like a military base, if you don't have a pass or an appointment with someone, you can't get in.

Meeting someone that works there isn't that easy. When you are one of the world's top theoretical physicists working on exploring the fundamental particles and forces that make up the universe, you are pretty much living in a personal time/space warp, where nothing matters but the work you are doing, and the 'normal' everyday world outside the lab seems remote and irrelevant. When you live, eat, and breathe nothing but cutting edge particle physics, you really don't have much interest in socializing with anyone except other particle physicists. Nobody else is going to understand a single thing you're saying. It's a hard group to break into. I think

Mike was sorry he had come to the party.

When I asked him what he thought about the letter that Murray Gell-Mann had written to the extremely prestigious publication *Physical Review,* and which had been published in their February 1st [1964] edition positing the existence of quarks—particles even more fundamental than protons and neutrons—I was afraid that he was either going to die or have a public orgasm. He mentally popped straight back into his space/time warp bubble and tried to pull me right along in with him.

I gently, but firmly declined—it just wasn't the right time or place—and I was getting very black looks from both his companion and mine. I said, "Mike, the noise level in here is just terrible. Let's all go back to my place for a drink after the party. I live about 25 minutes away from here, but it's nice and quiet and has spectacular views—even at night."

I think everyone breathed a sigh of relief when he somewhat reluctantly said, "Sure. That would be great."

We left *Bella Vista* a little before midnight. The house was a hit, but we decided to sit outside around the picnic table to continue with wine and cheese. I brought out big, heavy towels for everyone to wrap up in (even in August, when you're halfway up the Jura Mountains, the night breeze can be chilly). It was tough preventing Mike from constantly trying to turn the conversation into a detailed discussion of particle physics, but I think he finally got the idea that it didn't have to be just tonight that he and I could meet. I told him that maybe next weekend we could have a big picnic, where he could invite some of his buddies and their wives or girlfriends, and that we could talk physics all afternoon and night.

We chatted amiably until around 2:30 or so. It was clearly too late for them to drive back to Geneva, so I showed them the bedrooms on the mid-level, told them there were a bunch of brand-new, still in the package toothbrushes in the drawer under the sink in the bathroom, extra blankets in the closets, etc. and that I'd wake them in the morning for a pre-breakfast swim. Mike seemed a little nervous, and I wasn't quite sure why. I guessed him to be in his mid to late 20's and he didn't seem to be gay or anything, but I figured that whatever it was, the two of them would just have to work it out. They didn't have to sleep together if they didn't want to—they had three bedrooms to choose from. I certainly wasn't going to worry about it.

The next day we said our goodbyes just after lunch. Mike seemed to be in an extraordinarily good mood. He gave me his office and home phone numbers and said to be sure to call him, and he would arrange to show me around CERN. I repeated the offer to get together again the coming weekend, and said that if he wanted to bring some of his buddies, just to let me know. As they had a sedan, they took my companion back to Geneva with them, and I got to enjoy the rest of the day with a long run, a sauna, a swim, and a light supper.

Early the next morning I got a call from Martin who told me that he had received a number of messages that I might be interested in and 'to drop in on him at my convenience if I were interested.' I called my secretary at her home to tell her that I had some urgent business to attend to, and that I wasn't sure when I would be getting in to the office. I drove straight to the safe house, and read the blizzard of top secret signals, which chronicled the events surrounding the attack on the *Maddox* on August 2nd.

Though I watched in bewildered unbelief as events unfolded both in the United States and Vietnam in that August of 1964, I had to continue my life in Switzerland under the guise of a typical American ex-pat working abroad.

Mike called and asked if I had been serious about inviting him and a bunch of his buddies with their 'significant others'.

I answered, "Absolutely."

He asked if I thought that having twenty or so people would be going too far. I said I'd be delighted and to tell everybody to come on over around 2:00 p.m. on Saturday. To be truthful, there was more than just my love of particle physics in involved in the invitation. Though the opportunity to chat with ten or twelve (I assumed that everyone would be bringing a 'significant other') of the best experimental particle physicist in the world would be a major event for me, I had a hidden agenda.

The nuclear physicists at CERN are involved solely in exploring the building blocks of the universe, and how they interact with one another on a level which has *absolutely nothing* to do with nuclear weapons and the physicists who design them. While both groups share a keen interest in the implications of Einstein's famous $E=mc^2$ equation, the physicists at CERN ask themselves, for example, "If energy and mass are transposable, why isn't the universe composed entirely of energy? Why should there be any mass at all?" Nuclear physicists who design nuclear weapons spend most of their time trying to maximize the efficiency of the process that converts mass to explosive energy in a weapon. That said, the number of top-level nuclear physicists in the world is small indeed and the two groups often rub elbows at international symposia. Though in general there is something of a mutual disdain between the two groups—sometimes, on a purely personal level—friendships develop. In addition to enjoying the discussion of particle physics at its most advanced level, I would do what I could to probe my guests for personal contacts in China and behind the Iron Curtain.

To prepare for the gathering, I phoned the manager of *Bella Vista* and told him that I was hosting a party on Saturday at my house, and asked if he could recommend a caterer. It turned out that there was nothing scheduled for *Bella Vista* that entire weekend, and the IOS catering staff was delighted to have the opportunity to make some extra money. They were expensive, but they did a spectacular job.

Things worked out well. The pool, the sauna, the sound system, the elegant picnic tables that had been set out on the lawn, and the non-stop food and wine contributed to a memorable evening. I made some tentative friends and some tentative contacts. The majority of the crowd left by 10:00 p.m., but Mike and his companion wanted to stay, so we chatted away while the catering staff cleaned up and put everything back in order. I asked Mike about his background, and how and why his family ended up in Belgium. The explanation was long and convoluted but you'll see why it's important.

The summary is this: Mike's extended family had been part of China's ruling and intellectual upper class for centuries. His father had a medical degree from Harvard, and his father's brother had a PhD in mathematics from Stanford. Clearly, this family was not only extremely well educated, they must have had a lot of money as well.

In the late 40's, when Mike was seven years old, his father decided that the growing power of Mao Tse-tung was becoming threatening, and that he and his family should move while they still had the opportunity to do so. He tried to get his brother and his family to move as well, but his brother refused. Now, the only method of communication between the two brothers was by mail—heavily censored by the Chinese authorities.

I commented that it must be very hard on the entire family to be so cut off from one another, and Mike said that they weren't entirely cut off—his cousin was also a nuclear physicist, and the Communist Party would occasionally let him attend international symposia. He said his cousin's return to China after the symposia was guaranteed by the threat of harm to his parents if he did not. I asked when he had last seen his cousin, and was astonished to learn that they had both attended a symposium on 'Crystal Diffraction of Nuclear Gamma Rays' held in Athens from 15-17 June, 1964. By this time, I'd had enough of the family chat and suggested that we all turn in for the night.

The next morning while the women were in the kitchen preparing breakfast, Mike accompanied me into Aubonne to pick up croissants. I idly asked him what kind of research his cousin was doing in China. When he told me that his cousin was the chief engineer at their gaseous diffusion enrichment facility at Lanzhou, it was all I could do to keep from running off the road. If China was producing enriched U-235, it could only mean one thing. They were close to producing a nuclear weapon.

I tried to keep my voice calm and casual when I inquired if the plant had become fully operational, or was still in the design or start-up phase. He blithely assured me that the plant was fully operational and had been for some time.

"Sounds like they are getting ready to become the newest member of the world's nuclear weapon club," I remarked.

"Yeah," he responded. "I think they are going to run the first test around mid-autumn." Mike appeared to have no idea that he was casually providing some of the most highly classified information in the world. I'd heard enough anyway and turned the conversation towards more mundane matters.

Mike and Claire left for Geneva around 10:30. My companion, Monique, stayed with me, as I had to go into Geneva late that afternoon to meet with some managers at IOS to prepare for a conference that we were having the next day.

On our drive into Geneva she said, "Do you remember how strange Mike was acting when we left him with Claire as we were all preparing to go to bed last Saturday?"

I said that I remembered clearly, and asked if she knew what that was all about.

Monique giggled and said, "Mike was a virgin until last weekend. But don't worry. It seems he is trying diligently to make up for lost time."

After I had dropped her at her apartment, I drove to the safe house to file my report on China.

Frankly, I expected an immediate avalanche of kudos for an intelligence coup of that magnitude, and was puzzled and disappointed to receive no response at all for a week. What I finally got certainly wasn't what I had anticipated. General Carroll informed me as gently as he could that the overwhelming majority of intelligence analysts felt that I had been a target of disinformation. First of all, even the most pessimistic analysts had concluded that the earliest possible time for a Chinese nuclear test would be sometime in the first quarter of 1965, and most felt that the Chinese were a year or even two away from their first test. Since plutonium core bombs are far easier to fabricate than bombs based on enriched uranium, it was also assumed that plutonium technology would be used and that the enrichment plant at Lanzhou was nowhere near becoming operational. General Carroll warned me that if I were being targeted for disinformation, my 'reliable source' might suspect that there was more to me than met the eye and that I should drop any further contact with him or her.

I thought about that for a while but I could not imagine anyone more ingenuous than Mike. Up until a couple of weeks ago his immersion in particle physics had been had been so intense and monastic that he was still a virgin. Though the latter was apparently no longer the case, I just couldn't see Mike as a trained enemy intelligence agent. On top of that, I needed him as my entrée into CERN. I did realize though, that I had been pretty cavalier in assuming the impenetrability of my cover as just another ex-pat working for IOS. I needed to be more careful. What if Mike's cousin was feeding *him* disinformation? I needed to get busy trying to get operational cells set up. I still didn't know how I was going to use the beachhead that I had established in Italy, but I felt sure that Don Moretti could give me some help and advice. In the meantime, I had a job to do for IOS and I decided that the next office should be in France before

98

I tackled the huge installations that were going to be necessary in Germany and England.

I'd learned a lot of lessons while setting up the Italian operation, and I meant to make good use of that knowledge when setting up in Paris. I called Pierre and asked if we could get together the following weekend. I had a lot to tell him and several questions I wanted to ask.

Even though it was the end of August, it was chilly and raining when Pierre pulled up the following Friday evening. He had picked up Monique, whom I was glad to see again, and introduced me to the lovely companion that he had brought along. After dinner, I built a fire in the huge, open circular fireplace. We all sat around and chatted amiably for an hour or so, until I said that I had a little business that I needed to discuss with Pierre, and that we were going to go upstairs to my office and would rejoin the ladies soon.

Trust has to be based on honesty and openness, so I felt that I had to tell Pierre about Sally Boyle and her father. He was aghast, to put it mildly. His only comment, however, was to the effect that I must have some very powerful friends in order to keep something like that completely hushed up.

"Here in Switzerland, we frown pretty heavily on that sort of thing," he remarked dryly. "Honestly, it's a good thing you're my client or I would absolutely have to turn you in to the Police. Now I think I've absorbed all the information I'm capable of for the moment so why don't we go downstairs and rejoin the ladies?"

Over the weekend, I told him of my plans to open a French processing office for IOS, and asked him if he could recommend a nice, but modest hotel, and if he knew a good law firm in Paris. He told me I was in real luck on the latter point, as the father of one of his law-firm partners was the principal partner in the largest law firm in Paris. He said he would get contact information for me on Monday, but recommended that I contact the legal department in IOS to get their blessing if I intended to use the Paris firm as our local legal advisors. Once again, I was appalled that I hadn't thought of doing that. I thought of myself as such a 'loner' that I kept forgetting to maintain regular contact with both 'companies' that I reported to.

Bernard Monod

Maître Bernard Monod was even more striking in person than his mellifluous voice on the phone had led me to imagine. Tall, fit, elegant, probably in his late fifties or early sixties, 'salt and pepper' grey hair swept back on the sides, piercing bright blue eyes and easy smile. He looked every inch the successful head of the largest law firm in Paris. His receptionist had greeted me warmly in perfect English when I gave her my name and said that I had an appointment with Monsieur Monod; she assured me that he was looking forward to meeting me. When I told her in French that I was very much looking forward to meeting him as well, her smile broadened even more. I got some very curious looks from the dozen or so other clients in the reception area when he swept in and greeted me like a long lost friend.

Although I knew that Pierre would never divulge any of the information I had shared with him, his three law partners could scarcely overlook the amount of time that he and I spent together socially, or the fact that he was introducing me to some of the most prominent families in Geneva. I was clearly more than just an IOS employee, but when questioned, all Pierre would say was that I was a very honorable man. I later discovered that Pierre *had* made one slip in a conversation with his partners, and had intimated that I had direct access to people 'at the highest levels of the United States government.' It didn't take anywhere near the elevated levels of IQ of those guys to speculate that I was some sort of 'super spy' and I'm sure that Maître Monod's son had shared that speculation with his father.

I felt awkward when I explained to Maître Monod that I wasn't going to be a client—IOS had another law firm in Paris that they wanted to use—and I wanted to get that out on the table immediately. Although he was politely regretful, he assured me that he wanted me to regard him as a personal friend, and to feel totally free to call on him at any time in that capacity. He also said that he would be happy to put one of the firm's small conference rooms at my disposal to conduct interviews if that would be helpful. Finally he told me that his wife was most anxious to meet me, and wanted to know if I would be free for dinner the following evening. He gave me his personal card with his home address on Avenue Foch.

Avenue Foch is probably the most desirable street address in Paris. It runs east from the Porte Dauphine to the Arc de Triomphe where the famed Champs-Elysées begins. He pointed out that his home was within walking distance of the hotel that he had found for me, and asked if I found the hotel suitable. The hotel was only about a block north of Avenue Foch and not more than two to three blocks away from the Arc de Triomphe, and yet was on a quiet and secluded side street. It had a total of 16 rooms and though ostensibly open to the general public, unless someone important had called the manager to arrange your first visit, you simply weren't going to get in. I loved it.

Bearing a bouquet of fresh-cut flowers and a box of superb Swiss chocolates (which I had brought with me because they were unavailable in France), I rang their doorbell the next evening at 7:00. I was promptly ushered in by the butler, to expressions of delight by Madame Monod, who laughingly scolded me for bringing chocolate. If ever there were a lady (and lady is absolutely the right term) who didn't need to worry about eating the occasional chocolate, it was surely Mme. Monod. Although she was about the same age as her husband, she had the same incredible figure as did Emma and Ingrid, and she looked as though she played tennis and/or rode every day. They were truly a beautiful couple.

I shook her hand and murmured, "Enchanté, Madame Monod."

She gave me a dazzling smile and said, "Oh! No, no, no. It is Bernard and Sylvie. May we call you Bertie?"

It was a dinner I'll always remember. Although the food and wines were exquisite, it was the wonderful conversation that I remember most from that evening. We moved seamlessly over a vast range of topics: art, history, current events, literature, sports (Sylvie was heavily into equestrian show jumping, Bernard was devoted to blue water [open seas] sailing), and on and on. In a way, Bernard reminded me a little of Jack Kennedy with his ability to immediately create a relaxed atmosphere, and make you feel that the two of you had been good friends for years and years.

Just before I left, Bernard drew me aside and said, "Bertie, I have a very good friend who lives here in Paris and perhaps is someone you might like to meet. Although both he and his wife are naturalized French citizens, he was born in Vietnam and lived there for many years and maintains close contact with a number of people there. His wife is Thai by birth and also maintains close contact with her friends and extended family there. My Vietnamese/French friend, whose name is Teng Lo, is a close friend of General Vang Pao in Laos. Would you like to meet him?"

I stared hard at him before answering, "Yes. Thank you. I'd like that very much."

He smiled and gave me a gentle clap on the shoulder. "I thought you might," he said. "I like you, Bertie," he continued "and so does Sylvie. My son said we would. You and I have perhaps more in common than you know but we'll discuss that later. I'll try to set things up with Lo and I'll call you at your hotel." He pulled a small envelope from his inside suit coat pocket and gave it to me. "I prepared this before you arrived but I wanted to wait until after dinner to give it to you. We lawyers are a cautious lot you know. I found this evening to be delightful and I hope you enjoyed it as much as Sylvie and I have. The envelope contains a note card with the numbers for my private line in the office and my private line here at home. You are now the only person beside my son that has both numbers. I understand that you have a remarkable memory so if you would, please memorize them and destroy the card. I'll be in touch and thanks once again for a thoroughly enjoyable evening. We'll be good friends, you and I. If you need anything at all, please give me a call."

I walked back to my hotel with a heavy heart. I did *not* want anything more to do with Southeast Asia but it looked like I was going to get sucked in. One never passes up an opportunity to gather intelligence. I had a double Scotch on the rocks before I turned in.

Background — Laos and the 'Secret War'

Not much of what follows is going to be comprehensible without a little background. Whereas the phony 'Gulf of Tonkin' incident was used as a pretext by Johnson to drag us into the debacle of the Vietnam War, for quite some time the United States had been actively participating—via the CIA—in a secret war in Laos. As far back as 1954, the United States had been covertly (and illegally) supplying financial aid to the Royal Laotian Army (the U.S. paid one 100% of their salaries). And, in a total and blatant violation of the Geneva Accords, were supplying not only military equipment, but also military training by U.S. military personnel who were not wearing uniforms, and were posing as civilians reporting to the State Department.

Laos is a small Southeast Asian country which was formerly controlled by Siam (now Thailand) from the late 18th century until the late 19th century, when it became part of French Indochina. After the 1954 French defeat at Dien Bien Phu, Laos was recognized as an independent, neutral country. Laos is a small country—not much bigger than Utah (and like Utah is completely landlocked)—but it occupies a tremendously strategic position in Southeast Asia. It is bordered on the north by China, on the west by Burma and Thailand, and on the south by Cambodia. On the east, it is bordered entirely by Vietnam—both North and South Vietnam. Unfortunately, it also has a narrow valley that runs along that entire border, and the valley extends along part of the Cambodian/Vietnam border.

Ho Chi Minh considered it to be an ideal route for the transport of men and supplies into South Vietnam.

Laos is truly a strange little country. Most of the terrain consists of rugged, wooded mountains, although it has a few plains and plateaus. Only 4% of the land is arable. In 1962, *Time Magazine* wrote:

> Though it has a king, a government and an army, and can be found on a map, Laos does not really exist. Many of its estimated 2,000,000 people would be astonished to be called Laotians, since they know themselves to be Meo[22], or Black Thai, or Khalom tribesmen. It is a land without a railroad, a single paved highway or a newspaper. Its chief cash crop is opium.

Ho Chi Minh skillfully exploited this power vacuum and the communist, 'indigenous' Pathet Lao was born—trained and well-supplied by the North Vietnamese Army. The Ho Chi Minh Trail went from being primarily a jungle footpath, to a road that could accommodate trucks in the dry season. Desperate to prevent the takeover of Laos by the Pathet Lao, but prevented by the Geneva Accords to directly intervene militarily, the U.S. turned the job over to the CIA, who recruited the top officer in the Royal Laotian Army, General Vang Pao. He quickly recruited 7,000 Hmong guerillas, and would steadily increase that number to over 34,000. His

---

[22] The native Hmong tribesmen. The term Meo was widely used by Americans and other non-natives to refer to the Hmong people. Hopefully they did not realize that it is a highly pejorative term which roughly translates into 'ignorant savage' or 'barbarian.'

relationship with the CIA was uneasy, to put it mildly. Although he was highly effective at what he had been recruited to do, and thus invaluable to the CIA (and irreplaceable), he had such a violent hair-trigger temper and was so arrogant that they could not effectively control him. *Nobody* gave direct orders to General Vang.

Teng Lo

I got a call late the next day from Bernard informing me that his friends, Teng Lo and his wife, were out of town, and their butler didn't know how long they would be away, but thought it might be several weeks. I was relieved, somehow.

I spent the next three weeks arranging for the legal registration of the IOS data processing subsidiary, interviewing candidates, and searching for appropriate office space. Those were my daytime activities, anyway. The evenings and weekends I explored Paris, and began a love affair with the city that endures to this day. I learned how to use the Metro—which ran silently on rubber tires—and I explored Paris continuously. Paris is meant for walking, and I walked for hours on end. I explored the parks and museums, the major tourist attractions, but mostly I just wandered wherever my feet led me. I was endlessly fascinated. I explored the little cafés and bistros, as well as some of the more famous restaurants. I'm sure everyone has their favorite national cuisine, but mine is undoubtedly French. I found it astounding how often I would simply drop into some convenient, but totally unknown little restaurant just because I was starting to get hungry, and left thinking that's one of the best meals I've ever eaten.

Although it had taken me some three weeks, I had finally found someone who I thought would make an excellent head of the Paris operation. I hired him, and we flew back to Geneva together. I needed to introduce him around, and he needed to begin his orientation process, wherein he would learn our data processing procedures, meet the key IOS operations people in Geneva, etc. I had mixed feelings as we landed in Geneva. It was good to be home again, but I really missed Paris. I decided to ask Bernard if he could help me find a small apartment in Paris that I could use as a permanent *pied-à-terre*.

I got a call from Bernard a couple of weeks later informing me that Teng Lo was back in Paris, and had said that he would be pleased to meet with me. Bernard had set a tentative date of October 20, which I said would be fine with me. I took the occasion to ask Bernard if someone in his office could keep an eye out for a small apartment, on the Left Bank if possible. Bernard laughed and said he would see what he could do. Paris's Left Bank [*rive gauche*] is the student quarter of Paris, and has a history of being the home to intellectuals, dissidents, writers and artists such as Picasso, Apollinaire, Breton, Henry Miller, Anaïs Nin and Hemingway after World War I; Camus, Sartre, Juliette Greco and the Existentialists after World War II. Even in the early 1960's, it retained much of that student/bohemian/artist/intellectual flavor and I loved it.

On October 16, the Chinese surprised the world by conducting their first nuclear test, a 22-kiloton device installed atop a 102 meter tower at the Lop Nur Test Ground. Scientists sampling the atmospheric fallout dust were surprised—shocked, actually—to find that it used Uranium-235 as its core. My August cable to General Carroll had been correct on all counts. So much for the Washington 'experts.'

I met with Mr. Teng and Bernard in one of Bernard's conference rooms at his law firm. Mr. Teng was probably in his late fifties or so, and was small and rather plump for a Vietnamese, but I suppose that years of living in the gastronomic capitol of the world will do that to you unless you are extremely careful. He was a pleasant man but with an unmistakable aura of quiet authority. He spoke both French and English faultlessly.

Conversations, or negotiations (and I had no idea which one of these two applied) in Eastern countries tend to be very different from the Western way of holding such discussions. The Oriental way tends to be far more subtle and indirect, and I freely confess that at times, I wasn't even sure what subject we were supposed to be talking about.

When we had had dinner together, Bernard mentioned that Teng's wife's family in Thailand had been good friends with the family of General Vang for many decades, and that Teng had met Vang when he was a young major in the Royal Laotian Army. The only reason I had told Bernard I would be interested in meeting Mr. Teng, was to try to get some insight into Vang's personality from someone who knew him well, and then pass that information along to General Carroll, who presumably would relay it on to the CIA.

Anything having to do with the U.S. involvement in Laos was super classified, and though my security clearances were high enough for anything at all, I had no 'need to know' and was therefore not on the distribution list for Laotian activities. As a result, my knowledge of what was going on in Laos was really sketchy, but my impression was that the CIA was having great difficulty controlling Vang. Given the fact that Vang's name had not even been *mentioned* in the entire conversation, I was at a total loss to know what I was even doing in this meeting. Frankly, it was frustrating as hell. When the meeting finally ended and Mr. Teng and I had fully expressed how humbled and honored we were to have met, etc., Bernard accompanied him out, and I sat back down and waited, in utter bewilderment, for Bernard to return.

When he came back in, smiling broadly, I got up and started to thank him for the courtesy of the introduction. He laughed and motioned for me to sit back down. "Bertie, you did an outstanding job," he said. "Lo was very impressed with you. My strong guess is that in the near future, Lo is going to tell me that General Vang would be honored to meet with you, probably somewhere in Thailand."

I just sat there for a moment before asking, "How is that possible? To the best of my recollection, Vang's name never even came up in the conversation. How could Mr. Teng have possibly been impressed with me? I'm not even sure what we talked about. It seems to me that we just exchanged pleasantries about Switzerland, Vietnam, Paris, New York and Washington but the Washington conversation was simply about the city. We spoke nothing at all about the White House or even just governmental affairs in general."

"That's the whole point," he replied. "You never tried to force the conversation in a particular direction, never hinted that you might have access to people at very high levels in the administration—a subject we won't mention again—but personally, I feel quite confident that you do. You spoke with genuine warmth about your 'visit' to Vietnam, (and incidentally, nobody would have the kind of access to the areas you visited without approval from the highest level of your government), and you were always respectful and deferential. Only your eyes showed that you were a Westerner. They almost never left his eyes. Your gaze wasn't challenging; it was more inquisitive, as if you were trying to make sure you understood what he was saying. It's a minor mistake for a Westerner to make. Overall, I'd say you scored 95 out of 100. Good job. Now on another subject, I hope you're free for dinner tonight. Sylvie and I would like to take you as our guest to one of our favorite restaurants, and Sylvie thinks she may have some good news for you on your apartment search." We arranged to meet at the restaurant at 8:00.

Besides the pleasure of a wonderful meal and the company of two delightful people who were rapidly becoming good friends, Sylvie told me she had called a friend of hers who owned a lovely place on the Rue de Bernardins in the 5th arrondissement (the student quarter). British by birth, she had married a very well-known French writer when she was quite young, and they lived in his mansion on the Rue des Bernardins.

Sylvie said, "It's huge. I don't know how many rooms there are altogether but there must be close to forty. Her husband died of cancer about 15 years ago and she decided to turn some of the rooms into apartments —not because she needs the income—the art collection that she has in the part of the mansion she lives in is nearly priceless, but because she is afraid of living in such isolation. When I called her she said that she would welcome having a strong young man around, and that she has a lovely two bedroom apartment on the ground floor on the opposite side of the courtyard, which you can have. Would you like to go see it with me tomorrow? It is furnished and available immediately if you would like. Oh, yes. One more thing. It's very discrete. From the street, all you see is a very ordinary door set into a concrete wall. There is no hint of the courtyard and the mansion on the other side."

The apartment was beautiful and became my home in Paris for the next 20 years.

Defying Johnson

Just before I left Paris I got a call from 'American Express' informing me of a 'package' waiting for me in Geneva.

On my arrival I went straight from the airport to the safe house.

Martin grinned when he handed me the message, and said cryptically as he walked away, "Ah, dear. And just when I was beginning to like you." Bastard made no secret of reading all my mail.

It was an urgent message from General Carroll. He said there had been some very red faces in Washington—some red from anger and some red from embarrassment—when news of the Chinese nuclear test on October 16 broke, and instantly became world-wide news. Even in 1964, atmospheric tests of nuclear devices were impossible to hide, and the Chinese were not only *not* trying to hide it, they very much *wanted* the world to know that China was now a full-fledged member of the world's exclusive nuclear club. Some of the faces in Washington were particularly red when analysis of fall-out material showed traces of Uranium 235 instead of the expected plutonium. Carroll said in light of the fact that I had somehow been able to gain access to information at the highest levels in the Kremlin, and to the highest level of the Chinese nuclear leaders and planners; the decision had been made that I had become a national security intelligence asset too valuable to be left unguarded.

My old office in the White House was to be returned to me, as well as my old apartment in Washington. I was welcome to keep my house in Switzerland if I wanted, and if I did, a state-of-the-art security system would be installed. I was instructed to inform him of my expected date of return to Washington.

Martin, who had been sitting on a nearby couch watching me closely as I read the cable, came over and put his arm around my shoulders. "I'll get one of my guys to drive you home, old son. I don't think you're in any shape to drive. Feel free to call me at home if you need somebody to talk to."

I could only mumble my heart-felt thanks. Martin was definitely right about the inadvisability of my trying to drive. There were so many half-formed thoughts and ideas whizzing and tumbling around in my head that I was all but oblivious to the outside world. Go back to Washington? Go back to the political cauldron of the White House? Be at the direct beck and call of Johnson? If I am 'too valuable to be left unguarded' does that mean that upon my return I am going to have a 24-hour security detail following me wherever I go? Unimaginable. Well, I mused, even though they came from my so-called 'boss,' instructions weren't orders, and I decided that I was going to decline as politely as possible. If they ordered me, I was going to refuse. Since the only person that could issue such direct orders would be Johnson himself, I was going to be in huge trouble, but I was professionally trained to become invisible to anyone looking for me. On top of that, I had so many contacts in so many countries that owed me favors, I was sure that I could get at least one of them to grant me citizenship and issue me a passport.

106

By the time we pulled up outside my house, I had made my decision. I wasn't going back. Period. Try to force me and I'll vanish. If you want to keep me, you'll have to play by *my* rules.

I don't think that the vast majority of the world populace ever thinks very much about personal identity, and rightly so. Certainly if you are born in some tiny village in a truly remote area where you will probably spend your entire life, identity is a total non-issue. You are just simply you, and 'everybody' knows it. It's actually much the same in the more 'civilized' world where people have birth certificates, driver's licenses, residence addresses, school records, marriage licenses, bank accounts, credit cards, mortgages, medical and dental records, perhaps even a passport, etc. Your identity is a fixed and stable thing. Trying to change or hide it is something that would never even occur to most people, and if they did try it, unless they had some *very* unusual resources at their disposition, they would quickly realize the insightfulness of Cassius Clay's (later known as Muhammad Ali) observation (in a different context, of course): 'You can run, but you can't hide.'

Today of course, DNA can nail you, but even primitive DNA profiling wasn't available until around 1987, and it wasn't until the mid-90's that it started to be accepted as reliable evidence in some courts. Fingerprinting has been around since the early 1900's, but in the mid-1960's, there was no such thing as an international fingerprint file and white collar criminals—never mind *non*-criminals—don't usually get themselves into situations where fingerprints are collected in the first place.

Governments issue official documents, and if it is to their advantage to do so, are perfectly capable of supplying you with official documentation showing that you are a citizen of their country, and that your name is [whatever] and issue you a passport in that name. If you really want to vanish, it is extremely handy if you have more than one government which will issue you such documents.

Lawyers can set up all sorts of shell companies in tax-free havens, and establish bank accounts in the name of that company. Even now—if you have enough money—it's fairly easy to vanish. In the mid-60's, for someone with my contacts and training, it was almost trivially simple. Although at the moment I have no desire or reason to do so, if push came to shove, I could vanish in a flash. I have lots of passports and lots of names. They constitute another facet of my 'insurance policy.'

The next morning, I checked into my IOS office, went over some documents, and drafted a cable to send to General Carroll. Once I was satisfied with it, I took it over to the safe house for transmission. I told General Carroll that I had considered the contents of his previous cable at some length, but felt that I could be far more effective if I stayed in place rather than returning to Washington. I told him that I was deeply involved in cultivating some important contacts, and that it would be impossible for me to continue that development if I had to return to

Washington. I said that I sincerely appreciated his confidence in me and assured him that I would work hard to sustain it.

The answer wasn't long in coming but this time it was signed by McNamara, which meant it came from Johnson. I was briskly informed that the cable from General Carroll should not be construed as 'suggestions' and that I should comply with his instructions right away. I hoped that as the word 'instructions' rather than 'orders' had been used, that just maybe I had some wiggle room.

I composed my response and gave it to Martin, and asked him to wait until I was on the other side of the safe house gates before he sent it. I told him I didn't want to put him into an awkward position if he got orders to arrest me. I also asked him to please call me when he got the reply, and just say either "Bad reply" or "Good reply."

The cable I gave him read as follows:

> Mr. Secretary. I read your cable with considerable disappointment. I feel that I am performing my assigned task competently and am constantly expanding my contact base. I wish to serve my country well and effectively and will continue to exert every effort to do so if permitted to remain in my present post. I therefore respectfully decline to return to Washington as instructed. If it is insisted that I return, I will assume another identity and disappear permanently. I beg you not to force me to do so and to acknowledge your consent that I be permitted to remain in my present post performing the duties that have been assigned to me. Absent that acknowledgement, I will immediately make other arrangements. Respectfully, B. MacFarland.

Martin whistled when he read it. He told me he thought I had a whole lot more *cajones* than were good for my health. He sighed and said, "You've just told the President of the United States in no uncertain terms to go and stick it in his ear. Head for the hills, my friend. I'll call when I get the reply. And incidentally, if I were you I'd go home and quickly pack some essentials, then go check into a hotel somewhere. If the reply is negative, I don't think your house is going to be a very safe place for you to be. I'll call your secretary at IOS when I get the reply. God, I'm glad I'm not in McNamara's shoes. His boss is going to have a meltdown. Now get going, Bertie. Good luck."

I found an inexpensive hotel in Lausanne and settled in for the night. I was pretty sure I wouldn't get a reply until the following morning, and even if a reply did come back before then, there was no way for me to pick it up. I reflected uneasily on the fact that, one way or the other; the events of tomorrow were going to dramatically affect the rest of my life. I didn't sleep much that night. I called my secretary at nine the next morning, told her I had a meeting in Lausanne and wouldn't be in until later. I asked if anyone had left a message for me, and was disappointed when she said, 'No.' I figured that was not a good sign but there was sure no going back now. I'd thrown down the gauntlet and I was going to live with the consequences.

When I called again at 10:30, Marianne said she had received a very strange message from a Mr. Smith, which he had asked to be passed on to me. "He said that he had received a one-word response to the question you had asked. He said the response was simply 'Acknowledged'. Does that make any sense to you?"

I told her that yes it did, and it was the response I had hoped for. I drove back to the house and made sure that the little piece of thread that I had strung across the driveway was still intact, and that the blade of grass that I had closed the front door on when I left was still in place. It looked like this was going to remain my home for the indefinite future.

I called Martin to confirm that I had received his message and he invited me to come by for a drink after work.

Chapter 6 — A Visit to Stockholm

Christmas in Paris

Emma and I spoke on the phone at least once a week, often twice, but I hadn't seen her for months and missed her companionship. Christmas and New Year were coming up and that's usually the loneliest time of the year for me, so when we next spoke and I told her about my new apartment in Paris, I asked what her plans were for the holidays.

There was a long pause before she replied, "I have been dreaming that you would ask. Are you asking me to join you?"

"With all my heart," I replied, and then, "Would you want Ingrid to join us? Pierre is always asking about her. I haven't spoken to him at all about his end-of-year plans but if he asked her to join him and us, what do you think she would say? More importantly, what do *you* think about the idea?"

There was another long pause before she replied, "Although I think Ingrid's parents will be very disappointed, I think she would say 'Yes' to Pierre. And as far as I'm concerned, I can't imagine a more joyous time. Ingrid is my best friend and we both treasure the chance to be in each other's company. Sometimes when we're double-dating, I'm a little nervous because Ingrid's prettier than I am and, well, you know how men can be, sometimes I find my date paying more attention to her than he is to me. It's entirely different when we are with you and Pierre, I'm so comfortable and relaxed that sometimes I think I'm just as pretty as she is."

That was pure Emma. Honest and candid to the point of almost child-like vulnerability. I felt humbled by her unquestioning trust that I would never do anything to hurt her and that she could be totally, completely honest with me. All I said was, "Emma, in my opinion, you are at *least* as pretty as Ingrid and I love being with you. I don't know if Pierre enjoys Ingrid's company as much as I do yours, but he's a lucky man if he does. Now let me call Pierre and tell him what I have in mind so that if he doesn't have any plans that can't be broken, he can call Ingrid and see what she says. In any case, I can't wait to see you and spend the year-end holidays with you. I'll call you as soon as I hear back from Pierre and if it's not tonight, it will for sure be tomorrow."

She was laughing and crying when I hung up. I immediately called Pierre. First I told him how much I enjoyed spending time with Bernard and Sylvie—the parents of one of his law partners—and about my new apartment in Paris. I then recounted my conversation with Emma, and asked if he would like to ask Ingrid to spend the year-end holidays with him. I told him that if she accepted, I would very much enjoy making it a foursome.

He hesitated a moment before he said, "Bertie, don't you dare breathe a word of this to Emma, but I think I may be in love with Ingrid. I think about that woman every day. I just can't get her out of my mind. God, I'd love nothing better than to spend the holidays with her, but the only telephone number she left me was her office number at the Swedish Embassy in Moscow. I'm just not comfortable calling her there on a personal matter. Do you think you could call Emma and ask if she would give you Ingrid's home number or if not, would you give Emma my home number to give to Ingrid so she can call me if she wants? I'd give anything for the four of us to spend the holidays together, and you're welcome to tell Emma *that*."

I called Emma, and relayed Pierre's message.

She started crying again, much harder this time, and to my slightly exasperated question of what was going on she responded, "Oh! Ingrid will be so relieved! She was devastated by the fact that Pierre never called her and simply couldn't understand why not. She thought they had gotten along so well together and she couldn't understand how she had so badly misread his interest in her. She has been depressed for months. I can't wait to tell her but it's already 10:00 p.m. here and as you know, its three hours later in Moscow, and I don't want to wake her at 1:00 in the morning. She usually leaves for work between 7:30 and 8:00 so Pierre can't call her in the morning (unless he wants to try to do so at 4:00 a.m. our time) but he can certainly reach her at home tomorrow evening. Oh! Thank you my darling! You are so kind and gentle to me and to everyone. She will be thrilled to hear from him. I can't wait to see you! I'll be counting the days."

"Kind and gentle to me and to everyone." The words shook me up. Let's see. We have Cory, Genady, my Pentagon guard, Petr, Sally, three guys in Vietnam, Siddhi and his entire family—all of them dead—killed either by me or because of me. Martin almost made the list, but I had no doubt it would grow. I was sure that there would be other situations where I would have either to kill or be killed. Poor, sweet Emma. It was becoming another 'Chantal' situation. I was going to have to break it off, but I'd do my best to make the Christmas vacations a memorably happy time for all of us before I said anything. It was getting near midnight but I called Pierre anyway and passed on the information from Emma.

He was delirious with delight. I found out later that he stayed up until 4:00 to call Ingrid. They talked so long she was late for work. We were definitely going to be a foursome.

It was foggy and overcast in Geneva that Saturday, December 20, 1964 and I was afraid that Ingrid's plane (she was flying in directly from Moscow) might not be able to land. Pierre was picking her up around 11:00 a.m. Emma was catching the very first train out of Bern and would be arriving in Lausanne at 9:00 a.m., so she and I were happily ensconced in the house sitting around the central, open fireplace, finishing up our coffee and croissants when Pierre arrived with Ingrid shortly after noon.

After the shrieks and hugs and kisses of greeting, we all sat close together around the fire with wine and cheese and bread, enjoying the spectacle of Lac Leman and the snow-covered Alps, and Mt. Blanc on the other side of the lake. We were oddly quiet. There was hardly any conversation. We all just sat there smiling in an introspective kind of way and gazing at the fire. It somehow just felt so *right* for the four of us to be together.

I think we were all having the same thoughts—*this* is my family. We'll always be together, our children will grow up together, we'll always be there for one another, we'll go places together, grow old together—everything. I caught *myself* thinking that way and wondered if there weren't some possible way that I could make this work. I'd have to be away a lot. And then, with a jolt, I stopped myself from day-dreaming. I'd be putting Emma in horrible danger. As much as I wanted it, it just couldn't work. I think my involuntary sigh broke the mood. Emma unfortunately misinterpreted it and gave me a look and a smile that would have melted a heart of stone. It melted mine anyway, and I just felt worse.

We left for Paris two days later. Pierre sat in the front of the Mercedes with me and at one point asked me how much I knew about Bernard Monod. I told him I didn't know much other than the fact he was head of the largest law firm in Paris, was married to one of the most elegant women I had ever met, was very wealthy and well-connected, was an avid blue-water sailor and quickly was becoming a good friend. Pierre told me there were a couple of other things that I might like to know.

"He is almost a legendary figure in France. Bernard was head of the French *Résistance* during WWII. It's hard to know now how many of the stories about him are totally accurate, rather than somewhat exaggerated, but if even half of them are accurate, he more than deserves his legendary status. He was apparently a master planner and was fearless in battle. On top of that, he somehow motivated the French peasants to follow him and support him. That's no mean feat. French peasants are not known for their bravery. All they want is to be left alone to tend to their cows and their farms."

I immediately thought of the peasant farmers in Vietnam.

"Bernard was able to convince them that unless they followed him they weren't going to *have* any more cows or farms because the *Boche*[23] would take everything for themselves. If you asked them to fight for France you'd get a response like, 'Oh, I would instantly do so with honor at any

---

[23] Derogatory term for German soldiers in WWII.

other time but my mother is extremely ill and I must attend to her immediately. Promise you will ask me again!' Ask them to fight for their farms and cows? - 'Give me the pitchfork! Give me the rifle! Tell me where I am to find these *salauds*[24] - these *connards?*[25]

"Bernard received the *Légion d'honneur* from DeGaulle, and he and DeGaulle are close personal friends. I am told by my law partner that both Bernard and Sylvie like you very much. I'm impressed. Getting *approval*, much less friendship, from Bernard and Sylvie is quite an accomplishment. You should tell your friends in the United States of your coup."

I hesitated before replying, "Right now, I don't have any friends back in the United States. I just had a big—what shall I say?—'disagreement' with Johnson. I was told that he considered me to be a national intelligence asset, and he needed me near him. He wanted me to return to the States, all was forgiven, I was to have my old office and old apartment back, I could keep the house in Aubonne if I wanted, etc. I was to return right away. I knew that it was just a ruse to get me more fully under his direct control and I refused. Said if he tried to force me, I'd vanish. Nobody challenges Johnson that way and gets away with it, but for the moment at least, I seem to be safe. I need to talk to you privately about the implications. Pierre, my loyalty is to the United States, not to any particular Administration and especially not this one. God knows what's going to happen to me because of what I did."

He looked at me as if he didn't understand what I was saying. He said, "Do you mean that this whole thing between the four of us may not happen? Don't tell me you don't know what I'm talking about. When we were all sitting around the fire and the conversation just stopped, all of us—including you, Bertie—were sort of overcome with a kind of a feeling, or insight or something. I don't know how to describe it, but we were all connected in a special way. We were not just family, we were and are *bonded* somehow. Don't tell me that's not going to happen!"

I just said, "I'm scared for Emma's safety, Pierre. You know the risks of my job, and I don't have the choice of quitting. Johnson will never allow it. This isn't what I want but I can't put her in harm's way. Look, you and I will talk about it later after both of us have had some time to think about it. In the meantime, let's just enjoy ourselves."

And enjoy ourselves, we did. The weather was perfect for brisk walking, and there were an amazing number of things within less than a 30-minute walk from my apartment. Notre Dame Cathedral on the Île de la Cité was less than a ten minute walk, and exploring the lovely little hidden shops and cafés on the adjacent Île Saint-Louis occupied us for hours. We visited museums, the Eiffel tower, strolled up and down the Champs-Elysées, ate in some tiny *bistros* and some great restaurants, had a wonderful dinner with Bernard, Sylvie, their son and his

---

[24] Bastards
[25] <u>Really</u> bad term. Best not to print it. You can look it up.

wife, made the rounds of the night clubs, and arrived back at the apartment each night thoroughly, totally, delightfully exhausted—and sublimely happy. In some sort of strange way, we were all in love *with each other*. Emma and Ingrid thought this was the beginning of the most wonderful life they could ever imagine, much less hope for. They were truly on cloud nine. Pierre and I knew what was coming, however, and we both dreaded it.

We drove back to Geneva on Saturday, January 2, 1965. Both Emma and Ingrid were leaving the next day, as they had to be back to work on Monday.

When Emma and I got in bed, I turned to her and said, "I have to tell you something."

She immediately gasped and said, "I sensed it on the way back. You're going to leave me aren't you Bertie?" We talked for almost an hour before she really regained control of herself and I was startled to see an aspect of Emma that I had never seen before.

She said, "Bertie, I have something to tell you, too. When we first met, although I was very attracted to you, I never thought twice about having any serious relationship. I simply wasn't ready for any real involvement with anyone and didn't want one. I never told you much about me because, frankly, I didn't think it was any of your business. Then, when I realized that I was falling in love with you, I didn't know how to tell you. Ingrid and I discussed it a lot, and her only advice was to just wait. Surely an appropriate time would come. Well, this isn't exactly the moment I was hoping for, but it's time for me to make a confession. My family is very rich and my father is a very powerful man in Sweden. He is a personal friend of Tage Erlander, our Prime Minister, and he is head of one of the largest manufacturing conglomerates in Sweden. I have told him a lot about you, and he wants to meet you very badly. He wanted to give us all a Christmas present by sending his private plane to fly us from Geneva to Paris and setting up lavish dinners for us at several three-star restaurants[26] in Paris.

"I was horrified, and told him that you didn't know anything at all about my family, and would be shocked and maybe offended that I hadn't told you. He told me you were going to have to find out about the family sooner or later, and I should just be forthright and tell you.

"'It's not a crime to be rich and powerful,' he said. 'Just tell him the truth—and also tell him that I am very much looking forward to meeting him. It will be refreshing to meet a young man who I know for sure has no ulterior motives. He's not going to try to get into my good graces to help win you over—it looks like he has already accomplished that task. He's also not going to want to meet me because of who I am (and what I might be able to do for him). He knows nothing of me, and apparently hasn't cared enough to do any research on the subject. It looks like his only interest is you, and I'm delighted. I can't wait to meet this young man of yours.'"

---

[26] At the time, I believe that there were only 12 or 13 restaurants in <u>all of France</u> that had been awarded the coveted 3-star rating from the *Guide Michelin*.

The transformation from a sobbing, semi-hysterical woman to a calm, clear-eyed commanding general carefully and dispassionately assessing the state of battle was remarkable. Emma wasn't about to concede. I had realized from the moment I met her that Emma was very, very bright, but I'd never seen this incredibly tough side of her, and she was focusing all of that tough, powerful intellect on finding a solution to the problem at hand. By God, Emma was a fighter. It was a dimension of her that was totally unexpected, and I admired her tremendously for it. It made me wonder how many more dimensions Emma had which I had yet to see. This was one *very* special lady.

Emma was humming and singing in the kitchen, fixing breakfast for everyone and I was getting ready to go into Aubonne for *croissants* and *brioche* when Pierre and Ingrid tentatively came downstairs. I almost laughed at the expressions on both their faces when they saw and heard Emma, and Pierre shot me a sharp glance which clearly said, "Didn't you tell her?"

Emma came out of the kitchen, kissed them both and answered the unasked question. "Yes, Bertie told me everything last night. Let's sit down and have some coffee while Bertie goes to the *boulangerie.*" I hastily made my exit.

There was a pervasive mood of exuberance around the breakfast table upon my return, and Ingrid leapt up and gave me an excited kiss, and announced that this was the happiest day of her life. "Oh we really will all be together for the rest of our lives, Bertie—you'll see. Emma's father is very, very powerful; he can pull strings all over the world. I know he will fix things for us."

I wasn't about to break the happy mood with expressions of doubt so I simply said, "That's wonderful! I'm really looking forward to meeting Emma's father." At least everyone would leave with happy memories of our vacation. That meant a lot to me.

The Laotian Connection

I got a call from Bernard the next week thanking me for my note. My parents always taught me that one should always write a note of thanks (they called it a 'bread and butter' note)—within 24 hours, mind you—to the host and hostess who had invited you to dinner. Bernard said that he had heard from Teng Lo. General Vang Pao would be pleased to have the opportunity to meet with me in Thailand at my first convenience.

I thanked Bernard and asked him if I might call Mr. Teng directly to try to arrange a suitable date. "That's very considerate of you, Bertie. Thank you. It will be much more efficient for you and Teng Lo to make arrangements directly. Let me know if there is anything I can do to help."

I thought at some length about the protocol of meeting with General Vang. I would be really treading on CIA territory in a major way here. I wasn't even sure how much I was supposed to know about the *existence* of our totally illegal involvement in Laos. Our involvement there was not clandestine, it was *covert* and there is a big difference. In a clandestine operation, the sponsor conceals the existence of the operation. In a covert operation, the identity of the *sponsor* is concealed. Covert operations are designed and carried out in such a way that the sponsor's involvement in—and even knowledge of—the operation is completely deniable.

The first thing I did was to call Teng Lo to tell him that Bernard had relayed General Vang's message to me. I told him that I was humbled and honored by General Vang's invitation to meet with him in Thailand, but as he surely must realize, I would have to have my government's approval for a meeting with such a high-ranking officer. I told Mr. Teng that I would request such approval immediately, and re-contact him as soon as I received a reply.

He said he understood and would look forward to hearing from me.

I sent a short cable to General Carroll—the first cable I had sent to anyone in Washington since the 'showdown' cable, in which I refused to return to Washington. I explained that a contact of mine in Paris had a Thai friend (I suggested we call the friend "Joe") who was a personal friend of General Vang—their families had been friends for decades. I said that I had received a communication from Joe informing me that General Vang was seeking a direct communication channel with Washington, as he felt that his 'contact' in Laos was not transmitting his 'requests' to Washington, and Joe wanted to know if I could help. He said that General Vang would like to meet with me in Thailand. I had informed Joe that I was just an American working for IOS in Switzerland, but that I did have some contacts in the Administration and would approach them with General Vang's request and advise him when I had a response.

I gave the cable to Martin (who read it, of course) and commented, "Bertie, if you've got any asbestos underwear at home, my strong suggestion is to put it on, because I have no doubt that McCone[27] is going to fry your ass, but good. Did your momma drop you on your head when you were a boy or were you just born stupid?"

"Dropped," I replied. "I didn't think it still showed."

The response from Washington wasn't long in coming. My phone at home rang at 4:00 the next morning. 'American Express' was on the line informing me that I had a *large* package waiting to be picked up.

I drove to the safe house as quickly as I could. When I entered the reception area it looked like the whole place was on some kind of full alert status. Martin was in the middle of it of course,

---

[27]   John McCone, Director of the Central Intelligence Agency.

unshaven, disheveled, bellowing for fresh coffee and something to eat, and when he saw me he was apoplectic with rage. I was truly worried he was going to have a stroke or a heart attack or something. He managed to gasp out a greeting so colorful that I hesitate to try to repeat it for fear that inexactitude in doing so might diminish the truly Shakespearean eloquence of it.

Impressed, I followed his beckoning middle finger into his private study where I learned, between masterful expressions of calumny, that a conference call—over the ultra-secure, encrypted line—between me, John McCone and General Carroll was scheduled for 5:00 (11:00 a.m. Washington time) and ten minutes from now. I asked him if he would be listening in, which if anything, enraged him even further.

He said that he couldn't because the analysts could tell if anyone else was listening in; but apparently the worst insult of all was that McCone had ordered that the normally recorded transcripts on both ends of the line be immediately destroyed upon call termination. There would be no written records *anywhere* of the conversation about to take place. I was warned of the dire consequences that were to befall me if I didn't repeat every [expletive] word to him once the call was over.

I grabbed a cup of freshly brewed coffee from the table that somebody had placed just outside the door of his study (nobody had dared knock on his door), and sat down at the desk in the soundproof personal communication room just as the light beside the telephone glowed red.

I won't go into the details of the conversation. The upshot from McCone was that a line had been crossed which was never, ever to be crossed without special and direct authorization by him, the Secretary of State, or the President. He forcefully reminded me that my role was one of a passive intelligence gatherer. I had never been authorized to act as a field operational intelligence agent, and not only wasn't I authorized, I didn't know a damn thing about it and would almost certainly wind up getting myself killed in very short order if I tried to meddle in it. Worse than that, I might compromise some *real* agents and possibly get them killed as well. But much, *much* worse than any of those things, in this particular case I could cause irrevocable damage to our national security operations, and possibly even embarrassment to Johnson himself. I was to tell 'Joe' in no uncertain terms that as a simple civilian that just happened to know some (fairly unimportant) folks in Washington; I had been told in no uncertain terms that I was in no way authorized to meet with General Vang. *Did I understand?*

Before I had a chance to reply McCone continued, "Everybody knows your reputation for ignoring orders, Bertie, but I just want to make sure that you know the consequences of ignoring this one. Your name, passport photo and passport number have been distributed to every international airport in Thailand. I give you my personal promise; you'll be dead within 24 hours of arrival in Thailand. Got that?"

It was actually the first time in the whole 'conversation' that I'd had the opportunity to say anything at all except the occasional 'Yes, sir," or "No, sir, or "I understand, sir." I relished the opportunity to finally respond and I meant to do so in a way that would leave no room for misunderstanding. I tried to quell my anger and there was a long pause before I said:

"I'm not going to worry about that last threat for several reasons, John.[28] Chief among them is that I want absolutely nothing—and I truly mean *nothing*—to do with Southeast Asia. I want nothing to do with Thailand, I want nothing to do with Laos, and I want nothing to do with Vietnam. In *particular* I want nothing to do with Vietnam. You have no idea how happy I am to leave all of those countries in the good hands of the prescient and sagacious U.S. government, its military, and the multitude of its all-knowing experts who will doubtless lead us unscathed through the coming perils. Let me be clear. I love my country and will willingly die to protect it from its enemies, but I do *not*, repeat *not*, love this *Administration* and I particularly do not agree with what it is doing in Southeast Asia. So just to set your mind at rest John, and yours too Joe, I give you my solemn word that I will tell my contact's friend in Paris that I was informed in very definite terms that I am in no way, shape or form allowed to meet with or even speak with General Vang. I shall tell him that I have been personally informed by the highest sources in my own government that I will be assassinated with 24 hours should I dare to even set foot in Thailand.

"Now one last thing, if I may. I certainly never sought any contact with 'Joe.' He's a friend of a friend. It just turned out that his family and Vang's family go back a long way and that Vang had expressed a desire to establish contact directly with Washington. I have a very vague idea of the role that Vang is playing in the area and thought it was my duty to report his request to you. If in the future, something similar should pop up where there is a request from someone we are working with—or who wants to work with us—to establish a communication link to Washington, should I just ignore it or should I report it? I'd just as soon not have to wear asbestos underwear again to help protect against getting my ass fried. It's hot and it's scratchy."

There was a long pause on the other end before John said,

"No, it's O.K., Bertie. You did the right thing, and if something similar happens again, by all means let us know about it. I totally misinterpreted your intent, and I owe you a sincere apology for having gone off the deep end a little bit. I assure you, your anger comes through over the phone loud and clear, and I understand why you are so pissed. I thought you were trying to get involved with our operations in the area, and that would have been completely, totally unacceptable, and I wanted to make that point to you in a very unambiguous way. I realize now that you were simply alerting us to his request and trying to help. You were quite

---

[28] John McCone had told me back in 1962 to address him as 'John' but of course that was when Kennedy was President. He'd never since told me not to but then again, we'd had little occasion to speak directly. I addressed him now by his first name just to annoy him.

right to do so. I'll make sure your present travel restrictions to the area are lifted. After what you've told us, I can't imagine why you would want to travel to that part of the world anyway, but if it turns out you need to for some reason, you won't have to worry about being killed—at least not by us. It's dangerous out there though, so if you do visit the area—watch your step. Well, I've got to go now. You're doing great work, Bertie. All of us here are impressed—keep it up. Again, sorry for the misunderstanding."

As soon as I had hung up and opened the door, Martin unceremoniously hustled me right back into his private study and demanded to know absolutely everything that had been said. "Can't," I said. "Classified." His look of utter stupefaction was hilarious, but the reddening color of his face actually concerned me, so I apologized and gave him the entire conversation, blow by blow. He expressed his desolation that he was not going to have the satisfaction of seeing me hustled out into the courtyard to face the firing squad and that, even worse, the entire brouhaha and disruption of his schedule had essentially been for nothing. The worst thing of all was his regret that McCone had gone from threatening to kill me to giving me compliments on my good work. I expressed my deepest sympathy with his frustration, and left.

Around mid-morning I called Mr. Teng to tell him that I had been absolutely forbidden to have any contact of any nature with General Vang. I told him my understanding was that our government is already in contact with him on a number of matters, and that the government wanted no interference whatever with existing arrangements. I expressed my sincerest regrets to him, and asked if he would also pass those regrets on to his friend, the General. Mr. Teng took all this in with perfect equanimity, apologized for having disturbed me, and expressed the hope that we could have lunch together the next time I visited Paris. I hung up with a profound sense of relief. McCone's attitude towards me had swung 180° and I thought it was finally starting to get through to Washington that *nobody* there owned me. Additionally, I had successfully dodged the Vang bullet.

God, how wrong I was on the latter count.

A Visit to Stockholm

I got a call from Emma around the middle of February, telling me that her father would be returning from a business trip to Africa in about a week, and wanted to know if he could stop in Geneva and pick me up. He'd then pick her up in Bern, and we'd all continue to Stockholm for a long weekend together. I said I'd be delighted and couldn't wait to see her again, and meet her father.

Anders Dahlquist was a vibrant, charming, delightful human being and I was drawn to him immediately. We came from totally different worlds, but it was clear that this man was one of those rare individuals who could fit himself easily into any world at all. By the time we picked

Emma up in Bern, we were chatting away like old friends. It was only 4:30 p.m. when we landed in Stockholm, but it was pitch dark. It was also bitter cold, but none of us felt it much as Anders's car was pulled up only a few feet away from the airplane's bottom step.

The house—well, mansion, really—was lovely and there were vases of fresh-cut flowers everywhere. Where in the world do you find fresh flowers in Stockholm in February? Mrs. Dahlquist came running in from another room and literally threw herself into Anders' arms. She then turned to Emma, gave her a big hug and kiss and then turned to me. It was the first time I had gotten a good look at her, and there was only one word to describe her—stunning. Sabina Dahlquist was one of the most beautiful women I'd ever seen. It was as though someone had taken the best features of Grace Kelley and Ingrid Bergman and then created her.

I didn't have much time to admire that incredible face, because suddenly she was hugging me and giving me kisses on the cheek. "Oh, Bertie, Bertie," she said as she stepped back and held both my shoulders at arm's length to examine me in detail. "I finally get to meet you in person. Emma has told me so much about you and now, here you are. She said you were very handsome and I totally agree. Now let's all move into the family room and have a drink before dinner."

Emma grabbed my hand to lead the way and when she leaned over to kiss me on the cheek she whispered, "I think mother really likes you."

The real conversation didn't start until we sat down for dinner. At some point, Anders said, "Emma told us that when she first met you, you were a Special Assistant to President Kennedy. Did you know the President well?"

I was startled to realize that this was the first time anybody had ever asked me about my relationship with President and Mrs. Kennedy. It was a pleasure to bring up those fond memories. I told them about my nearly disastrous trip to Hyannis Port but which had finished by Mrs. Kennedy asking me to address her as 'Jackie,' etc. Eventually the story came out about how I came to be Special Assistant to the President. Anders and Sabina (she had quickly nixed the Mrs. Dahlquist form of address) were aghast. Emma (who was sitting beside me) was weeping and stroking the back of my neck and I was getting nervous about having divulged so much of my past.

I stopped and said, "I shouldn't be telling you about all this but I feel so comfortable here that it seems like the natural and the right thing to do. I must ask you to please not repeat a word of it to anyone. Emma, please, not even to Ingrid."

Anders said, "William Bertram MacFarland, you are an extraordinary young man. You are a credit to your nation, and it is a distinct pleasure to have you as our guest."

I started to thank him for his kind words then stopped, appalled, as Mrs. Dahlquist suddenly broke into tears and rushed over to collect Emma. I watched wordlessly as they left the room, sobbing and hugging each other tightly.

Before I could ask what in the world was going on, Anders came over and said, "Don't worry, Bertie. It's not your fault and it's not anything serious. Come on in my study and let's have a drink. I have some very old Laphroaig that I believe you'll enjoy.

The Laphroaig was magnificent but I was puzzled. "How did you know I like single malt scotch?" I asked.

"Oh, I know a good deal about you Bertie," he responded. "Fathers like to know about any young man that their daughters seem to be serious about. It's part of our job," he laughed. "I have lots of contacts all over the world," he continued. "Quite a few of them are in Washington and though few knew you personally, almost all of them knew something about you. I already knew much of what you told us tonight, though certainly not all. I also know about some parts which you left out—and thank you very much for doing so—those things would have upset Sabina and Emma terribly. I know about the two Russian KGB agents you killed, and I know what happened in Vietnam. But let's not talk any more about such things. We've all had a long day. Perhaps I can show you around Stockholm a little bit tomorrow. Would you enjoy that? I'm sure you didn't have the opportunity to look around much the last time you were here. But it's getting late. Let's go upstairs and get to bed."

As we were walking down the long upstairs hall, he stopped, pointed to a door and said, "You and Emma are in there, our bedroom is a little farther along." He paused and said, "Bertie, I do know a lot of people in Washington, and I think I can be of some real help in resolving your current situation, but we'll talk more about that tomorrow or the next day. Sleep well, my friend."

Emma was propped up in bed reading a book when I came in. She held out her arms and said, "Oh, darling! Come and give me a hug. You have utterly charmed both my parents. I was sure they would both adore you."

I kissed her and said, "Now hold that thought. I've got to take a shower but I'll be right back and we can take up where we left off."

When I came back she was sleeping so soundly that she didn't even wake up when I crawled into bed beside her. She had such a beautiful, serene smile on her face that I must have stared at her for a full minute before putting her book on the bedside table and turning out the light.

It was still dark outside when Emma and I came downstairs around 7:00 the next morning, but the breakfast room was brightly lit, and there was the wonderful aroma of freshly brewed coffee in the air. Anders and Sabina had been having a quiet conversation, but they both got up to greet us.

Sabina gave me a hug and a kiss on the cheek, and when we were all seated she said, "Bertie, I want to apologize for making such a scene last night. All of a sudden the image of you being beaten in that awful prison cell, and thinking about how hurt and lonely you must have been just overcame me and . . .," her lower lip started to quiver and she quickly finished with, "Oh!, I can't think about it anymore. Let's move on to cheerier subjects. Did you sleep well last night?"

I told her that I must have because the last thing I remembered was turning off the light. I said, "I think I'd probably still be sleeping if Emma hadn't waked me with stern instructions to go shave and get dressed or we'd be late for breakfast."

We didn't have much time for sightseeing. It didn't get light until around 8:00 and Anders said it would be dark again by 4:30. Sabina had begged off, saying that she had a huge list of things she needed to do, and she of course had already seen the sights of Stockholm as she was born and brought up in the city. "I still love it though," she said. "I wouldn't want to live anywhere else but I must admit that the winter months can be a little dreary. Our summers more than make up for it, though. They are simply idyllic," she added, "and I hope to see a lot of you this summer, Bertie."

"I hope so, too," I said as we left.

Stockholm is a fascinating city, and with Anders in the lead, we saw parts of it that most visitors (and most natives too, I suspect) never get to see. He greeted everyone as a friend and equal and it was clear wherever we went that he was not only deeply respected, he was genuinely liked.

We stopped for lunch at a small, unpretentious restaurant which was filled with workmen. I was prepared to wait for a table, and was astonished when several workmen, eating at a table by the front window, got up with their plates, waved and called out to Anders, and found places at other tables. The manager rushed up to shake Anders' hand and made a big fuss over Emma, who kissed him on the cheek to the accompaniment of whistles and cheers from the other diners. When we sat down, I remarked to Anders that he seemed to be rather well known here. He said his company had a big manufacturing plant nearby, and that a lot of the workmen came here for lunch. He also said that he wanted to introduce me to good plain Swedish food. "You can't get this in Paris," he joked. "Seriously, the food here is excellent. Try the meatballs. I think you'll like them." Served with mashed potatoes and lingonberry jam on the side, they were the best I'd ever eaten.

We got back just as it was starting to get really dark, and I spent the rest of the afternoon engaging in 'getting to know you' conversation with Anders and Sabina. Sabina wanted to show me the house and I trailed along (with Emma holding my hand) as we went from room to room.

The house was huge and beautifully furnished with a profusion of magnificent artwork. I was truly impressed and said so.

Sabina smiled and said, "Now let me show you my most marvelous and treasured room. I spend hours in it every day just admiring it. I hope you'll love it too."

When we finally got there and she opened the door I was staggered—first by the light, then by the size, then by the fragrance. It was a commercial-sized greenhouse! The profusion of flowers, spices, orchids, and heaven only knows what other kinds of plants was simply astonishing. It took my breath away. I finally blurted out some inanity like, "This is unbelievable! Here is a tropical paradise in the middle of Stockholm in February! Now I know where all those beautiful fresh-cut flowers come from. I also understand why you would want to spend as much time as you can in here. It's ethereal. It's enchanting. I don't know what else to say."

Sabina smiled and said, "I'm so glad you like it. Next time you're here, we'll walk through it together with Hjalmer, our gardener. He knows everything about all the plants. He treats them as though they're his children, and I suppose in a way they are. Well, let's all go and have a light dinner and then I think Anders wants to get together with you in his study so you two can discuss plans."

When Anders and I settled into his study and closed the door, he poured us a Scotch and quietly asked me, "Why do you and Lyndon Johnson hate each other so much?"

I reflected a few moments before answering, "Well, first of all, I am absolutely convinced that he was responsible for the assassination of President Kennedy. I can't prove it yet, but I'll die trying. Secondly, he is a totally dishonest, deceptive and untrustworthy man. Lastly, he is going to be the direct cause of the deaths of tens of thousands of Americans in Vietnam in addition to many times that many Vietnamese in both North and South Vietnam. In his arrogance and stupidity, he really believes that the mighty U.S. military can 'liberate' South Vietnam from the Communist influences that threaten it. He simply refuses to understand that the South Vietnamese peasants would rather have Ho Chi Minh as head of the government that oppresses them than being oppressed by a corrupt puppet government controlled by Washington."

In response to his query about why I felt I was safe from the wrath of such a powerful man, I told him about my 'insurance documents.' When he asked why Johnson refused to let me go, I explained that I thought Johnson was terrified of the idea of me being completely outside his control. "I'm skating on thin ice, though," I confessed. "He recently decided that I am a national security intelligence asset who is too valuable not to be under constant 'protection' of the Secret Service in Washington. He instructed me to return, said that I could have my old office in the West Wing, my old apartment, and that I could even keep my house in Switzerland. I refused and said that if he tried to make me return—I would vanish."

He sighed and said, "I don't know, Bertie. This problem is much deeper than I ever imagined. I don't know if I can be of help or not. I'll have to think about it." He slowly shook his head then looked up and said, "Just out of curiosity, I've heard several stories about some sort of gruesome knife you carry around with you. Is there any truth to that?"

"Well," I said, "I wouldn't call Excalibur gruesome but it is a very deadly weapon. And yes, I usually do wear it. I almost feel undressed without it. Emma knows about it and has seen it but she's never seen it unsheathed."

He asked if I were wearing it now and when I said that I was, he asked if he could see it. In expectation of his response to the warning I was going to give him, I unobtrusively stretched out my right leg a little bit.

I warned him that I didn't think he was going to like what he saw, but he insisted.

When you have practiced a movement for hundreds and hundreds of hours you really *do* become very good at it and with a movement so swift you had to wonder if it had really happened, Excalibur, in all its savage beauty, appeared as if by magic in my right hand, which was several feet away from where Anders was sitting.

His reaction was so violent that if the big leather chair in which he was sitting hadn't been so heavy, he would have pushed it over on its back. He kept his eyes tightly closed as he croaked, "Put it away, Bertie. Put it away. Please!" He only opened his eyes when I told him that I had done so. I was appalled by the severity of his reaction, and apologized profusely for giving him such a scare. He said, "I just saw a Bertie MacFarland that I've never seen before and I pray God that I never will again. It's not just that terrible weapon that so magically appeared in your hand—I saw the eyes of a killer. Your face was a stone mask but your eyes, your eyes—I can't get them out of my mind."

He straightened up slowly and said, "This isn't going to work, and after what I just saw, I'm not sure I'm completely unhappy about that. Your involvement is far too deep for me to be of help, and frankly, I'm not sure that you even want to be helped. I'll send the girls on a shopping trip tomorrow morning and take you out to the airport while they're gone. The pilots will fly you back to Geneva—or Paris, if you'd rather. Just let me know ahead of time as they'll have to file a flight plan. I'll call them now and tell them to have the plane ready for take-off at 10:00 tomorrow morning. Emma is going to be devastated; she's very much in love with you. I can't stop her from seeing you when she gets back, but I wish you wouldn't. It's going to be hard enough for her to re-build her life without constantly reminding herself of what it might have been. Sabina is going to be devastated, too. She's almost overwhelmed by you, and is so much hoping to have you as a permanent part of our lives. Frankly, so was I. I was starting to imagine all kinds of things we would be doing together as a family, or sometimes just you and me together.

"You're in way, way too deep for me, or anybody else, to extract you from the life you have chosen for yourself—or at least resigned yourself to. That's all I'll ever tell Sabina or Emma. I promise you I'll never mention the knife incident. Maybe I can actually be of some help to you in your 'business.' One of my companies sells quite a lot of non-military hardware—medical equipment, things like that—to the East German government, and I know the Head of State Procurement very well. He is quite close to both Walter Ulbricht who is Chairman of the Council of State, and Willi Stoph, Chairman of the Council of Ministers. He and I meet three or four times a year, and I will be your eyes and ears. I'll also be your friend, Bertie. I respect your values and I respect your patriotism. Let me know anytime you think I can be of help. Now let's try to put on a good face and go re-join the ladies. They'll ask lots of questions and if you would, please let me do the answering. I'm just going to say that it's a more difficult problem than it first appeared to be but that we are both working on it. Now let's go."

The next morning on the way to the airport, I turned to Anders and said, "Anders, I just want to tell you that last night's incident scared the hell out of me too. Other than continual practice to maintain technique, last night is the first time that I have *ever* taken Excalibur out of its sheath without intending to kill or seriously harm someone. When I did it last night, and was staring at you, waiting for you to make a move, I was on complete autopilot until I suddenly realized where I was, and what I was doing. I was just as horrified as you were. I've thought about it a lot and what I've realized is that I should never, ever again take Excalibur out *unless* I'm intending to kill or harm. Reflexes are everything; in close combat there's no time to think. If your lightning-quick reflexes don't take over—you're going to lose your life. Showing Excalibur to you was a really stupid thing to do, and I can't tell you how sorry I am for doing it. I now deeply understand that when I draw that weapon I enter a completely different state of mind and a completely different persona. All my intense training has made my use of Excalibur totally instinctual. Anders, I didn't choose this life.

"I did my best to resign and rejoin the real world after Jack was killed, but Johnson simply would *not* let me go. So much has happened since Jack's death that I'm afraid there is now no way for me to go back to a normal, civilian life. The good part is that I've discovered that I can make some meaningful contributions to the security of the United States, and as long as that's the case, I feel honor-bound to continue. I apologize again for my stupid, childish demonstration and I thank you for having taught me a painful lesson. I can't tell you how terribly sorry I am that it had to be *you* who taught me."

History of a Hero

Anders grinned ruefully and reached over and rumpled the hair on the back of my head. He dropped a bombshell when he said, "You know something Bertie, you remind me so much of a friend of mine. I can't claim I know him very well—I've only met him twice, and considered it an honor to do so because although he is a true hero, he is a total recluse. He must be around 70 or so now, and I don't think he is in very good health but he was one of the greatest Italian heroes of WW II. He's a legend in Italy to this day. Even little children know about him. It's an interesting story.

"When in early September, 1943, the Italians (behind the backs of the Nazis, with whom they were allied) signed an armistice with the allies, there was a period of great confusion in Italy. Were the fascists of Mussolini in control? Were the Germans in control? Were the allies in control? In many of the small towns and villages of Italy, nobody was really sure. The local Italian fascist leaders (who had control of most of the entire country) were 'loyal' to Mussolini, as long as he was sure to be *Il Duce*. As that was no longer sure to be the case, they abandoned their provincial posts *en masse,* slipping quietly away into the night to avoid reprisals from the villagers they had so brutally exploited.

"A young partisan who had vehemently opposed the Mussolini regime and who was even more outraged when Mussolini teamed up with Hitler, saw his chance. He assembled a team of raiders that would take over these temporarily abandoned villages' administrative offices, destroy tax and military service records, open the warehouses and distribute the wheat and whatever else was there to the peasants, and steal any abandoned military equipment they could find. This fearless young man was a remarkable leader and an organizational genius. By the time the German Army finally re-established control, he was a force to be reckoned with. He was so elusive that he was nicknamed the Mirage—il Miraggio, I think it is in Italian— because he seemed to have no substance. The name stuck. He recruited disaffected soldiers from the Italian Army, particularly specialists, and used them as trainers for his ever-growing number of followers.

"What had started out as a local guerilla movement grew larger and larger. With his ability to blow up bridges and disrupt German supply lines, he was becoming a major headache to the German Army in Italy. News of his exploits eventually reached Berlin, and Hitler himself ordered his capture and arrest, but to no avail. This *Miraggio* was a huge asset to the allies when they invaded Italy. Unfortunately, just after the allies had taken Rome, he was shot in the back by a German soldier, and while the wound wasn't fatal, the bullet lodged in the lower part of his spine and had to be removed. In the process, the nerves in one of his legs were permanently damaged, and whereas he used to be able to move around using just a cane, I believe he now has to use a wheelchair most of the time. Anyway, after the war, the Italian Government inundated him with honors, and he was also flooded with business opportunities and requests from very large companies to sit on their Board of Directors, etc. In a short time, he himself had become a very wealthy man with business interests all over the world. But his patriotism reminds me of you. I wish you could meet him."

126

"It's Don Moretti's left leg that is damaged," I said quietly as I tried to keep my voice from quavering. "I truly love him. The last time I saw him, he asked me to call him Umberto when we were alone or with just Mamma. He said he thinks of me as his son and wants me to come live with him and Mamma in Sardinia, but said that he knew that would never happen. I think of him and Mamma often and I very much miss being with them. It is so beautiful there, and it's one of the few places where I feel completely safe. I am very grateful to you Anders, for telling me his story. I know that I would never have gotten it from him. Why are you looking at me that way?"

He kept shaking his head as he said, "I'm literally speechless. I'm having a hard time taking this in. Don Moretti sees no one. He doesn't even like to have his name mentioned. He is probably more reclusive than was your Howard Hughes in his later years. I would never have told you his name and I *couldn't* have told you his first name because I've never heard it. My companies have extensive dealing with several of his companies, but everything goes through his law firm in Rome. Very few people know that he even *exists* any more. And you not only know of his existence, you have obviously been a guest in his home, call Signora Moretti 'Mamma' and have been invited by him to call him by his first name when you're in a private setting. You are the definition of unique, Bertie. There is no other man in the entire world who has that kind of knowledge of, and access to, Don Moretti. I'm out of my league with you Bertie. You have my profound respect and I will value our continued friendship even more. Well, there's the plane. Let's get you on it."

He got out of the car with me and I extended my hand, but he grabbed me instead and gave me a big bear hug. "Call me any time you need me," he repeated, "and rest assured that our conversation regarding our mutual friend will never be repeated. Not to anyone."

I thanked him and got on the plane. I thought a lot about Emma on the way home, and what it would be like to be a part of a family. I was really depressed, and tried to shake it off by concentrating on work. My original concept of what it meant to set up cells and recruit people to gather 'behind-enemy-lines' information, was beginning to undergo a massive transformation. I would have to really think this through. If somehow I could tap into trusted pipelines of communication that *already existed....*

When we landed in Geneva, before retrieving my car and going home, I called my office. I hadn't told anybody except Pierre that Emma and I were going to visit her parents, because I didn't think it was anybody else's business. My secretary damned well thought that it was hers, however. She was beside herself; she said that she kept getting calls from a Mr. Martin, who said that he had to speak to me urgently. She had tried calling me at home; she had tried calling the apartment in Paris; she had tried calling my friend Pierre (who *wouldn't* have told her anything because of our friendship, and *couldn't* say anything because of lawyer/client confidentiality); she called our new Italian office; she called our new French Président-Directeur Général in Paris. Nobody knew where I was. On top of that, this Mr. Martin kept calling her—

even at home—to see if she had any news. She said she felt like a complete idiot, and was sure that Mr. Martin thought that either she was lying to him or that I didn't trust her. She started to cry.

I apologized sincerely for all the phone calls, particularly at her house. I tried to calm her down and said that I had needed a few days to take care of some private business, and would call Mr. Martin right away. I also told her to take the rest of the day off.

This thing with Martin didn't sound too good to put it mildly. I called the safe house, and Martin came on the line almost immediately. I held the phone away from my ear while he greeted me at the top of his lungs and advised me to get myself over there 'RIGHT GOD-DAMN NOW!'

I did so and indeed, all hell had broken loose.

Chapter 7 — Death in Thailand

The Laotian Problem

There wasn't much mistaking the barely masked hysteria in Martin's voice. I was both puzzled and annoyed. Annoyed because I was tired and immensely saddened by the realization that I would probably never see Emma again. I needed the solitude of my mountain home with its soothing views of the lake and the Alps. I wanted some space and time to think and plan. I wanted to think about a paradigm shift in the way I was going to do intelligence gathering. I wanted some alone time. I was puzzled because I couldn't imagine what in the world had gotten Martin so upset. He sounded a bit scared actually. "Oh, Hell!" I thought. "I guess there's no way out of it. I suppose I'd better drive over there."

Martin wasted no time on greetings but waved me immediately into his office. "The fat's in the fire now, Bertie," he began. "You personally have shut down our entire military operation in Laos." I asked him what the hell he was talking about and he replied, "General Vang has announced that he is sure his messages are not getting through to Washington, and until he receives assurances that you are flying out to Thailand to meet with him, he is ceasing military operations."

"Well that's too damn bad," I said. "I'm not anybody's messenger boy. I've got real work to do. I don't work for your crowd (the CIA), and if your guys in the field out there are having problems with their *prima donna* General, they can solve it themselves. I'm not getting anywhere near that mess. Forget it! You guys have thousands of people working for you. Get one of your own to sort this out and play messenger boy if they have to. I'm not getting involved and that's final. Now, I've had a rough past few days and I'm going home." I closed his office door none too gently as I left.

I could hear the phone ringing incessantly as I opened the door to my house. It was General Carroll. He got straight to the point. "This is not a fully secure line, Bertie so I won't be able to speak entirely openly. I will call you on the fully secure line in Geneva tomorrow at 5:00 p.m. your time to discuss details. You're not going to like what I have to say, but hear me out before you reply. Martin relayed your comments about not being anybody's 'messenger boy' and refusal to get involved, and we all understand that. Believe me, everybody here—and I do mean *everybody*—understands your unbending aversion to having anything to do with Southeast

Asia. Nobody *wants* to see you involved in any way. Having said that, we have no choice—and you don't either, Bertie."

I began to sputter my disagreement but he cut me off short with, "Damn it, Bertie! I said hear me out— so *listen* to me! The General in question knows you were a Special Assistant to President Kennedy, and he's not buying the official line that you are no longer a Special Assistant. He's insisting on dealing with you—and nobody *but* you. To make his point, he's stopped all operations involving his people. Although he is responsible for all ground operations, air operations can't continue without the guidance of his people. So we are effectively totally shut down in the area he commands. As you know, the area he commands is the whole damn country."

He continued, "That has not gone unnoticed by the other side, and attacks on our assets which are stationed there have started to increase dramatically. Once they find there is little or no resistance to these attacks, they will mount a full-scale offensive which we will be powerless to resist. We've already lost two of our own people, and we're going to lose a lot more very quickly unless he takes up arms again. We don't know how to fight in that terrain and even if we did, our skin's the wrong color. So here's my question to you, Bertie. Do you want to be personally responsible for the loss of hundreds of American lives and the loss of a whole country, or do you want to get your contact in Paris to tell the General that you'll be getting your ass out to Thailand as quickly as possible? OK, *now* it's your turn to talk."

The thought of having *anything* to do with their dirty war was absolutely abhorrent but I know when I'm beat. After a long pause, I sighed deeply and said, "I'll try to get in touch with my contact in Paris as soon as I put the phone down. Get McCone's people to let the General know I'll be there in the next few days. Since he obviously doesn't trust them, tell them to tell him that his friend in Paris will confirm my consent. Meeting arrangements will be made through the Paris contact. I'll talk to you tomorrow at five. You guys in Washington really owe me one for this, Joe." I hung up without waiting for his reply and placed the call to Paris.

It was cold in the house but I was too tired and too melancholy to light a fire, so I just turned the heat up. I remembered all too clearly the almost surreal contentment of those pre-Christmas days, when Emma and I and Pierre and Ingrid had sat around this fireplace and dreamed of the happy days that we four would have together for the rest of our lives. Now, at least for Emma and me, those dreams were shattered completely and forever.

On the 'positive' side of my trip to Stockholm, I had learned something of the past of my beloved Don Moretti, and was also realizing that I might be able to do a lot better job of intelligence gathering than would be possible using the traditional 'cloak and dagger' method. Through his businesses, Anders had a direct pipeline into the East German government—a government deemed almost impossible to penetrate. Ingrid's suitor in Moscow had provided invaluable information on what was happening at the highest reaches in the Kremlin (the overthrow of

Khrushchev by Brezhnev), but that was a one-off, fortuitous event. However, Moscow had countless businesses and other commercial, cultural, legal, etc. ties to entities outside the Soviet Union. I had close ties to three people who had a vast network of companies, business associates and top-ranking political figures spanning the entire globe. They didn't have to use skullduggery or James Bond-type methods to penetrate the highest levels of every single country behind the 'Iron Curtain.' They dealt with these people on an everyday basis!

My reverie was demolished by the reality of a loudly ringing phone with Teng Lo on the other end. I apologized for the lateness of the hour and said that, upon further reflection, my government had decided —in order to show their deep respect for General Vang—that they would be pleased to honor his request to meet with me personally. I asked if he would be kind enough to convey my government's position to General Vang and to inform the General—if he should still wish to meet with me personally—that I would be honored to do so at his earliest convenience. I could almost *see* Mr. Teng's quiet, knowing smile as he informed me that he would be delighted to pass my message along to General Vang, and would contact me immediately upon receiving General Vang's reply.

I went to bed hungry, miserable, and lonely.

The next day, at my IOS office, I got a phone call from our family lawyer in Baltimore, informing me that during the night, my mother had finally succumbed to her very advanced Alzheimer's disease which she'd had for years. He expressed his sympathy and asked for instructions. I asked if he would have her cremated, and if he would please ask one of the younger men in his office to take her ashes to Elkridge Landing in the nearby Patapsco State Park (just outside Baltimore, MD), and scatter them in the Patapsco River. When I was growing up, my parents often took me to that enormous park and I had wonderful memories of our strolls, hikes and picnics there. The snow on the ground this time of year would mean a very arduous trip from the parking area to the river.

Nevertheless, he said that he would convey and scatter the ashes personally, expressed his sympathy again and rang off. It's strange, you know. My mother hadn't been able to recognize anyone at all for the last few years, and her fate was inevitable. So now, why did I feel like crying? Why did I feel so alone? It didn't make any sense at all—but it sure was the way I felt.

I was pretty depressed when I got to the safe house for the 5:00 phone call, and Martin's greeting was downright surly.

"What the hell have I done to deserve that kind of treatment?" I demanded.

He shook his head resignedly, then sighed and put his arm around my shoulders and said, "Nothing. I know it's not your fault. I also know that the last thing in the world you want to do is to get involved in Southeast Asia. So I apologize sincerely, but damn it Bertie, nothing's been the same around here from the moment you first walked through that front door. I miss the old days. Now get yourself into the secure communications room or you'll be late for your call."

I told him I'd give him a full briefing afterwards.

He startled me when he replied, "No you won't."

In contrast to Martin, Joe sounded quite spritely and cheerful and politely inquired about how my day had been going. I didn't want to talk about the death of my mother so I told him that things were going well. He said that he had received congratulations 'for getting me on board' from all and sundry. Even Johnson phoned him to tell him he was doing 'excellent work.' I told him I hadn't realized that I had developed such a wide reputation for recalcitrance. He said he wouldn't call it 'recalcitrance' exactly, but I did have a widely known aversion to following instructions I didn't agree with.

"Anyway, let's get down to business," he said. "I can't overemphasize the diplomatic sensitivity of your mission." He started to describe the situation surrounding our involvement in Laos, and continued, "Let's start with our relations with Thailand. The United States and Thailand have a 'gentlemen's agreement' which allows limited use by the U.S. Air Force of certain Royal Thai Air Force bases. As Thailand is officially neutral concerning the conflict going on in Southeast Asia, there is no public acknowledgement of our planes being stationed at their air bases. Now if you think *that's* delicate, let me tell you something about our operations in Laos. Laos is also officially neutral, but the Communist Pathet Lao forces are being trained and supported by North Vietnam, and they have infiltrated the entire country. CIA has recruited General Vang, and he has enlisted the support of the indigenous Hmong people who are fiercely loyal to him. They not only fight the Pathet Lao, but when they discover any kind of a fixed base, they call in our air support to bomb it out of existence. The U.S. is so afraid of being caught doing air support in Laos, our pilots have to resign their commissions in the Air Force and fly missions over Laos wearing civilian clothes and carrying fake I.D., so that in case they get shot down, they can claim to be mercenaries. Their aircraft either bears no markings at all or it bears the markings of the Royal Thai Air Force.

"The CIA is running the entire Laos operation and you need to be fully briefed on it before you meet with Vang. The problem is that the operation is so sensitive and so secret that only a very few people are given access to the information you need. Martin and his people are not on that list and you are not to share any of the information you will be receiving with him or any of his staff. Accordingly, Martin has been directed to provide you with an office that has a bullet-proof door fitted with a combination lock which can be set by you to any combination you choose. You are not to share that combination with anyone. Additionally, your new office is to be supplied with a large security file safe like the one you had in your office in the White House. Again, only you will know the combination to open it. By special flight, we are sending you tonight a complete briefing file via diplomatic courier. The files will be sealed and only you are authorized to break the seal. You may only handle these files in your new office. They may only be stored in your secure file cabinet in your office. Any notes or other written material that you may generate in the course of your studying these files must also be stored in the secure file cabinet or shredded with the ultra-secure shredder which will be installed in your office. If you have any questions before you leave for Thailand, call me on my secure private number. The briefing materials being sent to you will also contain a list of the secure private numbers of Director McCone, and Secretaries Rusk and McNamara. You are now authorized to originate such calls from any suitably secure facility world-wide. Questions?"

I said I wanted to review the materials that I was being sent before I started asking questions. After I hung up, I just sat there for a moment. What in God's name had I gotten myself into?

Martin was waiting for me when I exited the communications room. All he said was, "Let me show you to your new office." He led me down a corridor that I had never entered before, and there was no mistaking the door to my new office. It looked like the door to a bank vault.

Martin said that since I hadn't set the combination yet, the door was unlocked and we could look inside. It was pretty Spartan with precisely four items of furniture—a desk, a chair, a large security file cabinet set, and a really big shredding machine. The desk top was piled high with office supplies. Martin said to let him know if I needed anything else because he had received strict orders to supply me with absolutely anything I needed. Anything. He smiled grimly.

"Martin. Come on. Don't hate me. Please be my friend. I really need a friend. Emma and I have broken up permanently, my mother died last night, and I've now got this God-awful Southeast Asia assignment. Don't abandon me now, Martin. Help me get through this," I implored.

He looked at me hard for a few seconds then smiled sadly and said, "I'm sorry to hear about your mother. Many years ago, I lost mine to cancer. Even though I, like you, was fully cognizant of the inevitability of the outcome, I found that when it actually occurs, the blow is much harder than you've prepared yourself for. I *am* your friend Bertie. Digesting the fact that, for the moment at least, your orders take precedence over mine in my little fiefdom here took some getting used to, but I'm OK with it. I really am. Come on in my office and we'll open up the bar and you can tell me about Emma."

The next morning I went to see Kent, my boss at IOS, and told him that my mother had died the night before and that unfortunately, I was going to have to be making a number of trans-Atlantic trips to wind up the family's affairs. Although I would continue to live in Switzerland for the foreseeable future, I simply was not going to be able to give my job at IOS the attention it deserved. He was very nice about it, expressed his sympathy, and said that since I had already established a successful template for setting up regional processing offices, whoever followed in my footsteps would have a far easier job in establishing future centers. I called Bernie Cornfeld with the same story, and got pretty much the same response, but he added that he was making me an honorary IOS employee, and that I would be notified of all future social events at *Bella Vista*.

I went out and bought the biggest bouquet of roses I could find plus a box of Switzerland's finest chocolate, and delivered them to my long-suffering secretary along with an envelope containing a note of heart-felt thanks and SFr. 1,000. She surprised me by bursting into tears and saying that she was really going to miss me (I thought she hated me). I gratefully accepted her offer to pack up my few personal belongings in my office and send them to the house.

I then drove over to the safe house.

Martin greeted me cheerfully and insisted that I have a coffee with him while somebody went to the vault to fetch my briefing package. I was astounded when the employee reappeared pulling a freight trolley with eight really large cardboard boxes on it! Martin laughed, and followed along as the employee deposited the entire lot on the floor of my new office.

When he left, Martin said, "Well, good reading, Bertie. Let me know if you need anything. Don't forget to set your combination locks."

The boxes were numbered and when I opened the first one and saw how much material was in it, I realized that I was going to be at this for the next couple of days. The first thing I did was to call Mr. Teng in Paris to tell him that I had received the briefing material from my government but they had sent much more than I had expected. I told him that it was going to take me two or three days to get through it even though I would be working full-time on the project.

He said that he would notify General Vang of our communication. He also suggested that I depart for Bangkok from Paris because there were so many people of Vietnamese and Thai descent living in Paris there were always several direct flights every day. He said that he would like to meet with me briefly before I departed, and suggested that perhaps we could have lunch or dinner together. I told him I would look forward to that and would keep him advised of my progress.

Each box had a packing list detailing its content. I opened them one at a time, and put the contents into the security file cabinets. Once I had gotten everything stowed away, I sat down at my desk and went over the packing lists to decide where to start, and decided I would be better off to go through the material in pure chronologic order, rather than in the order in which they had been packed. It was almost noon before I really got started. I was appalled by what I discovered. *For years and years, the CIA had been actively involved with the illicit narcotic trade in Southeast Asia.*

The CIA is a curious organization. 'It' is always afraid that there is some idea or political philosophy or system out there which, if left unchecked, might mean the end of the United States as we know it. Motivated by this often paranoid hyper-nationalistic fervor, and given broad discretion to operate in secret, it is the national poster-child for the belief that the end justifies the means. Totally illegal activities, including killing, are just part of the normal, day-to-day business if such activities are believed to be useful in accomplishing their goals. Its original mission of intelligence-gathering (which is primarily a passive mission) has evolved into one in which it actively seeks to shape events—not just report on them.

The CIA has often participated in the overthrow of a democratically-elected government in order that a government more suitable to the United States be installed. It has become the nation's leading paramilitary organization, a mini Department of Defense operating totally outside the realm of normal oversight (and the Geneva conventions). Its budget is massive, and it is dubious that there is any single individual who can accurately say how much federal money is allocated to the Agency each year, far less how those funds are spent. Secrecy veils all. Step behind the veil with me for a little while.

Southeast Asia and the CIA

It's important to remember that at the end of World War II, the Western world was becoming increasingly nervous about the spread of Communism. Russia's leader, Joseph Stalin, had shown himself to be totally and brutally ruthless in his pursuit of communist domination in Europe, and the power of the communist leader Mao Tse-tung in China was rising rapidly. Whereas the Western European allies presented a nearly impenetrable barrier to Stalin's expansionism in Europe, there was no such alliance to challenge the rise of communism in China and Southeast Asia. When Mao Tse-tung drove Chiang Kai-Sheks's Kuomintang (KMT) Nationalist Army out of mainland China and onto Formosa (now called Taiwan) in the late 1940's, there was huge consternation in Western Europe and the United States. The total population and land mass of China and Russia dwarfed those of the United States and all of Western Europe combined.

Remnants of KMT troops were left behind on the mainland, and they migrated into neighboring Burma. President Truman had been shocked by the collapse of the KMT Army, and his administration scrambled to devise a plan to stop further Communist encroachment in the area. This was probably the most secretive CIA program ever devised to that point. The U.S. Ambassador to Burma (now called Myanmar) was not told, top State Department officials were not told, and even the CIA's own Deputy Director for Intelligence was not informed. In early 1951, unmarked C46 and C47 transport planes were seen making a minimum of five parachute drops of supplies per week to the KMT in Burma. Their leader, General Li Mi, quickly regrouped, reorganized and began rapidly expanding.

Training camps were set up and instructors were flown in from Formosa. Soon General Li had more than 4,000 well-trained, well-supplied troops under his command, and he marched north to Burma's border with China. The subsequent invasion of China was a disaster, and Li's troops suffered massive casualties. Undeterred, General Li launched a second attack which suffered similar results. The CIA's response was to redouble its efforts, and they reopened an abandoned WWII airstrip at Mong Hsat in Burma to accommodate direct supply flights from Bangkok and Formosa.

General Li flew to Formosa for a three month vacation and returned with plans to bring in 700 more troops directly from Formosa. The CIA set up a mysterious company in Bangkok—the Sea Supply Corporation—which began sending huge supplies of military equipment to Mong Hsat. These included mortars, anti-aircraft artillery bazookas, .50 calibre machine guns and brand new M-1 rifles. After a year of build-up, General Li once again launched a major offensive into China. He hoped that the peasants would rise up and support him, but such did not occur and once more, he was driven back with heavy losses. He finally realized that he was never going to succeed. He and his remaining troops turned their attention to the opium trade.

Even today, Burma [Myanmar] is the second largest producer of opium in the world (the honor of first place goes to Afghanistan). With their organization and military equipment, the KMT quickly became the *de facto* government in Eastern Burma, which was also Burma's richest opium-growing area. Soon the air strip at Mong Hsat was being used to transport opium to Bangkok and Formosa via CIA Air America cargo planes. In Bangkok, the opium was under the personal protection of the Chief of Police. The KMT continued their enormously profitable drug activities until finally, in 1961, the Burmese Army (with Chinese help) was able to drive them out. They immediately dispersed into the hills of neighboring Laos. The Burmese government sent an angry note to Washington, reporting that large quantities of American military equipment and ammunition had been left behind by the departing KMT army.

It could perhaps be claimed that the CIA knew nothing of the illegal activities of its KMT client, but as early as 1952, the *New York Times* had published an article detailing the KMT's drug activities in Burma. More damning however, was the fact that throughout this entire period, the shipments of opium to Thailand were done using CIA aircraft, and the shipments were under the protection of the commander of the Thai Police—General Phao—and General Phao was the CIA's man in Thailand. In any case, by the early 1960's the now infamous "Golden Triangle" —the intersection of Thailand, Burma, and Laos—had become the single largest opium growing region in the world. Not so coincidentally, General Phao had become the most powerful man in Thailand.

The political situation had changed rapidly in the region, and when the French Army was defeated at Dien Bien Phu in 1954, the feared communist threat became ever stronger. The United Nations declared Burma, Thailand, and Laos to be neutral and 'temporarily' divided

Vietnam into North and South at the 17th parallel. Starting with the Eisenhower Administration, the United States lavished its support on South Vietnam's fraudulently 'elected' President Ngo Dinh Diem, and sent U.S. 'advisory personnel' to South Vietnam to ensure there was no encroachment by the North. As the tension between North and South grew more intense and more hostile, the ability to control Laos became more and more of an issue for both sides. The 'Laotian people' could more accurately be described as a collection of tribes rather than as a quasi-unified nation. On the Vietnam side of Laos [the East], the tribes have always considered themselves as part of North Vietnam, and the Hmong tribes in the West see little distinction between themselves and the Hmong tribes on the other side of the Mekong river in Thailand.

The North Vietnamese had the advantage in trying to control Laos, however. The zealotry of their communist philosophy was attractive, and they were experts at organization. They quickly formed and organized the Pathet Lao into an effective guerilla organization, which began to infiltrate the entire country. In response, the CIA recruited the top-ranking officer of the Royal Laotian Army, General Vang Pao and gave him the funds to recruit Hmong tribesmen to fight the Pathet Lao. The U.S. sent in teams of 'Green Berets' in civilian clothes under the guise of 'advisors', but in actuality to train the newly recruited Hmong guerillas. Both the United States and the North Vietnamese were supplying their proxy armies by massive air drops. Both China and the Soviet Union supplied the planes and the equipment for the Pathet Lao, while the US flew its own unmarked (or marked with the insignia of the Royal Laotian Air Force) planes, and supplied American-made equipment to General Vang and his guerilla army.

The violations of Laos's neutrality became so blatant that in 1962, the UN demanded that both sides withdraw all foreign (non-Laotian) troops through UN staffed checkpoints. The US withdrew the majority of its personnel (666) through the checkpoints. The North Vietnamese withdrew exactly 40, leaving an estimated 10,000 behind.

At this point, the CIA introduced one of its most colorful—and effective—recruits into the mix. William Young, born in 1934, was the son of a Baptist missionary. Bill's grandfather, the Reverend William Marcus Young, had arrived in Kengtung in northern Burma in the 1880's to do missionary work there. The missionary tradition was carried on by his son Harold (Bill's father) who was recruited into the CIA to spy on activities in Southern China. The CIA is big on missionaries. They are local, they are respected, and they know the terrain, the languages and the culture.

After Bill had served a tour with the U.S. Army in Germany, he was recruited by the CIA and posted first to Bangkok and then to the northern Thai city of Chiang Mai. In 1962, he was sent to Laos to interface with General Vang, and to find a suitable place for a major airstrip. He discovered a hidden valley southwest of the strategic Plain of Jars in the Long Tieng Valley (also spelled Long Chieng, Long Chen or Long Cheng) and construction was started. By 1964, a 4,200 foot paved runway had been constructed and a nearby town had sprung up which grew to a size of 30,000 inhabitants. It had bars, noodle shops, prostitutes, and Hmong who cobbled shoes, repaired radios, tailored clothes, ran a military taxi service, and served as interpreters for American pilots and crewmen. It was also known as "the most secret place on earth." It appeared on no maps and even its name was highly classified.

It had taken me the better part of two days to sift through all this material, and I was getting more and more nervous about it. I was clearly going into an area rife with drug traffickers and those guys play rough. If I got into trouble when I was in Thailand, I couldn't expect any help, because the Chief of Police, General Phao, ran the whole drug trafficking industry in Thailand. After thinking about it for a while, I sent an urgent cable to General Carroll requesting that two diplomatic passports with accompanying State Department authentication documents be sent to me by overnight diplomatic courier. I further requested that the passports be issued in two different names—neither one of them mine. State was going to scream their heads off when they got the request but they had no choice but to comply.

I called Mr. Teng in Paris to inform him that I had gone through the briefing materials that I had been furnished, but had requested some other material which I expected to receive the next morning. I asked him if he would contact General Vang to see if perhaps we could meet in Thailand sometime late next week. I told Mr. Teng that as soon as I received word back from him, I would make the necessary travel arrangements and meet with him the evening before my departure from Paris. I then locked up the office and went to see if I could find Martin.

Over drinks in his office, I told Martin that I was leaving sometime next week to meet with one of his colleagues in Thailand, but that I was not at all comfortable with it. I told him that I had requested two U.S. diplomatic passports in two names other than my own and that they were supposed to be delivered to him by diplomatic courier the next morning, and to please get someone to call me from 'American Express' to tell me that I had a package waiting. I expressed my very considerable discomfort about making this trip because, with the drug culture permeating the highest levels of law enforcement in Thailand, I really had nobody to turn to if I got in trouble.

Martin just sighed and said, "Bertie, I'm sorry to say that I don't think there is a damn thing I can do to help you. Good luck, my friend." I drove home in a foul mood.

Bangkok Briefly

I called Pierre to see if he wanted to get together over the weekend but he begged off, citing family obligations. Although we had talked several times since my return from Stockholm, we hadn't seen each other once, and I was starting to get a bad feeling about it, but this was no time to be confrontational.

The next morning, I packed my small gym bag and drove into the safe house to pick up my new passports. I then drove straight to the airport and caught the next plane for Paris. I wanted to get this over with. I called and left word for Mr. Teng that he could reach me on my Paris number, and then went out to do a little shopping. I didn't want to keep having to haul clothes and my shaving kit back and forth between Geneva and Paris, so I bought some clothes, kitchen and bathroom supplies, another shaving kit, extra towels, etc. After stocking up the bar and the pantry, my Paris apartment started to feel like home.

Mr. Teng called Tuesday morning and said that General Vang would like to meet with me on Friday at the Udorn Air Force Base if that would be suitable. I said that I had hoped to meet him at the American Embassy in Bangkok, but Mr. Teng assured me that would not be possible. He gave me the address of a Thai restaurant, and asked if we might meet there for dinner around 8:00—he would explain everything then. I agreed, but I was getting more and more uncomfortable with this whole set-up. Did Teng know about the secret war in Laos? I had no idea how freely I might be able to talk to him, so decided that I would not bring up the subject of Laos at all.

Over a wonderful Thai dinner, Mr. Teng told me that General Vang was apparently engaged in some very dangerous work for the U.S. government, and did not feel safe traveling among the civilian population of Thailand. He had already made security arrangement at the Udorn Air Force base and could not possibly change them on short notice. We began to talk about more general matters, and I brought up the fact that I had been surprised to learn that there was so much opium trafficking in the area. This drew a very sharp look from Lo (Mr. Teng had insisted that I call him by his given name) who quickly changed the subject, and asked when I intended to fly out to Thailand. I told him that I would probably leave on Thursday. The next day (Wednesday), I boarded a plane for Bangkok. I didn't feel comfortable sharing my travel plans with anyone.

It was evening when I arrived, and I took a taxi to the American Embassy, which, of course was closed. I showed the Marine at the gate one of my diplomatic passports.

He examined it closely and said, "I'm sorry, sir. I wasn't notified that there would be an arriving diplomat. Let me call the night duty officer. I'll take you right to him."

The night duty officer hurriedly looked through the papers on his desk, then looked at me, then looked at the passport more closely, then asked if I had any supporting papers, which I gave him. He examined them with equal care, and then handed everything back to me saying, "These are perfectly in order sir, and even though they were issued only last week, there was plenty of time to notify us of your arrival. There's been a bad communications breakdown somewhere. Ambassador Martin is going to be furious that he wasn't here to meet you, but he is attending a diplomatic function in the city, and probably won't be back until quite late. I can get his security detail on the radio sir. Shall I call them and tell them to notify the Ambassador of your arrival?"

I told him that the Ambassador had not been notified because I was in Thailand on a covert mission and it was deemed advisable not to have any official cable traffic mentioning it. "You will of course log me in, but the Ambassador might not want to read that log in the morning to preserve his honest deniability of any knowledge of my presence. I would like to have an Embassy car take me to the Don Muang Royal Thai Air Force base in the morning and I would like to leave here around 5:00 a.m., well before the time I imagine Ambassador Martin begins conducting official business. The Embassy will not see me again after my departure tomorrow. I know the kitchen is probably closed but do you think somebody could rustle up something for me to eat? I know I'm asking a lot but could you also show me to one of the guest rooms and make sure somebody wakes me at 4:30 tomorrow morning?" I asked.

The night duty officer made a quick, quiet phone call and then surprised me by rising from behind his desk, snapping to attention, and giving me a smart salute with a big grin on his face. "I of course know better than to ask sir," he said. "But I'd put some strong money on a bet that you are one of ours, sir. Even though you are out of uniform, you look like a marine, you carry yourself like a marine, but more than anything else, you have the command voice of a high-ranking marine officer. I can't leave my duty post sir, but I've phoned for one of our house boys to come right away to show you to your room and get you a meal. If there's absolutely anything else you need, just pick up the phone beside your bed and dial 'zero' for the operator. It will ring straight through to me, sir. Your car will be waiting for you at precisely 0500 hours tomorrow sir. Your driver will be armed."

He hadn't finished speaking when we both heard the gentle slap of flip-flops scurrying down the hall and a middle-aged Thai emerged from the darkened hallway, introduced himself as 'Sam' and grabbed for my gym bag. I made it clear that I would carry it myself and the grin on the duty officer's face broadened to Cheshire cat proportions. We bade each other warm 'Good Evenings.'

The 40 kilometer trip from the Embassy to Don Muang was uneventful until we were stopped at the gate. I gave the Thai guard my *other* diplomatic passport and told him that I would like to be driven to the office of the commander of the U.S. forces. He looked at my passport and papers, saw that the car was an official U.S. Embassy car, and disappeared back into the guard shack and got on the phone. After a very animated discussion with somebody, he came back to the car, said that a jeep would pick me up, and told the driver of my car that he was not authorized to enter. I got out of the car, and my driver saluted me and left.

The guard was just opening the gate for me to enter when a jeep with U.S. markings screeched to a halt and the Air Force MP driving it ordered me in. The Colonel who was in command of the U.S. presence on the base (I don't remember his name so I'll just call him Col. Smith) was apoplectic. He demanded to know who the f---I was and what I was doing on his f------ air base.

When I replied mildly that I needed a ride to Udorn, I honestly thought he was going to burst a blood vessel. When his screaming attenuated to the point where he could make himself understood, he made it clear that 'his' air base was not running an air taxi service for itinerant State Department diplomats.

I asked him if he had a secure phone at his disposal. He said that he did not—all of his secure communications were by cable. At least the question calmed him down enough to pay attention. I told him that I was on a highly covert mission, and the only people who could confirm it were President Johnson, Secretaries Rusk and McNamara, the Director of the CIA and the Director of the DIA. I asked which one of them he wanted me to cable. He looked at me in disbelief, and ordered everybody out of the room.

He said, "In the Navy, we have a strict chain of command. Going outside it can get you into a whole heap of trouble. You're asking me to go so far outside it I could probably get court-martialed, but if you're really dealing on a level that high, write down the answer to this question. He scribbled something on a piece of paper and handed it to me.

The question was, 'Give me the name of a high-ranking officer in Laos that might be known to some of the people you just mentioned.' I smiled and immediately wrote 'General Vang Pao' and handed it back to him.

His hand was shaking when he burned the paper in his ash tray. "Jesus, God," he said. "No offense sir, but I'd like to get you off this airbase as quickly as possible. Do you want me to contact my counterpart at Udorn and tell him you're coming?"

"I'd be grateful," I replied. "When do you think I can catch a plane out of here?"

"I'm going to order somebody to fly you up there right now," he replied. "You ought to be airborne within 30 minutes. Now, if you'll excuse me, I need to talk with my staff sergeant for a couple of minutes, to make arrangements, you know. There's a comfortable sitting area just outside, and he'll take you to your plane. Nice to have met you, sir. I hope you'll forgive my earlier outburst?"

I shook his outstretched hand and asked, "What outburst, Colonel? I can't recall that you had one."

It had been quite warm when I arrived in Bangkok the previous evening, even though the sun had set. It hadn't been exactly cool, but it was comfortable when we left for Don Muang at 5:00 this morning, but the weather had warmed up quickly. It was damned hot when we took off. The cool temperatures at 20,000 feet had kept our flight quite comfortable, but when we taxied to a stop at Udorn and I opened the door to get out, the heat and humidity hit me like a hammer. So far, I had seen almost nothing of Thailand, but had been impressed by the lushness of it as we flew northeast. Even so, the ambient air, temperature augmented by the heat bouncing off the tarmac at the airport, was so overwhelming, I remember thinking, "God, I hope I never have to come back to this country."

A jeep rushed up driven by a sergeant whose uniform was drenched with sweat. "Hop in, sir," he said. "I'll take you right to the Colonel. He's expecting you."

I can't remember that Colonel's name either, so I'll just call him Colonel Jones. He greeted me brusquely but civilly. "I got a call from Col. Smith down at Don Muang saying you were on your way," he said. "Given his report, I can't say that I'm all that happy to have you here. How long do you intend to stay and what do you want from me?"

I tried to answer his questions in turn. "I hope to fly out either tomorrow evening or Saturday morning. All I know is that I am supposed to meet with a certain Laotian General here tomorrow. I don't know how long the meeting will take, but I'd be grateful if you could supply us with a secure meeting room or if not, perhaps you could take us to the most isolated part of the airbase you have, and he and I can meet there," I replied.

"So Vang's coming in tomorrow," he mused. "Well, he knows where my conference room is. I don't know what you're going to do between now and then, though. We don't have much entertainment here on the base, but if there are any Air America girls at the bar, maybe you can get lucky. I'll write you a base pass good through Saturday so you can move around the base if you want, and use the Officers' Club. The sergeant will run you over to the BOQ (Bachelor Officers' Quarters). There's a lockable closet in your room. Don't forget to replace the key in the lock when you leave. One last word. Watch your step. These guys operate daily in what is probably the most dangerous place on earth. They're tough and they're mean. Stay out of trouble."

There was a fan in my room, but it didn't do much more than just move the hot air around. A cold shower felt good, and I dressed in the loose clothes I had brought with me. My previous trip to Vietnam had taught me why the Viet peasants always dress in loose 'pajamas.' You stay much cooler that way. It seems counter-intuitive to wear long sleeves and pants in the searing heat, but it is actually much cooler than having the sun beat on bare skin. My trousers were unfortunately a little short (I think they'd shrunk in the wash) so I strapped Excalibur on the underside of my left wrist and far enough up towards my elbow that it couldn't be seen, then wandered over to the Officers' Club.

The noise level was overwhelming, but I found a place at the bar and ordered a sandwich and a beer. I hadn't eaten since the previous evening and I was really hungry. The guy on my right kept glancing at me, and when I got through with my sandwich he said, "You're new around here, aren't you? I don't think I've seen you before. What unit are you attached to? Incidentally, my name's Frank."

"I'm a civilian, actually, and am just here for a meeting tomorrow and then I'm gone," I answered. I gave him the name that was on the diplomatic passport I'd flown in on this morning.

"Ah, so you're the mystery man that got flown up here from Don Muang this morning. You must pull a lot of weight somewhere. There aren't too many civilians that get allowed onto these bases, and certainly not ones that get air taxi service." (Clearly, the 'grapevine' on this base was in full functioning order.)
"This your first time in Thailand?" he asked

When I told him it was, he said he didn't have anything to do until he flew out in the morning, and asked if I'd like to see some of the surrounding countryside. He said he knew a little Thai restaurant where we could stop for supper on the way back. "Besides good food, there are usually a few cuties wandering around in there too," he added. I told him I thought it would be great, and he asked me to stay put while he found a buddy of his who was wandering around somewhere in the Club. "I don't know if he'll want to go or not but he'll be pissed if I don't ask him," he added.

A Visit to the Countryside

His friend introduced himself simply as Jim, and observed that it would be good to get a little fresh air and to get off this God-forsaken base. We went outside and 'borrowed' the first jeep we found. I sat up front next to Frank, and Jim sat behind Frank in the rear. I don't think the two Thai guards even looked up as we roared through the exit gate. They seemed totally absorbed in some board game that they were playing. Frank drove over the miserable roads as if he was trying to get somewhere, rather than idly enjoying the countryside, and I was starting to get uncomfortable. That old prickly feeling that I had learned to trust was growing ever stronger.

After about 15 minutes, I asked Frank where the hell we were going, but it was Jim that replied, "Sorry to do this to you, pal but Vang's got to learn that he reports through us whether he likes it or not."

I turned to look at Jim and saw a .45 calibre automatic pointed directly at my spine. "Don't kid yourself by thinking that I'm not going to do this, because if you die, Vang will stop the ground war again. He may do it, but it won't be for long. He's making a fortune out of opium smuggling and he needs that airbase at Long Tieng. Besides, he needs to be taught a lesson about who is really running the show," he added.

The bullet ripped through the muscle of my right thigh as I threw myself sideways at Frank. At the same time that Excalibur was sliding through his ribs, I grabbed the steering wheel and yanked it as far to the right as it would go. The combination of the violently abrupt change in direction, along with the sudden deceleration was enough to fling Jim out of the jeep. To stop the jeep from turning over, I pushed the steering wheel back hard left and pushed Frank's body out. I moved behind the wheel, down-shifted and floored it. I wove back and forth over the miserable rural road hoping that Jim would find it more difficult to hit me but I never heard a shot. When I stopped after a few minutes, I was out of sight and way out of range of the .45 but facing a real dilemma. This road was leading me away from the base and the only alternative I could see was to turn around and go back. I turned the jeep around then pulled off the road.

I had something else to attend to first. I eased my pants down to assess the damage to my thigh. The bullet had passed laterally not too far under the skin from the entry wound just below my hip, to the exit wound above and to the right of my knee—a distance of about a foot and a half. It had bled pretty copiously, but the bullet didn't appear to have hit anything major. Unfortunately, both the entry and exit wounds were starting to clot, and I was going to have to do something about that. There was bound to be some material from my pants leg that the bullet had pushed in there, and with the wound closed at both ends, it would start to suppurate quickly.

I unscrewed the cap on Excalibur and took out my sewing kit, and the small packet of antiseptic powder. I then sliced my leg open down to the wound over its entire foot and a half-length, laid the wound open, and sprinkled in the powder. It stung like hell, but I thought that if I could just keep the flies out of it while I was sewing it back up, I might avoid infection. After I finished sewing, I cut off the bottom half of the pants leg and used my belt to secure it around the wound. As almost everyone who's been wounded in battle knows, the shock of the wound often (initially) keeps you from feeling much pain, both physically and emotionally. I'm sure that shock buffer helped me from feeling the full pain impact of slicing my own leg open, but nevertheless, it was tough to take.

Now came the really hard part. I was going to have to drive back and face Jim and his .45. I drove slowly and as quietly as I could until I could just see Frank's body on the side of the road. I saw Jim lying on the side of the road a little farther away, but curiously, he wasn't looking in my direction. It had to be a trap. I waited for another five minutes but he still didn't move. The damn flies were driving me crazy and I was looking around in the jeep to see if there was anything I could use to shoo them off, when I saw it. The .45 was on the floor in the back! Jim had dropped it. I picked it up carefully—the safety was still off—and put it on the seat beside me, and then drove back at full speed.

Frank had bled to death, which is a miserable way to die, but I don't think Jim had felt a thing. He must have landed on his head, because his head was lying on his right shoulder at an impossible angle. It dangled uselessly as I dragged his body into the back of the jeep. I heaped Frank on top of him, and started back. Although we had taken a fairly torturous route, I had learned the hard way to pay close attention to the roads being taken when I was being driven around. I did well for the first four or five turns but then became totally lost on the outskirts of a little village that I was sure I hadn't seen before.

I drove in and as soon as I saw an adult—children were everywhere—I stopped, got out of the jeep. I bowed my head with my palms pressed together in the traditional *wai* greeting, smiled, and with my shoulders hunched and my palms up in a gesture of being lost, extended my arms like airplane wings and made my best airplane sound. The lady smiled and was about to gesture when she was stopped dead by the sounds of children screaming in terror and running madly away from my jeep. Kids explore everything and my jeep was a magnet of attraction. The gruesome sight of the two dead bodies in the back was more than sufficient to quell their curiosity, however. I thought I better get out before farmers came with pitchforks or something.

I drove semi-aimlessly for a half hour. I was convinced that the air base had to be in *that* direction but there were no road signs, and even if there had been, they would have been in Thai, which I couldn't read. My gas gauge was starting to get dangerously low, and I could only hope that there was some gas in the jerry can strapped to the back. The thought of spending the night, out of gas and totally lost, with a bleeding leg and two dead bodies in the back of the jeep terrified me. All I could do was to take roads that seemed to lead in the general direction of where I thought Udorn should be located.

I was saved by the sound of actual airplane engines. I couldn't see the planes, but I could dimly hear them and I did indeed seem to be driving in the right general direction. It took another half hour, and I was running on the fumes in the gas tank when I pulled up to the Udorn entry gates. Exiting Udorn was one thing but entering was entirely another. I fished around in my pocket for my base pass and in fact found it, but I should have put it in my left pocket. Coming out of my right pocket, it was so soaked with blood that it was entirely illegible. This was going to be a really, really bad scene. The two dead bodies didn't help any.

Base Security (Air Force Military Police) showed up, jerked me out of the jeep, patted me down, but the idiots never checked my arms since they had handcuffed them behind my back. Two ambulances showed up, and Frank and Jim got one of their last rides. I got smacked around pretty good until Colonel Jones showed up. He had a hurried conference with the Captain of the MPs, who then unlocked my handcuffs and quickly left with the rest of his thugs. I think the Colonel completely exhausted his litany of scatological descriptive adjectives (delivered at the top of his lungs) before he told me to get into his God-damn jeep. It was a relief to sit down since the MPs had not only used their batons to professionally punch me repeatedly in the solar plexus, but had also demonstrated their displeasure by blows to my back, neck and particularly, to the wound on my right thigh, which was now bleeding so badly I was beginning to feel distinctly woozy.

Staff at the base hospital was great. I remember their professional comfort and care to this day. They complied with my request that the sheathed knife be left by my side, and that I was not to be given any general anesthesia. I simply had to stay awake no matter what. They cleaned me up thoroughly and put me on an IV drip to replace lost fluids before the surgeon came in to look at my leg. He looked at my stitches and said, "Well, whoever you are, you do a pretty good job at stitching, but I'm going to have to take them all out, clean out your wound, and do a bit better job of stitching you back up. If you insist on no general anesthesia, I'll give you a topical anesthetic but I'm sure you know it's going to hurt like hell anyway and when it wears off in an hour or two, you're going to be in a *world* of hurt. You sure you don't want general?"

I thanked him, told him I was sure and asked him to just get on with it. He was right about the hurt down to the last detail. All the anesthetic had worn off when they transferred me to a hospital bed, and my leg felt like it was literally on fire. The staff was good though. When they transferred me onto my hospital bed they asked what I wanted to do with my knife, and I told them to put it under the small of my back with the haft pointed towards my right side and sticking far enough out so that I could reach it if I had to. They did but somebody said, "Whoever you are man, you're sick in your head. You know that?"

I told him to shut the fuck up and get out.

I dozed on and off but the pain mostly kept me awake. Shortly after daylight, there was a perfunctory knock on my door, and a white-coated physician walked in and stopped dead as we stared at each other. "Oh my God! It's you again, isn't it?" he asked.

"Well I'm delighted to see you again as well, doctor," I remarked dryly. "Are you just visiting or have you transferred here from Bien Hoa where I believe we last met? I do apologize for always seeming to be in the supine position when we have these little get-togethers. Do tell me how you've been," I added. Before he could answer I said, "I *would* like to stay and chat but I really must get over to see Col. Jones. Since I can't go wearing a hospital gown, I'm afraid that once again I'm going to have to trouble you for some clothes, and I'd like to borrow a good sturdy cane as well, if you don't mind." Without a word, he turned on his heel and left.

About 15 minutes later, an orderly showed up and smilingly told me, "Man, you sure know how to get under Dr. Roberts' skin. I don't think I've ever seen him that mad. Anyway, I want to change the dressing on your wound, then I'll help you get up and get these surgical scrubs on. Just leave them in your room when you get your regular clothes on. Dr. Roberts told me not to give you any pain medication but I've got some aspirin you can take if you'd like." I thanked him and took a couple.

Vang's Complaint

Col. Jones was grim when I sat down in his office. "O.K. Let's have your story," he said.

146

After I finished he sighed and said, "Yeah. That checks out. There's one bullet hole in the back of the front passenger seat, the .45 was issued to Jim, and one shot's been fired. We found the spent bullet in the dashboard pretty much in front of your seat. The docs over at the infirmary confirmed your wound was caused by a bullet. The bruises on Jim are consistent with having been thrown from a moving vehicle. I guess you're in the clear legally, but I suppose you know what agency those two were working for."

I told him I didn't *know* but I could sure guess.

"Your guess would be absolutely right," he said "and these guys look after their own. Although I'm assigning you an armed guard, I can tell you for a fact that you're not safe on this base. I understand that you've got personal access to the director of the agency these guys worked for, and when you get back to wherever in the hell you came from, you better give him a personal report. If he doesn't stop them, these guys will hunt you down and kill you no matter where in the world you are.

"Vang's here—he's in the conference room down the hall. If I were you, I wouldn't stand on ceremony and get better dressed before you see him. He won't care what you're wearing, and he's been briefed on what happened yesterday. Report back here to my office when you two have finished and I'll get my sergeant to drive you and your guard over to your room in the BOQ. Again, if I were you, I wouldn't bother getting dressed. Your best bet would be to just grab your things and get off this base as quickly as you can. I'll call Col. Smith and have him meet you with an armed guard there as well. You'll be a lot safer there than here. They have a few guys from the agency on the base down there, but nothing like the crowd we've got here. Oh yeah, one last thing. Did you really make a foot and a half long slice along the bullet trajectory in your own leg, disinfect the wound, and then sew the whole thing back up?"

"Yeah," I said. "Hurt like hell too, but it seemed like a good idea at the time."

I could hear voices in the conference room but they fell immediately silent when I knocked. When I opened the door, everyone stood up and though I couldn't recognize the rank insignia, there was no question which one was General Vang. He was only about 5'7" tall, but his command bearing was unmistakable. He was partially bald, brown as a nut, and I don't believe there was even an ounce of fat on that hard, lean body. He was smiling with his mouth but his eyes were hard as steel. There was no question that this was one tough character, and that he probably richly deserved the comment that was often made about him—'Vang doesn't take orders from *anybody*.'

As the others left, we shook hands across the table, and before I could say anything, he said, "I have been told of your experiences of yesterday. Our mutual friend in Paris told me that you were a man of great honor. I will tell him that you are also a formidable warrior." He paused a moment and reflected, "It's odd. That doesn't sound right in English. It sounds much better in

French." We carried out the rest of our conversation in French, but I'll report it in English.

I told him in no uncertain terms that I was here to listen to his request, and to transmit them to the appropriate people in Washington but that I had no influence on, nor indeed any interest in, whether his requests were acted upon favorably or not. I told him that if whatever request he wanted to make had already been transmitted to Washington through the normal channels, he would be given proof that the request had been reviewed and denied. If his request had not been received, then the appropriate people would be advised not to let such a circumstance happen again. In any case, I would never, ever play this role of messenger boy again.

I thought he would explode at such a cold, blunt recitation. His temper was legendary. He surprised me by ignoring it, and quite mildly but very clearly describing the problems he was facing. He explained that his troops were badly outnumbered by the Pathet Lao, and the extensive training that the Pathet Lao troops had received from North Vietnam made them more effective on the ground. Our superior air power, equipment, and ability to keep his troops well supplied evened the playing field during the day but the Pathet Lao ruled the night. Using their superior manpower, they were able to overrun his outposts at night, and he was constantly losing both men and territory to these raids. Our superior air power was essentially useless at night. It was a war of attrition and he was losing it. He said he had constantly begged for night vision equipment, which both his men and our pilots could employ to stop, and even reverse the constant night-time encroachment of the Pathet Lao, but he was always told that Washington had refused his request. He didn't believe it, and felt that his requests never got any further than the local commanders. He gave me a list he had prepared, which set out the quantity and types of night vision equipment he was asking for. I was impressed. It was a detailed list which even included the specific U.S. military item identification number for each type of equipment.

He said he had hoped to take me back to Long Tieng to show me the operations there, but with the condition of my leg and after what had happened yesterday, it would not be advisable right now, but surely the next time. Although I told him firmly there would be no 'next time,' he just smiled and said, "We will get along well together, you and I."

I returned his smile, shook his hand and said I needed to be getting along.

Col. Smith and an armed MP met my plane when we arrived at Don Muang. He said he was taking me over to the hospital so I could shower and shave, and that they would re-dress my wound with a dry bandage. He asked me where I wanted to go afterwards. I told him I needed to get to the civilian airport in Bangkok, and he said his driver would take me. I felt much better after a shower and a shave, and the shower had given me a chance to finally re-hydrate myself. I had been reluctant to drink anything at Udorn, but I figured the shower water here was surely not poisoned so I just opened my mouth and gulped it down. After I had gotten a dry bandage on my wound, I got dressed, but left my shoes (which, along with the contents of my pants pockets, had been delivered to my room when I was meeting with Vang) because the right shoe was full of clotted blood. The sneakers I had packed would have to do.

At the airport, I found that the next flight to Paris wouldn't board for an hour and a half, which was just perfect. I hadn't had any food for more than 24 hours and I was famished, and the airport was full of small restaurants and cafés. Back in those days, airlines always fed you on the plane as well, so I was exhausted but stuffed by the time we landed in Paris. I took a cab straight to my apartment and collapsed.

When I woke up the next morning, I knew I had problems. During the night, my leg had bled all over the place and it hurt like hell. I needed some real medical help, but if I were to show up at a hospital like this, there were going to be some very awkward questions asked, and the French police would surely get involved. That would be a disaster. I cleaned up the best I could, and put on a dark pair of slacks so new blood stains wouldn't be as noticeable, limped outside, and caught a cab to the American Embassy.

When I showed the Marine guard my diplomatic passport and told him I needed a wheelchair, he was genuinely concerned, and one quickly appeared. I told the Marine who was pushing the chair that I needed to use the secure phone to Washington, and he said, "Sir, even with your diplomatic passport, you'll need an authorization code to use that phone."

I told him I had one, and would give it to the communications duty officer. The Paris Embassy had a continuously open secure line to Washington, and I immediately gave the Washington operator General Carroll's number only to learn from whoever answered that he was giving a speech (at the Air Force Academy, if I remember correctly) but could be interrupted if it were an urgent matter of national security. I told him it was not, but to please tell the General that Bertie Mac had returned from his mission.

I had better luck with John McCone. He said, "Give me your version of what happened, Bertie." After I had done so, he said, "I'm really sorry, Bertie. I'm telling you personally that no such operation was ever authorized and that I'm very upset about it. I think we probably need to reshuffle our staff out there. I'll make it personally known that the next one of my employees who so much as touches a hair on your head will regret it for the rest of his or her short life. Now, how bad is your wound?"

I told him I needed to get to a hospital, but was afraid that on seeing the type of wound, questions were going to be asked and that the police would almost certainly get involved.

He said, "I'll take care of that. Let me speak to the Embassy's communications duty officer for a minute. Take care of yourself. I'll make sure somebody from the Embassy gives us a daily progress report. Incidentally, what name are you using?" I told him, and opened the door and called for the duty officer.

I told him I had John McCone on the phone and that John wanted to speak to him. His face was as white as a sheet when he closed the door.

Whatever McCone said, it sure worked. I was being wheeled out to the front door just as an Embassy limo screeched to a halt. Two Marines lifted me out of the wheelchair and into the back seat. I don't remember much of the fairly short trip to the American Hospital (the American Hospital was founded in 1906, is privately funded and, at least at the time, had the reputation of being the best hospital in all of France). I remember white-coated orderlies lifting me out of the back of the limo and strapping me onto a gurney. Somebody else was hooking me up to an IV and another person was using a pair of scissors to cut my brand new slacks off me. I remember a guy in a surgical mask looking down at me and telling me that I had a bad infection, and had lost a lot of blood. He asked if I knew what kind of antibiotic I'd been getting.

I remember telling him that as far as I knew, nobody had given me any antibiotics and his incredulous response, "Good God, man! What were they trying to do? Kill you?"

"Probably," I mumbled; then consciousness fled.

Chapter 8 — Birth of a System

Rétablissement - Encore

I was slowly emerging from a deep, deliciously comfortable sleep but I didn't want to open my eyes just yet. It might break the spell and I wanted to enjoy it while I was so contentedly immersed in it. I had a sense of blissful well-being. I felt so relaxed, so secure, so peaceful. There was a beautifully fragrant smell in the air and it reminded me of something or somewhere, and I was dreamily trying to place it, when it suddenly came to me. Sabina had moved Emma's bed into the greenhouse! What a sweet, thoughtful thing to do. I stretched out my hand to find Emma's but couldn't find it. She'd probably gotten up to go to the bathroom or something. My beloved would be back in a moment. I smiled contentedly and fell back to sleep.

My body's next attempt at regaining consciousness was much more effective, and much more painful. This time I didn't open my eyes immediately, because I wasn't sure where I was and whether or not I was in danger. If I were, somebody might be watching me for signs of consciousness. I was in a bed someplace. I didn't seem to be restrained, but something was wrong with my right leg and it hurt like hell. I tried surreptitiously feeling around for Excalibur but I couldn't find it. That was definitely not a good sign. There was a lovely smell in the air, though. As my morphine-soaked brain slowly cleared, jumbled memories of being shot, Thailand, Vang, and Udorn began to slowly re-assemble themselves into a semi-coherent sequence.

Suddenly, I had an appalling thought. I still had Vang's request for night vision equipment that I was supposed to have passed along to Washington and I hadn't done it! Oh God! How could I have not done that?

Horrified, I sat up with a jerk and immediately regretted it. The first consequence other than the blinding pain in my head was that the nurse who had been sitting beside my bedside was so startled that when she jumped up and screamed, she also knocked over her chair in the process. The scream and the sharp bang of the overturned chair not only immensely increased the pain of what had to be the world's worst hangover, it brought in two orderlies asking the nurse—in shatteringly loud voices—what in the world was going on. Lastly, I had torn the IV out of my arm, and my ripped vein was blithely and copiously distributing its contents on anything that happened to be in the way of its journey to the floor.

The orderlies firmly and efficiently pressed my shoulders and head back onto the bed, and before I could tell them that there was something extremely urgent that I had to do right away, I felt a pinprick in my other arm and was immediately engulfed in a comforting sense of peace before the lights went out.

There's an old folk-saying that 'The third time's the charm.' Maybe it's true. It worked for me, anyway. This time, when I segued into consciousness, I remembered clearly what had happed the last time. (I also remembered some weird dream where Emma and I were sleeping in her mother's greenhouse. I couldn't make any sense at all of that, and tucked the thought away for later examination.) With my eyes still closed, I announced, "I'm awake now. I know where I am. I'm not a threat. Is there anybody in the hospital room with me who can hear me?"

I was startled to hear multiple voices confirming that I was not alone, so I opened my eyes to see a physician, a nurse and two orderlies who were 'at the ready' peering down at me. "Good morning," I croaked as cheerily as I could. "Sorry for the trouble the last time I woke up. I'm rational now, so I'm going to move my head so that I can look around. I promise not to make any sudden or threatening movements."

The source of the strange, but pleasant fragrance became clear at once. Arrangements of flowers were placed on every flat surface in the room, all with little envelopes propped up on the vases. Sunlight streamed through the blinds, but having no idea which direction the window faced, I couldn't judge if it were morning or afternoon sunlight. As I was looking around, I was simultaneously performing a mental check on my body parts, and was getting unsatisfactory feedback from two of them. My right leg was complaining mightily, and my right arm stated that its elbow was non-functioning. Neither sounded like anything I couldn't deal with, and mercifully, that nearly unbearable splitting headache from my previous waking episode seemed to have crept *almost* completely back into whatever hole in Hell it came from.

"First, what date and time is it, and second, could I please have a glass of water?" I asked. "My throat is so dry, I can barely speak."

After looking briefly at her watch for the time, the nurse answered briskly, "It is 3:47 in the afternoon on Sunday, March 14, 1965. I'll pour you a small amount of water from the carafe at your bedside. Please sip it very slowly."

The water was room temperature, but wonderfully refreshing. As I watched her pour it, I saw what my right arm had been complaining about. There was so much tape and bandaging around my IV that it would have taken industrial construction equipment to tear it out. As far as my elbow was concerned, it might as well have been in a cast. I turned to the physician and asked, "Sir, what's your opinion on when I can get out of here?"

He didn't answer but just asked, "How are you feeling?"

I told him my right leg hurt a little bit but other than that, I felt fine, and again asked when I could leave. I told him I needed to leave quickly because I had a number of urgent matters that needed to be attended to right away.

He shook his head and motioned for the others to leave the room. "Sir, I'm afraid we are going to have to keep you under observation for at least the next two days. You lost a lot of blood yesterday—not quite enough to force us to transfuse you—but your body will take at least two days to get your red cell count up to normal. Also, there was some infection starting in your wound, and we have been giving you massive amounts of antibiotics to clear it up. We need to make sure that they have done their work properly.

"Before you begin protesting, let me say that you appear to have a lot of quite important friends, both in your country and here in France. We of course recognized the names of your Secretary of State and your Secretary of Defense and of our own Maître Bernard Monod, but we can only speculate that the senders of the flowers sent by 'John', 'Joe' and 'Martin'—all sent through your Embassy here in Paris—wish to preserve some measure of anonymity. We of course wondered why. The staff was pretty unanimous, given the rank of your other senders, that the 'John' had to be John McCone, the Director of your CIA. We were stumped by your 'Joe' and 'Martin,' though. I don't suppose you would care to enlighten us?"

I just stared at him. "Ah, no. I didn't think so."

"Well, in any case, that seems to validate our understanding, vividly expressed by a trusted source, that you have a true *'tête de cochon'*—which translates perfectly to your English expression 'pig-headed'—and we are quite prepared to deal with it.

"We have a certain item in our possession which we will be glad to return to you when you leave the hospital *with our permission*. If on the other hand, you simply decamp in the middle of the night, adroitly avoiding our normal security precautions, we will send it immediately—via diplomatic pouch—to our Ambassador in Washington, with the request that he deliver it personally to your President Johnson. It's entirely up to you. Incidentally, I apologize for not addressing you by name. We have the diplomatic passport and authentication papers which you were carrying when you arrived here yesterday. We are a well-respected hospital here in Paris, and we regularly treat patients from all over the world who have diplomatic status. They come in all sorts of shapes and sizes of course, but although most are regrettably overweight and flabby, now and again we receive one that is quite trim and fit. As we have never encountered a *real* diplomat in your physical condition, and never encountered one carrying a weapon such as you were carrying, I hope you will forgive us for doubting your undeniably authentic passport and identification papers in the name of 'Dillard Bertram.' We can certainly address you as 'Dillard' if you wish. However, as we have explicit instructions from on high that your presence here is covered by the official secrets act, if you have another name you're more comfortable with, we'll be happy to accommodate you. It really doesn't matter to us. You are not even officially registered as a patient in this hospital."

I sighed and said, "Just call me Bertie."

"As you wish, Bertie," he replied. "I'm leaving now but I'll send the nurse back in to look after you and either I or one of my colleagues will be dropping in on you from time to time. Let us know if you need anything."

As he was leaving, I called out, "Excuse me sir, but could I please have the key to my apartment, which was in my pants pocket when I arrived here yesterday? There's some material in my apartment which needs to be delivered to our Embassy right away. I'll get somebody to come by and pick up the key and get the stuff to the Embassy."

I was taken aback when he replied, "We will leave the key in an envelope marked 'Bertie' at the main reception desk downstairs, where your 'somebody' can pick it up. You are not allowed to have any visitors who we don't personally know unless they have a signed authorization from your Embassy. We are running a respectable hospital here and refuse to have it used, no matter how temporarily, as a hub for other activities. Please don't misunderstand. We have no doubt, given the identities of the people who sent you flowers and messages, that you are a very honorable man deserving of a great deal of respect in matters of state. It is just that we do not wish to have such activities conducted from our hospital. We are simply not equipped to handle hordes of visitors coming and going at all hours, and our ageing switchboard is already at its limit. I hope you understand. It's truly nothing personal."

I certainly had to give them credit. They had blocked me at every turn. No wonder they had such a good reputation. Presuming their medical care was as good as their administrative efficiency (and I had no doubt that it was), their reputation as a leading hospital was well deserved indeed.

The nurse came back in and asked, "Well, Mr. Bertie. How are you feeling? Is there anything I can do for you?"

I said, "I'd like to sit up if I may, and I'd be grateful if you would bring me all those envelopes propped up on the flower vases. Oh, yes. On the subject of flowers. They are very pretty, of course, but they remind me of another place and time. Please choose the arrangement you like best, and inform the other nurses that the ones that are left are available on a first-come, first-served basis. Finally, I'm just plain 'Bertie.' What's your name?"

She said it was 'Marie' and as she was cranking me up, I told her, "Marie. Just to avoid any awkwardness or embarrassment, I'd like you to know that I speak French."

She stopped cranking up my bed for a moment and said, "I knew that, but it is very nice of you to mention it. And thank you very much for the flowers. I will enjoy my lovely bouquet, and I know the other nurses will enjoy theirs as well. I will tell Dr. Gautier that you are not at all the fearsome man he described to me. Now, let me get you just a little bit higher, and then I will go and fetch all the notes. Afterwards, if I may, I will telephone to the Head Nurse and tell her about the flowers."

The notes all pretty much said the same thing—shocked to hear of your injury; best wishes for a speedy recovery; grateful that you accepted this mission; etc. Since I had spoken directly to McCone on the secure phone in the Embassy yesterday, there was no mystery in how the others in Washington were informed so quickly, but that excluded Bernard. I wondered how he found out so fast. I'd know the answer to that question very soon, because I urgently needed to talk to him. I asked Marie if she would leave the room for a few minutes so that I could make a personal phone call, and she told me to use the call button by the bed when it was all right for her to come back in.

I dialed Bernard's private home number which he answered with a simple, *"J'écoute."* ("I am listening.")

"Bernard, it's Bertie," I began.

He immediately interrupted me with non-stop questions on how I was doing. How was I feeling? Was I in a great deal of pain? What did the doctors say? Was I comfortable, did I need anything? etc., etc.

When he finally ran out of steam enough so that I could get a word in edgewise, I thanked him for the flowers, and added that Dr. Gautier had told me that he had been advised by someone that I had a true *'tête de cochon'* and that I had some strong suspicions as to the identity of that advisor.

Bernard absolutely dissolved with laughter. He was laughing so hard he couldn't catch his breath until I finally heard him call out in a wavery voice, "Sylvie? Sylvie? Listen. Did you tell Gautier that Bertie had a *'tête de cochon'?"* He totally lost it again and I could hear Sylvie's higher pitched gales of laughter merged in with his. Finally, he shakily adopted his best, formal courtroom voice and said, "Monsieur. Everyone I have talked to in this household strongly denies giving such advice, but I will question the butler and the maid very sternly and inform you of the results immediately thereafter." He and Sylvie promptly lost it again.

When he had calmed down enough, I asked how in the world he had heard so quickly, and he instantly became serious and told me that Lo had called him yesterday and told him what had happened in Thailand. He'd immediately called my apartment, and when there was no answer, he decided that before sending someone around to bang on my door he would check the hospitals for an emergency admission of someone with my description. He said he knew lots of the senior staff at the American Hospital, and guessed that if I were going to a hospital I'd go to the best and that indeed, he had located me right away. He said that he and Sylvie were terribly upset of course, but that Lo was even more so, and said that everything was completely his fault.

I asked Bernard to tell Lo to please not be upset and that I certainly in no way blamed him for what happened. "Bernard. I've got a problem. I need to get some material to Washington urgently, and I can't do it personally because I'm a virtual prisoner here in the hospital."

He quickly interrupted, "Does it need to go out tonight?"

"Not really. Early tomorrow would be fine."

"Perfect. I'll send my personal assistant over to you first thing in the morning. She'll take care of everything, and you can trust her with your life."

I thanked him profusely and rang off. I suddenly realized with surprise that I was very tired, and rang the bell for Marie. She came in immediately, followed by five nurses who delightedly claimed the remaining flowers.

When I told Marie how tired I was, she picked up the phone and ordered my dinner, which arrived within minutes. There was a large amount of calves' liver (very rich in iron and great for red cell production), small portions of fresh vegetables, a lovely salad, fresh-baked bread, and several soft cheeses to finish with. The half bottle of red wine was a perfect accompaniment. There's hospital food—and there's French hospital food. I slept like the dead.

I woke up at 6:00 the next morning feeling completely refreshed and full of energy. There was a different nurse sitting by my bedside, and she appeared to be sound asleep, so I softly called out, "Madame? Madame? Madame?" until she woke up with a start. I bade her, *"Bonjour"* and told her I was going to ring for the orderlies to help me get into the bathroom to shave and shower. I said, "Why don't you take my temperature, pulse and blood pressure or something like that, so when they come in you'll be busy as a bee."

She kissed me on the forehead and said, "Marie told me that you are a very nice man. Thank you for saving me embarrassment."

I was propped up, comfortably ensconced in a newly made bed with fresh linens, properly shaved and showered, hair combed and enjoying the last cup of coffee after breakfast when promptly at 8:30 there was a soft knock on the door. Without waiting for it to be answered, an elegant, very attractive middle-aged woman with the quiet authority of someone who was a chief executive of a large company entered, and introduced herself to me as Carole St. Pierre, executive assistant to Maître Bernard Monod. She turned to the nurse and very politely inquired if it might be permissible for her to speak with me privately for a few minutes. The nurse didn't curtsey or anything but she left like a shot.

Carole asked if she might sit as we talked.

At my mumbled, "But of course," she pulled the nurse's chair to my bedside.

Before sitting down, she said, "First of all, I want to convey the very best personal wishes of Maître and Madame Monod for your prompt and complete recovery. They asked if it would be convenient for them to visit with you briefly around 6:00 this evening."

"It would be an honor and a pleasure."

"Thank you. I will so inform them. Maître Monod said that you had some instructions for me. I believe you have some personal papers in your apartment which you wish to deliver to the American Embassy on an urgent basis?"

"Madame St. Pierre . . ."

"Please call me Carole."

"Carole, I have some very important documents in my apartment that need to be taken to the American Embassy, and urgently transmitted by cable to John McCone, Director of the CIA. The reception desk downstairs has an envelope with my apartment key in it. Do you know the address of the apartment?"

She nodded her head, reached in her purse, and held up the envelope.

I was impressed. "Great. Now the documents in question are in a sealed envelope hidden underneath the towels in my bathroom linen closet. You won't have any problem finding the envelope, but I'm afraid the real problems will start at the Embassy. I don't think there is any way that they are going to allow you to deliver that envelope to the communications duty officer with instructions from somebody they've never heard of, named 'Bertie Mac'—to cable it 'Top Secret, Eyes Only' to John McCone. They'll think you're out of your mind. I have the authorization code that would allow it, but I simply can't give it to you. Do you have any ideas, Carole? And incidentally, please just call me Bertie."

She answered so effortlessly that I think she had already thought through the whole problem and come up with a solution. "Maître Monod knows your Ambassador Bohlen very well, and I also know his assistant very well. I'll call Ambassador Bohlen—I have his direct number—and explain the situation to him. I'm sure he will give his own authorization. He's a very busy man though, and it's quite possible that I won't be able to get through to him immediately, and if I can't, I'll call his assistant on her direct number and explain the situation. On all administrative matters, she speaks for the Ambassador. She'll know how to get the cable sent immediately. I'll get started right away, sir. Is there anything else?"

"Actually, there is and I'm quite embarrassed about it. When I woke up Saturday morning, I discovered that my wound had partially opened up during the night, and not only had the seeping blood gotten all over my bed, I couldn't stop the slow but steady leak. I'm afraid there is blood all over everything. Since I had locked all the windows as well as the door, I'm afraid it must stink in there, too. I'm deeply embarrassed, mortified actually, to have to ask you to go in there. I can't apologize enough."

She smiled, stood up and said enigmatically, "Please don't trouble yourself. I've handled much worse. I will report back to you as soon as I leave the Embassy."

She called at 10:30 to inform me that the cable had been duly sent. She also said that she had engaged a cleaning company to clean the bloodstains and 'freshen up' my apartment. She said that she had asked someone from the office to supervise their activities and to supervise the removal of my mattress, sheets and duvet, all of which were ruined. Suitable replacements had been ordered, and the cleaning company personnel would make up the new bed. There was one small rug that did not merit the effort of bloodstain removal, and it would be removed along with the mattress, etc. and a replacement had been ordered. She begged my pardon but she had also ordered a replacement for the flowers that Maître Monod had sent, as she thought that he and Madame Monod might be disappointed not to see them in my room. She would give Maître Monod my key to return to me when he and Madame visited this evening. She finished by telling me that it had been a pleasure to meet me and asked if there were anything else she could do.

I was dumfounded. This lady had first walked into my room only *two hours* ago! I was so thunderstruck that I was sputtering as I began offering my heartfelt thanks for all she had done. I expressed my absolute amazement that she could have done so much in such a short amount of time. She assured me that it was nothing at all, and she was delighted to have been of service and asked again if there were anything else I needed. I told her that if it would not be too much trouble, would she please have a copy of my apartment key made and to give it to Bernard to keep?

She assured me that it would be done, bade me a cheery 'Good Morning' and rang off.

As soon as I hung up, the phone rang again, and this time it was the personal assistant of Ambassador Bohlen. She said that the Ambassador sent his sincerest regrets not to be able to phone me personally, but he would be completely tied up in meetings until 10:00 tonight. She conveyed his sincerest wishes for a speedy recovery, etc. and said that he wanted me to know that any friend of Maître Monod was a friend of his and that I should call him personally if ever there were anything he could do for me. She gave me his private number and her own. She also said I wouldn't need my authorization code at the Embassy anymore. The Communications Department had standing orders to accept my instructions. Finally, she said that the Ambassador would like to invite me for lunch and asked if I could suggest a few dates when I might be free.

I told her I didn't have my calendar with me and asked if I might contact her later.

While I was pondering all this, the phone rang once again. This time it was Martin. He told me not to worry, old age does that sort of thing to people, but it saddened him to see what a toll advancing age was taking on me. Clearly, I could no longer move faster than a speeding bullet. He told me to turn in my cape the next time I was in his office. I ignored him and thanked him for the flowers. He told me that he had tried to get me a bouquet of Venus Flycatchers but apparently, the flower shop was all out. He then asked, "How're you feeling, old friend? I was really worried when I heard you'd been shot."

I thanked him and said that it hadn't been a very happy weekend, but now I was feeling pretty much back to normal. He said he was genuinely glad to hear it, but I should stop doing things that made him nervous. He already had enough things to worry about. When we hung up, I reflected that I had just gotten a phone call from a true friend.

Joe Carroll called to ask how I was doing. He said that the cable that I had sent this morning had caused a good deal of consternation, because it was the first time anybody had seen such a request. He said we would talk more about it later 'when I got to the office in Geneva' but that everybody, without exception, was very grateful for the job I'd done.

Somebody knocked on the door, and a delivery man came in carrying two bouquets of flowers. One was identical to the one that Marie had taken home yesterday, so I guess she thought Bernard's was the prettiest. The other was enormous, and carried an engraved card reading 'With the compliments of Ambassador Charles E. Bohlen.' My room was starting to look like a funeral parlor again and I asked the nurse if she would like to take the big bouquet home with her when she got off duty. She was ecstatic. So was I.

After lunch, Dr. Gautier came by, and I told him that I really felt fine and would be very grateful if he would release me from the hospital's care.

He unwrapped the bandages on my leg and looked closely at my wound before announcing, "It's really healing remarkably well. I think a much smaller bandage will suffice now. I also see no more signs of infection, but you will need to keep taking the antibiotics for a few more days. You certainly don't need the IV anymore, so let's take that out. I'm going to draw a blood sample and if your red cell count is close to normal range, we ought to be able to release you tomorrow morning, but I insist you remain here for one more night of observation."

I knew better than to try to argue so I just asked, "Once my IV is out and the new bandage is put on, do you have any objection to my getting up and walking around a little bit? I find it difficult to be so inactive." He said that would be acceptable but I was not to leave my room without his permission. God, this man was a tyrant.

When he left, I asked the nurse if he was that tough on all his patients, and was taken aback when she replied, "Oh, Dr. Gautier almost never personally sees any patients anymore. I think he would like to, but his duties as *Directeur* fully absorb his time."

"*Directeur? Directeur* of what?"

"Oh! You don't know? Dr. Gautier is in charge of the entire hospital."

I might have known.

I managed to work up a pretty good sweat doing push-ups, sit-ups and stretching exercises for the rest of the afternoon, but I was properly showered and scrubbed and propped up in my bed when Bernard and Sylvie came in around 6:00.

159

Sylvie surprised me greatly by rushing over, holding my face between her hands, and giving me a not-quite-motherly kiss, right on the lips. If this was normal French custom, I was all for it. She plopped down in the nurse's chair, put her elbows on the bed, and with her chin resting on the back of her folded hands said, "OK, Bertie. I want the whole story—right from the start—and don't you dare leave anything out."

Bernard had been watching this whole show with a big smile on his face, and suggested, "Sylvie, Bertie's going to be famished by the time he gets through. Why don't we all go out for dinner—Gautier says it's OK, Bertie—and he can tell us everything over a good meal."

I was delighted, when it suddenly occurred to me. I didn't have any clothes! When I'd arrived at the Emergency Room, they had cut off my slacks, probably thrown away my shoes because the right one was filled with blood, and God only knows what they had done with my underpants, shirt and undershirt. I was appalled. That's when I noticed the wide grin on both their faces as they stared at me.

As they left my room, Bernard called out over his shoulder, "Carole thinks of everything. I hope you like what she picked out of your closet and bureau drawers. Your nurse will bring in everything now. We'll be waiting for you in the reception area just down the hall."

It was a delightful dinner, and I didn't hesitate to tell them everything. Yes, it was highly classified information and they were well aware that I was committing an unforgivable security breach, but it was crucial for me to establish that our relationship was based on total, complete trust. I think Bernard knew that I was probably going to ask him to help me and certainly, if he agreed to do so, he would be incurring considerable risk. Unless he was confident that he could trust me completely, he would never agree. Like the master strategist he was, (Bernard died peacefully in his sleep in September, 1997. Sylvie followed soon after.), he maneuvered things so that the other side (me, in this case) had to move first. Life is full of risks, especially in my business, but I was comfortable with this one.

When Bernard put me in a taxi to take me back to the hospital, he cautioned me, "Listen, my friend. In case you have any ideas to the contrary, remember that Gautier still has a certain item of yours in his safe. Sleep well. Keep in touch."

It was 10:00 the next morning before all the blood tests, blood pressure checks, wound check and re-dressing, etc. were completed. There were a bunch of legal forms to sign—I think they were to release the hospital from all future responsibility—but I told them to send all that stuff to Maître Monod. I didn't want my signature on anything, and besides, I wasn't even sure in which name I should sign. Gautier came in, wordlessly shook my hand, and gave me a small, carefully wrapped package. He wished me well, turned and left.

Planning a Network

I took a cab to my apartment in a very reflective mood. Not only had I lost Emma forever, I had to face the fact that I was *never* going to be able to establish a permanent relationship with *any* woman. I was never going to have a wife, children, or a normal home life. The little cottage surrounded by a white picket fence with a loving wife and a couple of wonderful children inside—who were perfectly content with me being a nerdy particle physicist paid a subsistence salary—just wasn't going to happen. I'd made my choice of what I wanted to do and accomplish in my life, and this was one of the inescapable consequences. I was in far too deeply to turn back so it behooved me to man up and make the best of it.

It would be great if I could simply, and in a fairly detached and business-like sort of way, draw on the friendships I had with Don Moretti, Anders Dahlquist and Bernard to gather the information I sought. Their worldwide businesses and political networks already had the close relationships and trust of the most secretive and inaccessible heads of governments and governmental departments throughout the entire world. Clearly, however, I was going to have to figure out some way to reciprocate for all this information. They would all be incurring some degree of risk, and I could scarcely ask them to do that and offer nothing in return. But what? Then it struck me. They had all the contacts that I wanted, and although all of them had powerful contacts in Washington, I could open any government door in the city, up to and including that of the President himself. That seemed like a fair swap.

What I wanted to do was to operate as a classified information broker. The old "You tell me some of your secrets and I'll tell you some of mine" paradigm had worked for as long as the barter system for exchange of goods and services (and information) had existed. Either both sides come out with an acceptable swap—in which both sides feel they have gained—or a deal can't be struck, in which case neither side feels it has lost. As the information broker sitting in the middle, however, I could only gain, because both sides would have to submit their information to me (in order to protect their identities) and therefore I would gain knowledge of what both sides were offering, and the identities of the offerors. As time went on and that storehouse of knowledge increased, I would become increasingly able to identify fakes, and sanction them as such. It wouldn't take long for both sides to realize that trying to submit fake information would incur strong negative consequences. Hence, over time, it would become an information market known for the absolute purity of the goods offered. Only the price would remain to be settled between the interested parties.

Sounded good on paper, and though I had little doubt that I could enlist the participation of that mighty troika of my executive friends, the mechanics of information collection was going to take a lot more thought. This was not going to be simple, and I'd need to discuss it detail with my friends for their advice and counsel. The final mechanism would have to be one they were thoroughly comfortable with.

If I could just live long enough to set it up.

I wanted nothing to do with 'field operational intelligence.' John McCone's acerbic observation that I wasn't trained for it, and would be way out of my depth was, sadly perhaps, absolutely spot on. My recent little adventure in Thailand constituted iron-clad corroboration of my pathetic inability to cope in that area of intelligence. Even so, I had a very uncomfortable suspicion that my recent little episode would not be the last such mission I would be forced to take on. I thought it would be stupid to be forced to risk my life on some tactical mission, when I had the possibility of putting a strategic plan into operation that could have a global impact and might stay in place for decades. McCone and Carroll needed to realize that I was uniquely positioned to make that global spy plan happen. Somehow, I had to get that fact understood in Washington.

I wasn't really sure why I had come back to the apartment instead of just going straight to the airport. I guess I just wanted to see what had been done to 'freshened it up' and to make sure the stink of dried blood hadn't crept back in.

I was stunned at what Carole had done to it. Previously, even though it had a number of very large windows looking out onto the courtyard, the apartment had always seemed a little dark, due to the heavy velvet drapes that ensconced each window. They were so heavy and thick that it was impossible to draw them far enough to the side to prevent them from blocking a good portion of the light. They had vanished. In their place were beautiful, bright, colorful print replacements, which were pulled fully aside so that the light streaming through the windows was totally unobstructed. The difference in the light level in the apartment was amazing. I had an immediate reservation, though. As somber and light obstructive as the original curtains were, they did have a wonderfully useful quality. Once they were drawn, there was no way in the world that anyone could see what was happening inside the apartment. Drawing those curtains closed was like sliding a concrete wall across the inside of the windows. I guessed that Carole didn't realize that from time to time I was going to need that kind of absolute security. I shouldn't have underestimated Carole. On closer inspection of these bright, cheerful, colorful new curtains, I discovered that they were lined on the back with a sort of metallic-looking material that was just as pliable as the rest of the curtain but which admitted absolutely no light. My guess was that whatever that material was, it might go pretty far in attenuating other forms of electromagnetic radiation than just photons.

The apartment itself looked as though every square inch of it had been scrubbed, literally floor to ceiling. 'Spotless' really didn't do it justice. My bed, fresh with its new mattress, had new pillows and sheets in a pale baby blue, and was covered with a paisley-print, predominately blue duvet. My bathroom towels, washcloths, etc. were now in the same baby blue as my sheets, while the shower curtain matched my duvet. It was lovely, breath-taking even, but I wasn't entirely happy with the new look. It sure didn't look like a bachelor pad. I could only imagine what comments it might incite in someone invited to share the night with me. Well the hell with it. I'd deal with the situation when and if it arose. Right now, I just wanted to go home.

There was one other issue I had to deal with before I left. An exquisitely beautiful small bouquet of flowers stood on my bedside table, with a charming note from Bernard and Sylvie propped up on the vase. It seemed a shame to just throw them out, but I didn't know what else to do with them. I decided I'd dump them in a trash bin on the street. Rue des Bernardins is so small and narrow that there are no trash bins, and there are rarely any empty taxis cruising by, but the busy Boulevard Saint-Germain was only a short half-block from my front door. At this time of day, it would be full of lots of people, lots of traffic, lots of taxis and at least a few trash bins.

Paris seems to have more than its fair share of pretty young women, and I literally ran into one while I was rushing to hail a passing taxi. I didn't knock her down, but she definitely got a pretty good thump, and I apologized profusely for my carelessness. I held out the flowers and said, "Some friends had these sent to my apartment because I just got out of the hospital, but they obviously didn't know that I have to be out of town for several days. I really can't take them with me, but I was dreading to have to throw them away. I'd be very grateful if you would take them as part of an insufficient excuse for my clumsiness."

She took them, smiled and said, "*Merci, monsieur*. They are very pretty." She walked off without another word.

I called Martin from the airport just to tell him I was back. He told me General Carroll wanted to speak to me tomorrow, if possible, around 10:00 a.m. Geneva time. I asked him to cable Carroll that I would be 'in my office' at 10:00 tomorrow.

Before he hung up, he said, "Listen, my friend. Don't get upset if you see a light on in your house when you get there. We've been asked to keep an eye on it when you're not in town. I think they're going to install a high-tech security system and you can probably get 24-hour guard service if you want it. Frankly, at this point, I think you can get whatever the hell you ask for. Anyway, I sent Yolande out there about an hour ago, and she'll probably still be there when you arrive. You probably remember her, she was the gal that ordered your furniture and met you there when you first arrived. You'll probably see her Audi in the driveway."

I thanked him for telling me and drove home in a considerably better mood. I absolutely remembered Yolande.

I got into the safe house the next morning around 9:30 and Martin immediately waved me into his office. He of course wanted to hear every detail of what had happened in Thailand. By this time, I had it pretty well rehearsed and I got through the whole thing in about ten minutes. I asked him to catch me up on what had gone on during my absence.

"Quite a lot, actually," he said. "For starters, your office here is now permanent. McCone and Carroll both agree that they don't want you handling any classified material at home. And before you start protesting, no, they won't agree to have a big safe installed at your house. They're worried about you in transit. There's no safe way for you to carry classified material back and forth between here and your house. The other thing is that your little adventure in Thailand has had some big repercussions in the Agency. Heads have rolled and a few careers have been either ruined or sullied. It was their own fault, of course, but for those affected, knowing that doesn't make the pill any less bitter to swallow. I'm sorry to have to say this but I tell you as a friend, Bertie. Watch your back, especially when you travel. These guys play rough. Really rough. Now it's almost 10:00. Better get in the old phone booth."

Joe was both solicitous about my wound and quite complimentary. I was polite and let him finish without interruption and murmured my thanks when he was done. Then I got down to business. "Joe, I want to discuss a plan that I've partially developed but first, a couple of questions."

"Go ahead."

"First, do I understand that there will be some sort of high-tech security system installed at my house?"

"Yes. We'll secure the perimeter of the grounds with an ordinary-looking chain-link fence about six feet inside your property line to give us room to plant evergreen shrubs on the outside of the fence to conceal it. The fence will set off an alarm if anyone tries to cut it or climb it. You'll also be able to electrify the fence whenever you want. We'll install an attractive, residential-looking gate at the entrance to your driveway, but you'd pretty much need a tank to drive through it. We'll install automatic gate openers in both your cars and an intercom system for visitors to call you in the house, so you can open the gate for them. There'll be a camera disguised as a birdhouse, so you'll be able to see as well as hear the visitor. If you lock yourself out, you'll be able to enter a security code to open the gate. There'll be cameras monitoring every entrance to the main house and the guest house. There's a lot more but let's move on."

"Joe, I need a part time secretary. I don't have anybody to answer the phone when I'm out of the office or type for me, or help me with all the damn administrative tasks I'm supposed to keep up with."

"Done. We'll have to use one of Martin's existing employees who already have Top Secret clearance and then get her upgraded so she can handle the Laos material. Next."

"Whoa, whoa, whoa, Joe. She won't need that extra level of clearance. I'm going to personally pack up every scrap of material that you guys sent me and send it back to McCone via diplomatic courier. I'm never going back to Thailand again. I've damned well paid my dues—in spades! I don't want anything to do with Laos, or Vietnam, or Thailand. And I want your personal assurance that you'll never again ask me to get involved out there! Now I want to talk about my plan."

There was a long pause before he answered, "I can't give you that assurance, Bertie. You know the old saying about Vang. He trusts no one and he takes orders from no one. Well at least part of that is no longer true. He very much trusts you. I don't know if he trusts anybody else, but he definitely trusts you. The war in Laos is absolutely essential to our efforts in Vietnam, and Vang is absolutely essential to the war in Laos. If we lose Vang, we might well lose both wars.

It's as simple as that. I give you my word that I will do everything in my power to keep you from having another mission in that part of the world, but I can't guarantee it. Don't send back those documents just yet."

I thought about it and replied, "OK. But I'm telling you here and now that if you, or anybody else, ever give me a mission to go back there, I'm simply not going to obey. You can throw me in the stockade if you can find me but I'll vanish like spit on the desert sands. Now let me tell you about my plan."

It took a lot longer than I expected to explain it to him and I was surprised at his skepticism. I kept emphasizing the beauty of not having to try to penetrate hostile governments *because they already were penetrated,* and by people they knew and trusted.

He was uncomfortable with my belief that those contacts would supply reliable information to me and that the U.S. was going to have to give up something valuable in return. I pointed out that both sides would have to be satisfied that the bargain was fair before any information was swapped but he still was doubtful that it would work.

Finally, I said, "OK. I understand your hesitation and admittedly, the plan is far from fully formed. It's going to take a lot of time for me to try put everything together. I probably won't be in a position to start gathering information you want until sometime in the fall. I'll tell you when I'm ready for a test and we'll see how it works."

Joe bade me 'Good luck' and said to give him a call if I needed anything. He didn't sound too excited.

Martin wasn't too excited either when I recounted my conversation regarding a need for a secretary. He was good about it though and Madeline 'Maddie' Picard, became my new secretary/assistant and given a secure office next to mine. Maddie was a no-nonsense, extremely competent, trim, married woman with two teenage daughters and who, over time, almost became an *alter ego.*

It was a busy summer. I was saddened but not terribly surprised when John McCone resigned his post as Director of the CIA on April 28. John's increasingly pessimistic view of the situation in Vietnam was simply incompatible with Johnson's habit of surrounding himself with 'Yes-men.' John was replaced by Vice Admiral William Raborn. Raborn was a decorated WWII combat veteran, and when placed in charge of the Navy's Polaris submarine project (to use the Polaris as a mobile underwater launch pad for nuclear missiles), he delivered three *years* early and under budget. He knew nothing about the intelligence business however, was totally ineffective, and resigned 14 months later. We never spoke once.

Pierre called and invited me for dinner at his club in Geneva, where he informed me that he and Ingrid were getting married at the end of June. I was invited, but as the wedding was going to be held in Sweden at Ingrid's parent's tiny lake-side summer house, I told Pierre that for obvious reasons, I felt it best to gratefully decline. I think he knew I would, but he was relieved, anyway. Pierre would be a life-long friend and I visited with him and Ingrid frequently at their home in Geneva (they never once visited me at my house outside Aubonne). Some ten years later, Ingrid died in a freak skiing accident. Following Pierre down the mountain in a sudden snowstorm, she lost sight of him, took a wrong turn and plunged nearly 100 meters to her death. They never had children.

I don't really want to talk much about the war in Vietnam. Johnson was pumping in American men and women in the prime of their youth at a rate of more than 13,400 per *month*. Troop levels in 1965 would rise from an initial 16,300 to 184,000 by year-end. They were killed at the rate of 172 per month—2,064 for the year, and the rate would get worse—much worse.

It took more than two months to get my home security system installed. While it was being installed, the guest house was taken over by a hired Swiss security firm which not only supervised the installation of the system, but also provided two-man armed guard teams which patrolled the grounds 24/7. These guys weren't kidding either. They were all ex-Swiss Army paratroopers and looked hard as nails. I hadn't really thought about it much but had just assumed that it would take several years for the evergreen shrubs to hide the fence. Governments (and the very rich, I suppose) don't do it that way. They planted fully mature trees and inspected them on a regular basis. If one didn't look as though it was doing too well, boom! Out it went, the hole disinfected to remove any root fungus, and wham! In came the new one.

I travelled a lot that summer. I first went to Sardinia. Don Moretti listened carefully and said that he thought I was trying to go too far too fast and suggested an alternative which he thought would be easier to put in place initially, but which could possibly, over time, lead to the information exchange I wanted to implement. He asked me to work out the details with his law firm in Rome. He also said that he thought I was looking pale and a bit worn. Momma was distraught because she was convinced that I was in imminent danger of starving to death. Umberto smiled at me and said that in his considered medical opinion, nothing less than a three-week recuperation period would be required. When I surprised myself by hesitantly agreeing, I was so humiliated by the spontaneous reaction of incredulous joy that it was all I could do to keep from crying. Fortunately, everybody was so busy making arrangements that I don't think anybody noticed. Don Moretti's oldest daughter, Fiorina, flew in from Washington with her new husband, Alex Robinson, a Washington architect. He and I liked each other immediately. Don Moretti's other son-in-law, Gino (who lived nearby with the younger daughter and his two granddaughters), again let me use his souped-up Vespa to explore all the little back roads and villages. In short, it was a glorious three weeks and when I left Sardinia for Rome, I was happy, tanned, fit—and three pounds heavier.

I met with Anders on several occasions, and was not surprised that he voiced the same reservations as had Don Moretti. Additionally, he made it abundantly clear that he was totally against what the U.S. was doing in Southeast Asia. He noted, however, that he had no companies or businesses in that part of the world, but informed me very firmly that should that cease to be the case, any information from those new companies would not be included in the network.

As we got deeper and deeper into it, we came across some very difficult practical problems which had to be solved, but little by little, we came up with a plan that Anders thought would work for his organization. We had no idea how Don Moretti's far-flung empire was structured, however, so we flew to Rome and met for three entire days with the head of Don Moretti's law firm. There were a substantial number of additional difficulties that had to be worked out— particularly as some of his firms were operating in areas of the world where the governments were even more paranoid about information leaks than were the leaders of the Soviet Bloc. Serendipitously, in the process of doing all this, we discovered to our mutual astonishment that the top corporate levels of both organizations were routinely receiving information from the 'field' that had very substantial intelligence value, but were completely unaware of its potential use outside their normal corporate planning and governance. On top of that, a surprising amount of it was flowing in from subsidiaries located in countries that were close allies of the United States. The managers receiving it never gave it a thought except for its use in running the corporation's affairs. In all fairness, why would they? Anyway, talk about low-hanging fruit!

Bernard, of course, was an altogether different deal. His huge law firm did nothing but civil work. They handled no criminal cases. They were (and are) specialized in international contract law, and unless you have actually had to deal with it, it's nearly impossible to imagine how complicated it can be. For example, take a Swiss company that does corporate jet aircraft leasing. Their client might be a Belgian multinational conglomerate that wants to lease, say, a Cessna jet for the head of its Italian subsidiary. Cessnas are made in the United States, so the Swiss company will have to buy the jet in U.S. dollars, but the lease is to a Belgian company which will make monthly lease payment in Belgian Francs and the aircraft will be hangared in Italy. What language is the lease written in? If there is a dispute, which country has jurisdiction? The Swiss leasing company had to convert Swiss Francs into dollars to buy the aircraft and is getting paid in Belgian Francs, but has to keep its books in Swiss Francs. What happens if over the term of the lease, the exchange rate between Belgian and Swiss Francs changes? (And it will do so on a daily basis). What happens in the catastrophic case that one of the two currencies gets devalued with respect to the other? Get the picture?

These are the sorts of contracts that Bernard's law firm negotiated for its clients on a daily basis. Every country has its own laws and legal precedents. Except for unusual countries such as Switzerland, where a Swiss company could legally originate contracts in four different languages (German, French, English and Italian), in most counties, at least at the time, contracts had to be written in the principal language of that country, and were of course governed by the laws of that country. No wonder that Bernard's law firm was so sought after and was so successful.

I shouldn't have been surprised, as I already knew that he and General DeGaulle (who was President of France at the time) were personal friends, but it turned out that Bernard personally knew almost every Prime Minister and head of government in Europe and the Soviet Bloc. All he ever said to me was, "We'll keep our eyes and ears open for you Bertie and let you know when we come across something we think you might find interesting. Now, let's go have lunch."

I started to get a trickle of information flowing in from Anders and Don Moretti's firms (which from now on I will simply refer to as the "Firms") in mid-September, and frankly, I found it disappointing. There were lots of pretty trivial details from all over the place but nothing that would cause anyone to pay much attention. It wasn't until three or four weeks later that I began to notice recurring patterns, and once they were put together, the information was *definitely* interesting. It may not be of much interest if one department of a government wants to order a fairly large quantity of item x but when you find that two weeks later another department of that government has ordered a similar amount of item y, and a third department of the same government has issued a purchase order for item z, all of a sudden, it all comes together. *They're trying to manufacture an advanced sonar system!* That will definitely get somebody's attention in Washington.

It did, and as the trickle of incoming information became a stream and then a torrent, Maddie and I were strained to keep up with it. The problem became one not of information-gathering, but one of information processing. It's handy to have a computer background in these kinds of situations. The mid-60's well preceded the date of modern spreadsheet programs, but IBM's FORTRAN language provided a powerful way to process and analyze the information we were receiving. I worked 18-hour days, seven days a week, to get the initial version of the program going. By the end of November, my initial system was working fairly well. I needed a break.

I decided to go to Paris for a week. It was an eventful decision. Of course, I called Bernard to let him know I was in town and of course, he invited me for dinner.

Dinner with Bernard and Sylvie at their apartment was a treat, as usual, but at some point in the conversation Sylvie asked if I would like her to introduce me to the daughters of some of her friends, since I didn't seem to have any female friends my age in Paris. I gratefully declined, but she was not deterred. Over after-dinner cognac, she wheedled the story of Emma out of me.

I reluctantly told them about Emma, but I made a huge mistake when I said that since the same thing had happened once before, I no longer had any doubt that I was destined to be a life-long bachelor. I told them that I simply had to avoid getting myself into any situation where my companion might envision any sort of long term relationship. Of course, Sylvie had to know about what had happened previously, and when I started to recount how Chantal[29] and I had met, and the ever-deepening relationship which had developed, and the dinner with President

---

[29] A wonderful, beautiful French physician with whom I had become deeply involved during the Kennedy administration. See Book One.

and Mrs. Kennedy and Secretary and Mrs. McNamara, she suddenly gasped and said, "Oh, mais non! Non, non, non! Oh mon Dieu!"

I was appalled when she literally leapt up from the table and went rushing out of the room crying, and asking us to excuse her.

I was completely dumbfounded. Utterly bewildered, I turned to Bernard. His ashen face wore a look of profound shock. "Bernard, Bernard," I pleaded. "Please speak to me! Tell me what in the world is going on!"

He got up and said, "Wait here, please Bertie. Pour yourself another cognac. In fact, if you don't mind, pour one for Sylvie and me as well. We've both had quite a shock. I'll go make sure Sylvie is alright and we'll be back in a few minutes."

I suppose it *was* only a few minutes but to me it seemed like an eternity before they both reappeared.

Before she sat down, Sylvie came over to my chair, put her arms around me and kissed me on the cheek and stroked my hair. "I'm so, so sorry, Bertie. It would have been a match made in heaven." She sat down, took a sip of cognac and continued, "Chantal's parents are two of our best friends. He is a very accomplished surgeon, and she is a well-respected landscape artist. We have known and loved Chantal since she was born. When she returned to Paris after her Washington vacation in the summer of 1963, she was a changed person. Everyone wanted to know what had happened to her in Washington, but she would speak to no one about it, not her parents, not us, not her friends—absolutely no one.

"Her father was convinced that she had been physically abused and very badly traumatized by it. He was prepared to use his not inconsiderable influence in Washington to ensure that the culprit was tracked down and punished, but she finally convinced him that absolutely nothing like that had happened. She assured everyone that she had not been physically or mentally or in any other way abused, and asked that they all stop hounding her about it. She said that, quite to the contrary, it had been a very interesting vacation and that she had made some very interesting friends, and that she simply wasn't going to talk about it anymore. We definitely were convinced about the 'very interesting friends' part when she was seen sometime in the spring of the next year having lunch at a very private club with Jacqueline Kennedy. In addition, it was reported by more than one club member who 'just happened' to pass by their table, that they were so earnestly engaged in their conversation that they were almost head to head across the table. Astoundingly, they were also addressing each other as 'tu' and 'toi!' As you well know, only *very* close friends do that.

"In the meantime, she has apparently abandoned any semblance of social life. She does nothing but constantly work and study. Although she is beginning to establish an excellent professional reputation, socially she is almost a recluse. Now we know what happened—to both of you. God, what a horrible world we live in," she sobbed.

I was absolutely devastated. I seemed to do nothing but cause pain to my best friends. I got up from the table and went over to Sylvie, put my arm around her shoulders which were shaking with sobs and said, "I can't tell you how sorry I am. I hope that someday we can get together again, but I'm leaving now." I looked at Bernard and said, "I truly love you both and I'm so sorry to have ruined not only the evening but maybe our friendship as well. I'll call you tomorrow." I hadn't even gotten halfway to the door when I was grabbed by both of them.

We talked until the early hours of the morning. I was gently informed, among other things, that if I thought I could just simply walk away from our relationship that I had better think again. We were all going to work on this together. I wasn't real sure what the 'this' part was but I was happy about the 'together' part.

Sylvie wanted to know what I was going to do for Christmas and New Year and I told her I had no plans and hadn't really thought much about it. She implored me to spend Christmas with them and I politely but firmly declined. I declined for the same reason that, years before, I had declined similar invitations from Kenny O'Donnell and Jack Kennedy. I simply felt that I would be intruding on a family gathering, and I wasn't going to do it. I would have felt horribly uncomfortable and out of place.

Bernard made a different request that I did agree to, but wasn't real happy about. He said that Teng Lo blamed himself for my being wounded in Thailand and was nearly desperate to have the chance to meet with me to apologize. I thought that was crazy, but it was getting late and I was in no mood to argue, so I promised to call Teng before I went back to Geneva.

The Reemergence of Thailand

I think our non-stop sipping of cognac was making us all a bit fuzzy. I have a pretty good alcohol tolerance but as much as I love cognac, I have learned to avoid it because it not only makes me drunk, I wake up with a splitting headache the next morning. That was certainly true when I woke up around 10:00 in one of their guest bedrooms. My shoes had been shined and my shirt and pants had been neatly pressed. I was informed by the butler that Maître and Madam Monod had gone out. Declining his kind offer of breakfast and coffee, I grabbed my coat and left.

It was cold and rainy that miserable day in early December. Even after I had showered and shaved, and taken enough aspirin to attenuate my headache and feel normal enough to venture out to the neighborhood café for a light lunch washed down with lots of coffee, my mood was as bad as the weather. It certainly wasn't a walking or exploring day, and I just didn't feel like going to a museum. I decided I would just go back to the apartment and read and fulfill my promise to Bernard and call Mr. Teng. Hopefully he would be out of town.

He wasn't. He sounded truly delighted to get my call and wanted to know if I would do him the honor of having dinner with him and his wife the day after tomorrow. I figured I'd have to get it over with sooner or later, and tried the best I could to accept his invitation with an air of pleasure and anticipation. When I asked for his address, I was astonished to find that he also lived on Avenue Foch. I was even more surprised when he said that he would send his car to pick me up. I'd never even given a thought to what Mr. Teng's personal circumstances might be. Whatever they were, he certainly wasn't penurious.

The next day the weather was still nasty but now I had an enjoyable task to pursue—research. I had long ago accumulated a lot of knowledge about Vietnam, but I knew almost nothing about Thailand. Although Mr. Teng's family origins were Vietnamese, Bernard had told me that his wife's family was Thai, and I thought that before I met her, I should get a bit better educated. What little I did know about Thailand from my recent trip, I wanted to forget. Accordingly, I spent the entire day at the Bibliothèque nationale de France studying Thai history, tribes, religion, art, culture, architecture, social system, cuisine, political system, the differences between the four principal geographic areas, etc. It was fascinating, and my mental picture of Thailand was dramatically altered.

There was a small Thai restaurant on the Boulevard Saint-Germain about three blocks from my apartment, which I had passed countless times but never entered, and that's where I went for dinner. I used my newly acquired knowledge of Thai food to ask the waitress what I should order, and sent her into gales of friendly laughter trying to pronounce what was written on the menu. The meal was delicious but two rather unusual things happened.

First, the chef emerged from his kitchen to greet me, and while that's not very unusual, I had the distinct impression that it was not his ordinary habit, and that for some reason, he wanted to take a good look at me. I found nothing unusual when he inquired if I had enjoyed my meal, but found his further questions somewhat jarring. He wanted to know if this was my first time in Paris, and then if I lived in the neighborhood. Marginally, that was friendly small talk but when, after receiving two negative answers, he asked where I *did* live—he went too far. I told him I lived in Amsterdam and asked for the check.

The other strange thing was just as puzzling. The restaurant wasn't very busy, and I had the impression from the way that new arrivals were greeted by the staff, and their frequent salutations to already seated customers, that the vast majority of the patrons were 'regulars.' I was one of the few non-Orientals in the restaurant, but one of the others was a very attractive young woman who looked to be about my age, and who was seated by herself in a booth across the room from me. The strange thing was that I was sure that she was surreptitiously examining me out of the corner of her eye from time to time, but every time I turned to look at her directly, she was studiously eating her food and reading a book which was propped up on the table beside her plate. She had to know I was looking at her but she never acknowledged it. I could see that her left hand was free of any rings. Why wouldn't she look at me directly? To further complicate the puzzle, she looked vaguely familiar. I felt sure I'd seen her before but for the life of me, I couldn't think of where or when or in what context.

I walked back home absorbed in thought. I was just unlocking the outside entry door to the courtyard, when I heard a car driving down the street. Rue des Bernardins is a very old, and therefore very narrow street. As a consequence, it has very little traffic and especially not at night. I turned to look and as the late model Peugeot drove past, the hairs stood up on the back of my neck. Even though it was dark and the car passed quickly, I was sure that the driver was the girl from the restaurant. What the hell was going on? Was I being hunted again? Why? I entered my apartment very, very cautiously. It was empty. Was I making a mountain out of a molehill? Now that McCone was no longer around, did the CIA feel that his previous edict concerning me no longer mattered? As soon as I got back to Geneva, I was going to have a serious talk with Joe Carroll.

Although it was cold the next morning, it wasn't raining, but with the River Seine only a block away, it was still a damp, penetrating cold. I walked down to the library at the Sorbonne and asked the librarian if he knew of any reputable dealers in antique maps, particularly maps of Indo-China. He was a wealth of information and at the second dealer that I visited, I found a beautiful original map which had been drawn in 1683, of what was then called the Peninsula of India. It covered the entire area that we now call Thailand, Laos, Cambodia and Vietnam. It was damned expensive but I really wanted it. That afternoon, I went to a florist and picked up a lovely bouquet of flowers and was standing on the curb at the ready with my gifts when Mr. Teng's car arrived promptly at 7:00.

I'm not quite sure how to begin with the description of the Teng residence. The very first impression that I had was that the place was enormous. I couldn't even imagine how much something like this would cost here on Avenue Foch—the most exclusive and expensive address in Paris. The second thing that hit me was the light, the color, and the art. All the art was either Vietnamese or Thai and it was breathtakingly, exquisitely beautiful. I think I was probably staring in open-mouthed wonder when Mr. Teng rushed up, grabbed my right hand in both of his, and began welcoming me in an unconscious mixture of French and English. He nearly dragged me out of the entry foyer into the magnificent living room which had so stunned me and as I entered, and I saw to my astonishment that it was even bigger than I had thought. Frankly, I was overwhelmed.

Whereas Mr. Teng was dressed in a Western-style business suit, Mrs. Teng was dressed in a silk Thai Chakkri which was predominantly blue and silver, with both silver and gold threads woven in. I can't really describe a Thai Chakkri, but it is a dress style like nothing else. I can only suggest that you look it up on the web. Mr. Teng introduced her as Sunisa, and when I surprised her by greeting her with the traditional Thai *wai* greeting (a slight bow with hands pressed together in a prayer-like way and held against the chest), she was genuinely delighted.

Formalities accomplished, we sat down while the butler brought in my gifts. Another servant asked what I would like to drink, and two more servants started bringing in dish after dish of appetizers, which were first offered around and then put on the coffee table. Sunisa (I tried addressing her as Madam Teng but was quickly corrected by both of them), thanked me for the flowers, and gave them to a servant who disappeared and then brought them back in a cut crystal vase, which he placed on the coffee table. Mr. Teng (sorry, Lo), was truly intrigued by the map, so much so that after several moments Sunisa gently reminded him that he had a guest, and suggested that he could continue to examine all the details later. He blushed, thanked me profusely, and then gave the map to one of the servants in attendance with a rapid fire admonition (in Thai, I think) to (I suppose) treat it very carefully.

We chatted easily and comfortably, and when we moved into the dining room, I was beginning to genuinely like them both. After a superb but leisurely meal, we moved back into the living room for tea and to continue our conversation. I couldn't believe that I had found my meal of the previous evening so enjoyable. It didn't even belong in the same universe.

Sunisa asked if I would be visiting my family over the Christmas vacation, and when I replied that I didn't have any family and lived alone, she seemed truly shocked. "Will you be with friends, then?" she asked. She seemed really upset when I told her that all my friends would be spending time with their own families, and I wouldn't feel comfortable joining them.

She shot a quick look at Lo who immediately nodded before she continued. "Then you must come with us to Thailand and meet my family. We are not going to Thailand because of Christmas; we are Buddhists, but December and January are the very best months to visit Thailand. The monsoons are over, the weather is warm and sunny every day, the orchids and other flowers will be in full bloom, and all the countryside is lush and green. Come with us, Bertie. You must be our guest. Although we have no children, we know lots of young people about your age and of course, we know their parents as well. We can assure you that you will be in good company."

Wouldn't be good to mix with the riff-raff, I thought, but replied, "It's incredibly generous of you to offer but I'm really busy at work, and during the year-end holidays, when almost everyone else is gone, it's quiet in the office and a wonderful time to catch up. I'm sincerely touched by your offer however, and I do hope that we might be able to go together sometime in the future. Hopefully by this time next year, things will be a lot more settled, and if the offer is still open, I would love to take you up on it."

One thing I have learned about Thai women over the years is, although they may look like fragile, beautiful porcelain dolls, they can be subtly (and actually, sometimes not so subtly) tough as nails. What's hard for the inexperienced Western male to understand is that, though veiled with what appears to be extremely polite deference, inside that veiled, velvet glove, there is a fist of steel. I won't bore you with the details, but the bottom line was that when I left them that evening, I had agreed to go to Thailand with them. That decision would change my life forever—and a lot of other people's, too.

Chapter 9 — Journey to Bangkok

I almost never talk to people on airplanes. I like to use the time just to sit and think, and I was in a very reflective mood when I arrived at Geneva's Cointrin airport the next morning. I needed to try to make some sense of what was going on in my life.

On the intelligence gathering side, things looked promising. As new as it was, the system I had designed was already beginning to produce worthwhile results, and it appeared that it was on the right track to keep improving. (It was and it did. So much so that it wouldn't be appropriate to talk about it much further. It has become the core and the basis of a vastly more sophisticated system in active use today.) Its promise pleased me for a couple of reasons. First, although I had been sent to Geneva to establish an intelligence gathering network, I'm fairly sure no one expected me to succeed. I think that Johnson had agreed to the present arrangements simply because it kept me under his thumb and out of his hair. Geneva would be a convenient parking place for me. I had refused to work for the Defense Department on ways to win a bogus, immoral and unwinnable war but I had to be assigned *somewhere*.

I originally thought I would have to try to set up the sort of clandestine network one reads about in spy novels, but I had no idea of how to even get started with that sort of thing. The newly-formed DIA was just getting set up, and they would be happy to have some additional help in gathering military intelligence if it didn't cost them anything. From a government documentary standpoint, I didn't exist, and so was totally deniable, and if I happened to get myself killed while trying to do my job, well that was regrettable of course, but I knew the risks. On a professional level, I had exceeded everyone's expectations—very much including my own. The bottom line was that happily (for me), I wasn't so expendable anymore, and there seemed to be an increasing, though grudging, realization of that fact in Washington.

I had also dealt with another concern. I had often wondered what might happen to me if by some miracle I actually did manage to set up some sort of effective apparatus for gathering military intelligence. Once it was up and running, why would I be necessary any longer? The network would have been established based on the contacts I had formed of course, but as the operation grew, Washington would assign me a deputy to handle some of the workload. Over time, he'd gradually take over while I was given 'special assignments.' Most Washington bosses don't take well to having insubordinate and difficult-to-control employees in key positions. In my case, however, being conveniently 'reassigned' simply couldn't happen unless I wanted it to. There's a big difference between having 'contacts' and having loyal friends. Without me, the whole operation would simply fall apart. I was pretty sure Joe was aware of that, but I made a mental note to make absolutely sure that he knew. I also wanted to give him a reason to contact McCone's replacement at CIA to ensure that McCone's previous edict concerning my safety vis-à-vis CIA employees continued to be operative.

So much for the professional dimension, but what about the personal one? What did I want to do with my life? What was I really *passionate* about? What did I want to accomplish? What did I want to leave as my legacy? I sadly realized that I wasn't really sure. I also realized that, for the moment at least, my freedom to make any sort of career change was extremely limited.

In the emotional euphoria of Camelot, I was as happy as I believe a man can possibly be. I was running full out—top speed—for as many hours of the day as I could stay awake. I viewed the eventual but inevitable necessity of sleep as an unmitigated nuisance. I couldn't wait to get to 'work' in the morning. I was watching history being made every day that I lived and worked at that epicenter of global power. My state of infatuated dedication had ended overnight with the assassination of Jack Kennedy. All my energies and intellect had become immediately re-focused on merely surviving Johnson's hatred. It's a pretty thin excuse for not concentrating more on what I wanted to accomplish with my life, but it's the regrettable truth.

In addition to *that* stupid hole which I had dug for myself, I had another, related one. I realized that I needed *people* in my life—people my age, people I could hang out with. Unquestionably, in Umberto, Anders and Bernard I had three of the finest friends that anyone could ask for, but all three were of an age to be my father. I needed some peers as friends. Pierre and Ingrid were peers and friends but what happened with Emma created a barrier that never really completely dissipated. I had irreparably broken the deep unspoken bonding that had occurred when the four of us had been gathered around my fireplace late last December. My reasons for doing so were understood—but I was never truly forgiven.

I got into Geneva just after noon and drove straight to the office. Poor Maddie was overwhelmed. She had been loyally working 12-hour days in my absence but the workload just kept piling up. I had to get this fixed. I composed a long cable to General Carroll and sent it off. I asked for two of his people to be sent over immediately on tourist visas to work with Maddie until he could get work permits for two people (preferably chemical and weapons experts) to be assigned to my office on a permanent basis. I further told him that we were starting to seriously encroach on the CIA's facilities in terms of office space, computer time, and communications support personnel, and therefore it would be reasonable to think about setting up a small, separate operations office in the near future. I also said that I recently had a rather strange encounter in Paris, and asked him if he would verify that McCone's previous order concerning my personal safety was still in effect. I spent the rest of the afternoon and early evening trying to help Maddie catch up.

Joe's reply cable was waiting for me when I got in the next morning. I read it while having a cup of coffee with Martin (who of course had read my outgoing cable, as well as the incoming one that I hadn't read yet). As expected, Joe thought that it was far too close to the year-end holidays to ask some of his people to pick up and leave right away and wanted to know if soon after the New Year would be acceptable. He also said that McCone's order affecting me was a Director's Order and that no one but another Director could rescind it. As it was still very much in place, he wanted details of what had happened to me in Paris. He also said that he would send someone from administration over shortly after the New Year to look for suitable office space for a separate office. In addition, he asked me how I felt about having a team from the private Swiss security firm stay in the guest house on a permanent basis.

Martin was watching me read the cable with a quiet smile on his face, and when I put it down on the table, he cocked his head and said, "Well?" He quickly continued, "Before you explode or whatever you're going to do, I want to tell you that I very much appreciate your recognition of the increased burden your activities are putting on my staff. Thank you. And *I* want to hear about Paris as well. OK, now I'm done. Start the fireworks."

I told him there weren't going to be any fireworks. He'd read my outgoing cable and in fact, I *wanted* to tell him about Paris and get his opinion.

After I'd done so, he mused for several seconds before he finally said, "You know, if it were anybody else but you Bertie, I'd tell them I thought they were being completely paranoid. You've got very good 'antennae' however, so I'm reluctant to completely dismiss it. Having said that, I'd estimate that the chances of there having been anything out of the ordinary are less than one in a hundred, so I think I'd let it go. On the other hand, I wouldn't go back into that Thai restaurant any more. Maybe there's something going on in there."

I thanked him for his advice and went to see Maddie, who was up to her elbows in computer print-outs. I asked her to give me a minute to send a cable to Carroll, and in it, I told Joe that sending his temp staff after the end of the year was fine, but we were going to take a break starting December 24 and wouldn't be back until Jan. 2. The data would just have to pile up in the meantime. I told him that Maddie desperately needed a break, and that I was leaving on the 28th on an exploratory mission. I didn't elaborate, and though I'm sure he would wonder what the hell I was getting myself into, I doubted that he would ask. I was in a pretty foul mood and it probably came across in the cable.

I told him about the Paris incident in as few words as possible, and added it was almost certainly nothing, but I was overly sensitive to unusual incidents. I said having the Swiss security guards in the guest house was fine, as long as they dressed as caretakers and had no weapons visible. They would also have to be ready to move out immediately and without a trace anytime I needed the guest house for real guests.

By 8:00 that evening, Maddie and I had cleared out the backlog. I had identified several programming changes that needed to be made, and worked until around 2:00 in the morning to make them. I decided to ask Joe for a full-time programmer as well. While I was working, I received a reply cable from Joe, telling me that it was imperative that the data flow not stop, and that two of his employees were arriving at 8:10 a.m. on Swissair flight 111 and GSA had booked rooms for them both at the Hotel Intercontinental. I groaned, and hoped they were quick learners. They weren't going to have much time. It was nice to know that Washington was getting so enamored with the output of my system, though.

They *were* quick learners. In the morning, I phoned them at the hotel, told them to try to get a couple of hours sleep, and that someone from the office would pick them up at 1:00 p.m. sharp. They got a brief security orientation when they arrived at the safe house, then all four of us got down to work. They had already been working with the system's output in Washington so the real task was to show them how the raw information was entered into the system, and how to interpret the intermediate output. The next several days were a whirlwind of activity. I got a phone call from Lo saying that we were booked on a flight from Paris to Bangkok at 3:00 p.m. on the 28th which would get us in to Bangkok a little after 9:30 a.m. on the 29th. I really didn't want to go, but told him I was looking forward to seeing him and Sunisa again.

On the 24th, I called Pierre and Ingrid to wish them a Merry Christmas, but they were gone, so I left a message with the butler. I also called Umberto and Mamma (I had sent a card to Anders at his office address). I called Bernard and Sylvie, and while I was talking to Bernard, I told him of my forthcoming visit with the Tengs, and how I had finally succumbed to Sunisa's pleas that I visit with them in Thailand. He sounded strangely surprised, but then said he was sure I would have an enjoyable visit. I told him how astonished I had been by the opulence of their apartment, and asked Bernard what Lo did for a living. He said that although the only professional relation that his firm had with Lo was that of an investment advisor, the relationship qualified him as a client, and therefore he couldn't discuss Lo's source of wealth with me. He added parenthetically that he really didn't know what the source was although he could make a guess (which of course he couldn't share with me).

Once again, he wished me a pleasant trip, then after a curious pause added, "Keep safe, Bertie. Phone me when you get back."

I worked with the team every day, Christmas included, until I left for Paris on the 28th. I had asked the guys how they felt about working on Christmas day, but it didn't matter to either one of them. One was Jewish and the other an atheist, so as far as they were concerned, Christmas was just another work day.

Bangkok

The flight to Bangkok was long, but back in those days airlines served their passengers superb, leisurely, five-course meals (at least in first class). We arrived in Bangkok tired, but very well-fed. After seeing the Tengs' opulent Paris apartment, it was clear that they were very wealthy, but I still wasn't prepared for the reception in Bangkok. There were hordes of people greeting the Tengs—lots of family, lots of friends—and lots and lots of servants. I don't think there was any real middle class in Thailand at the time. You were either very wealthy or very poor. When a servant tried to take my passport, though, I made it very clear that that simply wasn't going to happen, until Lo came over and assured me that it was quite all right. Amazingly, we never went through customs. We just walked out of the airport to a chauffeured limo which led a procession of four or five other limos on a swift journey that ended up on an estate in a beautiful residential enclave.

The house was huge. It looked to be as big as Umberto's. It probably was, in terms of total floor area, but the layout was uniquely Thai. It had been built—perhaps 'started' is a better term—in 1905, but apparently had been added onto several times. I found out later that such adding—not adding rooms, but adding entire connecting houses—is (or at least, was) fairly typical in Thailand. The whole inter-connected complex was built on a low knoll, which gently rose to 20 feet or so above the surrounding land. Although given the age of the complex, the hillock was so well integrated with its surroundings that it looked perfectly natural; I had to wonder what had formed it. I had the sneaking suspicion that it might have been massive manual labor. The whole area around Bangkok is very flat. It's really an alluvial flood plain formed by the sediments washed down over the eons by the Chao Phraya River, which flows through it (and through the center of Bangkok), before emptying into the Gulf of Siam. As I found later in the visit when I explored the estate, the surrounding land angled gently down to the river itself, so even though the river regularly floods every year, apparently it never got high enough to threaten the house.

Thai architecture is like no other and this house was an exquisite example of it. All of the buildings in the complex were two stories high but they appeared much higher for two reasons. The most obvious was the two-tiered roof, which must have sloped at a fifty degree angle. Each tier was topped by a spire called a *cho fa* and the bottom of each side of the roof gables was graced by a golden *hang hong*, often called a *ngoa*. The roofs were covered with orange ceramic tile outlined by a border in green. The second reason is that all four sides of each house were very slightly angled inwards, not enough for the conscious eye to notice, but which unconsciously gave a sense of perspective which made the house seem taller. Thai architecture is so complicated that it would be ridiculous to try to describe it in any detail. Among countless other things, everything has a spiritual meaning. The end result however is an edifice that truly comforts your soul. Somehow, these incredibly ornate and complicated structures blend organically into the trees and natural environment that surrounds them. It's just impossible to describe the peace and tranquility that envelops you as you enter.

There was no such peace and tranquility when we arrived, however. I don't know how many people were there to greet the Tengs but there had to be somewhere around 100. I was introduced first to Sunisa's mother, a tiny, elegant lady who was probably in her late seventies, but who moved with the alacrity and grace of someone half her age. Thais tend to have impossibly long names, especially last names, and I was bewildered by hers, but it seemed to end in something that sounded like 'Ayuthaya.' I learned much later that the honorific appendage 'Ayuthaya' is given to someone descended from the royal family. I simply addressed her as 'Madam.'

Although the majority of the people there were around the same age as Lo and Sunisa, there was a small gaggle of perhaps ten or so that were in their late twenties—like me—and one of them asked if I would like to go with him the following evening to a disco club that he belonged to in Bangkok.

I said, 'Sure,' but asked if we could go a little early so I could see some of Bangkok. He said the best way to travel in the city (even in those days traffic was bad) was by bike, and asked if I knew how to ride. When I assured him that I did, he pulled out what looked to be a business card, wrote something on the back of it, and told me to give it to my driver. He said that he would see me 'tomorrow around three.' I thought his attitude was a bit preemptory, and somewhat condescendingly arrogant, but hey, maybe I was just tired and a bit edgy, and a bike ride and some sightseeing and little dancing sounded worth putting up with it.

When the crowd at the house finally thinned out a bit, I spotted Sunisa's mother sitting on one of the couches and she patted the cushion next to her and beckoned me to come sit beside her. She was an absolutely fascinating lady. In addition to her native Thai, she spoke fluent French and English (and heaven only knows how many other languages) and could charm the birds out of the trees. I was captivated by her. She said that Sunisa had told her all about me and I sounded so interesting. She also said that unless I had other plans, she and Sunisa were planning a 'little get-together' at the house to introduce me to some of the local people that she thought I would like, and who might, in some cases, be helpful for me to know. "We want you to have lots of friends in Thailand to entice you back to visit with us frequently," she said.

I gently declined her offer for a mid-afternoon lunch, and a servant showed me to my room where I gratefully collapsed.

It was still dark when I awoke a little before 5:00 the next morning. I dressed quietly and opened the door to the terrace outside my bedroom. It was all I could do to suppress a shout when I saw a lifeless form lying on a mat just outside my door. My silence was further challenged when, as I bent to inspect the body, it leapt up, bowed, and in broken but definitely understandable English begged my forgiveness. In a soft voice, he asked what I would like for breakfast. With what I hoped to be oriental imperturbability, I thanked him graciously, told him that I needed nothing, and simply wanted to sit quietly on the veranda and listen to the night sounds. I told him that if he would like to go back to sleep, it wouldn't bother me at all but he bowed, rolled up his mat and quickly scurried away.

Sitting there in the dark reminded me powerfully of my trip to Vietnam. President Kennedy had been getting conflicting reports about how the majority of the populace of South Vietnam felt about their government leaders, the increasing U.S. involvement in South Vietnam, and their feelings about re-unification with the North and the leadership of Ho Chi Minh. He had come to rely on the reports, summaries and analyses that I submitted to him after attending whatever high-level policy meetings that he either didn't want to attend himself or was unable to due to scheduling conflicts. Although it has faded quite a bit now, from birth I have been gifted with pretty much total recall. I never took a single note in any of the meetings that I attended for him. Once back in my office, I could just close my eyes and play the whole meeting back just as if I were watching a movie. Jack trusted me to give him the unadorned truth as I saw it, regardless of whether I thought he was going to like it or not.

Initially I didn't think I was the right person for him to send on that covert fact-finding mission, but Jack had made arrangements which made all the difference. I would be accompanied and guided by a Professor Siddhi who was Professor of Southeast Asia Studies at Georgetown University. I first met him as we were making our way to Washington National Airport to begin our journey to Saigon. I liked him right away and we quickly became a real team. He was well-known in Vietnam. He came from a large and prominent Vietnamese family, and his knowledge of Vietnam was encyclopedic. His warm and sympathetic questioning of the village elders that we visited, all the way from the Delta in the south of Vietnam to our last village destination near the 17th parallel, became astoundingly skillful as our trip progressed. It provided me with invaluable 'on the ground' information about how the Vietnamese *people* felt about Ho Chi Minh and the American presence in Vietnam. Our mission had ended tragically when agents of President Diem's brother, head of Vietnam's dreaded Special Police Force, tracked us down at that final mountain village. They had killed Siddhi. I killed the three policemen, but then I got hopelessly lost in the jungle surrounding the village. I didn't know whether the nearby Viet Cong or a Special Police search team would find me first, but my prospects of surviving an encounter with either were just about nil.

What a contrast. Here I was in the lap of luxury, safely and comfortably soaking up the smells and sounds of the surrounding (wild but well-tended) jungle. In Vietnam, I had been anything but comfortable—huddled up and hiding behind a tangle of vines, hoping for whatever shelter the giant tree next to me might provide, totally alone, scared to death—and waiting for the sounds of the people who were hunting me and intending to kill me.

Though it was about an hour before sunrise, there was plenty of soft moonlight here. In Vietnam, the jungle canopy had made the darkness total. Similar to Vietnam, however, despite the fact that my conversation with the servant had been made in soft whispers, it apparently had been loud enough to put all those animals, insects and the other jungle night creatures on full alert. But just as in Vietnam, within ten minutes of sitting there in total silence, the whole cacophony of night-time jungle noises swelled to its full crescendo.

The memories of that brief time there on the veranda are as vivid to me today as if they had happened yesterday. I sat there transfixed by the emotions evoked by the sounds and smells, and the sense of the deep primal energy of the jungle. I was overcome with a feeling of outrage at the blind and uncaring wheel of fate and human destiny. Total safety vs. mortal danger, peaceful, relaxed tranquility vs. all nerves and senses on total red alert, the sadness of remembering poor Siddhi's death and my responsibility for it—Oh God, the remembrance of the stark reality of that night in Vietnam became so overpowering that I broke out in a drenching sweat. I went back inside to put an end to this nightmare and take a shower.

Madam had invited me to join them for breakfast at 9:00 on the veranda outside the main house, but as I was showering, I realized that I didn't have a clue as to what to wear. I certainly wasn't going to wear jeans, but wearing a business suit seemed far too formal. I hoped that just shirt, slacks and loafers would be acceptable. I needn't have worried. After I had toweled off and gone back into my bedroom, I found my clothes laid out neatly on the bed. I'd never seen them before. They consisted of a brilliantly bright white shirt and a pair of coal-black pants. They were simple but elegant, and had clearly been tailored for me because they fit perfectly. Somebody must have measured my shirts and slacks when they unpacked my suitcase in order to get the measurements. The shirt (later I found out it is called a *raj pattern*) is kind of a mix between a shirt and a jacket. It is worn outside the pants, has five buttons up the front and a sort of Mao-type collar. It has long sleeves, which end at the juncture between the wrist and the hand, and the length of the shirt itself is about halfway between your thumb and index finger when your arms are hanging at your side. The pants are loose and have no crease. They are extremely comfortable. They also hid Excalibur perfectly. With black socks and black loafers added, I showed up for breakfast feeling distinctly spiffy.

Lo stood up, shook my hand and greeted me heartily, and Sunisa and her mother greeted me as though I was their long-lost son/grandson. They were terribly concerned that I hadn't slept well (the servant had obviously ratted on me), wanted to know if I would like to change my bed or my bedroom, if the outside noises were too loud for me, was I feeling lonely because I had wanted to sit outside in the dark, etc. At first, I thought they were just being effusive, somewhat overly-polite hosts but as they kept it up, I began to realize that they were truly concerned. I tried to convince them that my internal clock hadn't yet adjusted to the time difference between Paris and Bangkok, and assured them that I had slept well and comfortably, and that my bed and bedroom were more than satisfactory. I told them that I just enjoyed nature and wanted to take advantage of listening to the night sounds and watching the sun come up.

They seemed appeased but not entirely convinced. Next, they wanted to know if I felt comfortable riding a motorcycle all the way into Bangkok and spending the afternoon and evening with Thaksin—who they described as a good boy from a good family, but a little bit wild and impulsive at times. They said that the best way to see the most important sights in Bangkok was from the river, and that they had arranged a private river tour for me on a private boat with a lovely Thai guide who spoke impeccable English. Wouldn't I rather see Bangkok that way? Frankly, I was beginning to find all this concern a bit smothering, and it was a relief when, after a wonderful but hour-and-a-half long breakfast, they consented to my request to just wander around the estate by myself and get familiarized with it.

I don't think they understood the 'by myself' part. When I went back into my room, changed into shirt and jeans and went outside, there were no less than five servants waiting for me. They explained that they were there to show me the boundaries of the estate, the safest paths to take, the names of the flowers and birds and animals that we might see, and to make sure I didn't get lost because the estate was large. They were also carrying flasks of water and boxes of goodies in case I got thirsty or hungry. As politely and as gently as I could, I explained to them that I would like to explore on my own, and that I could assure them that I would not perish from either thirst or hunger while I was doing so. Reluctantly, they all went back inside but on several occasions, I caught a glimpse of one of them who was trying to shadow me as invisibly as possible.

The estate was large but not huge. I guessed it as 8 to10 acres or so. It was crisscrossed by well-tended paths, and several times the path would open up into a small clearing, where there would be a little spirit house, beautifully hand carved from solid teak and raised to about chest height on a sturdy teak pole. Each of the spirit houses was surrounded by fresh votive offerings. The natural landscape was lush and incredibly beautiful, full of flowers and orchids growing wild, tropical trees and bushes bearing berries and fruit. It was a beautifully tended tropical paradise. The river, when I finally got to it, was much broader than I had expected, and it bore an impressive amount of small boat traffic. There was a landing dock, and I was startled when boats started to come over to me offering an astonishing variety of food. Some had fresh vegetables from the farm; others offered freshly caught fish and shell fish; others had cooked pieces of chicken or pork or beef; there were noodles and rice; some had big pots of soup and would offer a bowl of it, etc. I neither spoke any Thai nor did I have any Thai money, so all I could do was to bow in courtesy, raise my hands with upturned palms in a gesture of helplessness, smile ruefully and beat a hasty retreat.

I enjoyed the bike ride into Bangkok although Thaksin was something of a wild man on the road. The temples and places that we drove by are among the most beautiful in the world, and I wished we had more time to explore them. I got to know Thaksin a little better over dinner, and I wasn't sure that I really liked him very much. I thought he was over-pampered, spoiled, physically soft, and slightly condescending. He was a good dancer though, and we didn't pull ourselves away from the myriad of unattached young women there to commence our ride back until around 2:00 in the morning.

At least the weather was relatively cool, and I was sure there would be a lot less traffic on the road. We hadn't been riding for more than three or four minutes when we heard two powerful bikes coming up behind us. They roared past and then came to a screeching halt, blocking our way. I asked Thaksin what was going on, and saw that he was literally shaking in his boots.

He said, "Give them whatever they want, absolutely anything. I recognize the gang insignia on their bikes. They are members of the most feared gang in Bangkok and they'll kill us if we try to resist."

All four of us dismounted and the guy who seemed to be the leader came over to me and shouted something in Thai. I gave him the finger.

The idiot actually tried to slug me. I just ducked and pushed up on his right elbow as it flew past, so that he not only gave himself a glancing blow to the chin, he'd put so much force behind his blow that he spun, lost his balance and fell onto the street. The look of unbelieving shock and rage on his face was so comic that I couldn't help but laugh—and that *really* infuriated him. When he got back up, he had a gun in his hand, but he was stupid enough to walk towards me, and when he got close enough, I kicked his wrist so hard that I could hear it snap as it broke.

At this point his buddy started to rush to his aid, but stopped dead when I looked at him, wagged my index finger at him and said, "No, no, no, no." I had to give the first one credit though; he got up and came at me again, this time with a well-executed kick to my face. Instead of my face, however, it was Excalibur that took the blow and it went straight through his foot. I took advantage of the momentum of his fall to rip the blade out. His screams were loud and plaintive enough to attract some bystanders but seeing the gang insignia on the bikes, all of them were content to watch from a discreet distance. I was getting a little tired of all the noise, so after retrieving the gun and making sure the safety was back in place, I gave our brave leader a little tap behind his left ear with the butt of the gun. Silence reigned once more. I beckoned his buddy over, doubled him up with a blow to the solar plexus and gave him a little tap of his own as he fell.

The crowd was dead silent.

I had a few more things to do before we left. I slashed both tires on both motorcycles, unloaded the gun and threw the bullets in one direction, and the empty gun in the opposite. Then I went over to both thugs and ripped their pants off. Their pockets were stuffed with money and jewelry. I dumped everything out in a long line near the crowd and then threw them the pants. Nobody moved; they just stared at me. I gave them the traditional *wai* greeting, which was instantly returned as a group, but still nobody took a single step towards the small fortune that was lying in front of them. I shrugged, put Excalibur back in its sheath, remounted my bike and told the ashen-faced Thaksin to lead the way. As we roared off, in my rear-view mirror I could see the crowd swarming over everything they could lay their hands on.

I arrived for breakfast punctually at 9:00. Although I got the same hearty greeting and hand-shake from Lo, and hugs and kisses from the ladies, I could sense there was something a little different in their attitude. As soon as I sat down, Lo put his newspaper down on the table and mildly inquired, "Well, Bertie, how was your day yesterday?"

Dutifully, I began with my tour of the grounds and commented on how lovely and peaceful I had found it.

I could tell I wasn't going to get away with anything when Lo continued, "And your trip into Bangkok?"

I told them of my awe at the beauty of the temples, and how much Thaksin and I had enjoyed meeting and dancing with the young women at the disco. When I finished, all three of them just stared at me, waiting. I also became aware of a far larger number of servants than usual doing busy work around the veranda. I gave up.

"It looks like news travels pretty fast around here," I said. "Yes, there was a bit of unpleasantness after Thaksin and I left the disco, but it was all over in less than 10 minutes. There were two young guys that tried to rob us, and I'm sorry to say that I had to hurt one of them, but the damage was fairly minor and I'm sure his wrist and foot will heal nicely. It was all over quickly, and neither Thaksin nor I was ever in any real danger, so there's really not much to talk about." All of a sudden, a thought struck me and I blanched as I stuttered out, "I hope my actions have not brought dishonor to your house."

There were enough hugs and back-pats and laughing protestations to make me feel comfortable that I hadn't done so, and it was Sunisa that finally said, "Well, that's probably all the information we're going to get out of you Bertie, so I guess we'll have to be content. I have to admit that I liked the description from Thaksin's mother much better, though. She said that Thaksin told her the whole story. He told her he was going to rush to help you but when he saw that you had the situation totally in hand, he didn't want to get in your way and just made sure that the other gang member didn't interfere."

Sunisa looked at me closely and asked, "Bertie, did Thaksin really try to come and help you?" I told her that I was concentrating so hard on the gang leader that I really hadn't noticed but if that's what he said, I'm sure that's what happened. I asked her to please tell Thaksin that I would thank him personally the next time I saw him.

Sunisa, her mother and Lo immediately broke out into peals of laughter. When I looked puzzled and asked what I had said that was so funny, Sunisa replied, "Everyone knows that Thaksin likes to 'exaggerate' and everyone knows that Thaksin is—how shall I say—not noted for his personal bravery. I think he probably described pretty accurately what you did. It sounds rather amazing, frankly. He is in awe of you. And he is scared to death of you. If we tell him that you are going to thank him personally for his 'help,' he is probably going to decide that he needs to immediately go see a long-neglected aunt in the Philippines or somewhere. So we won't tell him, but it was hilarious to picture what his reaction would have been. Thank you for taking care of him and protecting him, Bertie. His family is in your debt."

Those were happy days. The family chartered a beautiful river barge and equipped it with copious servants and enough provisions to last for days, and also equipped it with a strikingly lovely young architectural history student as my guide. The best way to see the architectural and cultural treasures of Bangkok is definitely by boat, and this young lady was a true storehouse of information. I really learned a lot that day. I wish I had had a camera. On the way back to the landing at the estate, I asked my guide to ask the servants if they would take all the extra food we were carrying, but as they were employees of Madam, they were shocked by the idea.

Our barge driver said that he would be happy to take some home to his family, but there was far too much for him to carry, and it would spoil in any case. I didn't want him to take all the food back to Bangkok on the barge and give it to the people who were always standing around the docks, as that would be grossly unfair to all the 'mom and pop' food sellers on their boats. My guide solved the problem by saying that there was a small village about another mile upriver from the landing at the estate and she would be happy to take the food and distribute it there. I thanked her and asked her to never mention the name of Madam outright but to make sure the villagers would guess that the gift was from her. She surprised me by kissing me full on the mouth and then telling me how much the villagers would appreciate the gift. The servants and the boat driver clapped. It was a good day.

Prime Minister Thanom Kittikachorn

The 'little get-together' that Madam threw for me was a gas. Apparently, an invitation from Madam was little short of a command. There was an astounding array of accomplished guests, prominent businessmen and bankers, artists, politicians, etc. I don't think I have ever collected so many business and calling cards in a single gathering. Everybody felt compelled to write down their private telephone number on the back and some even included their home telephone number. There are only three guests that I remember, however.

One was an absolutely stunningly beautiful young lady named Cheranand something (for some reason or another, she told me to call her Lek). She was Miss Thailand, 1965 and I couldn't begin to imagine anyone who could be more deserving of the title. She was truly spectacular. I heard later on that she became a Thai film star but that might not be accurate. All I remember is that beautiful face and body.

The second person was Graham Martin, the U.S. Ambassador to Thailand. When we met, he smiled and took me aside and said, "I take it you're not travelling on a diplomatic passport on this visit to Thailand, Mr. MacFarland?"

I just shook my head and answered, "There really are *no* secrets in Washington, are there?"

He laughed and said, "Thailand's probably worse. I trust that you are not treating last week's little incident as a warm-up for further forays into law enforcement?" I groaned, but he smiled and said, "It's quite all right. In fact, I wish there were more people capable of standing up as you did to these thugs. Please consider the Embassy as your home away from home whenever you visit. You can even have your old bedroom back if you'd like. Before you leave to go back to Paris and Geneva, I'd very much enjoy the opportunity to have a private lunch together. Here's my direct line and the private line to my quarters. Do try to make lunch if you can." He gave me his card and melted back into the crowd. I never saw him again.

The third person caused a distinct ripple, even in that august crowd. He arrived about an hour later than everybody else—probably to heighten the effect of his arrival. When he was announced, everyone gasped and turned to look. The new arrival was none other than Field Marshall Thanom Kittikachorn—the Prime Minister of Thailand. He and Madam greeted each other like long-lost friends and after the traditional *wai* greeting, Sunisa joined with her mother in what looked almost like a family chat. People were crowded around the threesome at a respectful distance but clearly waiting for it to break up so that they could have their own chance to greet and be recognized by the Prime Minister. I wasn't among them but I was definitely impressed that the Prime Minister would respond to a social invitation by Madam.

There are few advantages to being a Westerner in Asian society but one of them is height. Everybody else was crowded around in that little surrounding circle, but at a height of just over 6 feet, I could gaze serenely over the heads of all of them to see what was going on. What happened next was a surprise. As the three of them started to draw apart, Sunisa scanned the room and nodded discretely in my direction. The Prime Minister strode purposefully towards me. Watching the crowd part before him reminded me of the story of Moses parting the waters of the Red Sea. He didn't waste any time, and he didn't even introduce himself. He simply shook my hand and asked if I had a few minutes to talk to him out on the veranda.

I didn't like the way that he hadn't waited for my answer, but simply proceeded to the veranda and assumed I'd follow him. I hesitated but decided that I couldn't embarrass Madam, so I reluctantly followed. We were well out of earshot of anyone when he stopped and asked me abruptly how I was enjoying my second visit to Thailand. I answered dryly that I found it much more enjoyable than the first one.

He laughed and added, "I understand that you are aiding us in our efforts to rid the streets of Bangkok of undesirables, and I thank you for your assistance. Like any large metropolis, Bangkok has a dark side, an underworld, and its inhabitants can be extremely vicious. I would suggest that during this trip at least, you would be well advised not to stroll the streets of Bangkok alone—particularly not at night." He paused and continued. "I wish the problems

186

facing this nation were confined to dealing with criminal elements within our own borders. Unfortunately, as you know, that is far from being the case. My country is in your debt for the aid that you have provided to my brother-in-arms, General Vang, and I hope that both he and I will be able to count on your invaluable aid in our continuing struggle against Communism in the future. Communism is an existential threat to us, and we shall not survive as a nation if we cannot defeat it. May I count on your support in time of need?"

I was absolutely aghast. I quickly protested, "Mr. Prime Minister[30], I fear that you have been *very* badly informed as to my powers to help you or anyone else. I am a minor functionary in my government. There is no use trying to deny to someone such as you that I was a Special Assistant to President Kennedy, but I can assure you with equal honesty that President Johnson hates my guts. Even if I *could* help you sir, I have no authority to make any promises of any kind to a head of government. I probably shouldn't even be talking to you."

He examined me intently for a few seconds before replying, "You speak frankly and you speak honestly and I respect that. I can see why General Vang trusts you. Of course you cannot make any promises that would commit your government. That's the business of the *front*, formal channel. I would like to rely on you in the same way as General Vang did, as the *back* channel. I am well aware of the fact that President Johnson 'hates your guts' as you put it, but my sources in Washington think that in some way he is a little afraid of you. On more than one occasion, you have directly refused to obey his instructions, but you are still very much alive and have access to the highest centers of power. You know of course that General Vang's trust in you makes you even more valuable and more powerful in Washington. That will be multiplied by many times if I let it be known that *I* trust you as well. Your government's use of the Royal Thai Air Bases is at my pleasure, you know."

What an arrogant bastard! I took a deep breath to calm myself and replied, "With respect Prime Minister, the only thing that you can count on me for is to be totally, brutally honest with you. If you ask for my opinion, I will give it to you as honestly as I know how with no regard whatsoever as to whether you may like it or not. For example, your veiled threat concerning the U.S. use of your air bases strikes me as total nonsense. If you are as interested in fighting Communism as you profess to be (and frankly, I think you are), you know damned well that you need those planes there just as much as we do. If you know as much about me as you appear to, you know I don't deal well with threats, and the only way I'll talk to you in the future is if you agree to those terms. If you ever break your agreement, I'll slam my door shut to you forever."

It was interesting to watch his face. With the moonlight and our dark-adapted eyes, it was clearly visible. I doubt if he had been spoken to this way since childhood—if then. I was mildly

---

[30] Formally, he should be referred to as Prime Minister Thanom. On a person-to-person basis, I always addressed him as Mr. Prime Minister but throughout the rest of this book, I often refer to him as Kittikachorn because that's how Madam addressed him.

alarmed at the way his face was being engorged with the blood, brought along by his mounting rage. I wasn't concerned for my safety. I was concerned for his. I was afraid he might be going to have a heart attack or a stroke or something. Curiously, he was a little like Johnson in regard to rage, although I've never, ever seen anyone even approach Johnson's ability to switch moods 180 degrees almost instantaneously.

It took Kittikachorn a couple of minutes. He finally replied, "I see much more clearly now why Johnson hates your guts. Let me give you fair warning though. I accept your terms on the following condition: if you ever again dare to speak to me as you have tonight within the hearing of anyone else, I will kill you—and I mean that very seriously."

I told him that was fine with me, and that I thought we ought to go back in now. I started to walk back when he grabbed my arm and asked, "Do you like elephants?"

I was beginning to wonder what he'd had to drink before he arrived. "I've never really been up close and personal with an elephant," I answered, "but why do you ask?"

"I have a very good friend who runs a teak logging operation in a place about 150 miles from here," he said. "His father started it about 60 years ago and it has grown ever since. It's very interesting. I think you would enjoy spending a day there. May I send a car for you—day after tomorrow, perhaps?"

I had absolutely no idea what was going on, but I had the definite impression that to refuse would not be the right thing to do; so, reluctantly, I nodded my assent.

"Good, good!" he exclaimed. "Now I have to be running along, so let's go back inside so I can thank my hostess. It's been good to meet you Bertie. Call me if you need me."

Maybe protocol dictates that guests are not supposed to depart before high-ranking dignitaries, but immediately after his departure, all the other guests were lined up to express their thanks to Madam, who motioned to me to stand beside her so they could all shake my hand as well. I thought the whole thing was as bizarre an evening as I had ever experienced.

When everyone was gone, Madam said, "Well Bertie, you've had quite an evening." She vaguely reminded me of someone (Rose Kennedy maybe?) when she said, "I imagine you'll want a good stiff whiskey now. Am I right?"

"I'd kill for one," I replied. Lo proclaimed himself exhausted, said his goodnights and exited stage right. It suddenly struck me that Lo never seemed to be part of the conversation. It was always Sunisa and her mother that made all the plans and all the decisions. His opinion was never asked and indeed, now that I thought about it, I never really saw him very much. It had been Sunisa and her mother that had been in close conversation with Kittikachorn. I hadn't even seen Lo in the room. Definitely strange.

Over a generous and delicious 'whiskey' (in Thailand, at least at the time, 'whiskey' only referred to Scotch whiskey. Bourbon and other such spirits were called by their proper names but considered somewhat barbaric). Sunisa and her mother said that Kittikachorn had paid me a high compliment on leaving. Apparently, he had said, "He is a very direct man, your Mr. MacFarland. I don't know whether or not I like him but I definitely trust him." Madam continued, "You know Bertie, he didn't come here tonight to see me. He came to see you."

Sunisa added, "You bring honor to our house, Bertie. We have heard of what you did with the surplus food on the barge. Your guide told us. Your instructions were followed exactly and my mother's name was never mentioned, but everyone in the village is convinced that the food was her gift. Our family has always given generously to museums and universities and hospitals, and temples and such. However, you have shown us that we have neglected to follow the path of the Buddha. It shall never be abandoned again. One of the Buddhist teachings is that wealth does not guarantee happiness, and also that wealth is impermanent. We are taught from an early age to be compassionate, and that compassion includes qualities of sharing, readiness to give comfort, sympathy, concern, caring. We are grateful to you for reminding us of these basic teachings."

It was definitely time for me to go to bed.

An Unusual Logging Camp

The car that arrived for me at dawn two days later was definitely not what I had expected. It was a beat-up old Chevy four-door sedan that looked to be at least three or four years old, and was dusty, scratched and dented. I figured if this was Kittikachorn's way of paying me back for being excessively straightforward with him, our relationship wasn't going to proceed very well. I shouldn't have worried. When the driver hopped out, saluted me and held the back door open for me, the unmistakable smell of good leather wafted out. I also noticed that the door was substantially thicker than was normal, and so was the window glass. It was actually pretty luxurious back there. Beautiful leather seats, thick carpeting, air conditioning controls and two radios—one normal and the other shortwave. The front seat was the standard, cloth Chevrolet bench seat, but what wasn't standard was the unnaturally thick back of it.

My driver showed me the button to press to raise the bullet-proof glass that it contained in order to completely seal off the back passenger compartment. The final touch was the front seat passenger that the driver introduced as our guard. The driver said that he was both a martial arts expert and was heavily armed. The passenger stopped the ceaseless swiveling of his head long enough to nod respectfully to me and silently show me the AK-47 that had been resting in his lap. I couldn't make head nor tail of it. Surely the elephants weren't armed? I figured the hell with it, and settled back to enjoy the ride.

The ride was a lot shorter than I had anticipated. I wasn't keeping close track of the time, and anticipating a long ride, I wasn't paying a lot of attention to the scenery, but it surely couldn't have been much more than 30 minutes or so when the driver sounded his horn and we started slowing down. Startled, I looked up and was flabbergasted to see that we were approaching the gates of Don Muang Air Base! We never stopped. The gates had been flung wide by the guards, who were standing at rigid attention and saluting as we swept past. We drove right up to a helicopter pad, where an American helicopter with Royal Thai Air Force markings was waiting, and once again, the driver hopped out to open my door.

The Thai Air Force officer who greeted me saluted, and led me straight onto the chopper, closely followed by my guard with his AK-47 at the ready. The driver stayed behind with the car. This whole thing was getting more peculiar by the moment. The chopper blades started rotating immediately after I sat down, and even though the space separating me from the Thai officer and the guard sitting across from me was narrow, the damned motor was more than loud enough to drown out any attempt at conversation.

Our flight was less than an hour, and the terrain that we were flying over was getting increasingly mountainous. We landed in a small clearing that had been carved out of the surrounding jungle, and were met by a Thai in civilian clothes driving a jeep. The chopper lifted back off the moment we disembarked. Silence has rarely been more treasured.

I was really puzzled and a little angry but just shook my head and said, "Where the hell are we? This sure doesn't look to me like an elephant-infested logging camp. What the hell is going on here?"

The Thai officer that had greeted me back at Don Muang saluted me and finally introduced himself. He said that he was on special assignment and that his orders to obey any command that I might care to give him came directly from the commanding general of the Royal Thai Air Force. He told me that it was an honor to serve me. He introduced himself as Colonel (incredibly long and hopelessly unintelligible name), but graciously added that he knew that Thai names were often difficult for Westerners to understand and suggested that I call him 'Sam.'

Before I could reply, the jeep driver stepped up and announced, "Me Joe, sir." I turned to look at the guard, who stopped swiveling his head for a moment, gave me a faint smile and a respectful nod, and went right back to his incessant surveillance. "Guess he's the strong but silent type—Thai style," I reflected. "Probably goes over great with the ladies but his arrogance is starting to really annoy me."

Once again I noted that this didn't seem much like a logging camp, and if we were surrounded by elephants, they were damned well camouflaged. Joe started to laugh but choked it off immediately when Col. Sam whipped his head around to glare at him. Col. Sam said, "So sorry, sir. We are only about a mile and a half away. The road is private and very secure. We land here because the elephants are disturbed by the noise of the helicopter and can become frightened and unruly. So sorry, sir. We will take you to the camp immediately." Jeeps don't have any back doors but the Colonel and my guard vaulted effortlessly into the back seats while Joe ushered me into the front passenger seat. I have to confess that riding in a military jeep in Thailand, for the second time, with a passenger in the back seat carrying a very lethal weapon was not at all comfortable.

Now we get to the life-changing part.

Chapter 10 — Elephants, Boss and Bill

Boss

I was astonished at how dense the jungle was on either side of the one-lane, dirt road that led us to the logging camp. It seemed even thicker than the jungle in Vietnam. Siddhi had often warned me that it was extremely dangerous to wander off a path in the jungle. He said I would be amazed at how quickly one can become completely disoriented and then totally lost. Thai jungles have denizens such as tigers and Burmese pythons which can quickly ensure that the only destination you are ever going to reach is their digestive tract. I was beginning to feel a very uneasy sense of vulnerability. I hoped I was correct in my belief that Kittikachorn needed me a whole lot more than I needed him.

I was relieved when we emerged into a large clearing, whose principal feature was a long, one story wooden building nestled up near the surrounding jungle about a hundred yards in the distance. It was a distinctly un-Thai sort of building; it reminded me rather of a long bunk house of the type one might see on a ranch in the western United States. It was on stilts, which wasn't unusual in Thailand. It is common for Thai villagers to build their huts on stilts for two reasons. The first is to protect the house from the floods which are so frequent in the country, and the second is to protect the occupants from unwelcome night visitors. To that end, the 'steps' used to access the house are the steps on a simple wooden ladder —which is withdrawn at night. This building had a wide set of fixed stairs leading up to it, and that was *very* unusual.

This building had some other unusual features for a rural building. It had a corrugated tin roof, windows with real glass in them, and a front porch which ran the entire length of the building. To complete the Western ranch semblance, there was a man sitting on the porch in a chair propped up against the wall who was intently watching our arrival. When we pulled up in front of the house and he came down the stairs to greet us, I halfway expected to see him wearing cowboy boots (he wasn't). He was Thai but like Vang, I doubt that there was a single ounce of fat on his wiry frame. Quite unlike Vang, his smile seemed warm and genuine.

Ignoring everyone else and eschewing the traditional Thai *wai* greeting, he just stuck out his hand and asked with a flawless western American accent, "You come to fix the radio?" When I admitted that I hadn't, he said, "Shit, that damn thing's been broke for three days now. They were supposed to send somebody yesterday. Goddamn it, we're isolated enough up here even *with* a working radio." He examined me closely and asked, "How long you going to be up here? You an instructor or an observer? What's your name? Everybody around here just calls me 'Boss.'"

'Baffled' doesn't adequately express the depth of my bewilderment, but it's the best I can do. I just said, "Boss, my name's Bertie and if I've got to choose between being an instructor or an observer, I guess I'm an observer. To be totally honest however, I have no idea why I'm here. All I can tell you is that at a social gathering a couple of days ago, I met Prime Minister Kittikachorn and he sort of insisted that I come up here and look around. He sent a car for me this morning—I'm staying with some friends in Bangkok—and the next thing I knew, I was climbing on the helicopter that flew me up here. I don't have a Goddamn clue of what I'm supposed to be doing here. I was hoping you could tell me."

Before he could answer, we heard the unmistakable sound of automatic small arms fire in the distance, and I could vaguely hear the kind of visceral shouts men make when they are in close combat. My guard had dropped to a one-knee firing position and was aiming his AK-47 in the general direction of the noise, while Boss was screaming at the top of his lungs at Col. Sam.

Joe was laughing so hard he could barely stand up.

I just stood in motionless wonderment like the completely confused, uncomprehending lump that I was.

Boss stopped shouting, and chuckled as he turned to me and said, "Come on up here on the porch with me and we'll chat a little bit. You want a beer?" I followed him up the stairs and tried to ignore Col. Sam who was now screaming at the top of *his* lungs at my guard. Joe was oblivious of the black stares he was getting from both of them and still laughing his ass off.

Boss re-emerged from the bunkhouse with two frosty Singha's (to this day, one of my very favorite beers) and said, "So Thanom sent you up here, huh? You look kinda young to be that important, but it's none of my business. I don't know what kind of training your people are doing down there today, but we can drive down and watch whenever you want to. Hold on a minute while I get rid of this damn noise." I don't know what he said but all three guys shut up like somebody had shoved a pineapple in their mouths.

The guard placed his weapon on the back seat of the jeep, and all three of them walked hurriedly towards a road that led out of the clearing in the opposite direction from which we had heard the gunfire. Boss sat back down.

Before he could resume, I asked, "What did you mean when you mentioned that you didn't know what kind of training *my* people are doing today?"

The question clearly caught him off-guard, and he was visibly upset when he asked, "You *are* with the CIA aren't you?" He was even more upset when I told him that I was not. He was almost ashen-faced when he groaned, "Oh shit! Have I let the cat out of the bag or something?"

I told him not to worry and told him that, whereas I had not previously known about this particular training camp, I was well aware of what was going on in a neighboring country, and in fact knew and had met with the army officer in charge of ground operations there.

He seemed considerably mollified, but then asked, "But why did Thanom send you up here, then? I don't understand."

I told him that I wasn't fully sure that I understood either, but had a glimmer of an idea that I would have to mull over. I then asked him, "Is this really a logging camp with elephants and all? I haven't seen an elephant since I've been here."

It turned out to be exactly the right thing to say to put him at his ease. He said, "Bertie, this is the best damn teak logging operation in the country. My old man started it and I grew up with it. Teak is getting more valuable every day, and between the land my old man bought and what I've added to it since he died, we have one of the largest teak holdings in the country. I run the operation just like he did, and if I have anything to say about it, we'll always use elephants to do our logging. Some of the other operations are switching to using tractors now because they are so much faster, but tractors aren't suited to jungle paths. These guys just go in and mow down everything that's standing, young trees and all. It takes 30-40 years for a teak tree to fully mature although they can live for up to 200 years. If you want to sustain your operation, you have to be careful to let the young trees stay and grow. I've got enough land here to keep this operation going forever, but I don't know what's going to happen to it when I die. My son will inherit it but he doesn't want anything to do with it. Too much work and too isolated. Anyway, let's go have a look. Before we go though, Bill Young's here. I'll send somebody to fetch him."

When I told him I'd never heard of Bill Young, he just shook his head and said, "Well, you two need to meet. I'm sure he'll want to meet you. Now let's go see some elephants."

Elephants

I about got myself killed but it was one of the most amazing experiences of my life. We drove down the same road that Col. Sam and his bunch had taken, and soon emerged into another much, much larger clearing which was a beehive of activity. There were several long railroad spurs which merged in the distance with what looked to be the main railroad line. Elephants, effortlessly dragging huge teak logs, were constantly emerging from the surrounding jungle, and there was an indescribable majesty to their movements. The humans on the ground as well as their mahouts on their back were simply their companions and associates—some, perhaps, were even friends—but in no sense were the humans their masters. The elephants and they alone, were the natives—and masters—of the jungle. Those beautiful beings moved their incredibly powerful bodies with an almost surreal grace and dignity. I was amazed, wonderstruck, and humbled somehow.

This was the beginning of my life-long love affair with elephants.

There was kind of a log depot which was parallel to the nearest rail spur, and when the elephant had pulled its chained log up to the unloading area, the mahout guiding it would descend (with the elephant's help), unhook the chain, remount the elephant and then disappear back into the forest. The forest looked pretty civilized for as far into it as I could see, which was a pretty long way. The combination of all the log-dragging and the elephants' tendency to eat any grass or shrub which had the temerity to try to grow anywhere within trunk's reach made the area around the growing trees pretty clear.

Watching the logs getting loaded for transport was a real wonder. The land sloped down gently and at the low end of the nearest spur, where there was a collection of 60 or so curious railroad cars, each of which consisted of nothing more than a four-wheeled, eight-foot square open steel frame resting on its two axles, and with a standard rail car coupling device at either end. The truly bizarre feature of these little cars (I think they were referred to as 'sleds') was a heavy steel inverted arch welded crossways to the middle of each sled, and cut so that the upward facing part of the arch consisted of nasty-looking triangular steel teeth.

Two elephants were in charge of the loading, and each had a human helper on the ground. The elephants would first separate out a log to load from the depot pile and, with their feet, roll it parallel to and about six feet away from the near rail spur. Then the elephant on the downhill side would grab one of these 'sleds,' get behind it in the middle of the track, and with a firm shove from one of its mighty forefeet, send the sled uphill where the other elephant, standing in the middle of the track even with the end of the waiting log would stop it. That elephant would hold the sled in place long enough so the human helper could place chocks behind the wheels to keep it from rolling back downhill. The first elephant would then grab another sled and position it at the lower end of the log while its human helper chocked it into place.

Both elephants would then grab a heavy wooden ramp specially made so that it just covered the highest exposed tooth of the arc, and then the elephants started rolling the log up the ramp, this time using their massive heads. Because the bottom of the log is bigger than the top, whichever elephant was rolling the top part had to roll it faster than the other elephant. It was amazing to see how smoothly they coordinated their motions so that both top and bottom ends reached the top of the ramp at the same time. Once it was pushed over the top, the log crashed down and impaled itself on those fearsome teeth such that now, the two sleds were firmly connected to one another via the log. If there was room for more than one log on the sled, the elephants would repeat the operation until the human helpers signaled them to stop, and then chained the additional log(s) to the first one. At that point, the chocks behind the top sled were removed, the train engine would come and haul off the newly created 'car' and attach it to other such cars on another siding, and the whole process would start all over again.

Well away from this work area was an adjoining clearing that looked to be something of a nursery area, as there were four or five young elephants wandering about and playfully jostling one another while a couple of adults watched them benignly from a distance. Curious, I went over to get a better look at one of the younger ones, and promptly had my waist encircled by his trunk, the end of which was searching around in my pants pocket. I couldn't move. These guys weigh over 200 pounds at birth and this one was perhaps three to four years old. Not knowing how to make him release his grip, I gave him a smack on his trunk with the palm of my hand. Big, big mistake. Not in the least hurt but very surprised, he backed off and shrieked and was instantly answered by a bellow from one of the adult elephants, who immediately came charging right at me.

It's a mesmerizing experience to be charged by a fully-grown elephant. There's nowhere to run, you can't hide. I've never stood in the middle of a set of railroad tracks watching in horror as a freight train hurtled towards me, but I imagine the feeling has to be the same. If Boss hadn't been there, the end result would have been the same, too. He came running towards me, waving his arms and yelling in Thai at the charging elephant, which finally stopped with a snort about 10 feet away from me. The 'little' guy ran behind her and watched me from the safety of one of her massive rear legs. Boss spoke gently to them both and reached into one of his pants pockets and pulled out a fistful of peanuts which he divided between the two of them. I stood rooted to the spot. The big elephant turned and led the 'little' one away but not without her first fixing me with a distinctly baleful glare of warning. My knees were literally shaking as I followed Boss back to the jeep.

As we rode back to the house, Boss explained that the 'aunts' are extremely protective of their charges and won't hesitate for a heartbeat to kill whatever they think is threatening them. He observed dryly that it was a good thing for me that he was close by. Apparently, he always carried some peanuts in his pants pockets and that was why the little guy was feeling around in mine. He told me that if I ever visited him again, he would give me a big bag of peanuts and take me by the nursery and personally introduce me to everybody. He said that after that, I'd be fine wandering around the nursery by myself, and that additionally, they would remember me for years and years. At the time, I had no intention of ever, ever coming back.

I asked why he spoke such idiomatically perfect American English, and why his accent sounded like he'd just arrived from a ranch somewhere in the American far west. He said that many, many years ago his dad used to make a little extra money by letting tourist groups come by to watch the logging operation. Boss had met his future wife on one of those tours. She had grown up on a ranch that her father owned in Montana, had never been outside Montana before, had never seen a jungle before, had never seen an elephant before and had become instantly and totally convinced that the logging camp was the tropical paradise she had always dreamed of.

"I learned my English from her," he said. "Words, accent, and all. The Thai hut that my father had built when he was young felt pretty cramped with the four of us living in it, and when our son arrived, it was clear that something had to be done. Beth, my wife, said that what we needed was a big old rambling bunkhouse, and since we had plenty of lumber and materials, that's what my Dad and I built. Those were happy times when the five of us were sharing the house. It started to seem a little big for us when my dad died, and even bigger when my mom died a few years afterwards. When our son Jason left, we wished we had the old hut back again. I thought about selling the whole operation when Beth died of breast cancer 'bout four years ago, but I can't never leave. My mahouts and my elephants are all the family I got. I don't know what would happen to them and the camp if I left. I got to find somebody I can train up and take over from me when I get too old. You wouldn't be interested, would you?"

You know, I actually seriously thought about it before I shook my head and said, "Thanks. It's tempting, but I'm afraid not." Many, *many* times I've wondered whether or not I made the right decision.

Bill

There was a guy about my age sitting on the porch drinking a beer when we pulled up to the bunkhouse. He was handsome, a little shorter than me, well-proportioned, and looked hard as a rock.

He cordially greeted Boss who continued on into the house to get a couple of beers then turned to me and said: "You Bertie?"

"Who's asking?"

After a pause—"My name's Bill. Bill Young."

"Do I know you?"

"Not yet. You kill Bill and Frank?"

Pause on my part, then—"Yep. Friends of yours?"

"Not close, but yeah."

"Well look, Bill. I didn't ask for this meeting and I have no idea why Boss sent for you. In fact,

197

I have no idea what I'm doing in this fucking camp to begin with. Ten minutes ago, I nearly got myself run over by an elephant, I don't like your questions, I'm thirsty and I'm hungry and I'm not moving off this damn porch until my helicopter comes. You're more than welcome to leave as far as I'm concerned. You got a problem with any of that?"

Boss broke the tension by arriving with two beers in his hands. He handed me one and said, "Heard you say you were hungry. I never eat lunch so I never thought of it. Set this beer down besides my chair and I'll go find you something to eat. You want something, Bill?" Bill shook his head 'No' and observing the two of us glaring at each other, Boss asked, "You two girls gettin' along OK?"

Bill surprised me by smiling at Boss, exchanging his apparently empty beer bottle for the full one Boss was carrying and saying, "We're doing fine, Boss. We were just going to sit down and reminisce about old times over a beer, weren't we, Bertie?"

"I believe we were," I replied. When we sat down, I turned to Bill and remarked, "Well Bill, you seem to have me at a disadvantage. You know at least something about me but I know nothing about you. How about filling me in a little bit?"

I won't recount the whole story, but these are the basics:

Bill's grandfather came to Burma in the late 1880's as a Baptist missionary. His son Harold also became a missionary and grew up travelling with his father throughout Burma, southern China, and northern Thailand and Laos. The CIA, fearing a possible invasion of the region by the armies of Mao Tse Tung, recruited Harold after WWII to spy for them as he knew the tribes, terrain, customs and languages of southern China. Bill was born in 1934 and accompanied his father on his travels. In addition to English and French, he was reasonably fluent in four, perhaps five, of the local languages of the tribes in eastern Burma, southern China, and northern Thailand and Laos. He served in the US Army in post-war Germany and after his return to his father's house in Chiang Mai, (Thailand) was recruited by the CIA and initially posted to Bangkok. The CIA loves American missionaries who are long-term residents of foreign countries. They are respected and know the terrain, languages and customs of the local people. The story of how Bill got involved with the secret war in Laos, General Vang Pao, hacked his way through the Laotian jungles to find the perfect place for an airstrip near the Plain of Jars, etc. is fascinating but far too long and complex for me to give an account here.

I was listening to Bill intently, though, when we heard the distant arrival of my chopper. He stopped and observed, "That's probably for you. Mind if I hitch a ride back to Don Muang with you?"

The sound of the chopper had stirred up a lot of activity. Col. Sam, Joe and my guard were running back from the work area as fast as they could and Boss re-emerged from the depths of the bunkhouse with a bowl of noodles. Bill and I shook his hand, thanked him for his hospitality and descended the steps to get in the jeep.

Col. Sam astounded me by objecting vehemently to Bill accompanying me. I asked him what the problem was. There followed a long and strenuous string of objections delivered in a mixture of French and English which included security risks, no unauthorized passengers, his possible demotion by the head of the Royal Thai Air Force for permitting such a thing, possible weight overload with resulting safety issues, and on and on.

I waited patiently for him to finish his litany then mildly remarked, "Colonel, it's my Goddamn helicopter and I not only decide who gets on it, I can decide where it goes if I want to. We'll ask the pilot about the weight issue and if there's a problem, you and that damn useless guard can stay here until your boss sends another chopper to pick you up. Joe, get in the jeep and drive. You coming with Bill and me, Colonel?"

Bill was trying not to grin as he climbed in the back and said, "I like your management style, Bertie. I appreciate the ride, too. I'll buy you a drink at Don Muang when we get back." I told him I'd look forward to it.

On the off-chance that there might be something to the weight issue, I asked the pilot about it before we boarded. He assured me that as far as weight was concerned, we could probably carry the jeep if we could figure out how to get it through the door.

The Colonel and the guard wordlessly followed Bill and I onto the chopper.

My car was waiting for me when we landed, but as the guard went to assume his place in the front passenger seat, I told the Colonel that I never wanted to see that guard again and that Bill and I were going to the American Officer's Club for a drink and some supper.

The driver looked like he was going to have a heart attack, and seemed to be pleading with the Colonel for instructions when Bill turned to him and addressed him briefly in some dialect that didn't even sound like Thai. The driver looked at Bill in astonishment, smiled, bowed and rushed to open the door for me and then for Bill.

We left the Colonel and the guard staring at our departing car in dumbfounded horror. "What the hell did you tell the driver," I asked, "and what language were you speaking?"

"I spoke to him in Lahu because I recognized his accent when he was talking to the Colonel. It's one of the dialects in northern Thailand and in China. I told him you were the honored guest of the Prime Minister and that to disobey your orders would mean very severe punishment—perhaps even death. Now that I think about it, I might not have been exaggerating. Kittikachorn isn't a man to fool around with. How do you know him, anyway?"

"How do you know that I'm his guest?"

"The man that Boss sent to pick me up told me. I would have made the assumption anyway. Vang says you've got a direct pipeline to 'the highest levels' in Washington. It's not surprising that Kittikachorn would want to try to tap into that pipeline. Anyway, let's not say too much here in the car. I presume it's wired. We can talk in the Club." I was really starting to like this guy.

Over dinner Bill said he thought I had more balls than good sense to show up in Thailand. He remarked that he knew I wasn't going to tell him anything that I didn't want to but, was I here to see Vang again? I think he was truly shocked when I told him that I was here at the invitation of some friends who probably felt sorry for me because I didn't have anywhere to go for the Christmas holidays. I could almost see the wheels turning in his head but his next question surprised me.

He asked, "How do you know Vang?"

"A friend of mine in Paris introduced me to someone who apparently knows him quite well."

"That wouldn't be a guy by the name of Teng Lo, would it?"

"You know I'm not going to tell you that."

He thought very carefully for a few moments before he said, "Bertie, if you don't know Teng, then none of this will make any sense and you can just tell me to shut up, but if it is Teng, there are a few things you ought to be aware of. You might already know all this but I'd be willing to bet that you don't.

"Both Teng and his wife come from very old and respected families, but there's a real difference between the families. His wife's family is directly related to the royal family. They are highly respected, very wealthy and very prominent socially. Teng's family is very highly respected as well, and they have been revered for generations in Vietnam as scholars, teachers and intellectuals of great wisdom. As a family, they are comfortably well-off but compared to the wealth of his wife's family, they are paupers. Teng and his wife met in London back in the 1930's. She fell in love with him for his knowledge, scholarship and enormous learning. He fell in love with her for her beauty and kindness. She took him back to Thailand for her mother's approval. Her father had died but I forget how, and Teng was stunned by the family's wealth. Although he had to do it, he was embarrassed to take her to meet his family, whereas it probably never even entered her mind to think about the difference in financial circumstances.

"Her mother had an apartment in Paris which she rarely used and she gave it to her daughter

200

as a wedding present. To the best of my knowledge, they both still live there. Anyway, to the great disappointment of both of them, they were unable to have children, and Teng kept feeling more and more worthless. Then, on one of their trips back to Thailand, General Phao Sriyanond, Chief of the Thai National Police and one of the most powerful men in the country, arranged to meet with Teng. From then on, everything was different."

I stopped Bill and asked, "Bill, how can you possibly know all this stuff?"

"Servants," he said. "Don't forget that I've lived here all my life. People with the wealth of Teng's wife and her family have so many servants that they don't even notice them. They speak in front of them as though they are furniture or something. But the servants listen—and they talk. Stories get around, and although they circulate in dialects incomprehensible to the majority of upper-class Thais (who would never be privy to servant gossip in the first place), I speak most of those dialects. But here's the part I'm getting to."

The Ugly Truth

Bill continued, "General Phao ran all the opium traffic in Thailand. Most of the opium originated in Burma and although there was heavy usage in Thailand itself, the supply vastly outweighed the local demand. I think Phao probably initiated the original conversation because he wanted to use Teng's connections in Vietnam—which he did—but Teng wanted to make sure that nothing could be traced back to him directly. That's when Phao brought Vang into the equation as a middleman. Teng could make the introductions for Vang but all direct contact with those connections was through Vang.

"At some point, Teng decided that Phao didn't need the Italian Mafia as distributors in Europe because, for France at least, Teng could handle it himself. Needless to say, Teng has become extremely wealthy in his own right. He has tried to explain it to his wife as having been very fortunate in some of his investment decisions, but according to the information that I get, she and her mother are becoming increasingly suspicious and are starting to distance themselves from Teng. OK, that's my piece."

I sat there in total silence, overcome with the enormity of what I had just been told. I finally managed to stutter out, "Why . . . why are you telling me all this, Bill?"

"Because I think it's to my advantage," he answered coolly. "I'm not sure if you and I will ever get to be friends—and I think we might—but I think we can probably be useful to one another. For that to be the case however, a basis of both trust and respect has to be established first. It's neither useful nor healthy for you not to know who you're dealing with and I don't want to see you get blind-sided by Teng.

"I don't like Vang very much but I've never seen him make a mistake in sizing up people. He clearly both respects and trusts you, and it looks like Kittikachorn is trying to establish a relationship with you as well. From what I hear, a lot of the people in Washington don't like you very much either, but somehow or another, you seem to have won their respect and trust as well, grudging though it may be. I needed to do something to make you understand that whereas you can tap into sources I could never get close to, I can do the same thing for you. I'd be willing to bet heavily on the fact that there's not another American anywhere in the world that could tell you what I've told you tonight. There are probably damn few Thais outside of the drug trade that could do so either. You've already established your *bona fides*. I needed to establish mine." We shook hands and I left.

Nobody was awake (but the servants, of course) when I arrived back at the house, but although I was dead tired, there was no way I was going to be able to sleep. I went out onto the veranda outside my bedroom to listen to the night noises and to think and to try to calm my rage and inner turmoil. What Bill had told me was absolutely mind-boggling. There was no proof of any of it of course, but some of the details rang true. I had already noticed the curious lack of interaction of Lo with Sunisa and her mother. If what Bill had told me were really true and became known, Sunisa and her family would be disgraced forever. It was simply incomprehensible that Lo could even imagine getting involved in such a thing. It was monstrous to think that he would be willing to betray his own sacred honor and every ethical principle that his family had upheld for generation after generation. What was even more grotesque was that he had no need whatsoever for the money. He had entered into this obscene trade for no other reason than to stroke his ego—to make himself feel more manly, more important, more of a provider to his wife. It was simply hideous. I hoped with all my heart that it wasn't true but I was very much afraid that it was. Until I felt more comfortable, I didn't even want to sleep under the same roof with him.

As it turned out, I didn't. I was still sitting on the veranda when I awoke with a start as the early morning sunlight stroked my face. I had slept so soundly that it took me a moment to gather my senses and get my bearings but then it hit me. I knew that Sunisa and her mother were looking forward to taking me down to their beach-front estate in Phuket, and I really wanted to go because in addition to truly enjoying the company of Sunisa and her mother, Phuket had the reputation of being one of the most beautiful islands in the world. (It is, actually—or at least was.) I went inside, packed, showered and shaved and used the telephone in my room to call the airport and make reservations on a noon flight back to Paris. When I arrived for breakfast promptly at 9:00, it was clear that something was wrong, as I was dressed in shirt and slacks rather than my usual Thai breakfast garb. Sunisa and her mother looked stunned. I couldn't keep the hostility out of my eyes when I nodded to Lo.

Sunisa and her mother came running over and I took one in each arm and hugged those two fragile, sweet, tiny, wonderful women with genuine love and a deep sadness as I told them that something had come up at the office, and I needed to get back to Geneva urgently. It broke my heart to see their tears and to realize how much distress I was causing them, and I wanted to kneel on one knee so I could look them directly in the eyes, but that would have been an unforgivable breach of etiquette. So I just looked down and kissed them both on the cheek and held them tightly as I earnestly told them how very sorry I was. I don't think either of them doubted that I was truly speaking from my heart, and that just made them cry even harder. I disentangled myself, went over to Lo and told him I was genuinely sorry for the disruption I was causing. I looked him hard in the eyes but he had to look away even as he told me how distressed he was. I felt sure right then that Bill had told me the truth.

Sunisa and her mother were still hugging each other and crying as I went over to them, bowed deeply and said how genuinely honored I was to have been their guest and to be able to count them as friends. I apologized again for my unforgivable disruption of their plans. I never even glanced at Lo as I left. One of the servants drove me to the airport.

Word travels fast in Thailand. When I got to the airport and went to the Air France counter to pick up and pay for my ticket, I was astounded when the agent bowed and handed me an envelope emblazoned with the governmental seal of Thailand and said, "With the compliments of the Prime Minister, Mr. MacFarland. Please follow me." I've been in a lot of VIP lounges in airports but this one must have been reserved for the very top rung of government officials. There was a huge portrait of the king, Bhumibol Adulyadej, on one wall but there were smaller portraits of a bunch of people I didn't recognize on another wall who were all lined up under a larger portrait of Kittikachorn. I was the only passenger in the lounge, and I know that all those airline attendants hovering about were only trying to be of service and make me comfortable. They stopped bothering me and instantly retreated when I told them I was really tired and asked them to be sure to wake me up in time to get on the plane.

I had a lot of time to think on the way back to Paris. I first thought about Kittikachorn and realized that I had never opened his envelope. When I did, I found a first-class ticket from Bangkok to Paris along with a sealed note. Looking with amazement at the ticket, I realized that when I had personally been escorted onto the plane as the first passenger boarding, no-one had ever asked for my ticket, and I had frankly forgotten all about it. When I tried to give it to the stewardess, she just smiled and said, "We have no need for it, Mr. MacFarland. Can I bring you something to eat or drink?"

Although the note was in a masculine handwriting, Kittikachorn must have dictated it to someone at the airport. It was a bit cryptic. It read:

'I hope you enjoyed your trip yesterday and found it informative. I thought you might also enjoy meeting your compatriot Mr. Young. I expect you two had a lot to discuss. I was disappointed to learn of your necessity to return urgently to your office, as I hoped we might have the opportunity to meet once again before you left. I'm sure we will have occasion to meet again in the future, however, and I look forward to working with you.

Cordially, K'

Crafty bastard, I thought. He had realized his mistake by hinting that he could remove the American planes from Thailand if he so wished, and I had called him on that bluff. He showed me yesterday that there are a lot more illegal American activities going on in Thailand that he *can* shut down, with no significant impact on his desire to keep Thailand free of communism. It might be a lot less convenient and a lot more costly, but the Americans could move those training operations to Laos or the Philippines. He was letting me know that he could definitely twist the tail of the tiger—and make it hurt, too.

I was less sure about his motivations for getting Bill and me together. Although Bill was apparently highly regarded by the CIA, he didn't seem to be in a position of great management power. Kittikachorn's reasoning escaped me. I was glancing idly through an Air France-supplied magazine, when a bizarre thought hit me. Was it somehow possible the Kittikachorn was using Bill to let me know about Lo? That really seemed way too far-fetched, but on the other hand, if I could somehow be informed of Lo's nefarious activities . . ..

Kittikachorn knew of my loathing of what the United States was doing in Vietnam, but on the other hand, I had felt patriotic enough to help Vang in order to prevent Americans from dying. Men who rise to the level of Kittikachorn always have a back-up plan to get what they want. I may not have known about Lo's activities, but I was sure that he did. He was probably surprised to find, when he visited with us, that Sunisa and her mother seemed to have developed a real affection for me, and probably guessed that the feeling was mutual. I knew that he wanted to use me, but would he be low enough to threaten to expose Lo's activities— with the resultant catastrophic disgrace to Sunisa and her mother—if appeals to my patriotism fell on deaf ears? I decided he wouldn't hesitate for a heartbeat.

It was good to be back in Paris. The new mattress on the bed in my apartment was a lot more comfortable than the old one, and although I woke to bright and cheery mid-January morning sunlight, I couldn't seem to get rid of my feeling of depression and sadness. For the second time I had come back from Thailand wounded by a significant traumatic experience. I wasn't wounded physically this time, but the emotional wound was almost worse.

I called my secretary, Maddie, in Geneva and was heartened by her report. She and Neal and Grant were getting along famously, and getting an amazing amount of work done. She said the she and her husband had invited them over to their house for New Year's, and their two teenage daughters had both been smitten by their good looks and the fact that they were intelligence service employees—sort of like 'James Bond' or something. We both had a good laugh over that, and when I told her I was calling from Paris and would be back in the office the next day; she said she would bring in cookies so we could have a little party to celebrate. I warned her not to let Martin know about the cookies—I could absolutely guarantee her that every last one of them would 'mysteriously' vanish. It was heart-warming to hear her laugh.

My next call wasn't so pleasant. I called Bernard on his private office line, told him I was back in Paris and would be really grateful if he could find some time for me to meet with him in the office. He ignored my question and asked,

"Are you hurt?"

"Not physically," I replied.

He let out a long breath and said, "I've got an extremely busy day today. Come have dinner with Sylvie and me at the apartment tonight. Eight o'clock work?"

"Bernard, I need to discuss some things with you that I don't think you would want Sylvie to be aware of. Could you and I meet at a restaurant or something?"

"Bertie, I'm pretty sure I know what you want to talk about. Sylvie and I always share that kind of information. See you tonight?

"I'll be there," I said.

I spent all day thinking about Lo; Kittikachorn; CIA training camps; elephants; Sunisa and her mother; a tropical paradise in the jungle; breast cancer; Bill Young; Vang; the war in Vietnam; the obscenity of the drug trade; the unthinkable perfidy which humans are so uniquely capable of; the blindness of love; the betrayal of trust; the unquenchable greed of powerful people; the beauty of night sounds in the jungle; motorcycles and gang members; the eight-fold way of Buddhism; and the compassion of kind people.

My face must have reflected the turmoil of my thoughts when I rang Bernard's doorbell that evening. Sylvie didn't even give me a chance to shake Bernard's hand, but just grabbed me, gave me a big hug and kissed me, and kept murmuring to me like a mother to a distraught child, "Don't be so upset sweetheart, it will all work out, everything will be OK ,you'll see, etc., etc." She sat me down on the family room couch, poured me a huge whiskey, put a big platter of hors d'oeuvres in front of me and said, "OK. Now tell us everything from the beginning. Don't leave out anything."

I don't even remember when we moved into the dining room, but that's where we were when I finally got through my story. Their faces were quite a contrast. Bernard's was dark with rage and Sylvie's was white with shock and horror. Bernard said nothing at first, but Sylvie was asking of no-one in particular, "How long has she known? How long has she had to bear this by herself? Oh! My poor, poor dear Sunisa."

Bernard looked at me and said, "We mustn't do anything precipitous, Bertie. We have to remember that we have no definite proof yet although I'm confident I can get it. I'm sure some of the people I know have access to that dark underworld. We must have firm, unshakable proof before we do anything. Having said that, I think you and I ought to be thinking about what actions we should take if and when we do get such proof. Poor Bertie. Two trips to Thailand and two disasters. I'm so sorry you didn't spend the holidays with us."

He paused for several seconds before continuing as though he was deciding on how to phrase his next comment. He sighed and said, "As if you didn't have enough things weighing on your head, I'm afraid I have to add another burden, and it's very heavy. DeGaulle is going to pull completely out of NATO. He told me so himself. I'm sorry to have to lay this on you but I see no other choice. As you know, your Ambassador Bohlen is a close personal friend of mine and on several occasions I have served as a 'back channel' between DeGaulle and Bohlen, with DeGaulle's full knowledge and approval. This time however, he specifically forbade it. I have spoken to Couve de Murville, our Minister of Foreign Affairs, about it, and he agrees with me that the U.S. should be informed as quickly as possible provided they can keep their foreknowledge of the pull-out totally secret. I want the two of you to meet and agree on a plan before anything is done, and before you say anything to Washington. Can you come back to Paris next week? I'm sorry old friend, but the Minister certainly couldn't meet with you in Switzerland without, literally, the whole world knowing about it."

"Of course I'll come back," I said "but why is DeGaulle doing this?"

"It's getting late and it would take hours for me to try to explain it, but you and I will talk next week before we meet with Maurice [Couve de Murville]. Good night, my friend. I'll see you next week."

Chapter 11 — DeGaulle and NATO

When I arrived back in Geneva, I drove straight from the airport to the office. Martin greeted me cheerfully, asked if I had enjoyed my trip to Thailand, and airily informed me that, "Your General Carroll would be grateful if you would give him a call—at your earliest convenience, please. Kill anybody in Thailand this trip, Bertie?"

I just glared at him and said, "And a Happy damn New Year to you too, Martin!" As I walked away, I thought, *Crap! I didn't tell Martin or anyone other than Bernard that I was going to Thailand. What the hell is going on now? Why can't people just leave me alone and let me get on with the information-gathering business?*

Before I called Joe, I went to my office to greet Maddie and the guys. Maddie had made a few changes to our offices. There were now two desks in my office—hers and mine—and two desks in what used to be her office. In addition, there was now an inside door connecting the two offices. I was kind of surprised, but thought it was pretty neat and said so. I think Maddie was relieved. The energy level in the office was impressive, and the three of them were really becoming a team. I told them I had to make a phone call to Washington but would be back to help as soon as I could.

Joe was both frosty and exasperated. He said that given the job I'd done so far, everybody had cut me a lot of slack up to this point, but having a private chat with the prime minister of another country was really over the top and what the hell did I think I was doing, anyway?

It took me a long time to explain the whole thing, starting with the fact that I had no idea that my host family would invite the Prime Minister to their social event, and no reason to think he would come if they did. I told him I didn't know that they would invite Ambassador Martin, either, but I supposed Martin had reported the encounter. I asked Joe to let *me* tell the story of what had happened—after all, nobody else was out there on the veranda with us, so unless they had gotten a report from Kittikachorn directly, nobody else could possibly tell them what had transpired or what we talked about.

In what I thought was an unnecessarily icy tone, Joe said, "Please do, Bertie, but first, I'm going to turn on a recorder. There are a hell of a lot of people who are going to want to hear this." I heard a small 'Click' and he continued, "O.K. Say your piece."

Even though Joe was good about not interrupting too much, it took me over a half hour to relate exactly what had transpired and what had been said. I then told him of my visit to the logging/CIA training camp (I didn't mention Bill Young). I said that I had decided to return to Paris the day after my logging camp visit, but that when I got to the airport, I found that Kittikachorn had bought my return ticket and the envelope I was given had a note from him , which I related from memory. Finally I said, "Joe, when the Prime Minister of the country you're visiting tells you to come and speak privately with him, how do you politely refuse? Maybe if I were a State Department employee I'd know the answer to that question—if there is one—I'm not and I didn't."

He let out a long breath and said, "Bertie, I swear I've never seen anyone who could get himself embroiled in as many unorthodox situations as you can. From what you've told me, I guess you didn't do anything to damage U.S. - Thai relations, but would you do all of us here in Washington a huge favor? Would you please not go back to that part of the world again without giving us an opportunity to discuss it with you? You have no idea how sincerely grateful we all would be."

I gave him my heartfelt promise.

He threw me off balance when he asked, "How much do you know about the Teng family?"

My first reaction was, "How does he know that name?" Then I immediately realized that Ambassador Martin would have named the Tengs as the hosts of the now-infamous 'get together.' I answered, "Not very well, really. Their permanent home is in Paris, and I was introduced to them by another friend in Paris. I was having dinner with them one evening, and when Mrs. Teng learned that I had no plans for the year-end holidays, she invited me to accompany them on a visit to her mother's home in the suburbs of Bangkok. I couldn't think of any graceful way to decline, so I accepted. As I found out when I got there, her mother—in addition to being a delightful, warm and fascinating lady, by the way—is also enormously wealthy, very respected, and very prominent socially—and a direct descendant of the royal family. She really is a very special lady, and her daughter is just like her. I sort of fell in love with both of them. They are kind, compassionate, and caring people."

"What do you know about the husband," Joe asked

"Not a lot. Apparently, he comes from a long line of highly respected Vietnamese scholars, teachers and intellectuals. That's about the extent of my knowledge, though. I don't even know what he does for a living. If indeed he does anything."

"What about this friend who introduced you to him? As far as you know, is he reasonably respectable?"

"Impeccable. He is well-known and highly regarded by some of the top people in France." I paused and asked, "Why are you asking me all these questions? Is there something wrong that you're not telling me?"

"Not that I know of. State has done a little probing. Everything you said about Mrs. Teng and her mother matches up perfectly with what they found. So does your information about Mr. Teng's illustrious family. It's Mr. Teng himself that gives us a little pause. We have nothing definite, but in some quarters, he seems to have a slightly unsavory reputation. I just thought you should know. OK. I guess that's it. I feel better now and I think the others will as well, but don't forget your promise."

Before he could hang up, I said, "Joe. It would appear that I may have the opportunity to pass along some extremely important and highly secret information concerning one of our allies. If I am permitted to do so however, I will have to meet with one of their top officials to agree on what I will be allowed to say. I already know the subject matter. It will be of major international importance, and we should have as much time as we can to prepare ourselves for it. I will simply be an information carrier, nothing else. I know full well that this sort of thing should be handled exclusively by State. However, until the announcement is formally made by the government in question, they don't have anything unusual to discuss with State. If I am allowed to transmit the information, I have to have air-tight guarantees that Washington's foreknowledge of impending events will be held in complete, total secrecy at a level that surpasses even that of Laos secrecy. How do you want me to proceed? I am requested to meet next week on this matter."

The silence on the other end was so long that I thought our connection had been broken when Joe finally said, "Bertie, I'm beginning to rue the day we ever met. It just never ends with you. No doubt about it, nobody believed you when you told us that Brezhnev was going to overthrow Khrushchev. But then it happened. Next, you come to us with some ridiculous story to the effect that not only were the Chinese ready to test a nuclear bomb right now; they were going to use U-235 rather than plutonium to do it. We thought we had you then. Our leading scientists knew for *sure* that one couldn't be true—but it was, and it happened. Then Vang shuts us down until he can meet with you personally. Then you have an intimate and totally private little chat with the Prime Minister of the most important strategic ally we've got in the Vietnam situation. Now you tell me that agents from another government want to use you as a back channel to pass along some sort of earth-shaking information, and they won't even talk to the appropriate people in the State Department."

There was another very long pause and in a resigned voice he added, "I don't have a clue as to what to tell you Bertie. This one is literally way beyond my pay grade. I'll discuss it with McNamara, he'll discuss it with Rusk, and then they will probably both discuss it with Johnson. I don't suppose you'd tell me what country we're talking about, would you?"

"I'm sorry, Joe."

"Are we talking political upheaval, military threat, trade relation rupture . . .?

"I'm sorry, Joe. I can't play '20 Questions' on this one. I *would* like to make one very emphatic point though. I want nothing to do with all this stuff. Nothing! I just want to be left alone to work on the military information acquisition system. I actually enjoy doing that, and the two temps that you sent over have turned out to be great assets, speedy learners, very knowledgeable, and great team players. I'm looking forward to working with them. You have no idea how sincerely I mean it when I tell you I want nothing to do with this other crap. However, in my opinion, it is something of grave national importance. It is certainly something that I had to bring up with you. I've done so and now the ball is entirely in your court. Kick the can further down the road and make the other guys earn their pay."

"Major, that is a flippant way to address me and to refer to my superiors and to the President of the United States. I suggest that you not do that again. I'll get back to you in due time. This conversation is ended."
He slammed the phone down.

I couldn't blame him. He was mad and frustrated and didn't know what to do. I thought he handled it better than I would have been able to if the situations had been reversed. I went back to start work with Maddie and the guys.

The system was really progressing well and with the additional experience that Maddie and the guys had gained with it during my absence, the alterations to the system design that were needed had become well defined. The additional human skills that we needed were also becoming very clear. I was truly pleased. It was comfortable to know exactly what needed to be created, what needed to be fixed and tweaked, etc. Interesting, useful, fun and eminently doable projects stretched ahead as far as the eye could see.

Having an extra pair of hands (mine) was helpful, and we decided to call it quits a little after 5:30. We spent the next half hour chatting like old friends and doing serious damage to the cookies that Maddie had made, as well as to the bottle of wine that Grant contributed.

I met Yolande on the way to the car, wished her a belated Happy New Year and then asked her if she'd like to have dinner. "Here in Geneva or somewhere around your place?" she asked. I asked which she'd prefer. She smiled and told me my place, but said that she needed to go home first and would meet me at the house. I told her I'd look forward to it.

It had snowed in Aubonne, but with typical Swiss efficiency, the roads were clear and dry. Somebody—probably the farmer—had plowed the little dirt road leading to his farm and my driveway and as I approached, the electronics for the gate sensed the security device installed in my car and silently swung it open. The new lights lining the driveway were a nice touch, as was the fact that the lights by the front door turned themselves on. I recognized the 'caretaker' who stepped out of the shadows and doffed his workman's cap to reveal the military brush-cut which it concealed. I told him that I was going to unpack and take a shower, but if a 1965 Audi A4 convertible driven by a young lady arrived to please let her in.

When I got out of the shower, Yolande was waiting for me in the bedroom and after kissing me 'hello' she asked, "Bertie, is it alright if I leave a few things here when I leave tomorrow morning? I assure you I'm not trying to move in but it's a little embarrassing to show up at the office wearing the same clothes that I had on the day before, and wearing a minimal amount of make-up. I've brought a couple of changes of clothes and shoes plus a make-up kit that I'd like to leave here. If you have someone else visiting, everything is easily moved to one of the closets in the servant's quarters. Would you mind?" I told her I didn't mind at all and thought it was a great idea.

In many ways, Yolande was the ideal companion. We both sincerely enjoyed each other's company. I didn't have to make up any stories about where I worked or what I did for a living. Whenever I travelled —which was frequently—she had complete use of the house if she wanted. The only hard and fast rule was that if she invited a male friend to sleep over, they couldn't use my bed. It was a comfortable arrangement for both of us and it lasted for several years.

I very much liked the guy she married, and was looking forward to being friends with them both but he hated city life and she was happy to go back with him to his native Australia.

It took two days for Joe to get back to me. When he did so it was to tell me that State insisted I use our Ambassador in whatever country I was talking about to be the information conduit to Washington. I thought about this for a moment. DeGaulle had forbidden Bernard to serve as the back-channel conduit to Ambassador Bohlen, but if the information flowed to me from someone in the French government and I subsequently passed it along to Bohlen, that might work. I told Joe the condition was fine with me if it was acceptable to the other side. I said I would of course have to explain Washington's caveat to my interlocutor and get his approval for the arrangement. I said if he did approve, I would send him (Joe) a two word cable—'Approval obtained'—and subsequent information flow would be the responsibility of the Ambassador. I emphasized that Rusk would have to give the Ambassador his personal assurance that the Ambassador's communications in this matter be treated with the highest level of security. If not, the high government official giving me the information would have his head handed to him by his own government. Joe said he would pass my comments along. I called Bernard to inform him of my conversation with Joe and he said he thought Maurice would find those terms acceptable.

I flew to Paris early the next week to talk to Bernard and to meet with Maurice Couve de

Murville. I met with Bernard first. Our discussion was centered on why De Gaulle would want to completely withdraw from NATO (the North Atlantic Treaty Organization), but before I recount our conversation, for those readers who know little or nothing of General Charles De Gaulle, a little background information is in order. The following was taken from the BBC's history archives:

'Charles de Gaulle was born in Lille on 22 November 1890 and grew up in Paris, where his father was a teacher. De Gaulle chose a military career and served with distinction in World War One.

During the 1930s he wrote books and articles on military subjects, criticizing France's reliance on the Maginot Line for defense against Germany and advocating the formation of mechanized armored columns. His advice went unheeded and, in June 1940, German forces easily overran France. As under-secretary of national defense and war, de Gaulle refused to accept the French government's truce with the Germans and escaped to London, where he announced the formation of a French government in exile. He became leader of the Free French.

After the liberation of Paris in August 1944, de Gaulle was given a hero's welcome in the French capital. As president of the provisional government, he guided France through the writing of the constitution on which the Fourth Republic was based. However, when his desires for a strong presidency were ignored, he resigned. An attempt to transform the political scene with a new party failed, and in 1953 he withdrew into retirement again.

In 1958, a revolt in French-held Algeria, combined with serious instability within France, destroyed the Fourth Republic. De Gaulle returned to lead France once more. The French people approved a new constitution and voted de Gaulle president of the Fifth Republic. Strongly nationalistic, de Gaulle sought to strengthen his country financially and militarily. He sanctioned the development of nuclear weapons, withdrew France from NATO and vetoed the entry of Britain into the Common Market. He also granted independence to Algeria in the face of strong opposition at home and from French settlers in Algeria.

In May 1968, violent demonstrations by university students shook de Gaulle's government. A general strike followed, paralyzing France and jeopardizing the Fifth Republic. De Gaulle held elections and the country rallied to him, ending the crisis. In April 1969, De Gaulle resigned the presidency after losing a referendum on a reform proposal. He retired to his estate at Colombey-les-Deux-Eglises and died of a heart attack on 9 November 1970.'

Bernard filled me in with a little more immediate background. De Gaulle was indeed intensely nationalistic and was by nature extremely autocratic. He did not care overly much about what the French people thought; he was quite sure that he (alone?) knew what was good for France, and what was in her best interests. The constitution of the Fifth Republic over which he ruled, granted its President sweeping powers, and he used them to their fullest. He did not bother to consult with his allies when he decided to formally recognize the communist Chinese government of Mao Tse Tung in January 1964. Nor had he consulted them about his recently announced plans to pay a state visit to Moscow in July of this year [1966] to meet with Brezhnev and Kosygin.

In the aftermath of WW II, the United States was playing a powerful role in the reconstruction of Europe. De Gaulle was extremely concerned about what he viewed as steadily increasing U.S. dominance—if not downright hegemony—in European affairs. He was also acutely concerned about the very strong ties between the U.S. and Britain. Viewing Britain as little more than a puppet government of the United States, he did everything possible to minimize its influence in continental European affairs. Consequently, he twice vetoed England's application to join the European Common Market. He saw the world as being increasingly dominated by three super-powers—the U.S., the Soviet Union, and communist China.

He wanted France to play a dominant and pivotal role as the leader of a unified Europe. Under such a scenario, France would be the essential power broker in global affairs. Militarily, Europe was united by NATO but De Gaulle wanted to change that. He felt that if France withdrew, NATO would be seriously compromised. Although the U.K. was a nuclear power, it was a very weak one. Building and maintaining a full-scale nuclear military capability is an exorbitantly expensive affair and the U.K. simply couldn't afford it. They depended on the U.S. The entire equation would change overnight if Germany became a nuclear power, but with the memories of both World Wars still uncomfortably fresh, it was nearly inconceivable that a nuclear Germany would be permitted.

I asked Bernard if the French withdrawal from NATO meant that France would no longer feel bound to come to the defense of its neighbors if they were attacked. He explained that while France was going to leave NATO, they were not leaving the Alliance. In the event of an actual attack on one of its European allies, France would commit its military to the defense.

Lastly, I asked why Couve de Murville would risk his career by informing the U.S. of De Gaulle's intentions. "You can ask him yourself," he replied. "He'll be here in about 15 minutes."

Maurice Couve de Murville was one of the most charming men I have ever met. Although this was a man who could—and did—move effortlessly through the halls of power throughout the world, when I shook his hand as we met, and started to address him as *Monsieur le Ministre*, he immediately said, "Oh! No, no, no, Bertie. My name is Maurice. Bernard has told me so much about you that I feel as though we are already old friends. Come sit and let's talk. I understand that you will once again reprise your role as 'back channel,' this time between Chip and me?"

I thought quickly (I'd never heard of Ambassador Bohlen being referred to as 'Chip' so I wasn't actually sure who he was referring to) and said, "Only with your approval, sir. You have my word that I will convey no information that you have not expressly permitted."

He spoke to me as an equal. I hadn't been treated with such courtesy by a government official since I had worked for Jack. He said, "Of course there is nothing that I—or anyone else, for that matter—can do about the President's decision to withdraw entirely from NATO, but I think it is in our government's best interests to do what we can to try to alleviate the discomfort of the withdrawal as much as possible. In my opinion, the most helpful thing that we can do for you and the other NATO members is to give you as much time as possible to plan for, and discretely commence, the disentanglement process.

"As you know, at present, your government has eleven air bases on French soil. The relocation process will, I imagine, be most difficult. I'm not sure exactly how much time the President will give you to withdraw all of your military resources currently located on French soil but my guess would be one year. I also don't know exactly when he intends to inform NATO and your government of his decision to withdraw from NATO, but I believe it will be soon—perhaps even this month. (I don't remember the exact date of our meeting but it was very early February 1966. The formal announcement was made on March 11.) Therefore, the only firm information that I can give you at the moment is simply that the decision has already been made by the President and it is irreversible. It is of course imperative that your government's awareness that such an announcement is forthcoming be held in the highest secrecy. There is nothing that has been said here tonight that you are not allowed to pass along to Chip. Please give him my sincerest and best compliments. Let me give you my card, and please feel free to call on me at any time. I know Bernard has all your numbers, and if I think something important is imminent, he will contact you. It is fortunate that there are so many flights per day between Paris and Geneva and that now the flight time is so short." (The newly introduced French-manufactured Caravelle twin-engine jet had reduced the flight time to 31 minutes.)

After he left, I remarked to Bernard, "As you know, I have yet to meet Ambassador Bohlen, but I gather his friends call him 'Chip.'"

Bernard laughed and said, "Quite right. You handled that well, Bertie. I can't help but wonder if Maurice was subtly tossing you a curve ball to see how you would react. If he was testing you, you passed with flying colors." He glanced at his watch and said, "It's 8:00 and I've made dinner reservations at a new restaurant that has gotten excellent reviews. Pour yourself a drink if you'd like and I'll go tell Sylvie that we're ready when she is."

The atmosphere in my meeting with Ambassador Bohlen the next evening was very different. 'Chip' was all business. He certainly wasn't unkind or impolite. He greeted me warmly, asked about my leg, etc., but there was nothing of the relaxed informality that I had felt with Maurice. However, when I told him why we were meeting, he was visibly stunned.

He turned to Bernard and asked, "Are you sure De Gaulle means to pull out of NATO *completely?*"

Bernard answered rather sternly, "Chip, your interlocutor is Bertie, not me. I gave my word to the President that I would not discuss this affair with you. I am providing my home as a meeting place and since it is known that you, Maurice and Bertie are personal friends, there is nothing unusual about any of you being here. I can assure you however that Bertie is very unhappy that he is being thrust into this role. He wants nothing to do with it. If you have any hesitation about information being routed through him, let's all have a drink and part as friends."

There's a reason why Bohlen was regarded so highly by the U.S. State Department. A Harvard graduate, he was a brilliant analyst, spoke fluent French and Russian and was an expert on Russian affairs. He had served as the U.S. Ambassador to Russia from 1953 to 1957. He had established a well-deserved reputation as being a pragmatic, non-partisan, realistic diplomat and later became known as one of the elite foreign policy advisors known collectively as "The Wise Men." After Bernard's reprimand, without hesitation, he immediately apologized to us both.

With what I thought was real sincerity, he said, "Bertie, I'm truly sorry. I in no way meant to offend you or slight you. It's just that the news you have just given me was so startling that instinctively I turned to Bernard, who has been a close friend for many years. I apologize to you both. Bertie, please tell me what you can. My understanding is that whatever you tell me, I am allowed to pass along to the Secretary (Dean Rusk, Secretary of State). I understand that you have received assurances, acceptable to you, that all such information will be treated by the Secretary as extremely sensitive top secret material. You can be sure that I will personally treat it as such."

After I recounted the information I had received from Maurice the previous evening, he commented, "Well, we certainly have no doubt about the reliability of your source. Maurice is a brave and patriotic man to assist us in this way. I can only hope that we will be able to find some way to repay the debt of gratitude which we owe him. There will be major political and military consequences which will flow from De Gaulle's decision and we need to start work immediately on analyzing those and how best to handle them. I will contact the Secretary privately to see how he wants to proceed. Bertie, how long will you be in Paris?"

I told him that I had planned to fly back to Geneva in the morning but could postpone that if it were necessary. He asked if I would please do so and join him at his club for dinner the following evening.

When we met for dinner the following evening he looked as though he hadn't slept since I saw him last, and he probably hadn't. Washington was outraged that De Gaulle would unilaterally (and illegally) break the treaties which bound him not only to NATO but also, in some instances, to direct bilateral military agreements with the United States. There was a general acceptance of the fact that there wasn't a damned thing that the U.S. or anybody else could do about it however, and planning was already beginning on how best to handle the multiple disasters which were going to have to be faced. One of the most difficult problems was going to be how to relocate the eleven U.S. air bases in France, and McNamara was sending over an ex-Defense Department official, E.P. McGuire, to do an 'inspection' of our bases in France.

Chip mused, "I knew him slightly when he was serving as Deputy Assistant Secretary of Defense for International Security Affairs back in the mid-fifties and later when he was Assistant Secretary of Defense for Supply and Logistics. For some reason, he didn't stay in that post for very long and I have no idea what he's doing now. I think he's working in intelligence somewhere, maybe with the DIA. Do you know him?" He laughed when I told him that the only person I knew in the DIA was Joe Carroll. He said, "I believe you may know one other person in that department but that's none of my business."

He then explained that the only reason he had brought up the subject of McGuire was that McGuire would have a temporary office in the Embassy and that other than himself; McGuire would be the only person in the Embassy who knew about De Gaulle's impending announcement. He gave me McGuire's office number, and the telephone number of the apartment the Embassy had provided for him. He said that since he personally was often in meetings all day long, if I couldn't reach him directly, I should contact McGuire as an alternative.

Things were starting to move pretty quickly in Geneva. The search for separate office space had taken a serendipitous turn with the possibility that we might be able to use excess space in a building occupied by another U.S. diplomatic entity with offices in Geneva. If the details could be worked out, it would be a great match, as the other entity was already established with diplomatic immunity and as such, had secure communications lines with the United States. We could slide into that facility without making the slightest ripple. It was the perfect 'cover' for our activities. (Note: To the best of my knowledge that relationship in Geneva still exists today. A rather good demonstration of the old observation that 'things are not always what they seem to be.')

I received a phone call about mid-February from Sunisa (who was now back in Paris), thanking me for the thank-you note that I had sent upon my return from Thailand. I apologized once more for my precipitous departure, but told her how sincerely I had enjoyed my stay. I also told her that I thought I had fallen in love with her mother. She shocked me by starting to cry.

I am completely incompetent in situations like this because, for starters, I'm totally bewildered as to what the hell is going on. It truly upsets me when women that I very much care about start to cry. Especially if I have no clue as to why they are crying. I apologized profusely and assured her that I had no intention whatsoever of causing any offence, and how sorry I was that I had upset her. To my relief, she assured me that quite to the contrary, no offence had been taken and that she would be so happy to tell her mother what I had said because she thought her mother felt the same way about me. She added, "I think I do too, Bertie. Your visit was a great gift to us. You made us think very deeply about how we should be living our lives."

She started to cry again. All I wanted to do was to get off the phone, but she was clearly extremely disturbed about something, and I told her that if she had a problem, I would do everything in my power to try to help. In a very tremulous voice, she asked if we could have lunch together the next time I was in Paris. She told me that she would promise not to cry. I told her that I would almost certainly be coming to Paris within the next two weeks and that I would call her just as soon as I knew my schedule.

I got a call a few days later from someone introducing himself as 'Perky' McGuire. He also asked when I would be in Paris next, and I told him that I had tentatively scheduled a trip for February 23rd. He asked if we could meet. He suggested that it would be best if we could meet somewhere outside the Embassy and I told him that perhaps we could meet for lunch somewhere. He said he would tentatively schedule lunch for the 24th and to please let him know if that had to be changed.

I called Sunisa to see if the 23rd would work. She said it would, and asked where I lived; she didn't want to unnecessarily inconvenience me so perhaps there was a nice restaurant nearby. When I gave her the address of the apartment, she thought for a moment and said, "Oh! Lo owns a Thai restaurant very near you. Do you know it? I can't remember the name—he owns so many."

I about fell out of my chair but tried to be nonchalant as I replied, "Actually, I've eaten there once. It's not bad, but I think you would be disappointed." I suggested an excellent nearby restaurant that specialized in seafood dishes from the south of France.

We both were truly pleased to see each other again, and over an excellent lunch she burbled happily along about how many people who had attended our 'get together' had called to set up a meeting with me and how disappointed they had been to learn that I had been called back to Geneva on urgent business. She told me that she and her mother had had a wonderful time together at their beach house in Phuket and when I asked if Lo had accompanied them, she said, "Bertie, that's what I need to talk to you about. Lo always seems to be off on business somewhere. Our marriage just doesn't seem to exist anymore for him.

"Over the past several years, he has opened dozens of Thai restaurants all over France. I think he has five or six here in Paris. He imports a lot of food directly from Thailand for his restaurants, and he tells me that now he has an import/export business, but there's something that just doesn't seem right. He never told me he was interested in the restaurant business—or any other business for that matter. He doesn't know anything about restaurants, but he keeps opening new ones and they must be very successful because apparently they are making an astonishing amount of money. He is starting to get a lot of phone calls at the house, but if I walk into a room and he's on the phone, he always tells the person he's talking to that 'he has to go now and will call him back later.' Sometimes if I answer the phone, whoever is calling just hangs up. When we were in Thailand, he was forever going to business meetings in Bangkok, but when I would ask him who he was meeting, he would never tell me. He would just say, 'It's someone in the restaurant supply business. You wouldn't know them.' Bertie, I can't help feeling uncomfortable. Do you think I'm just being silly? I talked to mother about it but she just said that she thought that men who were in business did things like that but of course, she wouldn't know. Although she didn't say so, I think she's a little worried, too."

I was at a loss to try to respond. I asked her if it would be all right for me to speak with Bernard about it. I told her that I thought Lo was a client of his firm so Bernard might not be able to discuss it but he might have some advice and it was worth asking. She brightened up immediately and said, "Oh, Bertie! You have taken such a load off my shoulders. I can't thank you enough. I couldn't ask for two better friends than you and Bernard." She paused for a moment and said, "Oh, dear. I almost forgot and my mother would kill me if I had. She sends you her deep affection and says that from now on, whenever you are in Thailand, you must absolutely stay at our house if you are going to be anywhere near Bangkok. She says you will break her heart if you stay anywhere else." I told her to tell her mother that I was truly honored and that I would not break her heart for anything in the world.

As we were leaving the restaurant, she grabbed my arm and asked, "Bertie, Lo doesn't have to know about this lunch and our discussion, does he?" She was almost giddy with relief when I assured her that he absolutely didn't have to know anything at all about it.

I called Bernard at the office only to learn that he was out of town for conference or something and wouldn't be back in Paris until Sunday evening. I spent the rest of the afternoon perusing the wonders of the Louvre.

The next morning I called McGuire at his office to confirm our lunch date and choose a restaurant. Later that morning I was surprised to get a call from Couve du Murville who seemed very relieved to find that I was in Paris. He said that he had tried to get Bernard to call me only to find, as I did, that he was out of town. Sylvie had given him all my numbers and the Paris apartment was the first one he tried. He told me that no-one could know for sure, but his instincts were telling him that developments were probably imminent. He apologized for asking but said it would be extremely helpful if I could either stay by my telephone or if it were absolutely necessary for me to leave my apartment, to let his secretary know where I could be reached. I told him where I was going for lunch but didn't know their phone number.

It's hard to remember what life was like before mobile phones.

Lunch with McGuire was pleasant but not particularly useful. He was clearly very bright and extremely knowledgeable about the logistical problems involved with getting all of our military assets out of France (the eleven air bases were a major headache but they were far from being the only elements of our military presence). I didn't envy his job. I told him about the phone call I had received earlier from Couve de Murville and observed that the secret fuse seemed to be getting fairly short. He just groaned. He said that he and Chip had discussed how to indicate in Chip's correspondence with the Secretary that I was the source of any future information on the withdrawal, and had decided on "High-level Foreign Office source known to you." I told him I didn't care what term they used as long as it couldn't be traced back to me.

I had dinner that evening with Sylvie at Bernard's apartment (after dutifully informing Maurice's secretary of where I could be reached by telephone) and scooted out of my apartment very early the next morning (Friday, February 25th, 1966) to visit the local *boulangerie* for croissants and coffee. I caught up on some of my reading during the morning and was thinking about what I could do for lunch when the phone rang. Maurice asked if I could get to his office at the Quai d'Orsay right away. I did and later that day Chip sent following cable:[31]

'Paris, February 25, 1966, 1605Z.

"5247. For Secretary From Ambassador. High-level Foreign Office source known to you this afternoon told McGuire that subsequent to my seeing Alphand this morning (Embtel 5243) De Gaulle saw Couve de Murville and issued peremptory instructions to him to prepare papers by 7 o'clock tonight (1) denouncing all multilateral agreements connected with NATO except the North Atlantic Treaty itself, and (2) all military bilateral agreements with U.S.

'Source continued that whether agreements were denunciable or not, De Gaulle intended to denounce them. Later De Gaulle will be prepared to discuss with U.S. arrangements for facilities in France in the event of a war in which France would be willing to participate. Timing is not yet established but De Gaulle said possibly rather quickly, and certainly before his visit to Moscow.

'While we have no reason to doubt authenticity of this information, which was relayed to source by Couve immediately on arrival at Quai from Elysee, it nevertheless is extremely curious. It counter-acts specifically and definitely De

---

[31] U.S Department of State, *Foreign Relations of the United States,* 1964-1968 Volume XII, Western Europe, Document 54

Gaulle's own statement in press conference that these changes would be accomplished progressively and that French allies would not suddenly be inconvenienced, and would seem to represent a sudden and abrupt change of his policy and tactics in this respect for as yet undisclosed reasons. In fact source said de Gaulle had changed his position in last five days, i.e., since press conference.

'Source added that after denunciation issued, method and timing of U.S. withdrawal was less important to De Gaulle and presumably could be carried out in manner to minimize difficulties for us. Source described these decisions as a declaration of neutralism on the part of France. Will have further comments in subsequent telegram.

Bohlen'

That cable plus the rest is recorded history. I flew back to Geneva the next morning.

Chapter 12 — War and Fishing

Even though I was far removed from the White House, I still got classified communiqués regarding Vietnam, and things were going badly there. On December 24, Johnson, hoping to break the cycle of ever-increasing escalation, had decided to temporarily halt all bombing in North Vietnam. He hoped to establish a meaningful dialogue with North Vietnam. A subsequent effort to seek informal contact with North Vietnam's trade representative in Paris was rebuffed, and the U.S. had received no positive signals of any kind from Hanoi.

Hanoi was however, taking full advantage of the pause to move additional men and supplies into South Vietnam as quickly as possible. Llewellyn Thompson, the U.S. Ambassador to the Soviet Union was instructed to contact North Vietnam's diplomatic representative in Moscow, but there was no official response from Hanoi to the cessation of bombing. Hanoi seemed quite willing to 'pay any price, bear any burden' to achieve the re-unification of Vietnam—on their terms, not ours. Johnson was beginning to realize how absolutely determined and unbending the North Vietnamese really were. In spite of that realization, however, he and his hawkish staff totally failed to realize an even more important truth—it is impossible to bomb an idea.

In South Vietnam, inflation was rampant due to the massive influx of U.S. dollars. Furthermore, the Buddhist majority was threatening political chaos if the South Vietnamese government did not bow to their demands for a peaceful settlement with North Vietnam, and the formation of an interim coalition government which would include representatives of the Viet Cong. The United States signaled Hanoi that they were willing to accept reunification if a free and fair vote could be held in both North and South Vietnam. Hanoi responded that a 'free and fair vote' would be impossible as long as there were U.S. troops stationed in South Vietnam.

As January wore on, Johnson was being assailed on all sides. Hanoi was spurning his every effort and continuing the build-up in South Vietnam. The Joint Chiefs of Staff were clamoring for a resumption of the bombing. Our Ambassador to South Vietnam—Henry Cabot Lodge, Jr.—opined in a memo to Johnson, that if the U.S. didn't 'completely break the back' of the North Vietnamese military during the course of 1966, we would lose the war. A bill was introduced in the U.S. Senate to withdraw authorization of U.S. military force in South Vietnam. Senators Robert F. Kennedy and J. William Fulbright were drawing national attention to their strong opposition to the war, and Fulbright, in an essay entitled "The Arrogance of Power," wrote:

'We are now engaged in a war to "defend freedom" in South Vietnam. Unlike the Republic of Korea, South Vietnam has an army which [is] without notable success and a weak, dictatorial government which does not command the loyalty of the South Vietnamese people. The official war aims of the United States Government, as I understand them, are to defeat what is regarded as North Vietnamese aggression, to demonstrate the futility of what the communists call 'wars of national liberation,' and to create conditions under which the South Vietnamese people will be able freely to determine their own future. I have not the slightest doubt of the sincerity of the President and the Vice President and the Secretaries of State and Defense in propounding these aims. What I do doubt—and doubt very much—is the ability of the United States to achieve these aims by the means being used. I do not question the power of our weapons and the efficiency of our logistics; I cannot say these things delight me as they seem to delight some of our officials, but they are certainly impressive. What I do question is the ability of the United States, or France or any other Western nation, to go into a small, alien, undeveloped Asian nation and create stability where there is chaos; the will to fight where there is defeatism; democracy where there is no tradition of it; and honest government where corruption is almost a way of life. Our handicap is well expressed in the pungent Chinese proverb: 'In shallow waters dragons become the sport of shrimps.'

We were in very shallow waters indeed. Even as beleaguered as he was, I felt no sympathy for Johnson. He had knowingly started this war *based on an event that never happened.* My sympathies were reserved for the families and friends of the 2,064 Americans that had needlessly perished in Vietnam the previous year [1965]—sacrificed on the altar of Johnson's (and the military's) arrogance. Many more thousands of North and South Vietnamese soldiers and civilians had suffered the same fate. 1966 would prove far more deadly. The bombing resumed on January 31. The pause had lasted for 34 days. McNamara privately told Johnson that he thought we had a one-in-three chance of winning the war. Johnson's response was to escalate.

The spring of 1966 passed rapidly and pleasantly for me. Much to the relief of Martin, my group had quietly vacated his fiefdom and moved into our new headquarters in Geneva (which also conferred partial diplomatic immunity on our staff and operations); acquired a much larger computer system; and added considerable staff. We added input devices with keyboards in Cyrillic and other language-specific alphabets to simplify inputting the data that we were receiving from a variety of countries. We added native speakers of several different languages who were also trained in disciplines such as chemistry and physics, and who additionally had knowledge of advanced weapons systems. My system was developing very nicely indeed and I was beginning to settle into a comfortable, relaxed and enjoyable existence.

Things were going nicely on the domestic front as well. Yolande hadn't moved in—she kept her little apartment in Geneva—but she now had her own closet in my bedroom, and we spent most weekends together. She introduced me to a large number of her friends and acquaintances, and I introduced her to a number of people I had met at IOS, plus several CERN physicists who had become good friends.

I really cherished my friends at CERN. It was wonderful to have the opportunity to talk to people who shared my passion for particle physics and who were on the cutting edge of research in the field. Oftentimes, to the dismay of Yolande and the physicist's wives or girlfriends, they would find us gathered in a tightly knit little group arguing passionately until the wee hours of the morning about things which were totally incomprehensible to them. In sum, we had a social circle that was more than sufficient to provide as busy a social life as we were in the mood for.

Yolande was a wonderful hostess and we gave some truly memorable parties at the house that summer. I don't think any of our guests had a clue that the gardeners/caretakers, whom they occasionally caught a glimpse of, were actually armed guards. From time to time, I reflected that my life had settled into a totally unnatural peaceful normalcy that surely couldn't last.

It didn't.

Teng Lo

I got a call from Bernard one early April weekend. It was about Teng Lo. I don't know if Bernard knew any underworld figures personally, but with his vast network of contacts all over France, he could certainly reach anybody or any organization that he wished. The information he had gotten concerning Teng was even worse than we had feared. Much worse. Bernard asked when I would next be in Paris. We agreed to meet after business hours on Wednesday— this time in my apartment. Sylvie was not going to be privy to our conversation.

In our meeting, Bernard outlined the grim facts he had garnered from his contacts. He said he had received 'irrefutable proof' that Teng was becoming the largest importer and distributor of heroin in France, and that his business was growing daily. The narcotics trade does not take kindly to newcomers but apparently, Teng could supply very high quality product at prices well below those of his competitors. In the drug business, distributor loyalty follows profit, and more and more distributors were beginning to desert their former suppliers as they found they could substantially increase their profits by buying his lower-priced drugs.

Teng was no longer operating from his apartment; he had acquired rather opulent office space in a prestigious business area of central Paris and had hired about a half-dozen employees. His second-in-command seemed to be his chief accountant. In itself, that was hardly unusual but what *was* surprising was that his chief accountant happened to be a fairly young (late twenties

/early thirties) woman. Bernard said that by all accounts, the woman in question had graduated from one of France's better law schools, was extremely good at her job, was tough as nails—and was sleeping with Teng.

The litany of transgressions didn't end there. Although Bernard's information source couldn't provide hard proof of culpability, in the last year or so, several of France's more notorious drug king-pins had been found dead. Curiously, except for one victim who had been garroted, none of the corpses had shown any obvious external signs of trauma. No knife wounds, no gunshot wounds, etc. They had all died of massive internal wounds or broken necks, etc. Bernard's source claimed that Teng hired martial arts experts from Thailand or Vietnam who flew in, accomplished their mission, and flew right back out again. If true, Teng wasn't hesitating to use lethal force to further his business objectives.

Teng's operation was certainly a big part of France's growing drug problem. Drugs produce their own sub-culture of addicts who are constantly committing all sorts of crimes to get enough money to feed their insatiable addiction, and France's crime rate was becoming a real concern to the national leadership, not to mention ordinary citizens whose once-safe neighborhoods were becoming infested with aggressively menacing pan-handlers. Additionally, Teng's business plan of distributing through his chain of restaurants was extremely clever. Instead of having to venture to or through dangerous parts of town to get drugs (where undercover police were constantly a threat), clients could find what they needed in a perfectly respectable restaurant in a perfectly respectable, safe part of town, without raising any suspicion whatsoever. Restaurants are hard to monitor. They receive constant daily deliveries of the food that they need, and it's impossible to inspect every bag of rice or noodles or melons, etc. for hidden drugs. Additionally, restaurants commonly do a large cash business, so cash payments are a totally normal part of doing business. Finally, when the staff is all bound by a certain ethnicity and are exceptionally well paid in addition, it's extremely difficult to either recruit or insert an informant.

When Bernard finished speaking, we just stared at one another. Finally, I sighed and said, "He's really gone off the deep end, hasn't he? He's in far too deeply to simply quit and try to turn back. Neither his source nor his distributors would permit it. On top of that, he's a physical coward. He would never have the courage to even try it. He definitely has to be stopped though. What do you think we ought to—or can do?"

"God, I simply don't know, Bertie. I've been wrestling with this ever since I got this report. I've spent my entire life finding or creating solutions to seemingly intractable problems, but I have to confess, this one has me stumped. What's your opinion?"

I thought hard about it before replying, "Well, I don't see a lot of options. The usual one—having Teng arrested and tried in court—would be a disaster on a number of levels. I doubt strongly that the person who gave you this information would like to see himself in the public spotlight, and grilled in court by Teng's defense lawyers on his own background and activities, and how he acquired the knowledge he has. Secondly, even if he were willing to go to court, unless he was provided with 24-hour police protection, it's doubtful that he would live long enough to testify. A public trial would be a devastating humiliation for Sunisa and her family as well as for Teng's prestigious family in Vietnam.

"Speaking of Sunisa, I think Teng has placed her in terrible danger. Until we've resolved this, I think she should be back in Bangkok with her mother. She'll have plenty of protection there but I have no idea how to suggest she leave for the visit. Do you think that Sylvie could do it?"

Bernard shook his head slowly and said, "I really want to keep Sylvie completely out of this if I can. I can't think of any way of asking her to suggest the trip to Sunisa without explaining why it's necessary. In any case, what in the world do we do about Teng? He doesn't seem to realize that he will surely be arrested by the police at some point."

I sighed, got up and looked out the window into the dark courtyard and thought long and hard before I turned and said, "Bernard, I hate to say this but I only see one alternative. I'm afraid we need to arrange a 'tragic accident.' I can guess what your reaction is going to be to that suggestion, and I don't blame you. In my opinion however, Lo has passed over a line that severs him from the usual compassion and forgiveness of friends. He's killed for profit. That's unforgivable in my book. It's time for him to pay the piper."

Bernard was aghast. "God, Bertie! You know I can't be complicit in such a thing!"

"Your call, Bernard. But I can't do it without the cover of your irreproachable reputation. I don't need you to do anything physically, but you'll have to be with me when it happens. You won't see anything; you won't hear anything. Look, Bernard, I don't want to do this but I've been trained to kill by my government—specifically, the U.S. Army. Killing is what armies do. It's their business. Usually they do it *en masse* but occasionally, it's necessary to do it on a more personal, one-on-one basis. I've been specially trained for that. I have never used that training unless it became absolutely necessary to protect the national interest or to protect my own personal safety. I think sanctioning people like Teng is not only in France's national interest, it is in the *global* interest and that's the only reason I'm willing to do it. People like Teng are virulent cancerous tumors in the body of humanity, and they need to be extirpated. Now, I've said my piece and it's up to you. I'll call Sunisa's mother in Bangkok and ask her to make up an excuse for Sunisa to come home for a few weeks. I think she should get out of Paris immediately. But for Teng, I'll need your help. I think we should take a deep-sea fishing trip with him sometime in the next couple of weeks. I sincerely believe you'll be doing your country a real service. Think about it and let me know."

Bernard looked like he'd aged ten years when he slowly stood up, put his hand on my shoulder, shook my hand and left.

A Primer on Assassination

I think I need to interrupt this narrative here to discuss assassination for a moment. It's not a pleasant subject and not one I like to discuss, but you need to know a little bit about it. The training for it is long and extremely tough—both mentally and physically. Assassins can be roughly divided into two groups—long range and short range. The long range guys are the snipers. I'm a short range guy. I won't discuss the hours of physical training, or the intense anatomy training which is necessary. I won't discuss the yoga-like training that permits you to wait for hours, often in challenging climactic conditions and/or very uncomfortable postures and positions, completely silent and immobile waiting for the arrival of your opponent. In passing, I'll mention that most short range assassins usually have a weapon of choice, and the vast majority choose guns. I don't like guns, although I'm well trained in their use and will use one if necessary. I find them bulky, noisy, and prone to mechanical failure. They have too many moving parts for my taste, and if they jam or you run out of bullets, they are essentially useless.

Another fact I need to mention is that short range assassins are essentially trained for one-on-one combat. If you're going to have to wade through a phalanx of bodyguards, get yourself a SWAT team. Our job is to create a plan to maneuver the opponent into a situation where he/she will be alone or, exceptionally, in the company of a single other person.

Now I have to get to the hardest part of all—the mental attitude and toughness of the assassin. The decision to assassinate is not made lightly. It's a horrible thing to kill another human being. The assassin must be categorically, thoughtfully, totally convinced that the assassination is absolutely necessary for the greater good of the country, or even for society as a whole, and that he or she is uniquely qualified or positioned to carry it out. Once that decision is made, it is final. Your mind-set must be that either you or your opponent is going to die. There will be no turning back, no second thoughts—and no mercy—just ruthless efficiency.

***

My conversation with Sunisa's mother went much more smoothly than I had anticipated. She was excited to hear my voice, and after the usual enquiries concerning health and happenings, she told me how much she and Sunisa had enjoyed my visit, and said she hoped the reason for this call was to tell her that I would be coming to Bangkok soon. I paused, dreading to explain the real reason for my call but before I could say a word, she said, "It's Lo, isn't it?"

"I'm sorry to say that it is. He is doing some bad things and dealing with some very bad men. His drug business is ruining the lives of thousands of people. Until the situation is settled, I don't think it's safe for Sunisa to be in Paris. Can you call her and ask her to come home to help you with some family business or something? I don't want her to know it has anything to do with Lo."

"Of course. But what must be done about Lo?"

"I will speak to him."

There was a long pause before she replied, "Yes, I understand."

As a descendent of the royal family, I'm sure she was brought up on stories of the unending intrigues that swirl around the royal court and the price most often paid by the loser. Her voice was filled with sadness when she continued, "What must be done, must be done. Like me, Sunisa will be alone for the rest of her life." In a resigned, but business-like voice she said, "I do not know how to arrange these things, but I know some people who probably do. I will begin making phone calls immediately. How can I contact you, Bertie?"

I was appalled. She thought I wanted her to supply a 'hit man!' I quickly told her she had misunderstood and that I didn't want her to do anything but invite Sunisa to come home. She sounded greatly relieved, but then asked me to tell her where, and in what amount she should wire the money, and thanked me repeatedly for being willing to help her so much with this. I think the truth only dawned on her when I told her that there was no need for any money and that I wanted her to know she should never say anything to *anyone*—especially Sunisa—about this phone call.

She gasped, "No! No! That's impossible! You mustn't even *think* about being personally involved! I could never ask you to do such a thing! You mustn't even imagine something like that!"

"You aren't asking me to do anything," I replied. "I think of you and Sunisa as family and I feel a duty to protect you. I don't want you involved in any way because you don't know what to do, and even if you did, you would put yourself in danger of blackmail. Lo has crossed a line which must never be crossed. He has killed for profit and damaged the lives of countless individuals with his drug business. His activities have put Sunisa's life and the honor of your family in jeopardy. I don't want to do this but I'm trained for it. Lo will never feel a thing, and there will be only three people in the entire world who will know what happened. It's best this way. Now call Sunisa and get her out of Paris."

She began to cry and I told her I loved her and hung up. The ball was now in Bernard's court.

About a week later, I got a call from Bernard, who said Sylvie had told him that Sunisa had received a unexpected call from her mother asking her to return to Bangkok to assist her with some family business. Although Sunisa was surprised given that her mother's lawyers were the best in Thailand, she dutifully left immediately.

"What am I supposed to do now," he asked.

I'd already made a plan. "Tell your source that you have a well-to-do friend that lives in Switzerland, but who spends a lot of time in France, and who is interested in buying a modest-sized, seaworthy boat. Ask him if he knows a boat dealer somewhere on the coast that might give him a good deal. Suggest that your preference would be Brest as he knows a number of people in the area. My strong guess is that he will recommend a dealer who is also connected to the *'famiglia'*. When he calls back, give him my name—call me William—and ask him to tell the dealer I'll be contacting him directly. Just get the boat dealer's telephone number and I'll handle the arrangements.

Call Lo and tell him that you understand he's a 'bachelor' for the moment and invite him for lunch or dinner at your club. It's important that you be seen together publicly in a social setting. While you're having lunch, tell him I'm thinking about buying a boat and am trying to arrange to rent a demonstrator for a weekend of deep-sea fishing, and I suggested that it might be fun for the three of us to go together. I've already been with him in a social setting in Bangkok, and he'll be deeply honored that you are inviting him to share some personal time with you. I'll try to make arrangements for the weekend after next so please keep that date open. I'll wait to hear back from you. Oh, one last thing. I'm presuming that your contact has a good reason to do as you ask and to keep his mouth shut?"

"I've got enough hard evidence to put him away for life," Bernard replied.

Good old Bernard.

Deep Sea Fishing

He called back a couple of days later with the name and phone number of the boat dealer. I contacted him right away. I instantly felt better when I heard the dealer speak French. You could have cut his Sicilian accent with a knife. I told him that I wanted to rent a boat for the next weekend for a fishing trip with some friends, but that I was also interested in perhaps buying a boat, and asked if he could dock it for me if I did. He asked what kind of boat I was interested in, and armed with my freshly acquired knowledge from the library and a friend who knew a lot about boats, I gave him some highly detailed specifications. I'll skip the details, but basically I told him that I wanted a cabin cruiser somewhere around 14 meters long, twin inboard diesel engines, stand-up interior with galley and toilet/shower facilities, capable of carrying ten adults and sleeping six.

He was ecstatic, and told me he had just the thing, and launched into a long, enthusiastic description. I asked him if he had a demonstration model which I could rent for the fishing trip, and he said he had a used model that had just been traded in (fabulous condition, almost like new, extremely low motor hours, had only been driven on weekends by a little old lady from St. Pol, etc., etc.). We haggled over the price for the rental, the price for equipping the boat with fishing equipment, coolers, with ice, food and wine for three people for the weekend, the price if I bought the used boat, the price if I bought the new one, etc. until we were both convinced that we couldn't get anything more from the other. Then I dropped the hammer.

I told him I wanted him to prepare two contracts for me to sign when I arrived the next weekend. The first was a straight rental contract for the used boat for the weekend, plus the supplies that I had ordered. The second would be for the conditional sale of the used boat at the price we had negotiated. It would be conditioned on satisfactory inspection of the boat, including my satisfaction on the way the boat handled during the inspection period. If I was not satisfied for any reason, the contract would be null and void and he would immediately refund my 20% deposit. I told him that one of my friends who would be accompanying me was the head of a very large law firm so it would be unwise for him to put any other terms into the contract. When he agreed, I told him that I wanted some additional items to be loaded onto the boat and placed into a locked storage area before my arrival. The items I wanted were simple—two concrete blocks weighing about 30 kilos [66 pounds] each, with a stainless steel ring set firmly and permanently into each block. I also wanted 10 meters [33 feet] of heavy marine steel chain of a size that would fit through the rings, and five padlocks whose shackles were of a size and length to fit through at least two links of the chain.

There was a long moment of shocked silence before he screamed, "Are you completely crazy? What kind of business do you think I'm running? I'm going to report you to the police!"

In reply, I shouted, "I know exactly what kind of business you're running (I didn't). If you want to go to the police and report me—go right ahead, but who are you going to report? Do you think I would be stupid enough to give you my real name and address for the contracts? (In fact, I *had* given him my real name and address.) Now shut up and listen to me! My lawyer friend is a very powerful man in France. He is personal friends with President De Gaulle. If you don't want to cooperate, I'll guarantee you that tomorrow morning you will have so many police and federal tax agents swarming over your establishment that you won't be able to count them all. They will be investigating you personally, all your financial and business records, your contacts, clients and every possible detail about you, your family and your business. In addition, they will force you to close your business until their investigation is complete, and that could take several months—maybe even a year. You want that? You think I'm kidding? Call your friend and ask him what he thinks.

"Now listen, we're both businessmen. We understand how business works and there has to be something good for everybody in a good deal. So here's what I'm going to do. I'm going to give you the 20% good faith purchase deposit in cash. (This was going to make a huge hole in my personal bank account.) You're going to counter-sign the conditional purchase contract acknowledging receipt. When we return, I'm going to tell you that I'm not satisfied with the boat—and then walk away. You keep the deposit and the rental money and that's it. We'll never see each other again. If you dare to try to get funny with me later on, you'll be sued for illegally keeping my good faith deposit, *and* you'll have the police and tax agents on your doorstep doing exactly the kind of investigation that you'll get if you refuse my initial terms. Now what do you say?"

There was a long pause before he shouted, "I say God damn you! I also say OK. I'll see you next weekend."

"Good. See you then. Oh yes, one last thing. Make sure the radio doesn't work. Loose wire or something."

Lo had been thrilled to be invited by Bernard and was extremely jovial on the early-morning flight from Paris to Brest the following Saturday. He wandered around the boat dealership while Bernard went over the contracts and I gave the dealer the rental money and the deposit. Bernard, who was an avid blue-water sailor and who had crossed the Atlantic several times in his own sailboat, more than satisfied the license requirements for the rental. The boat itself was beautiful, and the dealer had done an excellent job of equipping it with food, wine, beer and fishing equipment.

 As he was showing us the boat, he nodded surreptitiously towards one of the storage lockers and later slipped me the key. Orientation complete, the dealer left the boat and untied us from the dock. With Bernard at the helm, the twin diesels roared into life and we navigated out into the open Atlantic headed southwest. Our journey had begun.

Though the temperature on shore had been pleasantly mild, once we were out to sea, it dropped sharply. Bernard had warned us both that even on the hottest of summer days, as long as your boat is underway, it's chilly or downright cold on the North Atlantic. Lo and I bundled up but Bernard, in his completely enclosed flybridge helm station, was toasty warm. A stiff breeze was blowing, and the ocean was choppy, but the size and weight of the boat along with Bernard's experienced helmsmanship made the ride reasonably smooth and fairly enjoyable.

We were moving far too quickly to attempt trolling. I told Lo that Bernard was taking us to an area where he had always had good luck fishing, but suggested that until we got there, we would be far more comfortable in the main cabin I was starting to get damned cold even with my coat on. I didn't know how to turn on the heat in the cabin, so we kept our coats on, but at least we were out of the wind.

I knew this was the moment I had so carefully planned for. It didn't make it any easier. As I said before, turning back is not an option.

I put a pot of water on to make some tea and turned to Lo and said, "Lo, sit down on the couch there. I want to talk to you." He looked at me with astonishment as I said, "Bernard and I know about your drug business and we are both very disappointed in you." Over his babbled protestations and feigned shock, I said, "Don't even try, Lo. Bernard has proof which will stand up in court, so there's no use trying to deny it. You're lucky we're your friends because we want to avoid bringing dishonor to you, Sunisa and your families. The public must never know what you've been doing and we must quickly dismantle this vast network you've set up."

I'll have to give him credit that he at least felt some shame. I think his grief was genuine as he fell to his knees, weeping uncontrollably as he gasped out, "Does Sunisa know?" I told him I thought she didn't know for sure but I knew she had suspicions.

"Her mother knows, though. I told her and asked her to make up some excuse to get Sunisa out of Paris and back in Bangkok where she would be safe. It was simply outrageous of you to put her in such danger. Now look, Bernard is going to quietly dismantle this empire that you have built—and you're going to help. Now quit your crying and sit back down on the couch and answer some questions. First of all, what's the name of your chief accountant?"

"What's going to happen to her?"

"She's not going to be your chief accountant anymore. Now what's her name?"

"Alexia Lafitte. Her father was a Colonel in the French Army and she grew up in Vietnam. She speaks both Vietnamese and Thai—in addition to French and English, of course." He actually sounded proud of her.

"Do you have a single source in Thailand for your heroin or do you have multiple sources?"

"I only deal with one source."

"Who is it?"

He gave me the name of a company.

"Who owns the company? What's the name of the man you deal with there?"

He was sweating when he told me and Vietnamese don't usually sweat.

"Do you do the ordering or does Alexia do the ordering?"

"Oh, no. Only I do the ordering. Alexia tells me how much we need and then I do the ordering personally."

"Does Alexia know the name of your supplier?"

"I don't know. She might. But he will only deal with me personally."

It was time. I looked deeply into his eyes and said in a hard voice, "I'm sorry Lo, but it's finished for you. You have recklessly risked Sunisa's safety. You have selfishly risked bringing great dishonor to your house, your family, your honored ancestors, Sunisa and Sunisa's family. I am giving you this one last chance to act honorably so that they—and the rest of the world— will never know of your disgraceful actions. You have taken the lives of other people just so you would have less competition and make more profit. *Your* life must end now. Because I am your friend, I am giving you a choice. It is your last chance to act with courage, to be a man, and to do the right thing. You know what is strapped to my leg?"
His eyes grew wide with horror as he nodded.

"I will use it if I have to but I am giving you another option. I am offering you this small vial of liquid as an alternative. It may burn a little on the way down. It acts very quickly. You will simply fall asleep—but you will never wake up. It is your last chance to act with honor. You must make a choice and make it now. Which do you choose?"

"Is there truly no other way?"

I shook my head.

His eyes never left mine as he drank it.

I waited until I was sure he was dead before I dragged him back out onto the aft deck. The amount of poison I gave him would have killed a man twice his size within seconds. I knocked on the door of the flybridge helm station to signal Bernard to stop, and he immediately throttled back, but continued to look straight ahead.

When wrapping Lo in the chains, I attached one weight to the chest area and the other to the calf area, and used all five padlocks to ensure that the chain couldn't possibly become unattached from his body. I checked the horizon again. There wasn't a ship in sight. He was heavy as hell with the chains and weights attached, and it took every bit of strength I had to wrestle his body over the side. I watched as he quickly disappeared then knocked on Bernard's door again.

Bernard finally emerged. To his enquiring look, I nodded and said, "Yeah. It's all over."

We went below and had a couple of stiff whiskeys and something to eat. I told him I had offered Lo the alternative of suicide and he had accepted it. There had been no violence, no bloodshed.

We didn't talk very much. We mostly just sipped our whiskeys and looked at each other from time to time, shaking our heads. I don't know if Bernard had personally killed anyone when he was in the *résistance,* but if not, he had certainly been personally responsible for the deaths of many of the German occupiers.

I'd been a lot more personally involved with the deaths of a number of people, but all of them would have killed me if they could have. I hadn't killed Lo; he'd chosen suicide. Technically and legally, I hadn't killed Lo, but it sure felt like it. I'm sure Bernard felt the same about his involvement.

We both felt miserable.

The Alexia Problem

I told Bernard what Lo had told me and told him I was worried a little bit about this Alexia person. "I know the principle is that if you cut off the head of the snake, the rest of it will die, but I'm worried Alexia might be able to assume Lo's role and keep the operation going."

Bernard said he didn't think there would be a problem. Teng owned all of his many restaurants personally so there would be no corporate partners to deal with. Bernard's firm would represent Sunisa in selling off all the restaurants and other unwanted assets. He felt once the word got out that Teng was dead, most of the restaurants would close up anyway. After all, food was only their secondary business. The whole operation would quickly lose all its 'retail' outlets. On top of that, on Monday morning, Bernard would take action to impound all Teng's bank accounts until his estate was probated. Ordering illegal drugs which you can't pay for is usually a fatal lapse of judgment. Alexia would surely be aware of that.

Resignedly, Bernard took the helm again and turned the boat due north. I dumped about half the fish bait over the side and took two of the fishing poles, dirtied them up a little bit, made sure there were a few fragments of bait on the hooks and left them lying on the aft deck. After an hour or so, Bernard throttled back, turned on the radio and tried to use the emergency frequency. The radio didn't work (he knew it wouldn't) but if it came to it, he could testify truthfully that he had tried. He used the boat's horn to signal SOS in Morse code but there was no-one to hear. In fact, we didn't see another boat of any kind until we were almost back to Brest but by that time, it was dark, and we were so close to harbor he decided not to try hailing one.

The dealership was closed when we docked and Bernard used a pay phone to contact the police.

Both Bernard and I had almost finished giving the police our testimony when the boat dealer arrived. He was loudly proclaiming his shock and horror when the police Captain scowled at him and curtly ordered him to shut up and sit down. There didn't seem to be a lot of love lost between the police and the boat dealer.

I testified that soon after we had left port, gotten clear of local traffic and well out to sea, Lo and I had cast our lines, but although we got a few nibbles, we couldn't get anything to hit hard enough so we could set a hook. The fish were just stealing our bait. I admitted with a sheepish grin that neither Lo nor I had any real experience in deep-sea fishing, and essentially, we were just fooling around a little bit until Bernard got to wherever he was going and stopped the boat and showed us what to do.

I told them the sea was pretty choppy and Lo was starting to feel a bit sea-sick, and I went below to make some tea because I thought hot tea might help settle his stomach. I said before I had even had a chance to get started, we were hit so violently by a wave that it threw me across the galley. I had hit my head with such force on the corner of a cabinet I was afraid I was going to pass out. I said it probably took me a couple of minutes to clear my head enough to go back on deck and when I got there, Lo had disappeared. When I signaled Bernard to stop the boat and asked if he'd seen Lo, Bernard said he saw me going below and thought he had seen Lo following me.

Of course he had immediately turned the boat around and retraced our path. He had tried to radio for help but then discovered our radio was out of order. The police chief shouted at the dealer that he was going to be in serious trouble and silenced his protestations with another curt command to shut up. I resumed my testimony and said that because it was cold on deck, Lo and I had bundled up with heavy coats and if Lo had been thrown overboard, it would have been nearly impossible to stay afloat encased in that wet coat.

Bernard came to the defense of the boat dealer by saying that the radio might well have been in working order when we left port but the rogue wave had slammed the boat so hard it could have knocked a wire loose inside. The police were treating Bernard with a deference that bordered on the obsequious and replied, "Of course if such is your opinion Maître Monod, we will not press charges."

Finally, there was much consulting of nautical charts, with Bernard pointing out an area that was *north*west of Brest, whereas in actuality, we had sailed *south*west. There would probably be a totally perfunctory check of the area sometime tomorrow, but nobody could survive a night in those frigid waters.

Case closed. Tragic accident at sea. Happens all the time.

We'd missed the last flight back to Paris. We found a hotel and had something to eat, and Bernard said he was going to call Sylvie and go to bed. I asked him to ask Sylvie not to call Sunisa. I'd call her mother in the morning.

There was one last thing which was worrying me and I brought it up with Bernard. "I'm certain this is going to be in the local papers tomorrow, and I'm worried they may publish our pictures as well. If the story gets no farther than Brest, I don't care; but if the Paris papers pick it up, it's going to be very awkward for me. I definitely don't want my picture in the newspapers."

Bernard said not to worry-he'd already taken care of it. After we'd had our photos taken by the police photographer, he'd taken the chief aside and told him that at the direction of the President himself, I was doing some highly secret work for the Republic. It was imperative to keep my photograph out of the newspapers. Indeed; it would be appreciated if the negative were destroyed. Also, it would be helpful if my name was misspelled when talking to any newspaper reporters. He said, "I think you'll be OK, Bertie."

Good old Bernard.

We perused the local newspaper on the flight back to Paris the next morning, and indeed, the story had made the front page. I think it was mostly because 'the distinguished and nationally-known lawyer, Maître Bernard Monod, whose prestigious Paris law firm is also one of the largest law firms in the nation,' was involved. I think his presence was bigger news than the drowning. His 'distinguished guest' Monsieur William Furland, was barely mentioned. Lo was not even named, but described simply as a 'Vietnamese client of Maître Monod's law firm.' I told Bernard that I felt honored to be sitting beside such an exalted *personage* and, nose uplifted, he told me in his best British accent that, "Given my celestial status, I feel you are being a trifle cheeky speaking to me so sarcastically, but I shall graciously overlook it—just this once." We had a laugh, and for the first time since this whole sordid situation had arisen, I felt comfortable that our friendship would survive unscathed. Perhaps it had even strengthened, in a way. I think he felt the same.

When we landed in Paris, I decided to stay, rather than to return to Geneva, and took a taxi to the apartment. Before calling Bangkok, I sort of collapsed on my sofa. I hadn't realized how deeply this whole thing would affect me. My thoughts and emotions were in a turmoil.

I suspect my voice reflected my emotional state when the call to Bangkok came through, because Sunisa instantly said, "Bertie, what's wrong?"

I told her that I had some very bad news to report and asked if her mother could pick up an extension phone, so that I could tell them both at the same time. When her mother joined us on the line, I related the exact same story I had given to the Brest police.

There was a long pause before Sunisa's mother said quietly, "Sunisa knows. I had to tell her while there was still time to change plans. Tell us, why were you willing to risk your life for us, Bertie? You barely know us."

It sounded almost like a challenge and my voice was much stronger when I replied, "First of all, rightly or wrongly, I think of you as family and I sincerely love you both. No, no! Wait. Let me finish. I believe that in his heart, Lo was a good man, but for whatever reason, he decided to do a horrible thing. Lo was anything but stupid, and he had to know that sooner or later he would be caught, maybe go to jail and certainly ruin the reputation of both his family and yours. That angered me greatly, but what made me even angrier was that he must have known that in the meantime, he was putting Sunisa at risk of physical danger. Had that been the extent of things, I would have simply done whatever I could to ensure Sunisa's safety. I also probably would have had a very strong talk with Lo to try to convince him to stop doing criminal things. But supplying drugs is not like robbing a bank or stealing jewels. Drugs steal human lives. It's almost worse than war, because in this case, the victims kill themselves while recruiting others to do the same thing, and ruin the lives of everyone who ever loved them. Making money based on the misery of others is an unforgivable offense. Lo had to be stopped. His actions were affecting far more than just your family.

"I could only see two alternatives. The first was to give the police all the evidence which we had and let the judicial system run its course. Lo was wealthy and would have hired the best defense lawyers in the country. The trial would have dragged on for years. Both of you, as well as his family members in Vietnam, would have been called to publicly testify. Key witnesses might have been persuaded to change their testimony against him. Some of them might even have mysteriously disappeared, or been the victims of a 'tragic accident.' At the end of it all, he might possibly have been acquitted, but if not, he would have started the appeal process—which usually takes years and years to resolve. In the meantime, he would have been a free man. With his exceptional intelligence, it would have been easy for him to simply turn the operations over to a proxy, and keep right on operating. He would have enjoyed the game of wits.

"Now let me tell you something which I think may make you feel better. Lo understood, and agreed that there was no way for him to turn back. I offered him the opportunity to take his own life by swallowing a vial of poison I had brought with me. He took it willingly and with courage, and asked me to apologize profoundly to both of you for causing you so much pain and sorrow. He asked me to tell you that although he didn't show it as much as he should have, he loved you both and always felt deep respect for both of you. His end came by his own hand and he acted as a man with courage. That is my report."

He hadn't said any of those things of course, but I hoped the lie would soften their loss somewhat.

Through their sobs and tears, they responded with effusive praise and copious thank-yous, etc. but I was in no mood for it. I was probably a little abrupt when I interrupted with, "Thanks, but that's really not necessary. I simply did what I thought I had to do and let's not speak of it again. Sunisa, Bernard says he'll help in dismantling Lo's empire and selling off his unwanted assets. Real estate prices keep going up so I expect all those restaurants will bring in quite a lot of money. I presume his will leaves everything to you?"

She confirmed that it did but said she wouldn't touch a penny of the money. "Mother and I talked about it, and we think half the money should go to his family in Vietnam—his mother is still alive—and the other half should go to you."

I thanked her but said I wouldn't touch it either, and to give it all to his mother. I told them I loved them both and hung up.

I was in a weird mood. I was happy, sad, relieved, tense, full of nervous energy, yet drained, somehow. I don't know. It was all jumbled up. I needed to get out, get some fresh air, and walk. I made a mental note to ask Bernard if he knew of a good fitness club or gymnasium in Paris that I could join.

It was wonderful to be outside and walking vigorously—it was April in Paris, after all. I walked south along the Seine for about an hour before turning back, and as I approached my apartment, I realized I hadn't had anything to eat since breakfast and was really hungry. It seemed a little ironic but Lo's restaurant was only a half-block away. By Paris standards, it was rather early to be eating dinner, and there were only six or so other tables which were occupied when I got there. As a result, service was speedy, but the restaurant was starting to fill quickly as I paid my check and started to leave.

As I was heading for the door, the same woman that I'd seen on my previous visit to the restaurant was coming in, and this time I stopped her. "Excuse me. I know this must seem like a tired old pick-up line, but I keep thinking that you look familiar somehow, and I'm usually pretty good at recalling faces. I know I've seen you *once* before—here in this restaurant, actually—but I have the nagging feeling that we had actually met previously. Am I totally mistaken?"

"No, we met once before and you even gave me flowers." I stared at her blankly and she continued, "You said some friends had them delivered to your apartment, but hadn't realized you had to go out of town, and you didn't want to throw them away. I wasn't very pleased at being your alternative to a trash can, but they were very pretty so I took them anyway. You also said you had just gotten out of the hospital. Are you feeling well now?"

"Yes, I'm fine thank you, and I apologize again for nearly knocking you down trying to hail a taxi. Incidentally, do you drive a late model Peugot?"

There was a very long pause before she answered, "Yes, you saw me, obviously."

"I did. Why did you follow me the last time I was here? And why wouldn't you look at me when we were eating? You must have seen me looking at you."

"Let's not stand here talking. Come over to my table and we'll continue."

Her table turned out to be the same one at which she was sitting when I saw her last. As soon as she sat down, a waitress appeared immediately and without benefit of a menu, she gave the waitress her order—in Thai. She smiled at my look of astonishment and continued. "Yes, I saw you were looking at me but I had just spent a long day doing some work in Versailles—that's why I had my car, which I almost never use—and I didn't feel like talking to anybody. I heard you tell the chef that you didn't live anywhere around here and yet you had told me that you did. I found that strange. I left here just after you did, and as I happened to see you turn into the rue des Bernardins; out of pure curiosity, I followed. That's all there is to it."

"So you live around here as well?"

"Yes."

"Why do you speak Thai?"

"I grew up in that part of the world."

It made all the sense in the world but I still had to make sure. I stood up and said, "Thanks for clearing all that up for me. I've got to run now but I hope to see you again, perhaps here as you seem to be a regular. My name's Bertie MacFarland."

"I look forward to seeing you again as well, Bertie. I'm Alexia Lafitte."

Chapter 13 — Confronting the Snake

White House Meetings

The office in Geneva was running well and we were adding staff at a steady pace. Relieved of the necessity of getting Swiss work permits because of our cover diplomatic status, Joe was offering me a choice of fabulously qualified intelligence specialists to add to the Geneva team. As a result, by mid-May 1966, I had nine people working for me in Geneva. Grant and Neal, the two 'temps' that Joe had sent me to help Maddie while I was gone over the year-end holidays had both fallen in love with Geneva, and desperately wanted to stay. I was delighted because they not only got along well with Maddie; they had worked on the development of the system in its most nascent form and had a deep understanding of it. Both begged me to ask Carroll to assign them permanently to the 'Geneva office.'

For me personally, the situation was becoming literally unmanageable. The last thing I wanted to do was to run a big office with all the attendant personnel and organizational issues. 'Ordinary' staffing—hiring secretaries, clerks, accountants, support staff, etc.—was no ordinary issue in my case. Clearly, such staff is absolutely necessary but the huge problem was that all my employees had to have a U.S. security clearance. Running a 'Help Wanted' ad in the *Tribune de Genève* wasn't an option. With a heavy heart, I called Joe Carroll and told him that I thought we needed to meet personally. Then we discussed the question of where to meet. Top intelligence officials don't fly around on commercial aircraft. They use secure military aircraft and are accompanied by staff and heavily-armed guards. Even if those airplanes only want to touch down at a non-U.S. airport in order to simply re-fuel, they have to get clearance from the government of the nation where the airport is located. I had to admit, the only meeting place that made any sense was Washington.

It felt a little spooky to be walking through Washington National Airport, where once again, I was stopped by a Secret Service agent. This one greeted me politely, handed me a large, sealed envelope and informed me that his instructions were to drive me to Blair House. It had been almost four years since I had last been a guest at Blair House, but the concierge greeted me like an old friend. I suppose he remembered me because all my previous stays at Blair House had been at the direct orders of President Kennedy.

The envelope held a significant surprise—a two day, unrestricted, 24 hr. per day pass to the

White House, and instructions to meet Joe in the 'Fish Room' at 10:00 the next morning. I think the formal name of the Fish Room is the Roosevelt Room, but Teddy called it the Fish Room because he had an enormous fish that he had caught, hanging on the wall. Jack had sort of revived the tradition by hanging a huge swordfish which he had caught on the same wall (Teddy's fish had been removed long ago). The room is diagonally across the hall from the Oval Office. I also had full White House limo privileges for two days. It sort of felt like old times.

I couldn't relax, and decided to go for a long walk before going to bed. Washington can be hot and humid in May—even in the evening—but mercifully, the temperature was mild, and the air was filled with the sweet fragrances of springtime. Unfortunately, I was oblivious to my surroundings. I was finding that being back in Washington was enormously unsettling. The kaleidoscope of flashing thoughts and emotions was like a high-speed, disconnected slide show, where the mind barely has time to recognize an image before it is instantly replaced with another slide depicting an altogether different image on a totally different subject—and the continuous slide show seems to never either slow down or reach its end. Kennedy; Genady; Vang Pao and getting shot; Teng Lo; Sardinia; the Pentagon; Johnson; the logging camp; Chantal; Sally Boyle; the war in Vietnam; Hyannis Port; Siddhi; sitting around my fireplace with Emma, Pierre and Ingrid; Umberto; where my life was heading and where I wanted it to go; Couve de Murville—the 'slides' went on and on. I simply couldn't turn my head off. I don't think I walked for much more than two hours but I was mentally drained by the time I got back.

I got up at 6:00 the next morning and, clad in sweat suit and sneakers, ran across the street to the White House security gate. I wish I had a video of the guard's face as it changed from sternly forbidding to puzzled uncertainty as he inspected my pass.

"Excuse me sir, but for what purpose do you wish to enter the White House?"

"I want to use the gym."

"The White House gym?"

"Correct."

"Can you tell me where it's located?"

I told him in detail. He looked astonished and totally flustered. In desperation, he asked if I had any other form of identification. I'd anticipated this and gave him my passport, and asked him if he would keep it while I was working out, because I didn't want it to get soaked with sweat. Totally bewildered, he returned to the guardhouse, and I watched an animated phone conversation with much hand waving while I jogged in place.

He shook his head in resignation, and the gate silently swung open. He stuck his head out the guardhouse window as I passed, and waving my passport, he said, "I'll keep this safe and dry for you sir and meaning no disrespect, I hope the rest of my day is a whole lot less interesting than these last three or four minutes have been."

I jogged on up the hill to the entry of the West Wing. He hadn't even inspected my gym bag.

I worked out hard, almost violently, for more than an hour, but after a hot shower with an ice cold rinse, I felt immeasurably better when I got back to Blair House and had a light breakfast. While dressing for my meeting with Joe, I re-acquainted myself with American TV, switching channels between the 'morning shows' looking for news and marveling at the vacuous parochialism of what I was watching. One thing did impress me though. If you had the patience to piece together the few snippets of *real* local [i.e., American] news tucked between relentless commercials and pseudo-comedic commentators, there did seem to be a growing groundswell of popular opposition to the war in Vietnam. I wondered how or even if that would affect Johnson. My guess was that it would simply harden his resolve. Johnson could never be wrong. He could never lose. He'd show 'em. I sighed and went across the street for my meeting with Joe.

After the usual handshakes and formalities, we sat down, and Joe started to explain why he thought it was better to meet at the White House rather than DIA headquarters. I assured him no explanation was necessary. After all, I wasn't officially a DIA employee. He and I only had a handshake agreement, and I continued to be paid directly by the U.S. Treasury out of Presidential discretionary funds. As far as my Army status went, Joe could neither promote me nor demote me. I reported directly to the Commanding Officer of the United States—the President. All that aside, we needed to resolve a problem. Staff. My system was getting better and better as we ironed out the kinks, and the intelligence it was producing far exceeded anyone's expectations. The problem was that DIA had to supply, pay, administratively support, and administer the staff needed to run it and analyze its output. I not only couldn't perform that administrative function, I had no interest in doing it even if I could. On the DIA organization chart, somebody else had to be shown as occupying the top slot. As far as I was concerned, I'd accomplished the mission I'd been given. I'd make sure that the system continued to grow. I'd refine it; I'd try to add more Umberto's and Anders' and Bernard's to the system; I'd oversee the Geneva operation, but only on a strategic, not a tactical, day-to-day basis. As far as the Geneva employees went, I'd be some remote, high-level consultant. The ball was really in Joe's court but I needed to know how he was going to handle it.

He gazed at me thoughtfully before asking, "So what exactly do you want me to do, Bertie?"

"I think you need to appoint a really competent administrator to run the Geneva office. We need somebody that both you and I trust completely, and who has a proven track record of setting up and administering start-up operations. Ideally, he or she should also have lived and worked outside the United States for a significant amount of time; read, write and speak French (and hopefully a couple of other languages); and have some knowledge of computers and systems design. The latter is not absolutely necessary, as both Neal and Grant have a deep and nearly irreplaceable knowledge of the system, and both have begged me to ask you to let them stay permanently. I think highly of both of them and strongly support their request."

"Well that's done," he said quickly, "and I agree that you'd make a lousy administrator, and that we'd better find you one pronto. I don't mean that in a disparaging way. Good administrators are not only good at managing the day-to-day emergencies of all large operations; they are good politicians as well. They have to engage the loyalty and support of the people that report to them, but also have to win the loyalty and support of the people to whom they report. You, my friend, are the antithesis of that model—at least on the 'people to whom they report' part. I do admit that you seem to do well on the other part, but there are damn few people that report to you. On the other hand, you have managed to seriously piss off everybody from the President all the way down to me. Literally—the President, the Secretary of State, the Secretary of Defense, the Director of the CIA, me—you've got a fabulous track record. Maybe unprecedented in its scope. And you've done it repeatedly. Constantly. It's a wonder you're still walking around.

"That said, you've done an impressive job. To be honest, even though everybody knew how much President Kennedy liked and respected you, after his death you were an unwanted 'legacy.' Nonetheless, for reasons known only to you and him, Johnson insisted that you remain onboard. You were—and still are—a very competent, but totally uncontrollable loose cannon. I agreed to take you on because you didn't cost me anything, and you were completely deniable. Additionally, everybody from Johnson on down grudgingly agreed that you had extremely good insight and analysis talents. Under the circumstances, assigning you to explore setting up a European network for us didn't seem to have any downside that we couldn't easily handle.

"Then you come up with news that Khrushchev is going to be deposed. To be honest Bertie, we still don't have that level of penetration in the Kremlin. I don't know how you did it and I know you won't tell me, but that was kind of earth-shaking. When you came up with the Chinese nuclear test thing, there was sort of a sigh of relief. By whatever fluke you had done the Soviet thing, this erased it all. The Khrushchev overthrow was political; nuclear was scientific and on a whole different level of reality. The old hands considered you to be a 'one-shot wonder'—laughable, really. Then the damn test shot happens just as you said. Red faces all over Washington and a serious reassessment of your capabilities. And you kept going on and on. Honestly, this system you've put together has surprised everybody and we're becoming increasingly reliant on its output, but I'm delighted that you don't want to run it. I'll line up a half-dozen of the best people I can put my hands on for you to interview, and you can choose whomever you like the best. Give me a couple of weeks to get them lined up."

I told him that would be great but I wasn't going to do the interviewing. I'd send Maddie over to choose her new boss. I'd already asked her if she'd like to run the operation, but she'd decided that it would become too much of a responsibility and leave her no time for family life. I was happy she'd made that decision because there would need to be so much administrative coordination with DIA headquarters that it would be truly preferable to have someone who was already a part of the DIA system. I told Joe that I had no idea of what Maddie was being paid, but whatever it was, it wasn't nearly enough.

"She's worked tirelessly on this thing," I said. "She's never hesitated to work nights and weekends whenever she thought it was necessary, without my ever asking her to do so. She's really the glue that keeps the whole thing together and even though she's a pretty tough taskmaster, nobody complains because she's so fair and works so hard herself. She's priceless. Give her a thumping good raise and give her the royal treatment at headquarters when she comes over. You'll never have a more loyal employee." I paused for a few moments and changed the subject. "Joe, I've got a question. As far as I'm concerned, I've completed the mission I was assigned to accomplish. Do you have something you want me to do next?"

"Not really. Just keep your eye on the system and keep in touch from time to time."

"Fine, but what do I do with the rest of my time?"

"You'd better take it up with your boss."

Speak of the devil. We were just getting ready to leave when the door crashed open and in burst Johnson, bellowing, "Bertie, Bertie. I heard you were in town! I've been wantin' to talk to you for months and months. Now I don't want to break up your meetin' here with Joe— Hey, Joe! How're you doin'?—but when you're done, Bertie, walk across the hall and chat with me for a few minutes. I've got about 15 minutes before my next meetin'.'"

I told him that in fact, we were just leaving, and he allowed as how the timing was nigh onto providential and steered me across the hall into his office.

The man never stopped talking as he burst into his own office, slammed the door behind us (I swear he didn't even *know* how to open or shut a door normally), and immediately peppered me with questions. I was surprised at how much he knew about what I had been doing.

He asked how my leg was healing, congratulated me on my system, thanked me for the heads-up on the impending French withdrawal from NATO, wanted to know what Joe and I had been discussing and finally got around to the war in Vietnam. He said he knew I thought we ought to have pulled out of there, but observed we couldn't just walk away and turn over the entire region to the communists. He was convinced that if we turned up the pressure enough, 'old Uncle Ho' would finally recognize the futility of what he was doing, pull his people back to North Vietnam and leave the South alone.

I just said, "I hope you're right, Mr. President."

He looked at me hard and said, "You know something Bertie? I'm going to be sitting in this office for the next six years and when I get this Vietnam thing squared away—which ought to be pretty soon—you're coming back here and you're going to be working for me, just like you worked for Jack. Believe me, I won't take 'No' for an answer, either. Now I might have been a little short with you when you got back from your unauthorized jaunt to Italy, but those early days after Jack's death were the toughest days I've ever had. So let's bury the hatchet and be friends again. Next time you come to Washington, don't you forget to stick your head in the door and say, 'Hello.' And let's drop the 'Mr. President' stuff and go back to being Bertie and Lyndon. You OK with that?"

I gave him a wan smile, thanked him and left. I had no idea of what to make of what had just happened. I was sure of only two things. First, if we really could come to some sort of acceptable solution to Vietnam I was going to have to come back to Washington, and until then I had no real assignment. Secondly, I thought Johnson would find 'old Uncle Ho' to be a far more formidable opponent than he thought.

I flew back to Geneva that night. I'd had enough of Washington. I also reflected that once Maddie had selected her new boss, I was going to be essentially out of a job.

Grant and Neal were overjoyed to hear that they could now consider themselves permanently assigned to the Geneva office and Maddie was overwhelmed that she was going to be the one who chose her new boss. Then a curious thing happened. When I happened to mention that Johnson had been very complimentary about how well the new system was doing, Neal asked how I'd heard that. When I told them that he had told me during a brief meeting that I had with him after I'd met with Joe (I referred to him as General Carroll), I was bombarded with questions.

"Do you mean that you were actually inside the White House and that the President spoke to you personally?"

"Well, yes. General Carroll and I used one of the rooms in the West Wing to have our meeting, and Johnson barged in just as we were finishing up and dragged me across the hall to the Oval Office to talk to me privately. What's so strange about that?"

There was dead silence and a look of incomprehension on all of their faces. Suddenly, it hit me. None of them knew I had been a Special Assistant to President Kennedy, and in fact was currently a Special Assistant to Johnson. They knew nothing of my past. They knew I often had conversations with Washington sitting in the sound-proofed and super-secure 'telephone booth' but they had no idea of whom I was talking to or what it was about. They would never have dared even thinking about asking, either. They thought it was fabulous that I had not only been in the White House, but in the Oval Office itself and on top of that had actually met the President of the United States!

We'd all worked hard together, we'd put in some all-nighters, had often worked to past midnight and on the weekends, etc. We'd been out to dinner together on several occasions, and over the months all three of them had talked about their childhoods, where they went to school, etc. The guys had talked about their goals in life, and Maddie talked a lot about her husband and their two daughters (who often accompanied us at dinner). I knew them and they knew each other very well. However, they knew absolutely nothing about me or my background—and they never would. It was sad. I suddenly felt really lonely.

As I was leaving, Grant asked, "Sir, what are you going to be doing with all your free time now that you're not going to be baby-sitting the system—and us?"

I grinned and answered, "I'm not exactly sure but I never seem to have any difficulty in getting myself in trouble. In fact it usually comes looking for me." They laughed. They thought it was a joke.

It wasn't.

Thailand Beckons

Trouble didn't take long in coming, either.

A couple of nights later my phone rang and I was astonished to hear Bill Young on the other end. "Bill! This is a totally unexpected but very pleasant surprise! How're you doing and what's going on?"

"I'm afraid I'm the bearer of bad news, Bertie. Boss had a stroke about a week ago. The woman that cooks for him found him sprawled on the porch in front of the door when she came to cook dinner. He was unconscious, but they loaded him in a jeep and drove him to the hospital in Chiang Mai which is only about 50 miles away as the crow flies, but as you know, it's mountainous up there and the roads are terrible. It took them nearly two hours to make the trip, and Boss was almost dead when they got him to the hospital. After a few days, they transferred him by air to the main hospital in Bangkok where there are better facilities. He's going to make it but I doubt he will ever walk again. His speech is a little slurred but quite understandable and his mind seems to be pretty clear. He keeps asking for you though, Bertie. Apparently you made a big impression on him when you were up there. He's got nobody to look after him and I don't have either the time or resources. Can you come out here and make some arrangements for him?"

"Well yeah, I guess I could but what about his son? Jason, I think his name is. Where's he?"

"Shit. Nobody knows. The son of a bitch fancies himself as an international playboy, and might be anyplace in the world. He wouldn't be worth a damn anyway. He's always drunk or high on drugs or both. He spends every penny of his father's money that he can get his hands on, but is apparently deep in debt anyhow. Listen, Bertie. I know it's not your responsibility or even any of your business, but the poor old guy is totally alone in the world and doesn't have a single soul to help him out."

I had a sudden premonition of how I might end my days and said, "I'll get there as soon as I can. Maybe tomorrow if that's possible, but for sure the day after." He thanked me, told me that he would wait for me to get to Bangkok, and gave me a couple of telephone numbers where I could reach him there.

When I hung up, I groaned but got in the car to drive to Geneva so I could use the secure phone. I'd promised everybody that I wouldn't go back to that part of the world without letting them know. Even though Joe had a secure line at his home, it was 3:00 a.m. Washington time so I just left a message with his duty officer at headquarters. I emphasized that my visit was strictly personal to help an ailing friend, left him the telephone number of Sunisa's mother and said that unless I heard from him otherwise, I would presume that no-one had any objections.

In Bangkok, it was 3:00 p.m. so I had no hesitation in calling Sunisa's mother who was delighted to hear that I would be coming to stay with her. Because her first name was truly unpronounceable by me, I had always just addressed her as 'Madam' but she told me that as I was family now, I should call her Mémé. It's the familiar term that many French children use to address their grandmother and I was charmed.

It was impossible for me to get to Bangkok the next day, but Mémé was there with a whole retinue of servants to greet me the day after. I saw Bill trying to look inconspicuous in the crowd, and ominously, there was also an officer of the Royal Thai Army in full dress uniform, who snapped to attention and saluted as I entered the Customs area. I suppressed the normal reaction to return the salute but instead silently accepted the envelope emblazoned with the seal of the Government of Thailand from his gloved hand.

Mémé rushed to greet me, while the servants squabbled over who was going to carry my one bag. After giving Mémé a kiss and a hug, I told her I saw a friend who I thought was here to meet me as well and introduced her to the bemused Bill, who surprised me by bowing to her and greeting her in fluent Thai. It must have flustered her a little bit because she turned to me and complimented me on what a charming friend I had, and then turned back to Bill and insisted that he join us for dinner. There's nothing unusual about that except she had addressed us both in French. Not wishing to embarrass her, both Bill and I just continued along in French.

Bill gave the keys to his car to one of the servants, and the three of us climbed in Mémé's limo to make a detour to the hospital to see Boss. He was in a room with two other patients, but the nurse quickly drew the curtains around their beds so that only Boss was visible. He got a little choked up when he saw me, and apparently was rather astounded to see Mémé. There followed a long conversation in Thai which Bill later described to me as Boss expressing his deep shame that he was unable to stand in order to greet her properly. Mémé had tried to assure him that it was of no importance whatsoever. I told Boss I'd come to see him in the morning and we'd get things worked out, and his voice was pretty shaky when he thanked me.

As we were walking down the hall to the hospital exit, Mémé surprised me by addressing one of the nurses in the nursing station in quite a sharp tone of voice, and turning to me said (in English this time), "Excuse me Bertie, but the situation in there is intolerable. I must get this straightened out."

I had no idea what she was talking about, nor did I understand a word of the conversation she had with the two doctors, and a guy dressed in a business suit who had suddenly appeared, but there was no mistaking the steel in her voice. All three of them were bobbing their heads like mad as she talked. When she was through, the guy in the business suit pulled out a pad of paper and a pen from his pocket, which he gave to her to write something. She gave it back and inclined her head imperiously to them as they bowed to her while we left.

She said, "That poor, dear man. As if he didn't have enough problems. I told them I wanted him moved immediately to a much larger room—a private one—and that I wanted a phone installed immediately. I left them my telephone number so they could call and give us his number at the hospital as soon as the telephone is installed. Poor man, how could they treat him that way? I'm on the Board of that hospital. I think I'll have quite a lot to say at the next Board meeting."

I mumbled some inanity like, "That was very kind of you, Mémé," but privately thought that Boss was going to miss having some other patients to talk to. When we got to Mémé's estate, we were informed that Boss's private phone had been installed.

After dinner, Mémé said, "Well you men probably have a lot of things to talk about. I'll be in my sitting room if you need me."

Bill and I went out on the veranda. Before we even sat down, Bill said, "I'd open that envelope if I were you. I'd be willing to bet it's a note from Kittikachorn and if it is, it's not a real good idea to keep him waiting." I blanched. I had completely forgotten about it.

I pulled it out and tore it open. In beautiful calligraphy, it informed me of the Prime Minister's pleasure in welcoming me to Thailand, and that he would be honored to welcome me personally in his office at 9:00 the following morning. My car would arrive at 8:30. I was mad as hell to be summoned so peremptorily but there was nothing I could do about it.

Bill laughed and remarked that it must be fun to know so many people in high places. He said he was returning to Laos in the morning.

I asked how he had found out about Boss's stroke.

"I heard the Agency was pulling out of the training camp up there, and was curious as to why, so I made a few phone calls. I had to be in Bangkok on business anyway last week so I dropped in on Boss at the hospital and got the whole story. That's when he asked me if I would call you. I don't know how you're going to handle this, Bertie. I can't see any way he can run the logging operation if he can't walk. Hell, he's not even going to be able to get up the stairs to the bunkhouse. It's going to kill him to sell it but I don't see that he has any other choice. You're a great guy to come all this way for someone you hardly know and my hat is off to you, but I don't envy your position. I don't know what I could possibly do to help and I'm very hard to contact once I'm back in the field but here's some numbers you can try."

"Why is the Agency pulling out?"

"The logging operation was our cover, and we have strong doubts about its ability to continue. We don't want to be around when a prospective new buyer flies up there to inspect the property."

It made sense.

Kittikachorn

Kittikachorn was in an expansive mood the next morning, and ushered me warmly into his office. After the usual preliminary chit-chat he casually asked me how my friend was doing, and if he found his new, private room suitable. I think he meant to impress me with his 'all-seeing eye' but I had actually anticipated something like this when I saw the reaction to Mémé at the hospital yesterday. It was the first time I had ever seen her in a public setting and the deference paid to her was astounding. Whether it was due to her royal heritage or her public and private charity work—or both—I didn't know, but it was clear that she was comfortable with all the homage and indeed expected it.

Even before I opened it, I had been quite sure that the envelope that I had been handed at the airport was from Kittikachorn, and that he would be following my movements. Heaven knows there was nothing subtle about my visit to the hospital, and I reflected while we were still there that Kittikachorn would certainly be informed. Accordingly, I responded just as casually to his question and thanked him for his concern.

We discussed how difficult it was going to be for Boss to resume his operations at the camp, and I said that I'd come to Thailand at Boss's request to see if there was anything I could do to help him. I mentioned that since the only time I had traveled to the camp I had been onboard a RTAF (Royal Thai Air Force) helicopter, I didn't even know exactly where the camp was or how to get to it.

He smiled and handed me a piece of paper with a telephone number typed on it and his signature underneath. "Helicopter is the easiest and quickest way to get back and forth. I have given standing orders for one to be put at your disposition for whenever you need it, and for as long as you need it. Just call that number at the Don Muang Air Force Base."

It was a stunningly generous offer and even as I was thanking him sincerely and profusely for it, I was wondering what my cost was going to be. It didn't take long to find out.

"Actually, I'm glad to have this opportunity to speak to you about the logging camp, Bertie. As I'm sure your friend Bill told you, CIA is moving their training operation out of the camp, and they have approached my government for permission to establish a new one on some of our land in the north of the country. I think I might consider it, but a price will have to be agreed to, and I will need some further concessions which I am not at liberty to discuss with you. These will be rather sensitive discussions and I do not believe they are suitable for the usual formal diplomatic channels through our respective Departments of State. I have written the name of one of my senior staff officers on this piece of paper and I would appreciate it if you would make Director Helms aware of our discussion this morning, and ask him if he would receive my representative at his earliest convenience."

"Mr. Prime Minister, Vice Admiral Raborn is the Director of the CIA. I believe you must be referring to Richard M. Helms, but he's Deputy Director for Plans and works under the direction of Admiral Raborn."

"Bertie, don't play with me. I'm sure you know as well as I do that Raborn is resigning at the end of this month, and that Johnson will appoint Helms to replace him. (I had no idea whatsoever.) I want to make sure that one of the first people he sees as Director is my representative. This will give him some time to prepare his position paper while he's waiting to be appointed.[32] Now as much as I'd like to continue our visit, I'm afraid I have another meeting which I need to get to but thanks so much for stopping by. It was good seeing you again."

As I was leaving he called out, "See, Bertie? I told you we'd work well together."

---

[32] Admiral Raborn did indeed resign his position on June 30, 1966 and Johnson immediately appointed Richard M. Helms to replace him.

I told the driver to take me to the hospital, and before I went in to see Boss, I stopped by the nurse's station and asked to see his doctor. I began to realize just how powerful Mémé was when the same three guys that greeted her yesterday also came running to meet me. It turned out that the guy in the civilian suit was the hospital's administrator, and he had a most worried look on his face. To his apprehensive questions I assured him that as far as I knew there was no problem at all with Boss's new room and Madam [Mémé's family name (which I *could* pronounce) is withheld] was most gratified that he had acted upon her requests of yesterday so promptly (I hoped it was the truth). I said I didn't want to detain him further as my remaining questions were of a strictly medical nature, but if he preferred to stay and listen he was of course perfectly welcome. He bowed (to me!) and told me what an honor it was to have made my acquaintance before scurrying off with a smile stretching from ear to ear.

One of the doctors was the head of the Neurology Department, and the other was the neurologist who was personally treating Boss. I asked for his prognosis and it wasn't good. Because of the time it had taken to get him to the hospital in Chiang Mai, Boss had suffered some irreversible nerve damage, and it was highly doubtful if he would ever walk again. They said about the best he and I could hope for was some very limited mobility for short distances using a cane or crutches. The good news was, his mental functions seemed to have survived largely unscathed, and although his speech was a bit slurred at the moment, they thought it would improve.

To my question of how much longer he needed to be in the hospital, they answered 7-10 days. I thanked them and went in to see Boss. I tried to cut short his effusive thanks by being very business-like. I thought he was dangerously close to crying, and although it wouldn't have bothered me at all, he would feel forever humiliated and it would ruin our relationship. He blanched when I told him I had to return to Geneva immediately, but breathed a sigh of relief when I told him I'd be back in less than a week.

As I passed by the nurses' station, I told the head nurse that unless his doctor absolutely forbade it, I wanted him to get two Singha beers per day. One in the late morning after his physical therapy, and the other in the late afternoon either before or with the evening meal—his choice.

With a heavy heart, I told the driver to take me back to Mémé's. I explained to her that I was going to have to go back to Geneva right away, because of something Kittikachorn had asked me to do. She said she had just gotten a call from the airport and she was so angry I think she was going to call Kittikachorn right then and there and raise hell with him. I quickly added he had given me something very valuable in return.

When I told her about the unlimited helicopter privileges she shook her head slowly and said, "Yes, that's something not even I could give you."

"Mémé, may I please ask you for a huge favor?"

"Bertie, Sunisa and I owe you a debt far greater than all the favors you could ever ask for."

"You owe me absolutely nothing, and if you think you do, then I will *never* ask you for a favor."

There was a long pause before she said with tears in her eyes, "I am appropriately reprimanded, my dear Bertie. You ask simply as one member of the family to another. I will never make that mistake again. Please continue."

"Do you have someone who works for you who is mature, caring and capable of dealing with problems with little outside guidance? If the answer is 'Yes,' could you spare him to help work out some of the problems which will have to be solved to get Boss back into operation—if that's even possible?"

"Of course. Just a moment."

Bill Young had been absolutely dead right when he spoke of servants always being present, but getting no more notice than the furniture. I had completely forgotten about the two or three presences making themselves silently inconspicuous against the wall, until Mémé turned to one of them and said something which had the effect of making him instantly disappear down one of the hallways.

He re-appeared quickly followed by a calm, handsome man who was probably in his mid-fifties and whose 'salt and pepper' hair was demarcated by a slightly receding hair line. He stood in front of Mémé and bowed deeply. For my benefit, she spoke to him in English, introduced me as a dear friend whom she considered to be a member of the family, and said I would explain to him what I wanted.

I in turn explained the situation with Boss, said I had to briefly return to Geneva on urgent business and asked if he could do some things for me while I was gone. I told him the first thing he needed to do was visit with Boss to see what Boss needed most. Then I thought he ought to fly up to the camp, get a feel for the situation there, and bring Boss's second-in-command back to Bangkok so the three of them could discuss matters and make plans. "We need to get him one of those electric wheelchairs and figure out some way to get him up the steps at the bunkhouse. There's a ton of stuff to do, and I'd be really grateful if you would get started on it."

He looked stunned, and Mémé said, "That's a rather tall order for anyone, and Akara is more accustomed to receiving instructions rather than issuing them, but I'll help him over the rough spots. Now you get along, Bertie. You'll be late for your flight if you don't hurry."

"Mémé, I haven't even booked a flight yet."

"You have far too much to deal with to worry about details like that. It's all been taken care of. The car's waiting for you in the courtyard. Now come give me a kiss."

At the airport, they handed me an envelope and hustled me to the gate where the flight was waiting for me. I later found out they had actually held it for me for five minutes. We were airborne almost immediately, headed for Paris. I had to hand it to Kittikachorn. He'd known all along that I would quickly realize that there was no way I could honor his request without returning to Geneva. I couldn't send a cable. There were only two sources available to me in Thailand—the U.S. Embassy in Bangkok and the secure line from the American section of the air base at Don Muang. The first was out because it was a State Department line. Don Muang was out because all their traffic was routed through Admiral Sharp, the Commander-in-Chief for the Pacific. As I had thought about it more, I realized a cable wouldn't work in any case. I needed to talk to Joe to explain all this.

I wondered, *what if he doesn't know about the impending resignation of Raborn and that Helms is going to be the new Director?*

I had a wonderful meal and slept so soundly they had to wake me up when we landed in Paris. I was fully awake when I arrived in Geneva, however. I could see the clock said it was 8:00 and since it was bright daylight, I figured it was 8:00 a.m., but I had no idea what day it was. In any case, it would still be normal working hours in Washington so I figured I might as well drive straight to the office and get it over with.

On the way there I thought, *Wow! Are they ever going to be surprised to see me!*— and then realized they wouldn't be surprised at all. They had no idea I'd gone to Thailand in the first place.

Carroll was surprisingly calm. He told me he had been sure that Kittikachorn would contact me, but he trusted me not to do anything before I'd talked to him. He thanked me for confirming his trust. He said he was not aware that Raborn was going to resign, and he had no idea whether Kittikachorn was correct or not but it really didn't matter. As far as he was concerned, the whole thing was really up to Helms.

He said, "Bertie, I'll give you his direct personal number at the Agency. Just call him and tell him exactly what you've told me. Let him figure out what to do. It's going to be the Agency's problem in any case. Thanks for telling me and I'm sincerely sorry you had to fly all the way back from Bangkok to do it but you did exactly the right thing. Good luck with Helms and I hope your friend gets well quickly. Oh, one other thing. I'm lining up some really, really good people for Maddie to talk to and we'll give her the royal treatment when she gets here. Bye."

It was an interesting but short conversation with Helms. We'd talked on a couple of occasions before so he knew my name but was definitely surprised by my call. I told him exactly what Kittikachorn had told me, including the bit about Raborn resigning and him being the new designee for the Directorship, but the only question he asked me was to confirm the spelling and pronunciation of Kittikachorn's delegate.

I did so and he said, "OK. Thanks, Bertie. I've got it. Appreciate the info. See you around. Bye."

I checked in with Maddie and told her what Joe had told me about the people he was lining up for her to interview. She thanked me but said, "Bertie, you look like hell. Are you all right? Excuse me for saying so but you need a shave and a bath. Have you been out all night?"

I told her I'd just gotten in from Bangkok at 8:00 and was probably going to fly back tomorrow or the next day, but not to tell anybody. She shook her sadly when I asked, "What day is it, anyway?"

"It's Friday," she said. "Are you OK to drive home? I'm really worried about you. You're going to kill yourself—unless somebody beats you to it."

I assured her I was fine, but I didn't feel it. I had this vague but deep, gut feeling that things weren't moving in the right direction.

They weren't.

I called Bernard from the Paris airport the next day. He said he had assigned someone from his office to carry out the liquidation of Teng's business assets, and it seemed to be going well. He was surprised when I told him I was on my way to Bangkok to visit a sick friend there, but said he hoped everything would turn out OK, and told me to keep in touch.

Rehab for Boss

It was a relief to be back in Bangkok. At least I knew I'd be there for several weeks. Akara had done a wonderful job. He had flown up to the camp and brought back Krasin, Boss's operations manager, for a planning session. Neither one of them had ever been on an aircraft of any kind before, and they both said it was the most terrifying thing they had ever done.

Boss himself was doing as well as could be expected, but the doctor's prognosis seemed to be correct. It was painful to watch his physical therapy sessions because try as he might, his legs simply would not support him. The nerve damage was extensive and it was permanent. As predicted, he could use a crutch to hobble short distances (about 5 yards, maximum) and he was becoming resigned to the fact that he was going to be mostly confined to a wheel chair for the rest of his life.

During the course of the next several days, I ordered him an electric wheelchair (the hospital staff said a Canadian company made the best ones), and asked Akara to find me the best metalworker in Bangkok. When the metalworker arrived, I gave him the dimensions of the wheel chair, told him the height of the porch from the ground was approximately 3 meters [10 feet] and asked him to design a crank-operated lift that would get Boss (in his wheel chair) from the ground up to his porch. I asked him to make it so it could be assembled and bolted together onsite at the logging camp. I figured we were going to need some carpentry work done as well (ramps and so forth), and asked Akara to line up a good carpenter for us.

Boss said there was plenty of excess lumber at the camp. I asked Boss if the bunkhouse had electricity and he told me he had a small generator which he used mostly to charge the battery for the two-way radio. I found a distributor in Bangkok who could supply a much larger one, and told him to design a sound-proof and weather-proof enclosure for it. I told Boss that I was sorry, but he was going to have to wait until we got all the equipment before he could go back to the camp.

In the meantime, Mémé was holding 'small dinners' for me every two or three days. The dinners were in fact reasonably small, usually three or four families, and I enjoyed meeting her friends in an atmosphere where it was truly possible to have real conversations. Although I'm sure that Mémé's stated reason of introducing me to her friends was truthful, I suspect I was also convenient excuse to simply increase her normal level of social activity, which by my standards was already exceptionally high.

I think another motive was to introduce me to eligible young ladies, because there was always at least one such individual at every dinner. I appreciated her efforts but I was usually much more interested in talking to the parents. It was an incredible array of highly accomplished— and sometimes internationally known—people. Artists in every medium—paint, music, theater; intellectuals and practitioners in every field from architecture to zoology; these people were fascinating. More than once, Mémé had unexpected overnight house guests. You can't fake genuine fascination, and some of these people were/are among the most fascinating people I've ever met.

On a more mundane level, I was trying to get Boss back to the camp as quickly as I could. Before taking Akara and Krasin with me, I told Mémé I needed to go to Chiang Mai city (Chiang Mai is also a province) and buy a four-wheel drive truck. I asked her if she could find the name of a reputable dealer in Chiang Mai, and if she would ask her bank to assure the dealer that my credit was good. (I was hoping it was. I was receiving a salary at the level of a U.S. Army Major which wasn't huge, but I had almost no expenses except for food, drink and entertainment. Nonetheless, the deposit for the boat in Brest had taken a big chunk of my savings.) When I asked her to get her bank to confirm my credit with my bank in Switzerland, she just smiled and told me not to worry. After a quick phone call, she gave me a piece of paper on which she had written something incomprehensible in Thai, and asked me to give it to Akara when we went to Chiang Mai.

It's actually a pretty ride from Bangkok to Chiang Mai, but I had difficulty in getting either Akara or Krasin to open their eyes to look out the window. When we landed, I told the pilot to fly to the logging camp and wait for me there. I was surprised to be greeted by a young Thai in a business suit, and even more surprised when he bowed to me and said he had a car waiting for me to take us to his father's truck dealership. We all piled in, and I handed Akara the note that Mémé had given me. He glanced at it, smiled, and after carefully folding it, put it in his jacket pocket.

I saw the truck I wanted right away. It was a straight-bed, four-wheel drive Mercedes diesel with a hydraulic back lift-gate and extended fuel tanks, which the dealer said would allow it to travel over 800 km [500 miles] without re-fueling. I was sure I couldn't afford it, but asked the dealer the price anyway. I was astounded when he said it was all taken care of. Mémé's bank had apparently called and told him to give me whatever truck I wanted.

It was then that Akara respectfully handed the dealer Mémé's note. He read it with an air of reverence and immediately said that he would treasure the note forever; it would be a family heirloom. His son read it and had the same reaction. He then began asking me to assure Mémé (he used her formal name and title, of course) that he would always be her most humble servant, her slightest wish was his command, etc., etc. I finally got him to shut up long enough for me to ask the son if he would show us how to drive and operate the truck. It wasn't that hard for Krasin and me—Krasin was used to driving Jeeps—but Akara had never driven anything that didn't have automatic transmission.

We dropped the son off at the dealership, and Krasin observed that as long as we were here, we might as well go to the market and pick up some supplies for the elephants, and some food for the camp employees. I suddenly remembered I didn't have a single cent on me. I had several thousand dollars in cash back at Mémé's, but that wasn't doing me any good here. I didn't even have any money to put fuel in the truck. I cursed myself for being such a fool, turned off the engine and went back inside the dealership where the son came running up with a look of horror on his face. He was followed closely by his father, wearing the same expression.

To their relief, I assured them the truck was wonderful and that we were extremely pleased with it, but I had another, totally unrelated problem. When I explained what it was, the sense of relief was palpable and the son went running into his father's office, and re-emerged with a huge bundle of cash, which he gave me with a bow. I thanked them profusely and said I would have the bank wire them replacement funds the moment I got back to Bangkok. I didn't count it immediately, but I kept careful track of everything we spent before getting on the road to the camp.

Krasin was driving so I had a chance to count up what we had spent and how much money was left. They'd given me the equivalent of over $5,000! That was a hell of a lot of money back then.

When we finally got back—God, those were awful roads—and Krasin dropped Akara and me off at the bunkhouse, we found Joe, my former Jeep driver, and my helicopter pilot on the porch drinking Singhas. Krasin screamed something at Joe, who jumped up and ran towards the clearing where the elephants loaded logs.

I hoped the pilot hadn't had too many Singhas, but told him to stay where he was while I went inside. I asked Krasin if he and his wife would sleep in the bunkhouse and check the radio from time to time during the day until I could get Boss back. I had asked Boss who kept his books, and had groaned when he told me that he did it himself. He had given me the key—which he always wore around his neck—and I used it to unlock the safe.

The contents were interesting. Besides the 'books' there was a pretty good amount of cash, an old Smith & Wesson .38 revolver plus two full boxes of ammo, and most interesting of all, a photo album with pictures of Boss, his parents, his wife Beth (she was a really handsome woman), and pictures of Jason from birth to teen-age years. There was also a really old .35mm Kodak camera and two rolls of film still in their boxes.

I took his financial records and flew back to Bangkok with Akara. The pilot seemed OK, but we landed in Bangkok with a bit more of a thump than I was used to. I thought Akara was going to have a heart attack.

I spent the next day going over the books. Boss was a surprisingly good bookkeeper and kept meticulous records. The logging operation was actually quite profitable. His net income was about $250-$300,000 per year. I noticed that about four years previously, he had switched his savings account from the Chiang Mai branch of Bangkok Bank (which was, and still is, the biggest Thai bank in the country) to a small bank in Bangkok I'd never heard of. I called Boss to ask why, and he told me his son Jason had asked him to because he knew the owner, and they would give him a better interest rate for a big account like his. He told me he'd kept his operating account at the Chiang Mai branch of Bangkok Bank but sent his monthly operating surpluses to the savings bank in Bangkok.

I shrugged. The monthly statements all seemed to be in order and he had a balance of over $2 million in savings. It was crazy for him to be sitting on so much cash, though. I needed to get him a good investment advisor. I had met so many people at Mémé's various functions I was sure I could find him a good one. I wasn't worried that I'd never heard of the bank either. In Geneva, there were dozens of so-called private banks that only dealt with very wealthy clients. In Geneva, you'd need a minimum opening deposit of $10 million or so but then Thailand wasn't Switzerland. Additionally, I figured with a bank account like that, Boss could easily afford the

256

wheel chair, generator, lift, etc. which I had ordered for him. I was beginning to feel a lot more comfortable about the state of my own bank account.

Niew

Mémé was having another of her 'small dinners' that night, but only two families had been invited, so the total number of guests was eight or nine, but as far as I was concerned, there was only one. She was one of the most astonishingly beautiful women I've met in my entire life. Her name was Niew [something] and she modestly lowered her head and dropped her eyes when we exchanged the traditional *wai* greeting. I could hardly take my eyes off her, and I caught Mémé, who knew me very well by this time, smiling in a serene, somewhat contented way. I knew her pretty well too, and she immediately changed her expression when she caught me looking at her, but I was sure I knew what she was thinking. Although she'd never expressed it openly, I think her fondest dream was to have Sunisa come back from Paris and live with her and for me to marry a Thai wife and live on the estate as well. I believe she thought she may have finally set the gears in motion to accomplish the latter.

I didn't get much of a chance to talk to Niew alone before she left with her family. In the little time we did have together, I learned that both she and her brother (who was four years older) had mostly been educated abroad. Both had gone to Le Rosey boarding school in Switzerland during their high school years and both had gone on to Cambridge for their university education. He had received his MD there and she had graduated with degrees in Philosophy and Botany. Both spent most of their time in remote Thai villages, he as a physician and she showing farmers how to cultivate their farms to increase crop yields. I told her I was a consultant to some U.S. government agencies in Geneva. I also asked if I could see her again and to my great delight, she agreed.

The next day was Boss's homecoming. The wheelchair had arrived, the metal worker had completed all the pieces for the lift. The generator was completed but it was too big and heavy to put in the chopper, so we sent it to Chiang Mai by rail. Boss was happy as he could be, and was busily writing checks for all the equipment. He said he wasn't sure how much money he had in his operating account, so for the first time was writing checks on his savings account. He'd mailed off a check for the wheelchair the preceding week, and he was now paying all of his Thai bills. I discovered that in a charming gesture of thanks, Boss had ordered huge bouquets of flowers for his nurses.

By the time we finally got the chopper loaded with all the pieces for Boss's lift, the metalworker's tools, the carpenter's tools, Boss's electric wheelchair, plus Boss, the metal worker, the carpenter and me, the chopper was pretty close to its weight capacity but it lifted off easily. Of the four of us, I was the only one that had been on a chopper before, but Boss was delighted by it and kept his face glued to the window, while the other two sat rigid as boards with eyes tightly shut.

Joe was there at the landing clearing to greet us and was so overwhelmed with joy at seeing Boss that his voice got very shaky as he tried to hold back his tears. I think he would have hugged him if he could, but Thai men definitely do not hug each other—at least they didn't back then. He and I carried Boss to the jeep, and put him in the passenger seat. I jumped in the back with the carpenter, and Joe told the metal worker that he would be right back to pick him up and start loading the jeep with all the equipment.

When we got to the bunkhouse, we carried Boss up the stairs, put him in his chair on the porch and I ran in the kitchen to get him a Singha. When I gave it to him he said, "You saved my life with this stuff Bertie. Having a couple of beers a day was about the only way I could stand being in that big old room all by myself all day long. I know it was kindly intended but I need to be around people."

Before Joe got back in the jeep, I asked him if he knew how to drive the new truck we'd bought, and he complained that Krasin wouldn't let anybody else touch it. I told him to go find Krasin and tell him to bring the truck here right now. When Krasin arrived, I told him that there needed to be at least one other person at the camp that knew how to drive the truck, and then told Joe to hop in beside me on the trip back to the helicopter. I left them loading the materials while I flew back to Bangkok.

That evening, Niew and I met for dinner at a private club to which her parents belonged in Bangkok. She was just as beautiful as I remembered, and I hadn't thought about much else all day long. She was barely five feet tall, probably weighed less than 100 pounds, long black hair, dark brown eyes full of intelligence and the most beautiful light brown skin I've ever seen. As delicate and fragile as she looked, I figured she had to be pretty tough to spend weeks at a time in remote, isolated Thai villages, where there is no running water, no electricity, no toilet facilities, etc., and where the villagers work all day every day to scratch out a living from the land.

She was fascinating to talk to. Her voice was soft and surprisingly low-pitched for such a tiny being. The lessons taught at Le Rosey and Cambridge had been well absorbed and she was amazingly knowledgeable about a vast array of subjects. She loved what she was doing and felt that she was really making a difference in a lot of people's lives. She also had an endless store of stories to tell about her adventures. I was becoming increasingly smitten. When I dropped her off at her parent's house at the end of a long evening, before she got out of the car she thanked me for a wonderful evening, then leaned across and gave me a soft kiss on the cheek. I felt like a schoolboy.

Just after breakfast the next morning, I got a call from a nearly hysterical Boss who told me that he had just gotten a phone call from the Canadian company that had sold us the wheelchair. The woman on the other end had been decidedly unhappy. His check had been returned marked "Insufficient Funds" and she wanted a wire transfer from a bank immediately.

All of a sudden, I got a sick feeling in my stomach. I told him I'd take care of it, not to worry, had to be a stupid mistake somewhere and I'd get if fixed and call him. I was aghast when I hung up the phone. Mémé walked in and as soon as she saw my face rushed over and asked apprehensively, "Bertie, what's wrong?" When I told her, she immediately relaxed and patted me on the shoulder and said, "Oh, that's not a problem at all. My, you gave me a scare! Don't even think about it again. I'll call my bank right now and they'll take care of everything."

"Mémé, you're such a kind sweetheart (she blushed) but I can't let you do that. You're incredible gift of the truck was outrageous enough. Really, I'm grateful, but I can't let you do it. I simply don't understand it. I saw his bank records. He's got over two million dollars in his savings account! How can this be?"

Mémé was shocked. She thought a moment and said, "Well, yes. Dear me. This seems to be much more serious than I'd thought. I'm going to call my banker and have him look into it. I expect he'll want to see all the books and papers you've got. Would it be all right if he sent someone to pick them up from you? He can have everything photocopied in his office and send the originals back to you. Now in the meantime, the other matters need to be handled right away and he'll need to make phone calls to all the people Boss has written checks to. I expect most of them are Thai companies or individuals and I doubt if your Swiss banker speaks Thai, so let me handle this.

"Oh, Bertie! One of the reasons I adore having you here is you make my life so exciting. There's always a whirlwind of activity swirling around you and I love being a part of it. I never know what's going to happen next, but I'm always sure that *something* is going to happen, and it always does. It's so different from my normal life which consists primarily of an endless round of dinners, parties, social gatherings, board meetings and so forth. Until you walked into my life, I thought my life was normal and I was perfectly content with it. Now when you're gone, I feel bored and lonely. I hope Niew can convince you to stay. We have plenty of room to add another two or three houses. Now I'm going into my sitting room to make my phone calls. Call me if you need me."

I started thinking about the implications of all this. If there was something wrong with Boss's bank, there was going to be a massive legal battle, and there would need to be some way to get documents to and from the camp to Bangkok other than by regular mail. Boss had a Post Office box in Chiang Mai but it only got cleaned out once a week when somebody went into the city to get supplies. Given that it could take five days for regular mail to get from Bangkok to Chiang Mai, it could easily take a month or even more for a lawyer in Bangkok to receive a reply to a letter.

I turned to one of the servants to ask him to find Akara for me. When Akara came, I asked him to use his contacts to see if he could find me a communications specialist—someone that knew all about telephones and telephone equipment. I said it would be necessary that the person spoke fluent English. Akara bowed and left.

The next call was to Boss. I reassured him that everything was being taken care of and that Mémé's banker was going to contact his banker in Bangkok to get things straightened out. I told him that until that happened; no more money should be transferred to the savings bank in Bangkok, and to please leave everything in his Chiang Mai account. It was clear that I was going to need a general power of attorney, and that the lawyer at Mémé's bank would need one too in order to fully investigate the savings bank in Bangkok. Boss said he had no objection and to draw up the papers and he'd sign them.

Things were starting to happen quickly. Mémé came back in and said her banker had tried to call Boss's bank but had gotten no answer. His lawyers were looking into the bank's registration as we spoke and would call as soon as they knew anything. I asked Mémé if she would make a telephone introduction for me with her banker, and she smiled and said I'd already met him but she'd be happy to do it anyway. When I spoke to him, I asked if he would get his lawyers to draw up a general power of attorney for the bank's lawyer and for me and I would fly up to the camp tomorrow to get them signed. He said he would be happy to do so and would have the documents delivered to the house as soon as they had been typed up. I said I'd get the signed documents back to him within three days—maximum.

Akara struck pay dirt with the communications specialist. I got a call from a man who introduced himself as Paul Kline and asked if I was the gentleman who was looking for a communications specialist. He told me he had retired from the U.S. Army Signal Corps the previous year, was married to a Thai wife and had been trying unsuccessfully to establish a little business ever since she had convinced him to move to Thailand from Fort Gordon, GA six months ago. I told him I wanted to install a fax machine in a remote logging camp in the north of the country, and had no idea how to go about it or even if it were possible. I told him I was going up there the next day and asked if he would accompany me. I said we'd take a chopper so would be back late afternoon.

There was dead silence on the other end of the phone and I was going to ask him if we were still connected when he said, "Ahhh, yeah. I understand—or at least I think I do. What time are we leaving? Are you at Don Muang now?"

I told him I wasn't but that's where we'd be leaving from, and asked him if he could get to a private house by 6:00 a.m. I put Akara on the phone to give him directions. He said he'd be here by 6:00. Then the papers arrived from the bank—the power of attorney forms that Boss needed to sign and his original accounting documents. On the spur of the moment, I called Niew and asked her if she'd like to go up to the camp for the day. She said she'd be delighted.

260

When I told her that we'd be leaving for Don Muang early—6:00 a.m., she laughed and said, "Oh, that's well after sunrise. I would normally be up at least a half hour before sunrise helping the women to prepare the morning meal."

Paul was a big, hefty guy in his mid-fifties, and he thoughtfully got into the front seat beside the driver when I told him we were also going to pick up a young lady. He sort of stared at me when I told him that but just answered, "Yes, sir." I think he was convinced I was CIA and I was going to let him stay that way.

When the guards at Don Muang opened the gates as soon as they saw our car approaching and stood at stiff attention, saluting as we whizzed through without stopping for any kind of identity check, I saw him snap back in his seat and start to turn around to look at me. Apparently thinking the better of it, I believe he decided it would be wiser to just keep his mouth tightly shut and stare straight ahead.

Niew loved the trip; she'd never flown in a chopper before, but she was intimately familiar with the land we were flying over. Now and again, she'd cry out, "Oh look, Bertie. I've spent weeks in that village." I'd look but oftentimes couldn't see anything but uninterrupted jungle. It was kind of a scary lesson.

She and Boss fell in love with each other immediately. They were kindred souls whose deepest instincts were a profound caring love for the very earth itself and all living things on it—plant, animal and human. Both were gregarious, and they chattered away non-stop in a strange mixture of English, Thai and dialect.

Boss was looking a little scruffy. He didn't shave on a regular basis in any case, but now he wasn't able to stand up to see himself in the mirror, and was too embarrassed to ask anyone to help him. Thai men have much less facial hair than Western men in any case, but he definitely needed a shave. The next thing I knew, the charcoal brazier was lit, there was a pot of fresh water on it, Boss had a towel draped around his neck and shoulders, and Niew was expertly stropping his straight razor. I watched, amazed, as she took a bar of soap, shaved some of it into a small bowl, added hot water, made lather, applied it, and then expertly shaved Boss's face until it looked like a newborn baby's.

She shocked me when looking directly into my astonished eyes, she said in a pure Scottish accent, "Ah then, Bertie, me love. Do you think that such a wee lass wouldn't know how to take care of a man?"

It seemed almost like a direct sexual allusion and I was so confused I didn't know what to say. She laughed so hard that there were tears in her eyes when she stood up, and with a surprisingly strong arm, pulled my head down and kissed me full on the lips. Whipping around she addressed the speechless Joe and Paul and said, "Well don't just stand there. Pick him up and get him out to his chair on the porch." After they'd done so under her watchful eye, she turned to Joe and said, "Now take me to the village; these men have business to attend to."

What village? I wondered as they drove off.

Paul broke the stunned silence saying, "If you'll excuse me saying so sir, that is one *hell* of a lady."

"No kidding," I mumbled. I pointed to the radio and said, "That's our communication system. What do we need to do to get a fax machine and an answering machine installed?"

"I'm on it sir. What kind of electrical system do we have?"

I took him out the back door and said, "That little generator is the only one that's working for the moment. The big one sitting beside it isn't hooked up yet. Can you help with that?"

"I'm a master electrician, sir. Just leave everything to me."

I went out to see Boss and noticed his electric wheelchair parked just inside the front door. Out of curiosity, I tried to turn it on. Nothing happened. Apparently, the battery was dead. I went back outside where Paul was inspecting the big generator. When I told him about the wheelchair, he stopped and came in to look.

His comment was simple. "Well, beside the fact you don't have an outlet that will take that plug shape—meaning there's nowhere to plug the charger in—the generator you've got produces 220 volt current and that charger is built to take 110 volts. We'll need a transformer. I'll add it to the list."

The whole damn day went like that. The only easy part was to get boss to sign the power of attorney papers. Both the metal worker and the carpenter were still there, and both had problems. The metal worker couldn't get the lift installed because the ground was too soft, and the support columns kept sinking into it. He needed a concrete base, but there was no cement in camp. The carpenter had run out of the lumber he needed. There was no shortage of teak logs, but the massive gas-powered saw to cut them into planks, studs, beams, etc. had engine problems and needed a new saw blade.

'Need' was the operative word. There seemed to be no end to the things that were needed, and where were we going to find the money to pay for them? Supposedly, Boss had a ton of money, but where was it? I called Mémé's banker. He was reassuring on that issue. He said that the logging operation had a verifiable gross income of $25-30,000 per month and now that there would be no further transfers to Bangkok there would soon be more than sufficient funds in the Chiang Mai account—if there weren't already. He said that he would call the manager of the bank in Chiang Mai and arrange for $20,000 of additional credit if we needed it. That was way more than we needed at the moment to pay for the new equipment, plus normal operating expenses. That was the good news.

The bad news was that the small bank in Bangkok, although it was properly registered as a bank, was wholly owned by a certain Nopparat Thanasukolwit who had a distinctly unsavory reputation. In addition, the bank's registered address was the same as Thanasukolwit's home address. My heart sank. I asked if he could possibly try to get us an appointment with Thanasukolwit tomorrow. He said he would try.

Discouraged, I went into the kitchen and opened the ice box where Boss kept the beer. It was filled with tepid water, and a couple of dozen bottles of Singha whose labels were floating at the surface. I went out on the porch to ask Boss about it. "Yep, looks like it burnt out when I was out sick. I don't know why. Guess we'll have to get a new one when we can." He looked at me with a face filled with desperation and shame and asked, "Bertie, I got to go something awful. Can you help me out to the outhouse?"

Perceptions are funny. Of course I knew that Boss was much smaller than I. Of course, if I thought about it, I knew that Boss couldn't possibly weigh anything close to my 185 pounds, but I never thought about it. I just viewed him as an equal. As a result, when I lifted him from his chair, I did so with such force that I literally had to wrap my hands over his shoulder and leg to keep him from flying out of them. It was good to hear him swear at me, and he kept up a non-stop litany of abuse which continued even after I placed him on the outhouse seat and shut the door behind me when I stepped outside. No question about it. Good old scratchy Boss was back.

It was around 2:00 and Boss and I were consuming a warm beer on the porch when we saw the jeep in the distance. As it got closer I was taken aback to see Niew in the driver's seat; a rather plain but husky (for a Thai) teenage girl sitting beside her, and an extremely disgruntled, glum-looking Joe occupying the back. Niew jumped out and ran happily up the stairs exclaiming, "Jeeps are really fun! I've never driven one before. In fact, I've never driven any kind of car before. It's a wonderful sense of freedom, don't you think?"

Before I had a chance to respond, she'd whirled around at the top of the steps and shouted something at the girl and Joe that Boss seemed to think was hilarious. Both Joe and the girl came running. Niew took the girl by the hand and led her to me and introduced her. "This is Chianaporn," she said. I have negotiated financial arrangements with her family. The family and I both believe that the terms we have agreed to are fair and honorable. Chianaporn will live here in the bunkhouse permanently. Her only duty is to look after Boss. She will cook for him, wash for him, clean for him and look after his every need—including his natural needs, of course."

I looked at her sharply and she blushed. "No, no. Not that. I mean the needs that every human being—and animal has. He can't get to the outhouse on his own, so she will either help him or empty his 'night soil' pot every morning. She will help him bathe and I will teach her how to shave him when he needs it. Perhaps in the West, good male friends might lend such assistance, but here in the East, women are expected to perform these tasks. Now mumble a few meaningless words and I will tell her that you said, 'Do not fail in your duties.' She speaks no English."

The words that I spoke very clearly were, "You are an absolutely incredible woman."

After introducing Chianaporn to Boss, she instructed Joe to go back and get the carpenter and the metal worker while she and Chianaporn explored the bunkhouse. Boss and I just stared at each other and finished our beers. I went back in the house to fetch two more.

When Joe came back, Niew asked Paul and me to come inside and join her. She first asked me if there was anything I needed from Chiang Mai. I said I wasn't sure but I turned to the metal worker and asked him if he could modify a motor scooter so that instead of a seat, it had a platform that Boss could get his wheelchair on. I told him it would probably need three wheels instead of two to give it stability, and support the extra weight.

He wasn't quite sure what I meant, and Niew took the pad of paper I'd brought and quickly sketched the kind of vehicle I had in mind. He got all excited and starting showing Niew how it should be modified to keep the center of gravity low, etc. She gave him the paper and he started madly scribbling on it, completely absorbed in the project.

Turning to me, she said, "Bertie, you clearly are welcome to stay if you'd like, but I know you're busy and probably need to get back. I'll call you tonight and give you a progress report. The four of us, plus Krasin are going to have a lot of shopping to do in Chiang Mai tomorrow. It's a good thing you bought that big truck. Oh, I absolutely adore this place. We're going to have so much fun. You have no idea how excited I am."

I was shocked. "Do you mean you're going to stay?"

"Of course! They really need me here. There are tons of things that need to get done. I expect I'll be here all summer. I don't have the right clothes or shoes, but I can get them in Chiang Mai tomorrow. I'll call my parents and let them know. They're quite used to me being away for months at a time." She paused and took my hand before continuing, "I'm going to miss you, Bertie. I hope you'll come and visit me often." More sternly, "Now go on. You've got to clear up what's going on with Boss's bank account. But give me a kiss before you go." I complied with earnest vigor.

Banking Issues

Mémé was on the phone when I walked in, and she immediately switched to English and said, "Oh, wait. He just walked through the door." She handed me the phone, kissed me on the cheek and left.

It was the bank manager. He said that he had called the savings bank repeatedly all day long and there was never any answer. He'd keep trying tomorrow. I thanked him, and asked if it was too late to send someone to pick up the power of attorney documents that Boss had signed. He said he'd send someone right away.

I went to look for Mémé. She was in what used to be her husband's study, but which was now used as the family sitting room. She looked up from pouring me a drink and asked, "Bad news?"

"I'm afraid so. It seems to be impossible to get anyone at the savings bank to answer the phone. I guess we're going to have to go over there. I'm not looking forward to it."

"Well I think I have some good news for you. I had a long talk with Sunisa today. Among other things, she scolded me for keeping you out of Paris for so long. She sends her deep love and affection. Now the good news is that Sunisa says that the sale of Lo's restaurants is bringing in an astonishing amount of money. She asked me to tell you that even in the short time that the liquidation has been going on, there is already more than enough money to cover Boss's possible loss of his $2,000,000 savings. Since she won't touch it anyway, she would be happy to see it go to such a good cause."

I was speechless. She quickly changed the subject. "I got a call about an hour ago from Niew's parents. Not only were they not upset about the fact that she has decided to stay at the camp for the rest of the summer, they said they had never heard her sound so happy in her entire life. They think it might have something to do with you. They told me that in fact, they hoped so. They are constantly worried that one day she is going to set off for one of these remote villages and that will be the last they ever hear of her. They want both of their children to settle down and produce lots of grandbabies. I'd love to see that too—as long as you're the father of Niew's babies. Do you like her, Bertie? Would you consider settling down in Bangkok?"

"Mémé, right now I'm kind of on emotional overload. It's been a long day. As far as Niew is concerned, I can tell you for sure that she is one of the most fascinating, extraordinary women I've ever met. But we've only known each other for a few days. I certainly like her; I like her very much, but it's far too soon to know if it goes beyond that. I think her parents may have misinterpreted the cause of her happiness. She loves the camp, she loves Boss, she's thrilled by the elephants, and she's taken complete charge of getting everything fixed up. I think all those things make her very happy. I doubt if I had much, if anything, to do with it at all.

"As far as me settling down in Bangkok, I don't know if I would be allowed to. As I think you know, I have certain ties to the U.S. government, and I don't know if the government would release me from my obligations. I'm extremely reluctant to form strong ties to a possible mate because the nature of my work might put her in danger. More than that, I just can't say right now."

The next morning, accompanied by a lawyer from the bank, I went to the address given for the savings bank. It was certainly in a nice residential section of town and the residence was large with a couple of very expensive cars parked in the courtyard. I couldn't find a doorbell, and no-one responded to my repeated polite knocking, so I pounded on the door. *Somebody* was home; I could hear them moving around inside. The door was opened by a disheveled, unshaven young man who shouted something at me that made the lawyer stiffen with indignation. As he started to slam the door shut, I pushed back hard and walked in.

His sunken, drug addict's eyes widened with surprise when I said, "Hello, Jason. I'm Bertram MacFarland. I recognize you from the pictures in your father's photo album. How long have you been in town?"

"It's none of your business and I don't know you. Who are you anyway and what do you want? How did you know where to find me?"

"Don't worry, Jason. I'm not the police and if you'll keep a civil tongue in your head, I probably won't tell them either. I'm a friend of your father's. Where's the owner of the house?"

A door on the far side of the room was opened by a surly, middle-aged, unshaven man dressed in a bathrobe who said, "I'm Nopparat Thanasulkowit. Westerners call me Nicky. Who are you two guys and what are you doing in my house?"

"I'm Bertram MacFarland, and this gentleman is a lawyer. I'm a friend of Jason's father—who I call 'Boss'—and we are both representing his interests. I believe he has a savings account in a bank which shares this address with you. We would like to verify the current amount in the account because recently, several drafts written on that account have been returned marked 'Insufficient Funds.' Boss believes that he has quite a lot of money in the account, and has given both of us a general power of attorney (the lawyer handed him a copy) so you can discuss this with us. No further funds will be deposited in the account until the matter is satisfactorily resolved."

Nicky looked flustered, but Jason looked like a bomb had hit him. Nicky was cool though and said, "Well of course all this is totally unexpected and I don't have Boss's records at my fingertips. In addition, I was just getting ready to make myself presentable for a luncheon appointment downtown. I will have the accountant prepare a complete account statement in my absence." He shouted something and a man immediately appeared in the doorway. He gave some rapid-fire instructions and the man disappeared again. Turning to us, he continued, "I have quite a full schedule this afternoon. I'm afraid I can't possibly meet with you before 6:30 this evening. I know that's very late so if you prefer, I don't have anything booked for tomorrow morning and I'd be happy to meet you then."

I looked at the lawyer who said, "6:30 this evening will be fine. We'll look forward to seeing you then."

As we left, I asked Jason, who still looked shell-shocked, "Did you know that your father had a stroke and was here in the hospital for several weeks? He's back at the camp now."

Jason nodded and said, "Yeah. I heard he was sick."

I was astonished and asked, "Why didn't you go see him in the hospital? Why haven't you called him?"

"We don't get along well anymore," he sullenly responded.

"I can definitely see why," I said and slammed the door behind me.

As we were being driven back to Mémé's, I turned to the lawyer and said, "I don't know about you, but I didn't have a good feeling about any of that. Did you see his so-called accountant? He sure didn't look like an accountant to me. Looked more like a thug or bodyguard."

"I didn't have a good feeling either," he replied, "but I guess we'll find out more this evening. I'll pick you up at your house around 6:00."

I wasn't terribly surprised when we got back there. The cars were gone and the house was dark and locked up tight. I turned to the lawyer who was scribbling furiously on something and said, "Can we get a warrant for their arrest?"

"That's what I'm working on right now," he growled.

When I got back to Mémé's, I told her what had happened and then called Niew at the camp and told her. I asked her not to tell Boss either about Jason, or his savings account—just that we were working to clear up the discrepancy, and we thought that his savings were safe.

When Niew asked how she could possibly tell him that, I just told her I thought I'd found a way to replace any missing funds. She was delighted and her normal, ebullient spirit returned as she excitedly told me of all the things they'd been able to get in Chiang Mai, and how well things were going. She asked me when I was coming to the camp, and I told her it would probably be a couple of weeks. I had decided to leave for Geneva the next day and then wanted to spend some time in Paris before I came back. She sounded disappointed.

Geneva, Paris — and Heroin

It was good to be back in Geneva. Summertime in Geneva is absolutely idyllic. Average high temperatures from May through September range [in Fahrenheit] from the low 60's to the high 70's and nighttime temperatures are in the mid-40's to low-50's range. The lake is sparkling blue, and filled with the colorful sails of hundreds of sailboats; vegetation is lush; there are flowers everywhere; the sky is a shade of translucent blue that is uniquely Swiss; and in the distance, Mont Blanc, cloaked in its eternal snows, completes a picture of almost surreal natural beauty.

Yolande had been mostly living in the house since late spring and I was happy to see her sunbathing on the lawn as I drove down the driveway. She scolded me good-naturedly for not giving her some advance notice, but was clearly happy to see me. We really were good friends and it was lovely to feel her warm body snuggled against mine under the blankets that night (Aubonne is colder than Geneva by at least ten degrees). Sleeping alone, for me at least, gets old very quickly.

I went into the office on Monday, and met Maddie's new boss. It was easy to see why she had chosen him. Unassuming, genial, obviously extremely bright and very competent, we were chatting away like old buddies within 10 minutes. Maddie was clearly very, very pleased to see us get along so well. After dropping by to say hello to Neal and Grant, I spent the next two hours in my small office going through the stacks of classified cables. They mostly just told me that the war in Vietnam was simply continuing to chew up the more than 17,000 U.S. troops that Johnson was adding to the conflict *every month*. They also detailed the huge internal conflict that was going on in South Vietnam, news of which was being completely withheld from the American people.

Briefly, the Buddhist majority in South Vietnam was getting increasingly incensed by the South Vietnamese government and the South Vietnamese military commanders. They wanted a negotiated settlement with North Vietnam (which also had a Buddhist majority), peace, and the removal of the Americans. The South Vietnamese military was organized into four Corps (numbered I, II, III & IV) and the generals who commanded these corps had enormous political as well as military power. They were authentic war lords.

The northernmost of these corps—I Corps—was commanded by General Nguyen Thi, a devout Buddhist. I Corps was huge, and extended far southward from its northern border—the demilitarized zone between North and South Vietnam, and contained the two largest cities outside Saigon. Thi backed the Buddhist uprising and their struggle, and the result was that he was militarily attacked by the commanders of the other three Corps. The story is long and convoluted but in the end, the corrupt South Vietnamese government survived, and Thi accepted an offer of exile in the United States. The roots of organized Buddhist opposition had taken firm hold however and would continue to flourish.

Regular (non-classified) news from the United States was depressing as well. The war was becoming increasingly unpopular and demonstrations against it were increasing. Inflation was having a pronounced effect on the U.S. economy, and costs for everything were rising. Housewives were becoming so angry that there was a determined attempt made to organize the opposition against rising food prices. Although that movement never became a serious reality, the argument the nation couldn't afford 'guns and butter' at the same time was beginning its climb to the political and moral high ground.

I stayed in Geneva a few more days before getting together with Bernard and Sylvie in Paris. They were both looking unusually fit and tanned, and Bernard said he and Sylvie were regularly taking three-day weekends and flying to Le Havre, where his sailboat was docked. They would leave Paris Friday afternoons, sleep on the boat, and set sail Saturday morning at dawn, returning late afternoon on Monday. The boat needed a crew of four, but if they didn't have available friends in Paris to go with them, they simply hired crew in Le Havre.

Sylvie said, "If you ever settle down enough to go with us, we'd adore having you, and I know lots of attractive young girls who'd be happy to accompany you." I promised to take them up on the offer as soon as I could get things settled in Thailand.

Bernard asked if I could tell them what I was doing out there, and I gladly told them all about Boss and the logging camp, my helicopter privileges, Niew, Jason, the savings bank, Boss's missing savings, etc.

At one point Sylvie interrupted and asked, "Who is this 'Granny' you keep talking about? Surely you don't have a grandmother in Bangkok?"

"Oh, no," I laughed. "My problem was that I couldn't pronounce Sunisa's mother's given name. I always just addressed her as 'Madam,' but she told me that she thinks of me as part of the family and asked me to call her Mémé."

They were shocked. "You know she's of royal blood, don't you?"

"Yes and that means she has some sort of honorific title attached to her name, which makes it even longer and even more impossible to pronounce."

"You should take it as a real compliment that she would allow you to address her that way. Does Sunisa know?"

"I really don't know, but I want to ask you something. Mémé never mentions her husband and I don't feel comfortable bringing up the subject. Do you know what happened to him? I understand he died many years ago. Sunisa never mentions him either."

"I don't know for sure," Bernard replied slowly, "but my understanding is that he got killed defending his uncle, the king, in some sort of palace coup."

"Surely that would make him a national hero or something."

"Well yes, but apparently he was the one who *organized* the coup, then changed his mind at the very last minute and turned against his own followers, saving the king's life. Although he killed several of them before being killed himself, I'm afraid his hero status is somewhat compromised."

I thought it was best to change the subject and asked how the sales of Lo's restaurants were going. Bernard said he understood that the sales were going very well, but if I'd like and had the time, he'd introduce me to the lawyer in his office that was handling the liquidation. I said I'd drop around his office in the morning.

The next morning as Bernard was leading me to the liquidator's office he said, "Bertie, there's something that puzzles me. Although our customs people probably intercept less than 10% of all the contraband, including illegal drugs, that come into this country, it would appear that imports of heroin from Thailand are increasing, not decreasing. The heroin Lo was importing is easily recognizable by customs because of its purity and unique chemical signature. Although we've only sold off about a third of his restaurants, I would have thought we would have seen some negative effect by now. I really don't understand it. Take a look at the sales we've made so far and see if anything pops out at you."

He introduced me to Giles, the lawyer who was handling the liquidation of Lo's assets. Giles was a nice guy, energetic, late 30's, and easy to get along with. I asked him if he had a list of the restaurants that had been sold so far, the original price paid by Lo, the sale price, and the name of the buyer. He pulled the list out of his desk drawer and went to make me a photocopy. The first restaurant I looked for was the one near me, and I discovered that it had been one of the first ones sold—and for a thumping good price, too. I didn't recognize the name of the company that bought it, which wasn't surprising, but I didn't recognize the corporate designation either, which was.

For example, U.S. company names are generally in the form of [company name], Corp. or LLC. English company names usually end with Ltd., Swiss with SA, Italian with SpA, German with GmbH, French with SARL, etc. This one, I didn't recognize at all. Most of the sales were either to individuals with French-sounding names or French companies with SARL at the end. A substantial number of buyers didn't fit that pattern, however, and they all had different corporate names.

I asked Giles if he knew the country of incorporation for the ones I didn't recognize, and he reeled off the place names effortlessly. They were places like Cyprus, San Marino, Netherland Antilles, Panama, Cayman Islands, Monaco, Seychelles, etc. He said, "If you're thinking about tracking down ownership of these companies, don't waste your time. It's next to impossible."

I thanked him, took my photocopy and left. The snake had grown another head. It was exactly what I'd been afraid of. A vague plan was beginning to form in my mind.

Alexia Redux

I decided to visit the snake, and hoped I'd find her in the Thai restaurant near my apartment. She not only was there, she seemed surprised and pleased to see me and beckoned me over to 'her' table.

"Bertie, what a pleasant surprise! Will you join me?"

"With pleasure. How are you Alexia? You're looking very well. I was hoping I might find you here but really wasn't expecting it. You don't eat here every night, do you?"

"No, but I eat here a lot more than I used to. The owner died and the restaurant was put up for sale. I managed to acquire a small part of the ownership. I thought it would be a good investment, because the food is good, the prices are fair, and it has a large and loyal clientele. But now I eat here 3-4 times a week to make sure the food and service are consistent and additionally," she laughed, "I can eat here for free."

I ordered a small meal, which appeared almost instantaneously. I guess you don't have to wait your turn in the kitchen if you're eating at the owner's table. I had to admit, the food *was* good. Not great, but really quite good. We chatted amiably for about half an hour after we were both through eating and I found her to be a good conversationalist and an interesting one. In fact, as our conversation was winding down, I asked her if she'd like to stop by the local bistro for a drink before going home.

She said she couldn't but was free the following evening. I said I wasn't but the day after worked for both of us and we agreed to meet at the bistro at 9:00.

I really had no particular plan at that point beyond simply getting to know her better and get a sense for what kind of person she was. Once I knew more about her personality and could build up a sort of psychological profile, I'd decide how best to proceed. She knew nothing about me other than I had an apartment nearby, whereas I knew almost everything about her past, her upbringing, the fact that she was an accountant with a law degree, worked for Lo as his second-in-command, and had taken over his past role in the drug business. I had a deadly serious reason to find out more about her. Her interest in me was confined to being a possible fling and occasional sex partner. I liked the way that particular deck was stacked.

Sunisa and I had dinner the next evening. She looked drawn and unhappy. She said Lo was the only man she'd ever really known and she was finding life difficult and lonely without him. She read my mind when she said, "It had to be done, of course, there was absolutely no other solution, and my mother and I will be forever in your debt for helping us. It's just that my life seems so empty now. Lo and I did a lot of things together and it was fun having people over for dinner, going to their houses for dinner, going to parties together—Lo was a marvelous dancer—and now that I'm a single woman, all the hostesses want to find me a companion for their social functions. I've yet to meet one that hasn't bored me to tears. I'm just now beginning to realize how much time Lo and I spent speaking to each other in either Thai or Vietnamese, and discussing affairs in East Asia. I have no friends that I can do that with. I knew I would miss him but I'm just now beginning to realize how much. I'm not sure what to do."

"I know your mother would love nothing better than for you to move back in with her. She's lonely, too."

"She actually told you that she was lonely?" Sunisa seemed astonished—astounded, actually.

"Not in so many words, but I know it's true. I've gotten to know Mémé pretty well."

"*What* did you just call her?"

"Mémé. She asked me to."

"I know you wouldn't lie to me, Bertie but that's so far out of character for her that it's hard to take in. When I was growing up, I was never allowed to use the informal 'Mom and Pop' to address my parents. It was always 'Mother and Father.' I was never even allowed to use the Thai equivalent of the 'tu' form of address when addressing my parents. I always had to use the more formal 'vous' form. For her to ask you to address her as Mémé is astonishing!"

"Well, maybe she's mellowing as she grows older. But the next time you talk to her, why don't you just mention that with Lo gone, you're finding life in Paris a little lonely, and see what she says. Maybe I've completely misread your mother, but I don't think so."

We spent more time talking about what I'd been doing in Thailand, Boss's problems, my invaluable helicopter privileges to commute back and forth (I said I'd done a favor for Kittikachorn), Niew—and Mémé's wish that I would settle down with her in Bangkok and give her some great-grand-babies, etc. Sunisa couldn't take it all in.

"My *mother* said that?"

"Word for word."

"Amazing. And are you going to do it? I think it would be wonderful, too."

"Well. I'm not quite sure how I feel about it frankly, but there are some important issues that would have to be settled first. Most importantly, I'm not in love with Niew and she's not in love with me. Besides the fact that I'm not sure I want to settle in Bangkok, I'm not sure my government would let me if I did. Given all that, it's really premature for me to give the question a lot of serious consideration. I'll keep you posted on any breaking news on the subject though."

I was surprised when Alexia showed up at the bistro the following evening. I'd never seen her dressed in anything other than a business suit, but this little black thing that she was wearing was definitely not a business suit. She had a knockout figure—and was well aware of it. She turned more than a few heads as she walked to my table.

"Wow, Alexia! You look fabulous! I had no idea!—Uhm, sorry, that didn't come out right. Let me make up for it and buy you a drink."

She was laughing as she sat down and said, "Bertie. Have you not noticed that some of us change our clothes from time to time? It's not that a black turtleneck, blue jeans and loafers don't look good on you —they definitely do—but don't you get tired of always wearing the same thing? How many sets of turtlenecks and jeans do you have, anyway?"

"Humm, that's sort of a wake-up call. I never actually pay much attention to what I'm wearing as long as it's suitable for the weather and the occasion. It just doesn't matter to me. When I get up in the morning and shave, in a way, I don't even look at myself. I'm simply looking at a face in the mirror that needs to be shaved and I want to be careful not to miss any bits. From the time I open my eyes, my head is engulfed by activity, usually on at least three levels of consciousness, and the rest of it—what I'm wearing etc.—seems so meaningless and trivial that I don't want to waste any time thinking about it. You know, I don't think I've ever said that to anybody before because I've never really thought about it, and I don't like talking about myself."

"Bertie, are you repressed?"

"I don't think so but you're welcome to make a close-up clinical analysis for yourself a little later on."

She laughed and she had a wonderfully warm, throaty laugh that was easy to listen to. She was fun to talk to as well, literate, well-read and well-informed. She had thoughtful opinions on current affairs, modern art and architecture, Emanuel Kant, and an extensive list of other subjects. At some point, and a lot of drinks later, we began discussing Marcel Proust, *Remembrances of Things Past,* and the revelation—scandalous at the time—that he was a homosexual. She had such strong views on homosexuality that I asked if she were homosexual as well. She surprised me by saying that she was *bi*-sexual. She liked sex with both men and women. "They're both very different but they both give me much pleasure," she said. "Do you feel like experimenting with a bisexual woman?"

"My place or yours?"

"Let's try yours." This was going better than I expected.

She was surprised when I opened the door and she looked around. "Somehow, this doesn't look like the masculine décor, or lack of any décor at all, that I had imagined. Bertie. Are *you* homosexual—or do you have a woman living with you?"

"Neither," I growled. "The apartment was pretty messed up when I moved in and I got a friend of mine—a woman—to fix it up. When I saw what she'd done, I was afraid I'd get a reaction like yours if I ever brought a woman in here. Well, you're the first woman I've invited in and your reaction is exactly what I was afraid of. All suggestions for remedying the situation will be gratefully accepted."

"Is it all right if I look around then?"

"Absolutely, help yourself."

I followed her around as she made her inspection, and when we returned to my bedroom she said, "Well I do have several suggestions but let's save them 'till later. Right now, I have to go pee and I want to wash up. First . . ." —and then with the smooth, continuous motion that only women can do, she threw her purse into one of my chairs, reached behind her back, unbuttoned or unzipped something, pushed her dress off her shoulders, stepped out of it, and kicked off her shoes.

The woman had an absolutely amazing body. I don't know what adjective to put first—athletic, luscious, gorgeous—I really don't know. It was the kind of body you'd fantasize about if you had that much imagination.

She smiled and said, "I'll be right back." This project was going to be a lot more fun than I thought.

I was in a bit of a panic, though. What the hell was I going to do with Excalibur? I unstrapped it and was looking around frantically for a place to hide it when I heard the water stop running in the bathroom. I just shoved it behind the seat cushion of a chair when she came back in and said, "My, aren't we modest? I expected to find you naked. Are you beginning to think that something doesn't feel quite right? Well, it doesn't matter, William Bertram MacFarland. This evening isn't going to wind up like you thought in any case. Sit down!"

I did. She plopped down in the other chair, opened he purse, and I found myself staring down the barrel of a small, but very deadly-looking pistol. Hell, at this range she couldn't miss.

As soon as she had addressed me as William Bertram MacFarland, I realized that I had made a very significant miscalculation. I'd never given her my full name. It looked like she had been doing some serious research on me and her next statement confirmed it. "It was a rather miserable way for a house-guest to treat his former host, don't you think?"

"Alexia, I don't know what the hell you're talking about, but put that gun down, for God's sake! Are you crazy or something?"

"If you try any more of that kind of kind of bullshit with me, I'll make you pay dearly for it. Just so you know, we don't intend to kill you this evening—just teach you a lesson you'll never forget. With your connections, you could be handy to us. However, keeping you alive doesn't necessarily mean keeping you whole. I understand that blowing off someone's kneecap not only causes nearly unbearable pain for the rest of their lives, it also makes them a pathetic cripple. You have two choices, you can either play ball with us, and have an easy and enjoyable life, or we'll injure you severely and permanently and start killing people close to you. We'll probably start with Sunisa, then her mother, then Bernard's son, then Sylvie—perhaps even Bernard himself. Our people can get to anybody—absolutely anybody. You can see we've already gotten to you, but as I say, we think we'd like to keep you alive for the moment, but that can change any time. Now tell me, why did you kill Mr. Teng?"

"I didn't kill him. He committed suicide."

"Why?"

"He was ashamed of what he'd been doing."

For some reason or another, my answer made her semi-hysterical. Maybe because she knew it was the truth and still had enough decency left in her to relate to it. In any case, her face hardened with fury as she hissed, "You moralizing bastard! I've got two guys parked outside on the Rue des Bernardins that will make you remember this night for the rest of your miserable life. In the meantime, I don't want you bothering me while I get dressed." She jammed the pistol into my knee. I dropped it, pivoted to the left and slammed my fist holding the haft of

Excalibur into her right wrist. The bullet just missed, but she didn't drop the gun. That taut, fit, athletic body was the real deal, and the second shot ripped through my left arm just below the shoulder as Excalibur slid between her ribs and found her heart.

Death from a clean knife wound to the heart is clinically interesting. The puncture wound to the skin, peritoneum and lungs is so fast that the body doesn't have time to register it before being overwhelmed by the massive shock to the heart. Even if the vagus nerve isn't hit directly, the vagus is a cranial nerve and instantaneously relays the news of damage to the heart to the brain. All motion of the victim stops for as much as a second as the brain realizes that some major damage has occurred, and the hands reflexively reach for the site of the wound. Alexia looked at me with stunned surprise as she dropped the gun and slumped to the floor. I kicked the gun under the bed and went into the bathroom to survey the damage.

It didn't look too bad. The bullet had missed the bone, and although there was a lot of blood, it hadn't hit an artery. I put some gauze and adhesive tape around the wound and went into the bedroom to call Bernard. It was 1:00 in the morning and he was not happy, but when I explained what had happened he was both solicitous and all business. I asked him if he would call the police—they're close. There is a major station right across the road in front of Notre Dame Cathedral. I asked him if he would ask them to block both ends of Rue des Bernardins before coming to me.

He told me not to worry and said he'd be right there, and also not to say a word to the police or anyone else until he arrived.

Bernard arrived, just behind the police, about 20 minutes later. I thought that the police in Brest had treated him with almost obsequious deference because they were, after all, a bit provincial. The Paris police were even more deferential. When he politely asked if he might have some privacy to speak to his client, they offered to completely leave the premises! They can't do that! It's a crime scene for God's sake!

Bernard just politely declined, asked them to do whatever they needed to do and assured them that he would only need a few minutes alone with me. We went into the other bedroom, he wordlessly examined my wound, told me I'd have to go to the hospital to get it treated but that it didn't look too bad, and asked me what had happened. When I told him he just simply said, "Good work. Where's Excalibur?" I told him where I'd hidden it in the bathroom, but told him that the sheath was still behind the cushion of the chair I'd been sitting in. He said he'd take care of it.

I'd told him about the threats that Alexia had made and I begged him to try to get Sunisa back to Thailand right away.

He just smiled when I told him of the threats to his son, wife and to him personally and said,

"Don't worry about it." He said, "I think we've got everything under control, Bertie. The two men waiting in the car outside are well known to the police, and will not be bothering society for many, many years to come.

I'll make sure that Sunisa gets back to Thailand safely, and you have nothing to worry about concerning Alexia's death. It was justifiable self-defense and there's a bullet wound in your arm, plus a bullet in the floor to prove it. Off you go now into the waiting arms of your best friend, Dr. Gautier. I doubt if he'll be there personally at this hour, but you can be sure he'll drop in on you first thing in the morning. Oh, and on a more serious note—congratulations, Bertie. I think that this time the snake is definitely dead—but I'd advise you to be very, very careful when you return to Thailand."

Chapter 14 — Unfathomable Darkness

A Happy Team

The American Hospital had insisted on doing a little needlework on my gunshot wound and then loaded me up with antibiotics, but didn't make me stay. I had to stay in Paris a few more days in order to give sworn testimony to the police before I could leave for Bangkok. Bernard's assurance to them that I was doing some highly confidential work for the government sufficed to keep the incident out of the newspapers. Out of curiosity, I walked by Lo's old restaurant near my apartment. There was a 'Closed' sign on the door. I remember thinking that for once, things finally looked as though they were all moving in the right direction.

I could scarcely have been more wrong.

Mémé was in an ebullient mood when she met me at the airport. She was happy to see me, but she was even more pleased about a recent conversation she had had with Sunisa. She said that during the conversation Sunisa had mentioned that she was lonely in her apartment all by herself, and that she had suggested that Sunisa come for an extended visit. My guess was that it would turn out to be *very* extended. I was happy for both of them.

The first item on my agenda was to get an update on Boss's missing funds. I called the lawyer at Mémé's bank and the news wasn't good. 'Nicky' had fled the country and for the moment at least, couldn't be found by Interpol. Jason was probably still in Thailand, but nobody knew where. The 'savings bank' was in liquidation. All Nicky's assets were being sold—his house and its contents, his cars (which had been recovered), and all other tangible assets which could be located. The problem was, as I understood it, that Nicky's direct creditors stood first in line for the proceeds and the bank's clients (of which there were only three) would pick up the crumbs if any were left after his direct debts had been paid. The prospects of that looked dim, as he owed back taxes, the house was heavily mortgaged, he was behind in his car payments, etc.

Next, I tried calling Niew. The phone was answered by a woman speaking Thai but when I asked (in English) for Niew, the same voice said excitedly, "You wait, please! You wait, please!"

The next voice I heard was that of Boss and when we had exchanged heartfelt greetings, he explained that Chianaporn now routinely answered the phone for him, and that Paul had installed an extra-long phone cord so she could run out to the porch and give him the phone. He said that Niew was trying to teach Chianaporn some English, but while it was slow going. Chianaporn had gotten the 'You wait, please!' phrase down pat. He told me that I simply wouldn't believe the changes that had been made in the camp, and wanted to know when I was coming up. I told him it would probably be the next day but when I asked him if I could speak to Niew, he just laughed.

"I'll get her to call you when she gets back around 7:00," he said. "That little gal is flat-out amazing. She's up before sunrise every day and she don't get back here 'till it's near dark. You won't believe the changes she's making. Bertie, I have to tell you, even taking into account that I can't walk no more, I ain't been this happy at the camp since Beth was alive." It was an incredible tribute to Niew.

When Niew called that evening, she sounded just as happy as Boss. She had truly fallen in love with Boss, the camp, the elephants, the village, the way of life there—just everything. She couldn't wait to tell me all about it, but first wanted to hear about everything I'd done since I'd been away. Everything. I was to leave nothing out. I thought for a second about what I really *had* done, but said it was all pretty mundane. I'd had to do some consulting work for some clients in Geneva, then I'd spent some time with some good friends in Paris, I'd had dinner with Sunisa, all that sort of thing. Nothing important, just taking care of business.

When I asked her about what she had been doing, the floodgates opened. She literally couldn't get the words out fast enough. After 15 minutes or so, I said, "Niew! Niew! Wait! It's more than I can take in! I'll be up tomorrow—early. Can't wait to see you. Boss says you're doing an amazing job. Bye. Sleep well."

The next morning when I got off the helicopter, I was greeted by Niew, who was alone in the Jeep. Once again, I was stunned by how beautiful she was. It's so difficult to describe her adequately. If I showed you a photograph of her, you would almost certainly say, "Wow, that's a beautiful woman." But your evaluation would have been based, obviously, on what was visible in the photograph. There was no question that she was physically beautiful—you could see *that* in the photograph—but what you wouldn't have been able to see was her incandescent joy; her energy and her boundless enthusiasm; the intelligence shining out of her eyes; the vivacity and the love that radiated from her. This beautifully unique woman was in love with the world, in love with the earth, in love with life—and in love with me. I wasn't even clear of the helicopter prop wash when she leapt into my arms, wrapped her arms around my neck and her legs around my waist and kissed me, tenderly at first and then passionately. If I could give a single gift to humanity, it would be to be greeted like that at least once in their lives.

The camp really was a changed place. When Boss saw us emerge into the bunkhouse clearing, he got up from his chair, hobbled over to his wheel chair, drove it to the newly-installed lift, and descended to ground level. It was hard to see exactly what happened next, because there was a new structure surrounding the bottom of the lift, but out of it roared Boss, driving his specially modified scooter, and motioning for us to follow him.

It was really my first tour of the camp. I'd seen the elephant operations and visited the bunkhouse, but not much more. Although I hadn't thought about it until Niew had ordered Joe to 'take her to the village' soon after her initial arrival at the camp, clearly all those mahouts and their families had to live somewhere.

Boss led us to an entire village consisting of some 30 huts behind and below the bunkhouse and separated from it by about a half mile of jungle. I'll describe the layout of the camp in more detail later, but what first struck me was not the village itself, but the jewel-like lake that it bordered. It wasn't huge; probably not more than 100 meters across, but it was beautiful. There were scores of colorful Thai wood ducks paddling around on it, and I had little doubt as to where the majority of them would eventually wind up. Thailand has lots of water; it rains a lot in Thailand, but as the water flows farther and farther down to the sea and the streams turn into broad rivers, the water gets dirtier and muddier. Here in the mountains, nothing had soiled the fresh water that fed this lake and it was wonderfully clear and clean, and beautifully reflected the sparkling blue sky above it. Long ago, Boss had stocked it with fish—catfish, carp, tilapia and barbell—so the villagers were never short of fresh fish.

Near the lake's outlet, there was a shallow area where the mahouts gave their elephants a bath and a scrub-down at the end of each day. Elephants love being bathed and scrubbed; there is probably nothing which bonds an elephant more to its mahout than this daily ritual.

The village was alive with activity, and the arrival of Boss and Niew was greeted with the excited screams of swarms of children and warm welcomes by their mothers, and a motley assortment of friendly dogs. There were two nearby structures being built, and Niew proudly led me to one of them. With a blackboard on the far wall and several rows of bench-type desks, there wasn't much doubt of its function.

For an hour a day, Niew was teaching the children, and their mothers, how to read and write. Niew said that the 'schoolhouse' was turning into kind of a community center, where the men would gather and smoke at the end of the workday (the walls only extended halfway up to the roof so there was plenty of ventilation), as well as serving as a convenient place for the women to gather and gossip.

I was curious about a charcoal brazier that was pushed into a corner, and Niew said that she was showing the women new ways to cook and teaching new recipes. Almost all the villagers were at least second generation at the camp and some of the younger ones were third. As a result, all of the food preparation menus and methods had been handed down from mother to daughter, and it never varied. The majority of the villagers had never left the camp and there was nothing to induce them to change their comfortable ways.

Niew was showing them tasty new meal options. She was also showing them how to improve the productivity of their farmland, introducing the principles of crop rotation, showing them how to compost to make fertilizer, demonstrating new methods to make rice noodles, etc. In most of the world outside the United States, teachers are not just deeply respected; they are honored or even revered. Niew was also deeply loved.

The other new building looked like a partially constructed house—not a hut but a house—and I asked Boss about it. He told me that Prem, the carpenter, had asked if he could bring his family and stay in the camp, and he had agreed because 'a cripple ain't worth a tinker's damn at carpentry work.' Prem's wife, who was born and raised in Bangkok, agreed only on the condition that he build them a small house. Boss said he thought she agreed to come mostly because her parents had grown up in a village near Chiang Mai and often spoke longingly of the life they had there. At the moment, they were staying in a large hut that had some extra room due to the death of the owner's parents, and the children loved it. There was no way they were going to live in a house and be different from all the other little kids. Besides that, living in a hut was an adventure.

"You can see how all that ended up," Boss said and pointed to the far end of the village. Sure enough, a brand new hut was under construction. I asked what was going to happen with the abandoned construction on the house and Boss said, "Paul is trying to convince his wife to come up here, too. The villagers won't mind them living in a house because he's a foreigner and don't know any better."

We spent the rest of the morning touring the camp, and I discovered all sorts of things. Within a ten minute walk from the village was a large pigsty containing six or seven pigs snuffling around contentedly. The amazing thing about the sty was that it was entirely built of solid, sturdy teak planks set about 4 or 5 inches apart. The top of it was also covered with the same planks, spaced at about the same distance.

I looked curiously at Boss and before I could ask the question he said, "Tiger proof. They wouldn't last a single night without it." When I asked about feeding them he said, "They eat leaves, grasses, roots, fruits and flowers and Lord knows we ain't short of any of that stuff around here. It's the job of one of the boys in the village to come out here each morning and feed them, and to make sure their water trough is filled to the top. We only slaughter one on special occasions, but they reproduce at a pretty steady rate."

I was beginning to understand how incredibly self-sufficient this camp was. They lived in a totally sustainable balance with nature. Everything reproduced itself. They truly wanted for nothing.

I spent the next three months shuttling back and forth between Bangkok and the camp. In general, I spent four or five days at the camp each week, and each day I spent there, my love for the way of life grew. Boss taught both Niew and me all about his beloved elephants, and we came to love and respect those gentle giants as much as he did. I guess that counting the babies and the juveniles, there were around 45-50 elephants in the camp, and over time, I became accepted and trusted by all of them. I became sort of adopted by one group however, and it is extraordinarily humbling to have several of these huge, beautiful, unbelievably intelligent creatures come running and trumpeting across the camp clearing to greet you when returning after a protracted absence. The ultimate expression of trust and affection is when you are led to view a newborn. You never forget having a group of "aunts" nudging you to touch and caress the newborn. It's like being in love with a being from another planet—and knowing that the love is not only felt by that being—it is genuinely returned. It will change your life forever. I promise.

On several occasions, I rode out to the teak forest sitting on one of the elephants behind its mahout, and marveled at the ability of those huge beings to travel through the jungle in absolute silence. You have to experience it to believe it. The mahouts showed me how they felled the teak trees using two-man hand saws, and then used axes to remove the limbs. It was a smooth operation.

I also learned a few unpleasant things on those trips. Whereas the various stinging and biting insects of the jungle were largely uninterested in the mahouts, they found me fascinating. I returned from my first trip covered with a plethora of welts and stings. I also learned that elephants are covered with short, bristly hairs that left my ankles in a bloody mess. Boss showed me some leaves that I could crush and rub all over my exposed skin to keep the insects away, and while it worked quite well, I had to scrub myself really hard on my return to get rid of the smell. Simple cloth wrappings solved the problem of getting my ankles chewed up.

Niew and I slept together but we didn't make love. She said she wanted to present herself as a virgin to her husband, and unless I promised to marry her, we were not going to make love. That was really tough on both of us, but she was adamant and had a will of steel. I loved Niew but I wasn't totally sure that I wanted to live the rest of my life in Thailand. However, the more time I spent at the camp, the more I thought that it really could be a rich, satisfying life. I would have to get Johnson to agree to let me go, and although that wouldn't be easy, he might feel that marginalizing me at some remote Thai logging camp could actually be a pretty good idea.

When I was in Bangkok, I spent most of my time with Prime Minister Kittikachorn and his senior staff. He viewed me as a valuable asset because of my knowledge of the principal members of Johnson's administration, their quirks, hot buttons, etc. I was comfortable talking to him and his people because the information that I was providing concerned only personalities, areas of interest, organizational structure, etc. Absolutely none of that was classified, you simply had to be—or have been—a Washington 'insider' to be knowledgeable of it. I thought it was a fair swap for my continuing helicopter privileges. It occurred to me that during this process, I was becoming a 'Thai insider.' Maybe that would help Johnson decide to just leave me in Thailand. My knowledge of the principal players and inner workings of the Thai government might prove quite helpful.

Although I spent a lot of time with Prime Minister Kittikachorn and his interesting crew, I treasured spending time with Mémé and Sunisa. I was now considered a full member of the family, but it was hard for me to get used to being deferred to, simply because I was a male. Life on the estate was about as stable as life can get, so having to make any important decision was a rare event indeed, but on the few occasions that the situation arose, Mémé and Sunisa would come to me together and ask me what they should do. Because most of the time I didn't understand the problem, I had to ask so many questions that the solution usually became apparent to all three of us during my questioning, but nonetheless, when I summarized the obvious, they would both nod gravely and say, "Yes, I think that is very wise. We shall do as you say." I thought about objecting once or twice but on reflection, realized that there was no way I was going to change thought patterns that had been inculcated in both of them from birth by a strongly male-dominated culture. I decided that since they were essentially making the decisions themselves anyway, there was no harm in it and if it somehow made them feel more comfortable I was pleased to participate in what was—for me, anyway—a charade.

Although at first I found it somewhat annoying, Niew would call me punctually every night at exactly 7:30 and relate to me in exquisite detail absolutely everything that had transpired in the camp that day. I confess that I mostly didn't have a whole lot of interest in the details of camp life, but I loved to hear her talk. It wasn't just her warm, rich voice. It was the excitement, the constant wonder, the concern and the love which always permeated her descriptions of those daily goings-on that made her such a treat to listen to. Almost against my will, I found myself looking forward to her nightly calls.

A Visit to Laos

Bill Young and I were getting to be good friends, too. He was in Bangkok pretty often (I have no idea why and I certainly never asked). He'd always call when he got in town, and though occasionally he'd come to the house for dinner, I usually joined him in Bangkok, which was always interesting. Both of us were definitely in the category that the Army calls 'bad asses.' To give you an idea of what that means, when I was in Ranger training, slogging and jogging in full combat gear all over hell and half of Georgia, the song we'd sing to the cadence of the jog was:

> "I wanna be an Airborne Ranger
> Live a life of fightin' and danger
> Blood, guts, sex, and lots of danger
> That's the life of an Airborne Ranger!"

I know it's crude and childish, but the truth is that both Bill and I really *did* love danger; we loved to get into a good brawl; we loved deliberately putting ourselves into truly perilous situations in bars and brothels in the worst parts of Bangkok and then fighting our way out of them. We used only our fists and feet. Bill was armed with a .357 Magnum, and of course I had Excalibur, but we never even revealed them. We fought for the sheer joy of it. Many years later, alone, I would do the same thing in some of the sleazier dives in Marseilles. Although I came out on top in the majority of situations, in quite a few, I was the one getting picked up from the floor. The curious thing was that no matter whether I was picking up my opponent or I was the one getting picked up, almost invariably the two of us would climb somewhat painfully onto our bar stools and spend the rest of the night getting absolutely blotto with the drinks ordered by an admiring crowd which had watched the fight.

On one of his visits to Bangkok, Bill seemed really preoccupied and even though we both started our usual carousing around, Bill was drinking almost non-stop when he said, "Bertie, I need you to do something for me. I've got some problems here in Bangkok that I need to take care of, but I'm scheduled to fly as crew chief on an equipment drop tomorrow over the Plain of Jars. It's no sweat, I've got a great jumpmaster (it's a WW II term for a person who is currently referred to as a drop master) and he'll do all the loading, weight distribution, and 'kicking' (another WW II term for getting the cargo out of the aircraft). You'll really just be a passenger. Please do it for me Bertie. It's important." How could I refuse?

It turned out to be one hell of a ride.

Bill was so out of it that I had to put him to bed in his hotel. About the last conscious act that he had performed was to give me the telephone number of his driver, and although I wasn't much better off, I called him. I immediately discovered that the driver spoke almost no English. After a lot of shouting (why is it that people think they can communicate more effectively with someone who doesn't speak their language if they shout at them?), I think I got him to understand to come to Bill's room in the hotel at 6:00 in the morning and bang on the door. I looked at my watch. That gave me about an hour and 45 minutes to sleep. I plopped down beside Bill and instantaneously passed out.

As I reluctantly segued into consciousness, I couldn't decide whether the pounding in my head or the pounding on the door was worse. Groggily, I figured I could at least stop one of them and weaved my way to the door on rubber legs. I certainly wasn't prepared for what happened when I opened the door. This small Thai man whom I had never seen before looked me over, effortlessly draped me over his shoulder, and padded down the hall. I vaguely remember being shoved into a car, and then pulled out of the car and shoved into a small plane at Don Muang, but I wasn't fully awake until we reached Udorn Air Force base and I was hustled onto a C-123 cargo plane that was fully loaded and already revving its motors. I was still strapping on my parachute as we were accelerating down the runway for take-off.

Harry, the drop master, was laughing so hard that there were tears in his eyes when he asked, "You ever jumped out of an airplane before?" He relaxed when I told him how many jumps I'd made and under what conditions and said, "Well, that's pretty good but for right now, it don't matter. The only things going out of this airplane are these pallets. Vang Pao's got some troops near the Plain of Jars that need re-supplying, so we'll just kick these out over the Plain and then land at Long Tieng to pick up some other stuff before going back to Udorn. With any luck we'll be back at Udorn before nightfall." We didn't have any luck.

The rear of the fuselage of the C-123 is actually a giant gate that can be lowered right down to the runway to facilitate loading when the plane is on the ground. It can also be lowered when the plane is in flight to allow cargo drops. The system is pretty simple. The floor of the cargo bay is covered with rollers which makes the pallets easy to load and to drop. Each pallet is equipped with a cargo parachute and once over the drop zone, the chute is thrown out of the rear of the aircraft. As soon as the drag chute has pulled out the main chute, the pallet is released from its hold-downs and the chute drags it out of the aircraft. That's how it's supposed to work anyway, and that how it *did* work for all except the last pallet. As it was being dragged out of the plane, it got twisted somehow and jammed into the sides of the cargo bay. By this time, its main chute had fully deployed and was pulling so hard on the pallet that it was impossible to budge it. Also, the chute was slowing down the whole airplane.

When you're in the air, the pilot is in total command of the aircraft and he has to be asked for permission to cut the chute free, so that's what I did. I was astonished when he said, "Hell, if we bring that pallet back, I'll be filling out 'Incident Forms' for three hours. Don't worry, I'll get it out." Without any further explanation or warning, he gunned the engines, went into a brief but steep dive, then pulled back hard on the controls. I was holding on for dear life as the plane went into a climbing, hard left bank.

I looked back into the cargo bay and sure enough—Whoosh! Out goes the pallet, and then Whoosh! Out goes Harry! I turned to the pilot and shouted, "You son of a bitch! You just dropped our drop master!"

"Oh God!" he groaned. "Let's make sure he's OK." We circled back but even from a distance I could see Harry's beet-red face, and there was no mistaking the gestures he was making towards the plane as he slowly descended towards earth.

When we got to Long Tieng, Vang Pao wasn't there, but the CIA guy who seemed to be in charge scoffed at my request to get a helicopter out there right away. He said that the whole area around the Plain of Jars was swarming with Pathet Lao troops, and an attempt at a night rescue mission would never be authorized. He said he doubted that Harry would be found alive in any case—the Pathet Lao take no prisoners—but we would surely lose the pilot and the chopper.

He said, "Shit like this happens in wartime, fella. I'll try to get authorization in the morning, but I can't promise anything. We're short on helicopters and helicopter pilots, so somebody would have to be pulled off another mission. Vang's troops will probably take care of him. I wouldn't worry about it if I were you."

I told him very quietly that I was going to take a jeep and go try to find Harry, and if either he or the pilot were on the base when I got back, I would kill them both. To his insulted and condescending inquiry of 'who the fuck I thought I was,' I just gave him my name. I must admit it had quite an effect. I not only was under Vang's wing, the Director of the CIA himself had personally issued a stern warning concerning my safety. I cut through his babbled apologies with a curt order to find me a jeep, make sure it was filled with gas and two extra jerry cans of gas. I wanted a submachine gun with lots of extra ammunition, a pistol—either a .45 or a .357 magnum—with lots of ammunition, a couple of gallons of drinking water, a first-aid kit, lots of sandwiches and a map of how to get to the Plain of Jars.

He said he would get all that for me right away but added, "Mr. MacFarland, I think it's my duty to tell you that the road—well it's not a road, just a track, really—through the jungle and those mountains, is hair-raisingly treacherous in full daylight. I've never heard of anybody using it at night. Besides that, there's tigers and wild elephants and God knows what else in the jungle. Don't try it, sir. I'll do my best to get a helicopter in the morning and when they know who's pushing for it; I may well be able to get one. I'll be honest with you, though. If they figure he's probably dead anyway, they'll deny the request even if it is from you." I told him to shut up and start packing my jeep. I also re-emphasized that he and the pilot had better find some damn way not to be at Long Tieng when I got back.

There were only two good things about that trip. I really didn't need a map. That road had no junctions. The other was that I couldn't see the mind-boggling drops that were just off to the side of the track. It was a terrifying ride anyway. The air distance from Long Tieng to the Plain of Jars is only about 25 miles. The road distance is at least five times that and while you're in the mountains—which is most of the time—it's rare to be able to get out of first gear.

There was just the barest hint of the coming dawn when the road finally began to level out a bit as it dropped into the plain. That's when I hit the log. I should have been paying more attention, but I was desperately tired and was probably going 30 miles an hour when I hit it. Just about everything but me and the jerry cans flew out of the jeep, and frankly, it was a close thing with me. Thoroughly awakened, I began to back up and use the headlights to locate my gear. I got all the way back to the log before I found everything, and was about to get back in the jeep when I took a good look at the log to see if I could move it out of the way. The hairs on the back of my neck had to be standing straight up as I stared at the log and realized with horror that *it was moving!* As I bent to look more closely, I discovered that it was not only moving; it didn't have any bark on it either! It was the biggest piece of a Burmese python I'd ever seen, and figuring that I might have pissed it off, I got the hell out of there as fast as I could. If he was doing a U-turn and coming back to make enquiries, I didn't want to be there to discuss things with him.

In my heightened state of awareness, I started to really worry about the reported presence of the Pathet Lao in the area. Those guys were tough, well-organized, reasonably well-trained, and fierce Laotian patriots. They viewed Americans (quite rightly, in my opinion), as imperialistic foreigners trying to usurp their leadership and exert cultural, political, and economic hegemony over their country. I wasn't going to stand a chance if they spotted me.

The trees started to clear as I reached the plain and I pulled the jeep off the road and peeked out from the cover to see what I could see. The Plain of Jars is a vast plateau, and things look very different on the ground than they do from the air, but I was pretty sure I was in the right area. I probably walked a mile, dodging in and out from behind trees before I saw him, some 200 yards away on the edge of the plain, sitting forlornly on a pallet with his parachute wrapped around him. At least he was alive, but when I whispered to him from behind a nearby tree it startled him so violently that I was afraid he might not stay that way.

He said Vang's army had come and sucked up all the supplies within minutes after he landed but told him, "We only ask for supplies. Have no need for Yankee trooper. You go home now."

I slept most of the way back but the few times I did open my eyes I was so terrified by the precipitous drops mere inches away from the edge of the track that I immediately shut them tightly again and gladly succumbed to the lures of the god Morpheus, the god of sleep and dreams. When Harry woke me up when we got back to Long Tieng, he was drenched in sweat. Admittedly it was hot, but Harry said he'd never been so scared in his life. He said that he couldn't even count the number of times we'd been inches away from a thousand foot drop. I thought he was going to slug me when I airily told him that it didn't bother me a bit.

After a much needed shower, shave and attention to other necessities, Harry and I piled into the small plane that had been sent to take us back to Udorn. Although I hadn't made a thorough search before we left, I could find no trace of either the CIA asshole or the pilot. In response to my queries, a couple of guys said that they had caught a flight back to Udorn. But you never know. CIA guys are professional liars.

Darkness

I was surprised, and initially a little bit miffed that neither Mémé nor Sunisa seemed at all surprised and certainly not worried by my three-night absence. More than once, I'd stayed out all night with Bill, but I thought they might find a three-night absence with no phone call just to let them know how long I intended to be away somewhat worrying or at least rather rude. Not a bit of it. Niew said she wasn't worried either.

"Men do these things," she said. "It's perfectly normal and we are taught not to inquire about where the men have been or what they were doing while they were there." It is truly a mistake to think that Eastern cultures and Western ones are essentially the same.

About three weeks later, I was relaxing with a Scotch after a wearying day of meetings with a half dozen of Kittikachorn's staff. I was waiting for my 7:30 phone call, when a curious thing happened. The phone didn't ring. Niew made a big thing of always calling at 7:30 on the dot, and when I had heard nothing by 7:45, I called the camp. It rang and rang—no answer. Every warning red flag I had was raised high and waving madly. I was terrified. Something was horribly wrong.

In a cold sweat, I called Kittikachorn on his private number but it was his night duty officer that answered. The night duty officer for a Prime Minister has far-reaching powers to act in the temporary absence of the Prime Minister. This particular duty officer, who knew me well, immediately agreed to my request for an emergency mobilization of a couple of dozen troops and/or police officers in Chiang Mai to immediately get on the road from Chiang Mai to the camp, and stop and search any cars or trucks coming in the opposite direction. He also took considerable initiative when he said, "I'll scramble a helicopter from Don Muang to pick you up. I'm pretty sure there's enough area to land, but I'm afraid we may damage some of the Princesses' flowers. If we do, please offer her the profound apologies of the Prime Minister, and assure her of his commitment to restore the damaged plants at once. The duty officer also told me that he would be in radio contact with both my pilot and the commander of the Chiang Mai task force, and would keep me advised of any developments.

The helicopter arrived in seven minutes. There were four heavily-armed Thai rangers wearing bullet-proof vests aboard. We took off like a shot, and must have traveled at top speed rather than cruising speed; because the pilot shaved nearly 15 minutes off the normal flight time. I asked him how he was going to find the landing clearing, and he told me that they had already sent in an assault team by helicopter from Chiang Mai using night vision equipment. The assault team had taken a jeep that they had found at the camp, and were shining its headlights on the landing area.

He said, "Look, I think that's it right up there." It is indeed pretty easy to see even a pinprick of light when you're flying over a pitch-black jungle.

I asked, "Look if these guys have already entered the camp, what have they found? Where are the people? Is everybody OK?" I knew he was lying when he told me that he hadn't received that report yet, and then looked away.

He told me he had received a report from the Chiang Mai task force commander, who said that his team had intercepted a small truck and a jeep coming from the camp and they were currently on their way to the camp and expected to arrive in approximately 15 minutes.

Although I was expecting the worst, I couldn't have possibly imagined what I found. I got a foretaste of it as we approached the bunkhouse, and I saw the wanton, senseless damage that had been done to it. The door was off its hinges, all the windows had been shot out, and the chairs destroyed and flung into the yard. By the light of the flashlight that Captain was holding, I saw Boss lying dead just inside the front door. He'd been shot in the head and the leg, and was lying in a pool of his own blood. I looked up the Captain and he just nodded his head towards Niew's bedroom.

What they had done to Niew and Chianaporn defies description. Both were on the floor, both were absolutely riddled with bullets and both had their skirts pulled up to their waists. The huge amount of blood all over their loins made it all too clear that they had both been repeatedly, savagely raped.

People who have never been in combat sometimes wonder why soldiers never want to talk about what they've seen. The first reason is that no soldier wants to experience having to look once again at the vivid, detailed image of an atrocity which is burned indelibly into his memory. The second is that there are simply no words to adequately describe that level of shock and revulsion. When the victim of the atrocity is someone you loved, the task of trying to describe your feelings is simply impossible. It is for me, at least.

I went over to the closet where we stored our linens and covered each of them with clean sheets. I had noticed that the key to Boss's safe, which he always wore on a leather thong around his neck, was gone, so we went into his office. The safe was open and completely empty. They had destroyed the radio, Boss's wheel chair, both generators and knocked over the outhouse. I was trembling so violently with the cold fury that was consuming me that the Captain put out his hand as if to steady me, but looked at my face and quickly retracted it.

We heard the sounds of lots of vehicles drawing up to the bunkhouse and went outside to meet them. It was an impressive gathering. Kittikachorn had not stinted. There were a total of 28 of our guys—all clad in black SWAT-team outfits surrounding six extremely nervous civilians. All the official cars and jeeps had been drawn up in a circle with their headlights pointed inwards. The effect for the prisoners was that they could only see the ominous outlines of the SWAT team members back-lit by headlights, completely motionless and staring at them through closed helmet faceplates.

I went in to talk to the prisoners, Excalibur in my hand. Five of them looked like standard thugs, but it was the sixth one that interested me. He was much smaller than the others. I stared into those terrified, sunken eyes and said, "Hello, Jason. I've been looking for you."

Having broken the silence, the ringleader of the thugs approached me with outstretched hands.

His English was broken, but understandable. He tried to tell me that it was Jason that led them here because his father owed him money and he needed to collect it. "He said he owned this place jointly with his father so we had every right to be here."

"Why is everybody dead?"

"Listen, that was a mistake. I didn't have anything to do with it. These other four had been drinking and smoking dope, and when they found those two women hiding in a bedroom, they just went crazy. I don't know what women were doing here anyway. Maybe Boss . . .," he grinned conspiratorially.

He knew he was a dead man when I quietly replied, "I was going to marry one of them."

In one lightening quick, smooth motion, I severed his outstretched, pleading hand so violently that there were involuntary gasps of "Unh!" from the troopers while he stared in uncomprehending shock at the blood spurting from the stump of his wrist.

I turned to the Captain and just nodded my head and about ten of his men moved in. I motioned to Jason and said, "Leave him here."

I grabbed Jason, who was literally groveling at my feet, by his neck, and hoisted him upright. I held him at arm's length because he'd soiled himself and he stunk. I had just begun to question him when we heard the staccato rattle of automatic gunfire in the distance. Jason soiled himself again.

I won't go into all the details but the gist of what Jason told me was this: Soon after leaving his father and the camp for Bangkok, he got swept up into a crowd of worldly young men and women—'top socialites', he said—who took him around to their clubs and cocktail parties and befriended him.

In fact, they were ruthless predators who manipulated him skillfully into financing their own drug habits, their travel together, their clothes, their parties, etc. They made him feel important and powerful, and very much a part of the 'in' crowd. Jason was burning through his father's money at an alarming pace. At some point, Jason sobered up long enough to realize that there wasn't all that much money left any more, and that his so-called friends were simply using him, and he dropped them. He said he had planned to make a real effort to stop using drugs, and knew that he could survive for a very, very long time on what money was left, and the monthly deposits that his father was making to the savings account every month.

He needed a place to stay until he could sort things out so went to his friend Nicky, the banker, who was divorced and had plenty of room. A few days after he'd moved in and was discussing his plans with Nicky, Nicky confessed that in fact, not only was there no longer any money at all in Boss's account, it was deeply in the red because Nicky had borrowed against it to finance his own drug and gambling habits. Worse, the lender was Waraporn 'Vitale' Buankrathok, possibly the largest drug lord in Thailand. I got goose bumps when I heard that name. That was the guy that had been selling heroin to Lo!

After our visit to Nicky and his subsequent flight, Jason started wandering the streets, occasionally selling himself as a male prostitute in order to scrape together enough money to live on, when he was picked up by one of Vitale's men. Vitale ran one of the larger prostitution rings in Bangkok—male, female and child—and didn't take kindly to having any 'freelancers' wandering around on his turf. However, when he realized who Jason was, he probably thought he'd died and gone to heaven.

Boss's camp was making a lot of money and Jason was his only son and heir. If Boss were to die, Jason would inherit everything, not only the money in the ever growing bank account in Chiang Mai, but the whole logging camp and teak forest as well. Vitale could sell it off and make a fortune. As soon as title and assets were legally transferred into Jason's name, Vitale would make Jason sign everything over to him to clear his outstanding debt. (My guess was that Jason wouldn't be around much longer after that.)

To Vitale, the path was clear. He'd have to send some of his men up to the camp to get rid of Boss. The camp was impossibly isolated; he'd have to send Jason along with his men to show them how to get to it, but the isolation was completely in his favor. Once his men had gone in and gotten out, there'd be no way for the Chiang Mai police to figure out who did it.

You know the rest.

When he'd finished his sad tale, I told Jason that if Boss had died intestate with no living heir, I guessed that the State would inherit the camp. I also told him that I was going to make sure that Boss had died intestate because there was no way in the world he was going to get his sorry hands on the estate. Over his receding sobs as he was being led away, I turned to the Captain and said, "Let's get Chianaporn's body back to the village and explain what's happened. There's a fellow in the village named Krasin who is Boss's second in command. Is there any way you could leave him a radio to contact your headquarters in Chiang Mai so that they can patch it in to the telephone system? Otherwise, there'll be no way to contact the camp at all." He said he'd not only leave a radio, he'd leave one of his men to man it and keep an eye on things until they got straightened out. There was no doubt about it; Kittikachorn had not stinted.

It was a horrible scene at the village. Although her family and friends would certainly mourn Chianaporn, the entire village was staggered by the loss of Boss and Niew. I told Krasin that I thought it would be best to try and keep the camp operating as normally as possible and I'd keep in touch daily. We went back to the bunkhouse clearing, and I opened the truck to see what they had tried to steal. Besides their weapons, the entire contents of Boss's safe were there. I took the cash and his ledgers. I asked the Captain if he would get someone to put everything else back in the safe and simply close it if they couldn't find the key.

A Sad Return

I wouldn't let anybody else touch Niew and I held her tiny, tightly-wrapped body on my lap as we drove to the helicopter to deposit it. I got the shock of my life when we went back to collect Boss's body. As I was wrapping him in a sheet, I felt him move and groan softly! The son of a bitch wasn't dead—or at least not yet! How could he possibly survive being shot in the head? He was shot in the leg too, but that wasn't fatal. We quickly grabbed some cloths and water, and I began to gently swab his wound. I discovered that although the skull was fractured, the bullet hadn't actually entered. He had a very deep and serious head wound, but it sure looked survivable to me. The shot had clearly knocked him out cold, and I suppose that when the thugs saw him totally motionless on the floor, bleeding copiously from a bullet wound to his head, they had made the same assumption all of us had. I told the pilot to get us to the main Bangkok hospital as quickly as he possibly could.

Boss had lost a lot of blood and while they had immediately hooked him up to an IV, everyone seemed pretty upbeat about his chances for making a full recovery. I insisted on carrying Niew in my arms down to the mortuary, where I reluctantly turned her over to the mortician. Thank God, her parents wouldn't have to see what I saw. I took a cab back to the house.

Although I was an emotional wreck, the fury still burned with a white-hot flame. *Vitale, you low-life scum*, I thought. *You owe me a huge debt. Your life. And by God, you're going to pay it. You will not escape my vengeance.*

It must have been around four or five in the morning when I got back to the house, and as I feared, there was a servant standing respectfully by the doorway. The main entrance to the house was far from being the only entrance, but I was quite sure that Mémé would have a servant posted at every one of them. As soon as I got out of the cab, the servant respectfully held the door open for me, bowed, and disappeared. I went into the sitting room and poured myself a large scotch, and then plopped down in my favorite chair and waited for Mémé.

She and Sunisa weren't long in coming, but when I stood up to greet them, they both let out a loud screech and came running to me with outstretched arms crying, "Oh my poor, dear Bertie. You're wounded." I had no idea what they were talking about until I looked down and saw that indeed, my right side was covered with dried blood. It must have spurted out from the severed wrist of the chief thug.

I asked one of the ubiquitous servants to run to my room and fetch me a clean shirt as I explained that I wasn't wounded, but there had been bloodshed at the camp, and apologized for not having checked my appearance as soon as I had arrived 'home.' I asked them both to sit and said that I had some very sad news to relate.

I cleaned up the story as much as I could. I told them that Boss's son had gotten involved with the wrong crowd in Bangkok and had become a drug addict. I said that he had returned to the camp in the company of several of his creditors to beg for money, and that when Boss had refused to pay his drug debts, his companions had flown into a rage and started shooting out all the windows of the bunkhouse. In their wild shooting spree one of the bullets had stuck Boss in the head wounding him badly but not killing him. I said that Niew had not been so fortunate and that one of the bullets had struck her directly in the heart, killing her instantly. Jason and his accomplices had all been arrested and were being held by the police in Chiang Mai.

I was surprised to find myself trembling as I finished my recitation, and even more surprised as I went to try to comfort Mémé and Sunisa, to find that they were trying to comfort *me*. I'm not sure if I have ever again been at such a nearly unbearable level of emotional overload. Despair; immeasurable sorrow; rage; helplessness; hopelessness; shame for not having been there to protect and defend everyone when Jason and his thugs arrived; shame for losing control; gratitude to Kittikachorn for his unsparing support; the ghastly image of poor Niew. I don't know.

All of these things were hammering at me at once. Mémé hugged me and stroked my hair while murmuring, "Bertie, my love, it's not your fault. You did everything you possibly could. You've been up for almost 24 hours and you're over-tired and overwrought. Go to bed and get some rest, my love. I'll call Niew's parents. Please, Bertie. For me. Go to bed now and get a little rest."

I obeyed numbly while thinking; *She's never addressed me as 'my love' before. Maybe she really is my 'Granny.'* I washed up and passed out on my bed.

The next several days were a true misery. I left messages for Bill Young at all his numbers to please call me urgently, but had no response. I wasn't too surprised. Having some first-hand experience with the jungles of Laos, I was very much aware of the lack of public telephone booths where you could stop and call your answering machines to check for messages.

I met with Niew's parents, who went to great lengths to assure me that not only did they hold me completely blameless; they thanked me for having given Niew the happiest days of her life. I met with Kittikachorn and his cabinet to thank them for their whole-hearted support, and was astonished when I entered the conference room to see them all rise and greet me with the traditional *wai* greeting that shows respect. Not only that, their hands were near their foreheads. Like almost everything else in Thailand, the *wai* greeting is complex. It is given first by a person who is of lower rank or status and then returned by the person to whom it is given. The position of the hands is also important. Chest height is normal but the more the hands are raised towards the forehead, the more respect is shown. Other than the king, of course, the only people in Thailand who get more respect than the Prime Minister are the Buddhist monks. For them to *wai* me first was remarkable.

The meeting was very short with them expressing condolences and me thanking them for all their assistance. As I was leaving, Kittikachorn drew me aside and said, "I know what you're planning, Bertie and I caution you to be very, very careful. He is one of the most powerful men in Thailand and has powerful connections everywhere in the country. I'm sorry to say that I doubt that I can be of any help to you, but I would be happy to see him gone, so I won't stand in your way. He has a small army that guards him—I don't think you have any hope of getting close to him. Goodbye, my friend."

I visited Boss in the hospital. When I entered his room he simply burst into tears. He didn't care if I saw him crying or not. In fact, he didn't care about anything. He seemed to have lost any incentive for living. I think his fondest dream was that Niew and I would marry and live at the camp, but if that didn't happen, I'm quite sure he would have just given the camp to Niew—who would have been more than capable of running it—and finding someone else to marry and give him 'grandkids' to spoil. I tried really hard to console him but it was useless. He had simply given up.

Niew was given a traditional Buddhist funeral.

I flew back to Geneva to plan Vitale's demise.

Chapter 15 — Desolate Dawn

Planning for Vitale

Bill Young called about two weeks after I'd gotten back to Geneva, and the first thing he did was to offer truly sincere condolences. The second thing he did was to tell me, "I know what you're planning and that's one tough target. What do you want me to do?"

I told him I didn't want him directly involved at all, but asked if he could introduce me to an English-speaking Thai contact that I could trust, and who could speak the dialect that most servants use when speaking among themselves. I added that the guy would also have to be honest, because I was going to entrust him with a fair amount of money.

Bill said he knew just the guy and remarked, "You can trust him completely, Bertie. He knows I'd kill him if he tried to screw you. His name is Chakrii. Here's his telephone number, but wait 'till tomorrow to call him so I have a chance to speak to him first. When are you planning to get back out here?"

"Somewhere around mid-January. Where's a good place to stay? I'm not even going to tell Mémé and Sunisa that I'm coming to Thailand, much less stay with them. I don't want them involved in any way, shape, or form."

"Stay in my hotel room. We rent it on an annual basis. It's safe and secure. My schedule is totally unpredictable, so if I show up while you're there, we'll take turns sleeping on the couch. Don't worry about making international phone calls from the room, either. They all go on the Agency's tab and no records are kept of the numbers that are called. I'm in it now, and the phone has a direct outside line. I think it's one of the numbers I gave you, but if not, here it is."

"I'm going to need to buy some transportation—probably an old Jeep. Does the hotel have parking facilities, and will they let me park it there?"

"I'll tell the manager that you're buying it for me, and to make sure it's got a parking place. Mine isn't the only room the Agency rents here on an annual basis. They'll do anything we ask them to. What name do you want use while you're here?"

"Mine."

There was a long pause before he answered, "So you're going to do this straight up, huh? At first, I was going to tell you that you're crazy to use your own name, but with the connections you have here, maybe it's actually a smart thing to do. OK. What else?"

"Nothing else. You're a good friend, Bill. Thanks."

I did a number of things over the next several days. One of the first things I did was to call my banker at UBS and ask him to set up a personal account for me at whatever bank he chose in Bangkok, and to fund it with $50,000 from my personal account. I needed the name and telephone number of a contact at the bank in Bangkok.

I spoke to Chakrii and told him I wanted to buy either an all-weather Jeep, or a small delivery truck. If it was a truck, it would have to have four-wheel drive. Whatever he bought, I didn't want anything new, and I wasn't very particular about how it looked, but it had to be in perfect mechanical shape. I asked him to start looking around, and call me when he'd found something suitable.

I next told him that I needed some information concerning Waraporn Buankrathok—aka 'Vitale.' There was a sharp intake of breath, and a long pause before he asked if I knew that he was a very powerful, very dangerous man.

I told him I was very much aware of those facts, but I needed the information anyway. I asked him if he thought he could get close to some of Vitale's servants. He responded, as I thought he would, that it was possible, but that he would probably have to make certain 'gifts.' I was surprised when he estimated $1,000. Even distributed among several servants, it was a lot of money, but I didn't argue with him. Bill had said that I could trust him absolutely, and I absolutely trusted Bill. In any case, I had another plan concerning his expenditures. I said I would call my banker in Bangkok, and would call him back when the money was available.

I told him that I wanted to know what the servants thought about Vitale. Was he a good employer or bad? Did they like him or not? How were they treated? What kinds of things interested him? What did he like to do? What didn't he like to do? Were there any things which he found particularly distasteful or scary? What kind of physical condition was he in? How tall was he, and how much did he weigh? Did he have an office in Bangkok or did he work from his house? Was he guarded 24 hours a day? How many guards? I needed a complete map of his house. I needed a recent picture. Chakrii said he thought his previous estimate might have been too low, but he would see how far he could get.

The next requirement I had was for him to buy some land which was absolutely worthless for agriculture or cattle grazing, or logging, or hunting, or just about anything else. I told him about 20 acres would be sufficient. It needed to be not more than about a two-hour drive from

Bangkok, totally isolated, but accessible by a four-wheel drive vehicle. I asked him if he grew up in Bangkok, and when he replied in the negative, I asked him how long it would take to drive to his native village. He caught on quickly, but said that although the straight-line distance from Bangkok to his village was only about 120 kilometers (73 miles), the roads were bad and not direct, and it would probably take close to three hours to drive there. On the good side, before one got to the village itself, there was an old trail leading off to the north that ended halfway up a hill that had been logged out some 15-20 years ago. The last he had seen it, there were scrub trees and brush growing on it, but the soil wasn't good, and it had too many steep parts to make it worth trying to farm. I told him it sounded perfect.

I knew that almost without exception, it was illegal for *farangs* (a rather pejorative Thai term for foreigners—particularly white-skinned Westerners) to own land in Thailand. I told Chakrii to tell the owner that he was purchasing the land for a crazy *farang* who wanted to experiment with planting different kinds of plants to see if they would grow and improve the soil. The land would be purchased in Chakrii's name but if the land-owner wanted to make the sale, he would have to keep quiet about it so that Chakrii wouldn't get into trouble.

Lastly, I asked him to go to a woodworking shop and get them to build a box, internally measuring approximately 4 feet by 4 feet on each side, and constructed using solid one-inch thick teak. Two one-inch wide air holes would be drilled on the bottom and top and all four sides. The top would be hinged, and the side opposite the hinges fitted with a securely lockable latch. The design imperative would be that any animal locked inside would not be able to get out, no matter how strong it was. The outside appearance was not important. I had no objection if metal straps needed to be added to strengthen it.

I think all this was quite a bit more than Chakrii had bargained for, and his voice was distinctly shaky when he said that he wasn't sure he could do all that.

I ignored him and told him I had deposited $50,000 in a Bangkok bank that he would be able to draw on freely for his purchases. Whatever was left over at the end was his to keep. "So bargain sharply and don't let me down. It's your money that you're spending, after all. In addition, for whatever it's worth, you really will own the land—and the vehicle, too."

After a few moments, he briskly assured me that he'd take care of everything, and not to worry about a thing.

I found it difficult to pull away from my intense focus on my plans to assassinate Vitale, but it was the Yuletide season after all, and it would be pleasant to be around some happy people. Yolande and I went Christmas shopping for Maddie, Grant and Neal. Yolande had known Maddie for years of course, and picked out a beautiful Hermès scarf that she knew Maddie would love. I bought a half-case of some wonderful local wines for each of the guys (these wines aren't cheap but amazing for two reasons. First is the taste, of course, and the second is they resolutely refuse to travel. Try transporting them more than 50 miles from the vineyard, and the taste fades rapidly). Lastly, I went to Davidoff and bought a box of superb Cuban cigars for Maddie's new boss. We invited them all with their families and/or girlfriends to my house for dinner the Sunday before Christmas.

Johnson's Betrayal

I spent a day in my little office going over a massive pile of classified information, and was absolutely appalled by what I was reading about Vietnam. Firstly, I was interested in the opening paragraphs of a long memo that the newly-appointed Under Secretary of State Nicholas Katzenbach had written to Johnson:

Washington, October 15, 1966.

SUBJECT

Administration of Revolutionary Development

You requested a position paper on the administration of the "other war"[33] in Viet-Nam. Let me begin by offering two powerful first impressions which I believe bear decisively on that question.

1. My overriding impression after five days in Viet-Nam is of a topic so common, it is all-too rarely reported, and so obvious it is all-too rarely considered: the unceasing, backbreaking toil of the peasant population.

To see rows of coolies bending down, hour after hour, tending rice plants in the exhausting sun, is to recognize that it is not so much water that their rice grows in; it is sweat. They seed, nurture, replant, irrigate, dig manure, harvest, dry, and carry day upon day, year upon year to squeeze only the barest of essentials from the land.

And to see all this is to recognize a political fact: how easy it is for these people not to give a whit whether they are governed by the GVN or by the VC or by anyone else. Given the dawn-to-dusk imperative of their work, what they may wish more devoutly than anything is simply to be left alone. They wish no longer to be bombed and shelled or knifed and shot, drafted or kidnapped, propagandized or harangued, gouged by landlords or "taxed" by guerrillas.

---

[33] The "other war" was the 'war' to win the hearts and minds of the peasants. The program created for that purpose was idiotically named 'Revolutionary Development.'

It was nice to know that someone in Washington 'got it.' Surely Johnson would remember the report that I had made to President Kennedy after my own, much longer, trip to Vietnam, interviewing the village elders with Siddhi all the way from the Delta in the South to the 17th parallel dividing North and South Vietnam. Jack had certainly learned from it, and although I can't claim that it was the deciding factor in his decision to withdraw all American troops from Vietnam by the end of 1965, it certainly figured strongly in that decision. Actually, my report went even further and concluded that, given the choice, the peasants would rather labor under a government headed by Ho Chi Minh—a fellow Vietnamese—than under a puppet government propped up by the Americans.

My sense of cautious encouragement was further bolstered by a Top Secret CIA report on the effectiveness of the campaign of continuous American bombardment of North Vietnamese targets, which was code-named 'Rolling Thunder.'[34] I will summarize what I consider to be its most salient details below. It's important to read it because in order to understand the enormity of Johnson's self-deception and betrayal of the trust of the American people, you have to have the facts. It commences as follows:

Washington, November 1966.

THE EFFECTIVENESS OF THE ROLLING THUNDER PROGRAM IN NORTH VIETNAM[35]

1 January-30 September 1966

The first paragraph reports the Rolling Thunder bombing campaign had accelerated sharply from the previous year when some 34,600 tons of ordnance had been dropped on North Vietnam. The 1966 total would be around 3½ times that amount—over 120,000 tons.

The report then goes on to say that the cost effectiveness of air strikes in 1966 diminished substantially from 1965. In 1966, it was costing the U.S. $8.70 in direct costs to for every dollar's worth of damage done to North Vietnam targets.

"The major measurable effects on North Vietnam of Rolling Thunder attacks

---

[34] The complete report is long and very detailed and can be found in its entirety on my website at www.bertiemacdocs.com.

[35] Johnson Library, National Security File, Country File, Vietnam, 3 H (1), Appraisal of Bombing of NVN. Top Secret; [*codeword not declassified*]. The CIA forwarded the memorandum to the President on November 5.

are:

(1) About 20 percent, or 70,000, of the total [North Vietnamese] military forces are engaged directly in defensive programs and countermeasures against the Rolling Thunder program.

(2) Physical damage to economic and military targets has also increased." [It would total approximately $126 million in 1966—at a cost to the U.S. of over a billion (1966) dollars.]

"Despite the increased weight of air attack, North Vietnam continues to increase its support to the insurgency in South Vietnam. [Italics are mine.] The Rolling Thunder program has not been able to prevent about a threefold increase in the level of personnel infiltration in 1966.

"Taking a broader view, during the course of the Rolling Thunder program the North Vietnamese capability to support the war effort has improved.

(1) The capacity of the transportation system, at least as it affects the ability to handle the flow of men and military supplies to South Vietnam, has been increased.

(2) The sizable manpower drain has peaked, unless there is a sharp increase in estimated VC/NVA[36] manpower losses in South Vietnam or a radical change in the nature of the air campaign against North Vietnam. In 1965 and 1966, North Vietnam had to mobilize 80 percent of its physically fit males as they reached draft age. Subject to the assumptions just delineated, this levy could be as low as 50 percent of the 1967 class.

(3) Aid from the USSR and Communist China received in 1965 and 1966 has amounted, in estimated value, to about five times the total [damage] caused by Rolling Thunder attacks.

"Nor has Rolling Thunder served visibly to reduce the determination of Hanoi to continue the war. We see no signs that the air attack has shaken the confidence of the regime, and with increased Soviet and Chinese aid to bolster its capabilities, North Vietnam in the short term at least, will apparently take no positive step toward a negotiated settlement."

---

[36]   Viet Cong/North Vietnamese Army

There's much more but you get the gist of it.

The U.S. was paying $8.60 in direct operating costs to inflict a single dollar's worth of damage to North Vietnam—and if one included indirect costs (airbase infrastructure, maintenance, equipment replacement, etc.)—the total cost was at least double that figure. More importantly, this hideously expensive campaign was not only *not* hindering the North Vietnamese infiltration of the South; they were actually *trebling* their rate of infiltration.

Johnson's response? He followed the advice of Secretary of Defense McNamara to *increase the level of bombing*. During 1966, he had more than doubled the end-of-year 1965 American troop level of 184,000 to 389,000 and intended to follow General Westmoreland's advice to further increase it to a 'permanent' level of around 500,000! 1966 American deaths in Vietnam were averaging 412 per month—almost 5,000 for the year. The number of seriously wounded ran about three times that number. I was astounded to learn of Johnson's approval of a billion-dollar 'infiltration barrier' across the entire border between North and South Vietnam. Construction began in November 1966. Had we learned nothing from the pre-WW II French attempt to defend its borders with Germany—the ridiculous Maginot Line? It was difficult to comprehend the level of absurdity and such stupidity except for one thing—American arms manufacturers, munitions suppliers, contractors, airplane and ship builders, etc. were making money hand over fist.

In my naïveté, I decided that despite the many good things that Johnson was accomplishing domestically, he would go down in history as the only U.S. president to ever have led this nation into a major war based solely on personal hubris, and justified to the American public based on 'facts' which he knew to be false. It was an outrageous and stunning betrayal of the public trust. Johnson's Vietnam betrayal would surely be recorded by history as the most scandalous, outrageous betrayal ever perpetrated by an American president.

Then sadly, in March, 2003, George W. Bush led the nation into war with Iraq the very same way. My God! What are they drinking down there in Texas?

Going Operational

I spent the next three weeks training and getting fit for the job that lay ahead—swimming, jogging, taking saunas and going to a local firing range to get used to the .357 Magnum I had removed from Sally Boyle. After a week or so at the range, I was reasonably competent, but a very long way from the marksmanship exhibited by most of the other people using the range. I wasn't concerned. My plans didn't include actually firing the thing, anyway.

Before I returned to Thailand, I had some shopping to do, and I decided to do it in Paris where I was far less well known. Prior to leaving Geneva, however, I contacted an acquaintance (who traveled in rather undesirable social circles) to procure a cosh for me. For those of you unfamiliar with the instrument, it consists of an 8-10 inch-long solid tube of very hard rubber covered with braided leather and equipped with a wrist strap. Although it's quite a bit shorter, it's about the same diameter as the batons used by police, but much more dangerous because, even though the rubber is very hard, it will bend slightly when it hits the rounded surface of an even harder object—the human head, for example. The force of the blow is therefore spread over a larger area, allowing the striker to be extremely forceful with his strike while still avoiding fracturing the skull. I told my acquaintance that the covering leather had to be black.

In Paris, I bought a black balaclava which covered the entire face, neck, and head, leaving only a slit for the eyes. At another store, I bought a black cotton shirt with a high 'coolie collar' and a pair of loose black cotton pants. At yet a different store, I bought a pair of supple black canvas shoes with non-slip soles which reached up and around the tips of the toes. I already owned plenty of black socks. I visited a lot of shops before I finally found the kind of gloves I was looking for—very tight-fitting black cotton gloves with non-slip pads at the end of each finger, and a rather larger pad on the palm.

I got a long, hard stare from the Japanese shop-owner that sold them to me, but when I'd paid and he handed me the gloves, he smiled and said, "Bonne chase, monsieur (Good hunting, sir)."

Back in my apartment, I took mental stock of things, and decided I was as ready as I was ever going to be. I called the hotel in Bangkok and told them I would be arriving the next day. I instructed them to give Chakrii a key to my room if he happened to arrive before I did. I then called Chakrii and asked him to get to the hotel at least an hour before my plane landed and to wait for me in my room.

When I presented my passport to Customs in Bangkok the next day, the Customs officer examined it normally and then just smiled and waved me through. I looked over my shoulder as I walked away and sure enough, he was talking excitedly on the phone. Kittikachorn now knew I was in town. When I got in a taxi outside, an airport security guard stopped the cab as we were pulling away and briefly spoke to the cab driver before waving us on our way. Kittikachorn would now know where I was staying, and since I wasn't staying with Mémé, he would also know what I was here to do.

I had anticipated all this and it was the reason I had asked Chakrii to get to the hotel an hour previous to my arrival in Bangkok. I hoped he'd done so, because as of right now, one of Kittikachorn's men would be carefully watching each new arrival at the hotel. I reckoned that eventually they would discover that Chakrii and I were working together, but I wanted to delay that moment for as long as possible. Vitale was an extremely powerful, well-connected man and I had no doubt that he had some very high-level informants within Kittikachorn's staff. However, I was also sure that Kittikachorn would know that as well and would probably keep his suspicions about the reason for my current trip to himself—but you never know.

302

Vitale had no particular reason to know my name but he probably did. Too many people knew about my connection to that awful night when Jason and Vitale's raiding party visited the logging camp. The helicopter pilot definitely knew my name, and while I was never introduced to any of the other policemen, people talk. Vitale obviously knew that neither Jason nor his raiding party ever returned, and would have made enquiries. The people at the hospital certainly knew of my connection with Boss. I had to assume that Vitale both knew my name and would be informed of my arrival. Because of my close connections with Kittikachorn and Mémé, I doubted that he would try to have me assassinated, but he would have absolutely no qualms about getting rid of Chakrii. In fact, he would probably be highly motivated to do so as it would most likely mess up my plans, and would certainly teach me that he was not a man to be trifled with.

I actually recognized the agent standing in the hotel lobby because I'd seen him before at Kittikachorn's headquarters, so I waved cheerfully to him as I entered. He quickly turned away, pretending that he hadn't seen me, but the desk clerk certainly had and could barely contain his mirth as he checked me in.

Chakrii turned out to be a trim, fit, intelligent man whom I guessed to be in his early to mid-forties. We spent the next couple of hours discussing the information he'd obtained. He showed me pictures of possible vehicles, but the one he thought most suitable was a small, slightly beat-up delivery van. It was the kind you see all over Thailand as they are cheap and reliable. (They also pollute like the dickens.) Because it had previously been used in the mountains, it had four-wheel drive, but Chakrii had taken it to a mechanic to have it checked out, and it needed about $1,000 worth of repairs. He said he was willing to spend the extra money because if I were going to let him keep it after the 'mission' was accomplished, he would put it to good use renting it to a friend of his who made custom-designed teak furniture.

When I asked him how long the repairs would take, he blushed and admitted that he had already authorized the mechanic to order the spare parts he needed so the truck could be delivered the day after tomorrow.

I laughed and told him to get on with it but to leave the existing signage on the truck's sides. The past owner would get a little free advertising and we'd get a little free camouflage.

The details he gave me about Vitale seriously increased my level of apprehension. The man was a monster; universally hated and despised by those who worked for him; and they were also terrified of him. Although his main business was distributing heroin to surrounding countries and parts of Western Europe, he ran a huge prostitution business, and owned brothels all over Thailand. The brothels supplied whatever the client wanted—women, men or children—it didn't matter to them. He made his money by ruining other people's lives. Tens of thousands of them.

It had to stop.

He lived in a huge house on a fairly small estate of only two or three acres, but the entire property was surrounded by a nine-foot high wall with electrified wire on the top. It was patrolled day and night by armed guards accompanied by attack dogs. All visitors—even Vitale's good friends—were thoroughly frisked in the reception hall before being allowed to enter the house proper. Without my having to ask, Chakrii said that female visitors were frisked behind a screen by a female security guard.

Visitors' cars were required to park behind a blast-proof wall that shielded the house; the drivers were required to stay in the cars; and the keys were required to be handed over to one of the security guards. Astonishingly, Chakrii had managed to procure a rough, hand-drawn 'map' of the interior, but with security precautions like that, the map was essentially useless. Even though Chakrii said that Vitale's servants hated him and would help me, I was never going to get inside that house.

His limousine was bullet-proof and always carried two heavily-armed guards in addition to his driver who was not only armed—he was also a highly trained martial arts expert. I had known from the outset that an assassination attempt on Vitale was not only going to be one of the most dangerous things I'd ever done in my life, I also expected it to be extraordinarily difficult technically. This didn't look difficult—it looked hopeless.

It got worse. He used his house as an office. He didn't smoke (which was astonishing), he rarely drank, and he didn't do drugs. Chakrii had a recent newspaper photo of him dedicating a wing of a hospital that he had had constructed in Surat Thani, a small city in the south of Thailand. (He apparently donated millions every year to charitable causes in Thailand.) From the picture, he looked to be in his mid-fifties, a little on the heavy side but hard and fit. He had divorced his wife some seven years ago and had immediately re-married a much younger woman. They had two children, currently aged four and six.

I sighed and sat back in my chair while Chakrii and I just stared at each other, lost in thought. I thought fleetingly of the current wife and children plus the ex-wife and children, but gave them not a second thought. I'm an assassin, not a kidnapper or a hostage-taker.

I thought about what kind of deliveries would be made to the house. Office supplies and food came to mind but they both had the same problem. Maybe I could get some sort of disguised explosive device smuggled in with a delivery of office supplies or perhaps I could contaminate their food with some sort of poison, but either plan would almost certainly wind up hurting or killing innocent people as well. I wanted no part of 'collateral damage.' I was after Vitale and Vitale alone.

What else could I do? Where else could I attack? The man had to have some weakness somewhere.

Then it hit me. I raised my head and asked, "Does he have a mistress? Does he bring in call girls? Does he visit whorehouses? I know he owns dozens."

Chakrii brightened visibly and said, "I have no idea but I can find out. It may take a couple of days, though." I thanked him and told him telephone me when he had the information. Additionally, I asked him to get his mechanic to fix the back door of the truck so that it could be opened from the inside as well as the outside.

I also suggested that he leave the hotel through the service entrance. "I want to take every precaution to make sure that you are never seen with me and never connected to me in any way. All of our future communication should be by telephone until I'm ready to act. If you are under stress when you call, address me as Mr. MacFarland. If everything is normal, just address me as Bertie. I will program the answering machine to answer, 'Leave a message for BY.' If you get the machine, just answer, 'Sorry, wrong number,' and hang up. I'll know you called and I'll call you back." He nodded gravely and left.

The next couple of days were kind of a lark actually. I did lots of sightseeing, particularly at the *wats* (temples). Thai temple art is stunningly spectacular and is unmatched anywhere in the world. Lines of countless carvings all covered in 24 karat gold-leaf just stagger the mind and eye. The beauty, grace and delicacy are simply overwhelming. Spend a few days exploring theses vast treasures and your conception of religious art will be forever altered.

I knew I would be followed—by one of Kittikachorn's men for sure, and probably one of Vitale's as well. I'm good at detecting tails; I almost seem to have a sixth sense for it. Since I didn't feel threatened by either one of them, I played with them. One of my favorite tricks is to lose a tail, then circle back around behind him/her while he/she is frantically looking everywhere (but behind them) for me.

When I discovered that I did indeed have two tails on me, and that apparently neither one of them knew what the other was doing, I played that trick and watched them both from behind with a huge grin on my face. I decided the one with the more military bearing had to be Kittikachorn's man, so I walked up behind him and tapped him on the shoulder. When he whirled around, he couldn't suppress a gasp of surprise which caught the attention of Vitale's man who then also stared at me wide-eyed.

Although he stood stock-still as I beckoned him over, he was definitely within earshot when I pointed him out and said, 'That's Buankrathok's man and you two are doing the same job. Why don't you get to know each other and then you can work in shifts or something?" I'm sorry to report that neither man seemed to be amused.

On a more serious note, I did take precautions. I bought all my meals from road-side or klong-side vendors. I chose them randomly and never frequented the ones that seemed to be popular with the *farangs*. I'd wait until a local man had chosen something that looked good and then point out his dish to the vendor, and then point to me and nod my head. It worked every time. I drank a lot of water before I left the hotel in the morning, but Bangkok is one of the hottest cities in the world and even in January, it's hot. If I felt as though I needed to re-hydrate while I was wandering around, I'd find a bar and order an unopened bottle of Singha beer. It's virtually impossible to poison the food or drink of someone with those habits, and I wasn't going to take any chances.

There was no message for me when I got back to the hotel at the end of the first day but I was neither surprised nor particularly disappointed. Assassins, like any stalking animal, quickly learn the necessity of patience. In the human instance however, that essential patience does not extend to being bothered by other humans, so within the first 30 minutes of the next day I lost both of my tails (two new ones, incidentally) for the rest of the day. I could almost see Kittikachorn laughing his head off when his guy had to report what happened. I was a great deal less sure of what Vitale's level of amusement might be. I was just glad that I didn't have to know.

Chakrii called a little after 9:00 on the evening of the second day. His report was interesting, to say the least. Vitale did very definitely have a mistress. She was housed (imprisoned, actually) in a luxurious, walled villa in a very exclusive residential enclave about a 20 minute drive from Vitale's mansion. I say imprisoned because though she had every imaginable comfort within her villa, she couldn't leave. She could walk outside her villa on the small grounds within the walls, but she had no key to the gate. The servants, of course, had to do their daily shopping, but they were picked up at 9:00 sharp every morning by a small delivery truck and their purchases inspected minutely before they were allowed back inside the grounds. Vitale apparently believed that sexual slavery was normal.

There was other good news, and other bad news. The good news was that whenever he went to visit his mistress—let's give her a name and call her 'Suzy'—he only traveled with his deadly driver. The driver would unlock the gate; wait in the car in the courtyard until Vitale re-emerged, then re-lock the gate when they left. That opened up a plethora of possibilities. The bad news was that Vitale made his visits whenever the mood struck him. There was no possible way to surprise him on one of his visits. He might visit twice on one day and then not visit for a week or ten days. He might visit in the morning, afternoon, or dead of night. There was no possible way to park a surveillance vehicle in that exclusive neighborhood for even a few hours, much less a day or more. Worse, it would take a minimum of an hour for Chakrii to bring the truck to my hotel, pick me up, and then drive to Suzy's house. That's if we started the operation at 3:00 in the morning, probably Bangkok's least congested hour. It could easily take twice that long depending on the time of day.

306

True randomness—a total lack of predictability—is an assassin's worst nightmare. No matter how well trained you are, no matter what your capabilities are, if you can't locate your subject or get close enough to him or her to carry out the assassination, you are totally useless.

I told Chakrii that it was great information but for the moment, I just couldn't figure out how to use it.

He continued, "Yes, I thought the same thing until my informant told me that once every two weeks or so, Vitale has a night-time meeting with eight or ten people at his house. My contact doesn't know who they are exactly, but they are some kind of business associates, according to the one servant allowed to be stationed in the conference room." He was apparently picked for the station because he had a very low IQ and neither cared about, nor could have understood the substance of the conversations taking place in front of him. He was grateful for any commands to fetch food or drink however, and responded immediately. Chakrii said that these meetings usually lasted for two hours or so, and that afterwards, Vitale almost always went to visit his mistress, and usually stayed overnight.

I asked Chakrii if he could get his contact (who almost certainly had to be the head servant) to immediately phone him the next time such a meeting occurred. Chakrii said he had already done so. The man was priceless.

An Evening at Suzy's

Now it was a waiting game, and waiting is hard. It gives you too much time to think. Although you go over your plans ceaselessly, you are always aware that something can, and often does, happen which will force you to completely change them. It gives you too much time to think about the fact that your chances of dying a very ugly death are about 50-50. If you're lucky. Even worse, when you have to harbor these thoughts and live with the constantly mounting tension day after day, it becomes ever more difficult to maintain the cool, calculating steadiness that is absolutely essential for success.

It was therefore a real relief when, after ten days of increasingly unbearable tension and frustration, the bedside phone jangled me out of a doze at around 10:00 in the evening. Chakrii said he'd be at the hotel loading dock in 30 minutes. I waited in my room for 20 minutes and then went downstairs to the loading dock. When Chakrii pulled up, I jumped in the back of the truck and started changing clothes. I was sweating profusely and not just because it was hot back there. Vitale was in a rough business, and when his driver was described as a highly trained martial arts expert, I had no illusions of just how good he would be. Vitale could, and would hire only the best when it came to protecting his personal safety. My abilities in the martial arts arena were good—very good, in fact, but this guy would be world-class and there's a *huge* difference between very good and world-class. If the slightest thing went wrong, I would never see another sunrise.

The noise of the city was beginning to fade when I'd finally pulled on my balaclava and donned my black gloves with the slip-proof pads. I unsheathed Excalibur and wedged myself into a corner of the cargo compartment, and began to meditate. Within moments, I began to feel the soothing calm and peace that meditation brings. I had completely lost track of time and place when I heard two sharp raps from the cab and felt the truck pull to a stop. I heard Chakrii leave the cab and open the hood of the truck before getting back in.

That was my signal. Raising the hood of the truck is a sort of universal sign that a vehicle has engine trouble, and the fact that he got back in the cab was my signal that the coast was clear and Vitale had not yet arrived. It was all up to me now.

I slithered out of the cargo compartment and hid between the truck and the wall of Suzy's villa to reconnoiter.

It was exactly as Chakrii had described. The wrought iron entry gate was about ten yards in front of us, and recessed far enough back from the street so that a car could pull up to it without blocking the roadway. There were lights on in the house, but the courtyard was dark. In fact, other than our truck's emergency blinking lights, there was very little light at all. Chakrii had smeared mud on the front lights so that although they could be seen blinking behind the mud, they projected no useful illumination whatsoever. I melted back next to the left front wheel and crouched down to wait.

I had finally entered my operational state. It's a strange state of being—kind of like suspended animation, I suppose. I could have waited for hours—perhaps as long as a day—totally motionless, but with all the unleashed energy of a coiled spring, and after I had struck, I would have no memory at all of ever having waited. Pain sensors get completely shut down. The only sensory organs that receive any conscious input are the eyes and the ears, and they receive 100% of the brain's attention.

I heard the car slow down as it approached the truck. Even though the truck was pulled almost entirely off the road, the driver was taking no chances. I think that when he saw a dejected Thai driver sitting alone in the cab and then saw the raised hood, he relaxed and continued the few remaining yards to Suzy's gate. When the driver opened his door, he didn't go straight to the gate to unlock it but instead walked out into the road and looked in all directions.

My blood ran cold. Watching this man move was bone chilling. I wasn't even in the same universe with this guy. He moved with the silent, silky, confident grace of a tiger stalking its prey. Apparently satisfied with his inspection, he returned to the gate and unlocked it, and I could hear the patter of flip-flops as a house servant ran across the courtyard to swing the gate

308

open for him.

As soon as the driver returned to the car and turned his back to get in, I ran towards him with all the speed of a totally desperate man. I struck him just as he had put his left foot into the car and was turning to slide into the driver's seat. Even though I hit him with the cosh with the full force of my left arm, augmented by the velocity of my sprint, he was so fast that his outstretched right arm deflected the blow enough so that I hit him in his face rather than on his temple.

I cursed myself for my plan to disable him rather than kill him, but in the split second that he took to recover from the blow, I slashed through his right shoulder, and then cut him deeply behind his right knee. His mistake was to try to launch himself back out of the car only to discover that his right leg would no longer support him, because the tendons were cut. It's a good thing that he was falling, because even so, the shot from the pistol that he was now holding in his right hand barely missed me. I figured the rules of the game had changed since he was now trying to kill me, so I slit his throat as he fell.

The servant who had rushed out of the house to open the gate, had started to run towards the car when he heard the commotion, and was now standing only a few feet away from me, frozen to the spot and babbling with terror. I brought my face to within inches of his and stared into his uncomprehending eyes as I raised my index finger to my lips to signal for silence. He shut up, all right. He fainted dead away.

I turned to Vitale and saw that he, too, had a gun pointed at me, but I wasn't very worried. Firing a gun while sitting inside a bullet-proof car with bullet-proof windows is a mighty risky undertaking. That bullet is going to ricochet all over the place until it loses all its force, and I was standing just behind the passenger door with my own gun drawn. I told him to throw his gun into the front seat.

When he heard me address him in English, I could see the shock in his face, and his shoulders slumped.
"You're Bertie, aren't you?"

"It's me, Vitale. Now throw your gun and your wallet in the front seat, then slide over here, open the door and slowly get out of the car with your hands behind your head. Do exactly as I say and I promise I won't kill you."

"You give me your word that you won't kill me?"

"I give you my word."

He threw his gun and his wallet in the front seat and slowly exited. I told him to lean his head up against the car and spread his legs while I frisked him. He was clean. I hit him so hard on the back of the head with the cosh that he dropped like a stone.

I had some quick clean-up work to do. I dragged the driver and the servant out of sight behind the wall, closed the gate, pulled the car over the pool of blood the driver had spilled, took the cash out of Vitale's wallet, turned off the motor and the headlights, locked the car and threw the keys over the wall.

Chakrii helped me drag Vitale into the back of the truck, and I leapt in beside him and closed the door.

 Chakrii closed the hood and started our journey towards his village. By the light of the battery-powered lantern I'd brought, I stripped Vitale down to his shorts, then bound his wrists and elbows behind his back and then bound his ankles. I crammed a rag into his mouth and sealed his mouth shut by wrapping several layers of duct tape around his head. Lastly, I took off my 'ninja' outfit and re-donned my 'street' clothes. After I had repacked my bag, I gave a couple of sharp raps on the back of the cab and waited.

It was Chakrii's signal to pull over whenever he found a convenient place so I could join him in the cab.

The Arrival of Dawn

The sky was just beginning to glow red when we pulled off the main road and onto a miserable dirt track. Chakrii stopped and put the truck into four-wheel drive before we continued along a tortuous path which led to the heavy teak box. Chakrii turned the truck around and backed up to it. We pushed up the back door to find Vitale writhing around and trying to signal wildly with his eyes. I told him to quit wiggling around, and to throw his legs over the back of the truck and to sit up like a grown man while I talked to him.

He continued to wriggle, so I took out the cosh, and whacked him on the knee. The effect was instantaneous. His head jerked back as he tried to howl in pain. I had no sympathy for him as Chakrii and I dragged him to the back, and propped him up, leaning on the side of the truck for support with his legs hanging over the rear.

"Look around, Vitale. This may not be the prettiest piece of the natural world that you've ever seen, but you'd give up every possession you have to simply be let loose in it, wouldn't you? All your money, houses, airplanes, boats—absolutely everything—if you could just be free to go. Am I right?"

He almost fell out of the truck he was nodding so vigorously.

"Vitale, why in the world did you decide to make your money by ruining the lives of others with drugs and/or prostitution? You're a very smart man. You could have easily made a legitimate fortune. Why did you choose to make it by making others suffer? I wonder if you even know or ever bothered to think about it. I promised not to kill you and I'll keep my promise. My guess is that you'll wish I had killed you, though."

Before he could react, I grabbed his legs and yanked him into the open box, and threw his clothes into a corner. They would probably make a good nest for some little critter. After closing the lid and locking it, I carefully wiped the lock to remove any fingerprints, did the same thing with the keys to the lock, and then threw them as far as I could into the bushes. I turned to Chakrii and said, "Let's go."

On the way back, I counted the astonishing amount of money that Vitale had been carrying in his wallet, and put it in the glove box of the truck. I asked Chakrii to put it in a special place in his house, and to use it whenever he came across someone who was truly in need and deserving of some help. "Do it anonymously," I advised him. "You don't want people to start to wonder why you have so much money that you can afford to just give it away, and you don't want to make bad guys think that your house would be a great house to rob. So do your good deeds discretely."

I also told him that there was a small bag of clothes in the back, and asked him to please just to keep them for me in case I ever needed them again.

I got him to drop me off about two blocks from the hotel.

I was surprised to see the hotel manager waving wildly at me as I walked through the lobby. He bowed deeply before he said excitedly, "Mr. MacFarland, the Prime Minister called and wants to speak to you. He said you have his number. We are honored to have you as our guest, Mr. MacFarland. Please contact me personally if there is the slightest thing that you need."

I thanked him and went up to my room to call. *Damn, but word travels fast around here*, I thought.

The White Tiger is Born

Kittikachorn was in a jovial mood when I called. "I understand you've had a busy evening."

"How much do you know?"

"Everything, of course."

"What are you going to do?"

"Absolutely nothing. He deserves that fate and he has long been a thorn in my side as well. You've become an overnight legend though."

"Excuse me, Mr. Prime Minister, but I don't follow at all."

"There's an old Thai legend about a protective deity taking the form of a tiger who strikes in the night to save people from evil beings. This ferocious tiger is often described as a white tiger with blue eyes. The servant that you scared so badly last night swears by all that's holy that he actually saw a portion of your white tiger skin, and that he felt the force coming from your savage blue eyes when you looked directly into his. He said that you had taken the form of a human, but you could not completely hide your white skin, nor could you hide your shining blue eyes. He said that you were completely silent, and moved just like a cat, and that you had made him sleep so that he would not see you carrying off the body of his mistress's tormentor. He says from now on, he will always include you in his daily prayers."

"Well, it's good to know that *somebody's* praying for me. I could sure use it."

"You know Bertie, Thai people are very superstitious and I'm not talking just about the servant class. When commencing to build a house for example, one must wait for a day when all the signs are propitious so that bad things will not befall the occupants and visitors to the house. Certain omens are considered to be bad luck, and the place where the omen was observed is shunned and avoided—sometimes for generations.

"The legend of the white tiger is widely believed, and news of his return has spread like wildfire. I mean it. Probably half of Thailand has already heard the news and by tomorrow, most of the rest of the country will have heard it too. It gives hope to the oppressed, and strikes real fear into the hearts of those who are guilty of the oppression. Knowing as much about politics as you do, I'm sure you won't mind me pointing out to our citizens that if indeed this legendary white tiger has returned, he may have done so to aid the beleaguered leader of this nation in pursuing his goal to bring evil people to justice. Perhaps the white tiger will strike again in the future to aid me and my people."

He laughed and hung up, and I pondered a little bit on what he had said. Was he implying that his government was actually unofficially sanctioning—as opposed to just looking the other away—not only what I had just done, but possible similar acts in the future?

I took a much needed cool shower, toweled off and lay on the bed to think. When had I started to think of myself as an assassin? I certainly didn't think of myself in those terms when I had killed Cory or Gennady. After all, both of them were trying to kill me and self-protection is not assassination. The killing of Lo, however, was definitely an assassination. I don't think I had ever truly allowed myself to explore how I felt about that but somehow, without my consciously thinking about it, my self-perception had begun to change. Now I'd done it again.

What the hell was I turning into?

I don't know how long it had been since I had any sleep at all but the adrenaline overload that I had been carrying around for weeks was slowly draining away and I fell into an anguished sleep.

Sadly, I was to learn that neither Thailand, nor the white tiger,[37] was anywhere near finished with me. Worse, nor was Johnson.

I'm glad I didn't know that as I flew back to Switzerland. I was feeling miserable enough as it was.

---

[37] It's interesting to note that there really are white (albino) tigers and that these very rare tigers really do have blue eyes. I cannot attest that they are occasionally inhabited by protective deities but albino tigers are in fact unusually ferocious. Given their lack of normal camouflage, few survive to adulthood and those that do owe their survival to abnormal aggression. Although the majority of all tigers usually hunt at night, with no camouflage–albino tigers hunt only at night.

Epilogue — a Farewell to 1967

My visit to my tiny office at DIA European Headquarters in Geneva raised no eyebrows as I read through the stacks of classified material that had accumulated in my absence. My assumption that I was going to be totally 'out of the loop' in the European operations proved incorrect, however. Often questions of access arose that could only be resolved by my discussing these issues with my contacts in Sweden, Paris and Sardinia and while the necessity to use these contacts was rare, being able to resolve the issues was of immense strategic importance to the Agency. It looked like I was going to be involved—albeit at the highest level—for the foreseeable future. At that time I had no idea that for many decades to come, I was going to be involved in U.S. foreign policy affairs at the very highest level, and that my Army rank would rise to reflect that.

For the rest of 1967, my personal life was free of the violence with which it had commenced, but that was certainly not true for the hundreds of thousands of U.S. troops in Vietnam. (At the end of the year American troop levels had risen to 485,000.) Protests against the war raged constantly throughout the year in the U.S. Johnson tried numerous 'back channel' efforts to engage the North Vietnamese in secret negotiations, but they were not only rebuffed, they were not even acknowledged. McNamara's position was beginning to shift towards the position that Kennedy had always held—we'll support South Vietnam with money, equipment, and intelligence services, but if the South Vietnamese are not willing to be primarily responsible for the defense of their own country, there is no reason that American troops should try to do that job for them.

Elsewhere, on June 5, Israel launched the Six Day War, and on June 17, The People's Republic of China tested its first hydrogen bomb. It was only 32 months after the testing of its first atomic (fission) bomb, and the shortest fission to fusion development known.

On June 23 – 25, Johnson met with the Soviet Union's Premier Alexi Kosygin in Glassboro, NJ prior to Kosygin's scheduled speech at the United Nations. Nothing of note was accomplished, but the two leaders established good personal relations.

On November 2, Johnson convened a day-long top-secret meeting of foreign policy and national security advisors at the White House to discuss U.S. policy on the war in Vietnam. You can read the lengthy summary at: "Johnson Library, Meeting Notes File, November 2, 1967— Meeting with Foreign Policy Advisors. Top Secret." Astonishingly, the broad consensus was to keep on doing everything that was being done and not to try to negotiate with the North Vietnamese. It was recommended that the U.S. public be constantly fed a stream of encouraging news!

In frustration and disgust, McNamara announced his impending resignation as Secretary of Defense. He would take up his new position as head of the World Bank in February of the following year.

I made the fateful decision to be with Mémé and Sunisa over the Christmas and New Year holidays. When I called to ask if I could come, they were ecstatic, and immediately started planning for all the things we were going to do and places we would go. I suggested an arrival date, and told them I would give them a call with my flight number and arrival time. I hoped they heard me, because when I hung up they were talking so excitedly to each other, I think they forgot I was on the line.

I knew I was in trouble the moment I arrived in Bangkok and went to clear my one bag through customs. As soon as I presented my passport, the customs officer *wai*ed me respectfully, and waved me through without even looking at my bag.

Mémé and Sunisa, along with a crowd of servants were waiting for me, but before we could throw our arms around one another, a high-ranking army officer in full dress uniform, white gloves and all, stepped in front of me, saluted, and handed me a manila envelope with the official seal of Thailand emblazoned on it.

"With the personal compliments of the Prime Minister," he said before turning and leaving.

I had this vague and foreboding sense of *déjà vu*.

DISCARD

Made in the USA
Lexington, KY
06 August 2015